UNDERSTANDING STATISTICS

UNDERSTANDING STATISTICS

A Research Perspective

Robert E. McGrath

Fairleigh Dickinson University

 LONGMAN

An imprint of Addison Wesley Longman, Inc.

New York • Reading, Massachusetts • Menlo Park, California • Harlow, England
Don Mills, Ontario • Sydney • Mexico City • Madrid • Amsterdam

Acquisitions Editor: Catherine Woods
Project Coordination and Text Design: Interactive Composition Corporation
Cover Design: Mary McDonnell
Cover Illustration: Still Life by Rivera 1915 from Planet Art
Art Studio: Interactive Composition Corporation
Electronic Production Manager: Eric Jorgensen
Manufacturing Manager: Hilda Koparanian
Electronic Page Makeup: Interactive Composition Corporation
Printer and Binder: RR Donnelley & Sons Company
Cover Printer: Phoenix Color Corp.

Library of Congress Cataloging-in-Publication Data

McGrath, Robert E.
   Understanding Statistics : A Research Perspective / Robert E. McGrath.
   p.   cm.
   Includes bibliographical references and index.
   ISBN 0-673-99058-3
   1. Statistics. 2. Social sciences—Statistical methods.
I. Title.
HA29.M43855   1996   CIP
519.5—dc20   96-557

ISBN 0-673-99058-3

12345678910-DOC-99989796

To Deborah
I would spend my days
in conversation with you

 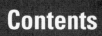

Contents

PART IV UNDERSTANDING INFERENTIAL STATISTICS

Chapter 9 Concepts Underlying Inferential Statistics   142

Chapter 10 The Logic of Hypothesis Testing   155

Chapter 17   The *t* Test for a Correlation Coefficient   242

Chapter 18   The One-Way Independent Groups Analysis of Variance   250

However much we detail a transmitted description, it will always be unnecessarily precise for some and fragmentary for others. (Lem, 1968/1983, p. 84)

TO THE READER

Many students interested in the behavioral sciences consider the required statistics course the most dreaded part of their curriculum. I think this perception is unfortunate, because I have found the study of statistics both fascinating and practically useful: fascinating because I am often struck by the logical beauty of the ideas that underlie statistical methods; practically useful because an understanding of statistical concepts such as probability and variability can help one think more effectively about both personal and social issues.

In writing this book I have attempted in several ways to address those fears. For one thing, I tried to focus as much on the *why* of statistics as on the *how*. It seems to me too many students finish their statistics course with a list of statistical methods they have studied, but little grasp of when and why they would be useful. I hope by the time you finish this course you will not only know how to use various statistics, but also when and why you would use them.

I also think it is important to provide a context for using statistics. Throughout this book I have emphasized practical issues that will emerge in the use of statistics in a research setting. Although this text is not meant to provide a full introduction to both research and statistical methods, enough research is thrown into the mix that I hope it gives life to the statistics.

I chose the aphorism at the beginning of this Preface because I think it is particularly appropriate to topics as complex as statistics. There is no way I can present this material so that it is equally accessible to all. I expect there will be times when you will find the material covered here difficult. I urge you to stick with it until it makes sense, and I hope that your efforts will be rewarded by seeing some of that logical beauty I mentioned above.

TO THE INSTRUCTOR

I originally decided to write this book because I could not find a well-written text that provided the level of understanding about statistics that I thought makes it most meaningful to the student. This textbook was written under the guiding principle that it has become less important for a student to know how to compute a *t* test or correlation coefficient than it is for a student to understand sampling distributions and hypothesis testing. While the former provides the student with information which may be useful in a particular research study, the latter has implications for almost any research project. In particular, understanding the concepts underlying statistics will help the student decide which statistics are appropriate for which research contexts.

In the course of working on the text, I have also tried to be innovative in the structure of the text. These innovations include the following:

- The text was written with flexibility in mind. Many chapters include supplements containing material which, while not essential or even necessary to understand the topic of the chapter, may enhance some students' understanding of statistics and research design. Instructors may also find some of the supplementary materials worth requiring, if the instructor wishes to emphasize certain topics addressed only in passing in the chapters themselves. In my own teaching of statistics I routinely require students to read the material on research design in the supplement to Chapter 3, since I like to cover research design issues in more detail than is standard for a statistics course.

- The first 12 chapters follow a traditional model for textbook chapters: each addresses a general topic, and includes all information relevant to the topic. After Chapter 12, the format is somewhat unusual. Each chapter is devoted to a single hypothesis testing statistic, and chapters are written so they can be read relatively independently of each other. This makes it easy for the instructor to eliminate material. Sections on confidence intervals are also clearly marked, and can be removed from the curriculum quite easily.

- Each hypothesis testing chapter follows the same sequence of topics: introduction, statistical hypotheses, testing the null hypothesis, making a decision about the null hypothesis, conditions for using the test, directional versus nondirectional hypotheses, power and sample size issues, and confidence intervals. This provides a common framework the student can use to organize information about hypothesis tests.

- I find most books provide at best an abstract discussion of power analysis. This model of instruction no doubt contributes to the disregard for power evident in behavioral research today. I have attempted to develop a practical approach to power analysis, presenting it in the context of sample size estimation for each statistic.

- Exercises were developed to reinforce basic principles. For example, almost every chapter has at least one question that asks about the type of study and the nature of the variables used, concepts that are raised in the first three chapters of the text.

- The final chapter is extremely integrative. It provides a model for choosing the correct statistics that draws upon information introduced from the first chapter on. The chapter also includes a table listing characteristics of each statistic that in my experience students tend to find particularly difficult to remember.

There are few references to computers in this text. This omission is not meant to imply that I do not consider it worthwhile to train students in the use of statistical software. To the contrary, I think this is an essential component of becoming a competent researcher in the behavioral sciences. However, many instructors do not find they have the time or resources for addressing computer use during the course. The text is written so a knowledge of computers is unnecessary (although in several places the discussion was slanted so it would be consistent with common standards among statistical software packages). For instructors who are able to integrate computer methods into their course, a supplementary text is planned.

GOALS

If I have been successful in achieving my goals with this text, upon completing the course the student should have a basic understanding of the following topics:

- the role statistics play in the research process.
- the types of situations in which each of the descriptive statistics are appropriate.
- the types of situations in which each of the inferential statistics are appropriate.
- the logic of hypothesis testing and interval estimation.
- the role samples, populations, and sampling distributions play in statistics.

These are the concepts I believe are most important to master if the student is to apply what has been learned in a flexible manner at a later point.

GENERAL ORGANIZATION

The text is divided into six sections. The first focuses on basic concepts that provide the context for subsequent discussions. This includes the introduction of some basic statistical concepts as well as research design issues common to all studies.

The second and third sections focus on descriptive statistics. Part 2 deals with statistics used to describe patterns in the data associated with a single variable, Part 3 with descriptive statistics used to describe relationships among two variables. This structure parallels the discussion of scientific hypotheses in Chapter 3, where a distinction is drawn between hypotheses about variable patterns and hypotheses about variable relationships.

Part 4 provides the context for the subsequent discussion of inferential statistics. Probability and sampling distributions, the logic of hypothesis testing, and interval estimation are outlined. The fifth and sixth sections focus on inferential statistics. Part 5 deals with statistics used to draw conclusions about a single variable in the population, Part 6 with statistics used to draw inferences about relationships among two or three variables in the population. With several exceptions, each chapter in Parts 5 and 6 focuses on a single statistic. This allows the instructor to modify the order of presentation or skip certain statistics with relative ease. In Parts 5 and 6 parametric statistics are discussed first, followed by non-parametric statistics. The final chapter attempts an integration of the material covered in the text by offering a model for determining the right statistics.

Two supplements are provided to accompany this text—a Study Guide for students (0-673-99424-4) and a Test Bank for instructors (0-673-55843-6). Both are authored by me. Addison Wesley Longman also publishes StatTutor, a student tutorial program available for both IBM and MacIntosh systems.

FINAL COMMENTS

There are several people whose contributions to this work deserve note. Christopher Capuano, Ph.D., John Herr, R.P., David Book, R.P., and Deborah Bernstein, Psy.D., provided important input into some of the examples used. I would also like to thank the reviewers whose invaluable feedback made this a much stronger work: Dr. Gordon Allen,

Miami University of Ohio; Dr. Nancy Anderson, University of Maryland; Dr. Timothy N. Ansley, University of Iowa; Dr. Amelia Barile, University of Oklahoma; Dr. D.K. Beale, Cerritos College; Dr. Charles F. Bond, Texas Christian University; Dr. Lizanne DeStefano, University of Illinois; Dr. Susan E. Dutch, Westfield State College; Dr. Warren Fass, University of Pittsburgh at Bradford; Dr. Michael Frank, Stockton State College; Dr. Dennis Jowaisas, Oklahoma City University; Dr. Gwen Murdock, Missouri Southern State College; Dr. Carrol Perrino, Morgan State University; Dr. Kirk Richardson, Georgia State University. Finally, I would like to thank my family, without whose patience and support this volume would not have been possible.

Robert E. McGrath

PART I

Introduction to Statistics and Research Design

Statistics are tools that are used as part of the scientific research process. The first three chapters of this text will offer an introduction to statistical concepts and the research process. Chapter 1 begins by describing the relationship between statistics and scientific research. Important topics in the first chapter include:

- the goals of the research process, including the role of statistics in research
- the nature of variables

Statistics is also a branch of mathematics, and understanding statistics requires some familiarity with basic mathematical operations. The supplement to the first chapter offers a refresher for students whose math skills may be a little rusty.

To help you develop a better understanding of the role statistics play in scientific research, Chapters 2 and 3 introduce some of the key concepts used in the development of research projects. Important topics in Chapter 2 include:

- the distinction between samples and populations
- sampling methods
- the different types of statistics

Important topics in Chapter 3 include:

- the scientific hypothesis
- the three types of research design

The supplement to Chapter 3 provides a brief introduction to the design of research projects. Although the information in this supplement is not necessary to understand the rest of the text, it may give you a richer sense of how research is conducted, and of the relationship between statistics and research design.

CHAPTER 1

Basic Statistical Concepts

1.1 SCIENTIFIC RESEARCH AND THE ROLE OF STATISTICS

The fact that you are reading these words suggests you are interested in the behavioral sciences. You are likely to be the type of person who wonders why people and animals do the things they do, and how their behavior can be changed for the better. What are the causes of poverty and ignorance? How can we improve teaching methods in our schools? How does learning take place?

Scientific Research. Scientific research provides a method for studying the types of questions that interest behavioral scientists. A researcher may observe naturally occurring events: a zoologist follows gorillas in their native habitat; a sociologist watches how a group of college students interact at a fraternity party; a political scientist reviews voter turn-out for an election. A researcher may actively request information: a teacher asks students their opinions of drugs and alcohol; a marketing consultant questions 1000 people about dental floss; a nurse surveys nursing home residents concerning their life satisfaction. Or a researcher may intervene in events to investigate the effect of the intervention: a physician examines the impact of a new drug on cancer patients; a psychologist studies whether making a person feel helpless increases feelings of depression; an educator studies whether fractions are better learned when lessons are spread out over time or grouped together. The common ingredient in each case is the *direct observation of real-life events*. This is the key element in all scientific research.

Statistics. Scientific research usually produces a great deal of information. Statistics are tools researchers can use to make sense of the information they gather. A **statistic** is *a number derived using mathematical methods that organize and summarize information*.[1] A statistic is a number, but it is a number that can summarize large amounts of information derived from a scientific study.

Besides being the plural of statistic, the term **statistics** also refers to *the branch of mathematics that has to do with statistical methods*. By allowing us to organize and summarize the information derived from scientific research, statistics make it easier for researchers to identify patterns in the results.

---

[1]Terms printed in **bold** are accompanied by a definition in *italics*. These terms are also listed at the end of the chapter under Key Terms, and are included in the glossary at the back of the text. A summary of basic mathematical concepts is provided in the supplement at the end of this chapter.

1.2 A SIMPLE STUDY

Describing the Study. To introduce some basic statistical concepts and demonstrate the role of statistics in the research process, a very simple example of a research study will be helpful. Suppose a researcher is interested in attitudes towards legalized abortion. Six hundred people are asked to indicate their opinions by choosing one of the following options:

1 = strongly opposed to legalized abortion

2 = opposed to legalized abortion

3 = neutral about legalized abortion

4 = supportive of legalized abortion

5 = strongly supportive of legalized abortion.

After each person responds the result is recorded as a number from 1 to 5. Each person's response represents a **datum**, *a single piece of information*. The datum produced by the first person might be a 1, indicating an individual strongly opposed to legalized abortion. The second person's response might be a 4, indicating support, and so on.

Since the plural of datum is data, the *entire set of information generated by a study* is referred to as the **data set**. The conditions under which people were selected to participate and asked their opinion, and the recording of their responses represent a **research study**, *a set of conditions and activities which produce a data set*.

Variables and Constants. Since the response can vary from one person to the next, attitude towards legalized abortion represents a variable. A **variable** is *a datum that can vary in value from one observation to the next*. In contrast, a **constant** is *a datum that has a fixed value in a given context*. The mathematical quantity π (the Greek letter pi) is a constant equal to 3.1416 in any context. Gender and religious affiliation would both be examples of constants if we were collecting data at a convention for Catholic priests.

The study on abortion attitudes has resulted in a data set consisting of 600 scores. Given the large number of data it might be difficult to identify patterns just by inspecting the scores. We might be able to make a few general statements, for example that 4 seemed to occur more frequently than 3, but more specific conclusions would probably be difficult. How much more common was a 4 than a 3? Which was more common, a 2 or a 4?

An Example of a Statistic. A statistic which would be helpful in this situation, and one that we use all the time without thinking of it as a statistic, is the **frequency**, *the number of times a particular variable value occurred in a data set*. Suppose we find the following frequencies for each value:

80 responded with a 1 (strongly opposed to abortion)

160 responded with a 2 (opposed)

50 responded with a 3 (neutral)

200 responded with a 4 (supportive)

110 responded with a 5 (strongly supportive).

We now know for certain there were more responses of 4 than 2. We can also say that an outcome of 4 occurred 4.0 times as often as an outcome of 3, since $200/50 = 4.0$. By computing these statistics we are able to detect patterns in the data, and improve our understanding of the results. This is the role of statistics in scientific research: *to help understand the data gathered in research studies by organizing that data in useful ways.* Statistics represent tools for organizing information about the variables we study.

1.3 TYPES OF VARIABLES

One of the most important points I would like to make about statistics is this: *the statistic that is most appropriate for organizing your data depends largely on the types of variables you are using* (see Davison & Sharma, 1988, 1990; Stevens, 1951). Two models have been suggested for classifying different types of variables. The first model was suggested by scientists interested in the measurement of behavioral variables, and can be called the measurement model of variables. The second model was suggested by mathematicians, and can be called the mathematical model of variables. The next two sections describe these models.

1.3.1 The Measurement Model

The **measurement model of variables** is *a model for classifying variables based on the extent to which variable values demonstrate the mathematical qualities of true numbers.* True numbers demonstrate the following mathematical qualities:

1. Different numbers indicate a difference: When we say Marie is 2 feet tall and Fred is 4 feet tall, we are saying there is a difference in their heights.
2. Different numbers indicate relative amount: When we say Marie is 2 feet tall and Fred is 4 feet tall, we are saying Fred is relatively taller than Marie.
3. Equal intervals between numbers indicate equal differences: When we say Marie is 2 feet tall, Fred is 4 feet tall, and John is 6 feet tall, we are saying the difference in height between Marie and Fred (2 feet) is equal to the difference in height between Fred and John (also 2 feet).
4. Ratios of numbers indicate proportional amounts: When we say Marie is 2 feet tall and Fred is 4 feet tall, the ratio of their heights is $4/2 = 2$. This indicates that Fred is twice as tall as Marie.

Although variable values are usually represented by numbers, these numbers may not demonstrate all the characteristics of true numbers. Stevens (1946) distinguished between four types of variables which differ in the extent to which variable values demonstrate the characteristics listed above. The four types are hierarchical, in that each includes all the characteristics of the preceding category plus an additional requirement.

Nominal Variables. A **nominal variable** is *a variable for which different values indicate only a qualitative difference in the characteristic being measured.* Gender is an example of a nominal variable with two possible values, male and female. Referring to one person as a male and another as a female indicates that a qualitative difference exists between them.

Numbers may be used to represent the values of a nominal variable, as with social security numbers or numbers assigned to horses in a race. These numbers are used for identification purposes only; identifying one horse with the number 2 and another with the number 6 does not indicate that horse 6 has more of some characteristic than horse 2. It only means that these are different horses. The choice of numbers for each horse is arbitrary.

Researchers often use numbers to represent the values of a nominal variable, for example using a 1 for females and a 2 for males when recording gender data. This practice is particularly common when a computer will be used to generate statistics.

Ordinal Variables. An **ordinal variable** is *a variable for which different values indicate a difference in relative amount of the characteristic being measured.* Any rank ordering is ordinal. If John's rank on a statistics test is 1, Fran's is 2, and Chet's is 3, we know the relative order of their scores. However, these numbers do not indicate equal intervals. The difference between John and Fran's scores on the test is not necessarily equal to the difference between Fran and Chet's scores.

Many of the variables used in the behavioral sciences are based on **rating scales**, *a method of collecting data in which people rate their opinions on topics of interest to the researcher.* Earlier in the chapter, 600 people were asked to rate their attitude towards legalized abortion on a scale from 1 (Strongly Opposed) to 5 (Strongly Supportive). The values 1 through 5 on this rating scale suggest order, since higher values imply greater support for legalized abortion. However, the difference between being Opposed (2) and Neutral (3) is not necessarily equal to the difference between being Strongly Opposed (1) and Opposed (2). For this reason, rating scales are usually considered ordinal variables.

Interval Variables. An **interval variable** is *a variable for which equal intervals between variable values indicate equal differences in amount of the characteristic being measured.* The Fahrenheit temperature scale is an interval variable. The amount of heat associated with a 3°F temperature change is always the same, so whether the temperature increases from 25°F to 28°F, or from 50°F to 53°F, the increase in heat is equivalent. Another example of an interval variable is years on the calendar. The earth revolved around the sun the same number of times between the years 1000 and 1005 as it will between 2000 and 2005.

Ratio Variables. A **ratio variable** is *a variable for which ratios of variable values indicate proportional amounts of the characteristic being measured.* Height is an example of a ratio variable, as indicated above when it was used to demonstrate the mathematical qualities of true numbers. If Fred is 6 feet tall and John is 3 feet tall, then we can say Fred is twice as tall as John, or that a ratio of 6 feet to 3 feet equals a ratio of 2 to 1.

In addition to equal intervals between values, ratio variables also have an absolute zero point, a value which represents the absence of the quality being measured. The division of 6 feet by 3 feet produces a meaningful value because there is an absolute zero point on the scale of height: the value 0 inches is associated with the absence of height.

This is not true of the Fahrenheit scale of temperature, since the value 0°F is not an absolute zero point. In contrast, 0° on the Kelvin scale of temperature refers to the point at which heat is absent. An object heated to 200°K is twice as hot as an object heated to 100° K. Similarly, calendar years would represent a ratio variable only if years were numbered from the birth of the solar system. Then, the earth would have revolved around the sun twice as many times in the year 2000 as it had in the year 1000.

A note of caution: an absolute zero point does not insure a ratio variable. Suppose a researcher studying smoking behavior asks people to describe their cigarette use on the following scale:

0 = does not smoke

1 = smokes less than $\frac{1}{2}$ pack per day

2 = smokes $\frac{1}{2}$–1 pack per day

3 = smokes 1–2 packs per day

4 = smokes more than 2 packs per day.

This is not a ratio scale. For example, a 4 on this scale is not twice as much as a 2. Even though this variable demonstrates an absolute zero point, the absence of equal intervals between variable values makes this an ordinal scale.

1.3.2 The Mathematical Model

The **mathematical model of variables** is *a model for classifying variables based on whether there are clear distinctions between variable values*. The model suggests dividing variables into two categories.

Continuous Variables. A **continuous variable** is *a variable for which there are no boundaries between adjoining values*. To get a sense of what this means, consider the variable distance. The distance between two points can be measured to tenths, hundredths, thousandths, millionths of an inch, and still not be measured exactly. Differences between adjoining values of the variable distance are so infinitely small that no real boundary exists between them. Each value essentially *continues* into the next. Because of this characteristic, exact measurement of the distance between two points would require an infinitely long number.

Other familiar continuous variables include temperature, height, and level of intelligence. Interval and ratio variables that do not involve counting a set of objects, and ordinal variables that do not involve rank ordering, are usually continuous variables.

Discrete Variables. A **discrete variable** is *a variable for which boundaries between values are clearly defined*. Suppose a supermarket takes inventory and counts the number of items presently in stock for each product. The number of items per product is a discrete variable, since an exact count is possible for each product. Whenever a variable is nominal, or the variable involves counting or rank ordering, the variable is discrete.

Measuring Continuous Variables. Since continuous variable values cannot be measured exactly, continuous variables are measured as if they were discrete. Saying someone is 65 inches tall is different than saying someone owns 65 books. The number of books someone owns is a discrete variable, and 65 represents an exact measurement of the number of books.

Height is a continuous variable. The value 65 inches is applied to anyone whose height falls in the interval between 64.5 and 65.5 inches. An **interval** is *a range of values grouped together for practical purposes*. In the interval from 64.5 inches to 65.5 inches, 64.5 inches represents the **lower real limit** of the interval, *the lower endpoint of an interval*. The value 65.5 inches represents the **upper real limit**, *the upper endpoint of an interval*. The value 65 is the **midpoint** of the interval, *the value half-way between the upper and* *lower real limits of an interval*, and is used to represent all values in the interval. Since height is a continuous variable, to say someone is 65 inches tall does not suggest that person's height is *exactly* 65 inches; it indicates only that the person's height falls within an interval represented by its midpoint 65.

1.3.3 Putting the Two Models Together

Seven different variable types can be defined by combining the two models, as demonstrated in Table 1.1. Part (a) of the table summarizes the two models, and Part (b) provides examples of the seven possible combinations. For example, calendar year represents a discrete variable because it involves counting years; at the same time it is also an interval variable.

Make sure to familiarize yourself with the different types of variables in Table 1.1. As each statistic is introduced in this book, I will indicate the types of variables for which the statistic is appropriate.

TABLE 1.1   A Summary of Variable Classification Models.

(a) Summary

Variable Type	Description
The Measurement Model	
Nominal	Different values indicate a difference in the characteristic being measured.
Ordinal	Different values indicate a difference in relative amount of the characteristic being measured.
Interval	Equal intervals indicate equal differences in amount of the characteristic being measured.
Ratio	Ratios of variable values indicate proportional amounts of the characteristic being measured.
The Mathematical Model	
Continuous	No boundaries between adjoining values. Includes most interval and ratio variables that do not involve counting, and ordinal variables that are not rank orders.
Discrete	Clear boundaries between values. Includes nominal variables, counting variables, and rank orders.

(b) Examples

		Measurement Model			
		Nominal	*Ordinal*	*Interval*	*Ratio*
Mathematical Model	Discrete	Telephone numbers; Marital status	Positions in a race; rank orders	Calendar years	Annual income
	Continuous	*This combination is not possible*	Responses to an abortion attitudes rating scale	Fahrenheit temperatures	Kelvin temperatures; height

KEY TERMS

constant	midpoint
continuous variable	nominal variable
data set	ordinal variable
datum	rating scale
discrete variable	ratio variable
frequency	research study
interval	statistic
interval variable	statistics
lower real limit	upper real limit
mathematical model of variables	variable
measurement model of variables	

EXERCISES

Answers to all exercises may be found in Appendix B.

1. I would suggest you begin the process of learning about statistics by learning about the structure of this book.
   a. Examine the Table of Contents. The book is divided into six Parts. Each Part begins with a statement of goals. By reading these statements, try to develop a sense of the format of the book. What is the purpose of the first part, called Introduction to Statistics and Research Design?
   b. Using the Table of Contents, locate the Glossary and Appendix B (Answers to Exercises).
   c. Review the Key Terms list for this chapter. Compare your memory of the meaning of these terms to the definitions provided in the Glossary.

2. Two students are interested in learning more about alcoholism. One decides to interview alcoholics about their experiences. The other reads several books about alcoholism. According to the description of scientific research provided in the chapter, can either of these methods be considered an example of scientific research?

3. Indicate whether each of the following is a *constant* or a *variable*:
   a. The distance from New York to Chicago
   b. The length of five different routes from New York to Chicago
   c. Every student received an A on the statistics midterm
   d. A researcher records age in months for a sample of 2-year-olds
   e. A researcher records age in years for a sample of 2-year-olds

4. For each of the following variables, indicate whether it is *nominal*, *ordinal*, *interval*, or *ratio*; and whether it is *discrete* or *continuous*.
   a. The number of votes each of 25 students receives in an election for class president
   b. On the basis of the vote in 4a, students are ranked from 1 (most votes) to 25 (least votes).
   c. The outcome of a single coin flip
   d. The number of heads out of 50 coin flips
   e. Zip codes
   f. Measurements made with a ruler
   g. Annual family income
   h. The length of time it takes to read this sentence
   i. The number of words in a sentence
   j. The Celsius (centigrade) temperature taken in four different cities at 12 noon
   k. Score on a rating scale of attitudes towards ethnic minorities
   l. The distance between two cities
   m. Olympic medalists came in either first, second, or third in their competition.
   n. Olympic medalists receive either a gold, silver, or bronze medal.

5. Each of the following is an example of a continuous variable interval. Indicate the upper and lower real limits and the midpoint for each interval.
   a. Height was measured to the nearest inch. Anthony was 68″ tall.
   b. Height was measured to the nearest half inch. James proved to be 71.5″ tall.
   c. Height was measured in half-inch intervals. Elliott was found to be 69″ tall.
   d. Ed's temperature was found to be 101.3°F.

It was noted earlier that statistics is a branch of mathematics, and as such requires some familiarity with basic arithmetic and algebra. You probably have already been exposed to all the mathematical concepts you will need to understand this text, but you may feel the need for a refresher. The pretest below can help you determine the topics on which you need to brush up; problems are divided according to the supplement section devoted to each topic. Answers may be found at the end of this Supplement (Section S10). A posttest is provided at the end of the Supplement if you would like to evaluate your mastery of the concepts once you are finished.

S1.1 PRETEST

(S1.2)   **1.** $|2| =$ **2.** $|-4| =$

(S1.3)   **3.** $\dfrac{3}{2} + \dfrac{6}{7} =$ **4.** $\dfrac{2}{13} + \dfrac{9}{13} =$ **5.** $\dfrac{3}{2} - \dfrac{6}{7} =$

       6. $\dfrac{4}{9}\left(\dfrac{7}{6}\right) =$ **7.** $\dfrac{\left(\dfrac{4}{9}\right)}{\left(\dfrac{7}{6}\right)} =$ **8.** $\dfrac{7}{14}$

       9. $\dfrac{42}{12} =$ **10.** $\dfrac{6}{12} =$ **11.** $\dfrac{-4}{2} =$

(S1.4)   **12.** $2^{-4} =$ **13.** $3^{0} =$

       14. $\sqrt{52} =$ **15.** $\sqrt[3]{27} =$

(S1.5)   Round each number to two decimal places:

       16. $26.759 \approx$ **17.** $0.135 \approx$

(S1.6)   **18.** $(2 + 5) \times 6 =$ **19.** $2 + 5 \times 6 =$

(S1.7)   **20.** $x(a + b + c) =$ **21.** $(x + y)^{2} =$

(S1.8) **22.** $4x - 16 = 12$ **23.** $18 - 3x = 6x$

$x =$ $x =$

S1.2 ABSOLUTE VALUES

The *absolute value* of a number is indicated by enclosing the number between two vertical lines. Taking the absolute value of a negative number makes it positive, but has no effect on positive numbers or zero.

Examples:

$$|-5| = 5$$
$$|5| = 5$$

S1.3 FRACTIONS

A *fraction* results from dividing one number by another, for example 3/4 (divide 3 by 4) or 5/2. The number on top is called the *numerator*, the number on the bottom the *denominator*.

    If fractions with the same denominator are added together, the resulting numerator is the sum of the two numerators and the denominator is unchanged. If fractions with different denominators are added together, the resulting numerator is the sum of the two numerators, each multiplied by the denominator of the other fraction. The denominator is the product of the two denominators.

Examples:

$$\frac{4}{3} + \frac{2}{3} = \frac{4+2}{3} = \frac{6}{3}$$

$$\frac{4}{3} + \frac{5}{2} = \frac{(4 \times 2) + (5 \times 3)}{(3 \times 2)} = \frac{23}{6}$$

$$\frac{4}{3} - \frac{5}{2} = \frac{(4 \times 2) - (5 \times 3)}{(3 \times 2)} = -\frac{7}{6}$$

    If two fractions are multiplied, the resulting numerator is the product of the two numerators, and the resulting denominator is the product of the two denominators. When one fraction is divided by another, the fraction in the numerator is multiplied by the *inverse* of the fraction in the denominator, the fraction flipped over.

Examples:

$$\frac{3}{4} \left(\frac{5}{2} \right) = \frac{(3 \times 5)}{(4 \times 2)} = \frac{15}{8}$$

$$\frac{\left(\dfrac{3}{4} \right)}{\left(\dfrac{5}{2} \right)} = \frac{3}{4} \left(\frac{2}{5} \right) = \frac{6}{20}$$

$$\frac{\left(\frac{3}{4}\right)}{1} = \left(\frac{3}{4}\right)1 = \frac{3}{4}$$

Fractions can be simplified in several ways:

1. If both the numerator and denominator can be divided by the same number, the fraction can be reduced by dividing each by that number.
2. If the numerator is greater than the denominator the number of times the denominator divides into the numerator is placed before the fraction, and the remainder serves as the new numerator.
3. If there is no remainder the fraction is removed.

Examples:

$$\frac{6}{3} = 2$$

$$\frac{23}{6} = 3\frac{5}{6}$$

$$-\frac{7}{6} = -1\frac{1}{6}$$

$$\frac{6}{20} = \frac{3}{10}$$

$$\frac{3}{3} = 1$$

$$\frac{-14}{-7} = 2$$

Fractions can be converted to decimal values by dividing the numerator by the denominator.

Examples:

$$\frac{3}{4} = 4\overline{)3.00} = 0.75$$

$$1\frac{1}{2} = 1 + 2\overline{)1.0} = 1.5$$

S1.4 EXPONENTS AND RADICALS

Exponents and radicals represent inverse operations. *Exponentiation* occurs when a number is multiplied by itself a given number of times. The number to be multiplied by itself is called the *base*. The number of times it is to be multiplied by itself is the *exponent*. Exponentiation is symbolized by following the base with the superscripted exponent. An exponent of 0 produces a value of 1 unless the base is also 0. A negative exponent produces the inverse of the value produced by the positive exponent.

Examples:

$$3^4 = 3 \times 3 \times 3 \times 3 = 81$$

$$-3^0 = 1$$

$$0^0 = 0$$

$$2^{-1} = \frac{1}{2}$$

$$2^{-3} = \frac{1}{2^3} = \frac{1}{8}$$

$$\frac{1}{2^{-3}} = 8$$

The *radical* symbol $\sqrt{}$ indicates the desired *root* of a given number. If the desired root is not indicated it is assumed to be 2 and the root is called the *square root*.

Examples:

$$\sqrt{9} = \sqrt[2]{9} = 3, \text{ since } 3^2 = 9$$

$$\sqrt[3]{8} = 2, \text{ since } 2^3 = 8$$

S1.5 ROUNDING

Rounding is almost inevitable when working with statistics, where numbers often extend for many decimal places. When reporting statistics, numbers should be rounded to one or two decimal places. When computing statistics, numbers should not be rounded to less than four decimal places. Rounding to fewer digits can substantially affect the accuracy of subsequent computations. For this reason, it is strongly recommended that all computations be completed using a calculator.

Suppose you want to round to three decimal places. When the fourth digit to the right of the decimal is less than 5, the third digit remains the same. When the fourth digit to the right of the decimal is 5 or greater, the third digit is increased by one.

Examples:

4.651   rounded to one decimal place $= 4.7$

4.651   rounded to two decimal places $= 4.65$

S1.6 ORDER OF OPERATIONS

An *expression* refers to a series of numbers and operation symbols that indicate the computations to be completed. The order in which operations in a mathematical expression are performed can change the outcome.

Examples:

$$2 + 3 \times 5 = 5 \times 5 = 25, \text{ or } 2 + 3 \times 5 = 2 + 15 = 17$$

$$2 + \frac{2}{6} = \frac{4}{6} = \frac{2}{3}, \text{ or } 2 + \frac{2}{6} = 2 + \frac{1}{3} = 2\frac{1}{3}$$

To deal with this problem, a standard order of performing operations has been developed. First, compute operations in parentheses or brackets. Next come exponents and roots, then multiplication and division, and finally addition and subtraction. Within these steps, operations are performed from left to right.

Examples:

$$2 + 3 \times 5 = 2 + 15 = 17$$

$$(2 + 3) \times 5 = 5 \times 5 = 25$$

$$2 + 4^2 = 2 + 16 = 18$$

$$(2 + 4)^2 = 6^2 = 36$$

$$2 + 3 + 5 = (2 + 3) + 5 = 10$$

S1.7 ALGEBRAIC OPERATIONS IN PARENTHESES

Many of the expressions in this book are *algebraic*, meaning that they include letters which serve as symbols for numbers. In working with these symbols, there are several rules for operations involving parentheses. Rules followed by a caption such as (S1.1) will be referred to in later supplements to prove formulas.

1. $a(b + c) = ab + ac$ (S1.1)

2. $(a + b)(c + d) = ac + ad + bc + bd$ (S1.2)

3. $(a + b)^2 = (a + b)(a + b)$
$$= aa + ab + ab + bb$$
$$= a^2 + 2ab + b^2$$

4. $(a - b)^2 = (a - b)(a - b)$
$$= aa - ab - ab + bb$$
$$= a^2 - 2ab + b^2 \tag{S1.3}$$

S1.8 EQUATIONS

An *equation* consists of two expressions separated by an equal sign. An equation indicates that the quantity to the left of the equal sign equals the quantity to the right of the equal sign. Equations in this book are usually algebraic, meaning symbols are used to represent unknown quantities. You can solve for the unknown quantity by performing the same operations on both sides of the equal sign.

Example:

$$-4x + 5 = 12$$

$$-4x + 5 - 5 = 12 - 5$$

$$-4x = 7$$

$$-4x\left(-\frac{1}{4}\right) = 7\left(-\frac{1}{4}\right)$$

$$x = -\frac{7}{4}$$

S1.9 POSTTEST

(S1.2)   **1.** $|-12| =$ **2.** $|0| =$

(S1.3)   **3.** $\dfrac{5}{3} + \dfrac{7}{12} =$ **4.** $\dfrac{6}{5} + \dfrac{5}{6} =$ **5.** $\dfrac{6}{5} - \dfrac{5}{6} =$

   6. $\dfrac{6}{5}\left(-\dfrac{5}{6}\right) =$ **7.** $-\dfrac{\left(\dfrac{6}{5}\right)}{\left(\dfrac{5}{6}\right)} =$ **8.** $\dfrac{27}{18} =$

   9. $\dfrac{12}{42} =$ **10.** $\dfrac{12}{8} =$ **11.** $\dfrac{-3}{-2} =$

(S1.4)   **12.** $4^3 =$ **13.** $12^1 =$

   14. $\sqrt{127} =$ **15.** $\sqrt[4]{16} =$

(S1.5)   Round each number to two decimal places:

   16. $26.795 \approx$ **17.** $17.014 \approx$

(S1.6)   **18.** $7^2 + 6 \div 2 =$ **19.** $7^2 \div \{5 + 3\} =$

(S1.7)   **20.** $(x + y)(a + b) =$ **21.** $(x - y)^2 =$

(S1.8)   **22.** $\dfrac{x^2}{3} + 12 = 13$ **23.** $16 = 22 - 2x^2$

$x =$ $x =$

S1.10 ANSWERS TO SUPPLEMENT PROBLEMS

Pretest

1. 2   **2.** 4   **3.** $\dfrac{3(7) + 6(2)}{2(7)} = \dfrac{21 + 12}{14} = \dfrac{33}{14} = 2\dfrac{5}{14}$

4. $\dfrac{11}{13}$ **5.** $\dfrac{3(7) - 6(2)}{2(7)} = \dfrac{21 - 12}{14} = \dfrac{9}{14}$ **6.** $\dfrac{28}{54} = \dfrac{14}{27}$

7. $\left(\dfrac{4}{9}\right)\left(\dfrac{6}{7}\right) = \dfrac{24}{63} = \dfrac{8}{21}$ **8.** $\dfrac{1}{2}$ **9.** $3\dfrac{6}{12} = 3\dfrac{1}{2}$

10. $\dfrac{1}{2}$ **11.** -2 **12.** $\dfrac{1}{2^4} = \dfrac{1}{16}$ **13.** 1

14. 7.2111   **15.** 3   **16.** 26.76   **17.** 0.14

18. 42   **19.** 32   **20.** $ax + bx + cx$ **21.** $x^2 + 2xy + y^2$

22. $4x - 16 + 16 = 12 + 16$ **23.** $18 - 3x + 3x = 6x + 3x$

$\qquad\qquad 4x = 28$ $\qquad\qquad 18 = 9x$

$\qquad\qquad x = \dfrac{28}{4}$ $\qquad\qquad \dfrac{18}{9} = x$

$\qquad\qquad x = 7$ $\qquad\qquad 2 = x$

Posttest

1. 12   **2.** 0   **3.** $\dfrac{5(12) + 7(3)}{3(12)} = \dfrac{60 + 21}{36} = \dfrac{81}{36} = 2\dfrac{1}{4}$

4. $\dfrac{61}{30} = 2\dfrac{1}{30}$ **5.** $\dfrac{6(6) - 5(5)}{5(6)} = \dfrac{36 - 25}{30} = \dfrac{11}{30}$

6. $-\dfrac{30}{30} = -1$ **7.** $-\left(\dfrac{6}{5}\right)\left(\dfrac{6}{5}\right) = -\dfrac{36}{25} = -1\dfrac{11}{25}$ **8.** $1\dfrac{1}{2}$ **9.** $\dfrac{2}{7}$

10. $1\dfrac{1}{2}$ **11.** $1\dfrac{1}{2}$ **12.** 64   **13.** 12

14. 11.2694   **15.** 2   **16.** 26.80   **17.** 17.01

18. $49 + 3 = 52$ **19.** $\dfrac{49}{8} = 6.125$

20. $ax + bx + ay + by$ **21.** $x^2 - 2xy + y^2$

22. $3\left(\dfrac{x^2}{3} + 12\right) = 3(13)$

$\qquad x^2 + 36 = 39$

$\qquad x^2 + 36 - 36 = 39 - 36$

$\qquad \sqrt{x^2} = \sqrt{3}$

$\qquad x = 1.7321$

23. $\dfrac{1}{2}(16) = \dfrac{1}{2}(22 - 2x^2)$

$\qquad 8 = 11 - x^2$

$\qquad 8 + x^2 - 8 = 11 - x^2 + x^2 - 8$

$\qquad \sqrt{x^2} = \sqrt{3}$

$\qquad x = 1.7321$

CHAPTER 2

Sampling

2.1 POPULATIONS AND SAMPLES

Suppose a research study was conducted concerning self-esteem among high school students. Students from several high schools were asked to rate their level of agreement with the statement "I feel good about myself" on the following scale:

1 = Strongly Disagree

2 = Disagree

3 = Neutral

4 = Agree

5 = Strongly Agree.

Of 826 students who participated, 27% responded with a 1 or 2, 16% responded with a 3, and 57% responded with a 4 or 5. The results suggest that 27% of the adolescents who responded did not report feeling good about themselves. Many people may consider this finding interesting, including parents of teenagers, politicians developing social policy, and educators. But when you think about it, there are millions of high school students in the United States; why should the opinions of these 826 students matter? The answer to this question requires an understanding of the difference between populations and samples.

2.1.1 Populations

A **population** is *the complete set of observations of interest to a researcher*. The entire set of possible dice rolls associated with a certain pair of dice would be an example of a population. Another would be the reading grade level for all American sixth grade students placed in special education. In the study I have been describing, the population of interest is the responses of all high school students to the self-esteem question.

There are cases where it is possible to collect the entire set of observations of interest. The complete set of batting averages in the American League East in 1990 is relatively small and easily gathered, for example. In most cases, however, the population is too large to be measured completely, as in the example of measuring reading grade level for all American sixth grade students placed in special education. There are many cases where measurement of the entire population is even impossible, as in the infinitely large population of possible dice rolls resulting from rolling a certain pair of dice. In such cases the researcher is limited to examining a sample of the population.

2.1.2 Samples

A **sample** is *a subset of a population*. In the self-esteem study mentioned above the sample consists of the 826 self-esteem scores from high school students who provided their responses to the rating scale. If the study involves measuring some variable produced by a sample of living things (rats, college freshmen, or whatever), then *the members of a sample* are referred to as the **subjects** of the study. For example, if the population consists of self-esteem scores for all American sixth grade students placed in special education, the subjects are those sixth graders in special education who participate in my study.

Samples are interesting because we believe they tell us something about a population. Data from a sample of 826 high school students are interesting to the extent members of that sample can be considered representative of some population of high school students that interests us.

The introduction of these new terms allow me to be more precise about the meaning of the term *statistic* than was possible in Chapter 1. A **statistic** technically refers to *a number derived using mathematical methods that organize and summarize information in a sample. A number derived using mathematical methods that organize and summarize information in a population* is called a **parameter**. The percentage of high school students in my sample who strongly agree with the statement "I feel good about myself" is a statistic; the percentage of all high school students in the country who strongly agree with the statement "I feel good about myself" is a parameter.

2.2 SAMPLING METHODS

There are three popular strategies for selecting a sample of subjects from the population of interest: random sampling, stratified random sampling, and convenience sampling. The next three sections will discuss these strategies.

2.2.1 Random Sampling

Random sampling is *a procedure for selecting a sample which insures that all members of the population have an equal chance of being chosen*. If random sampling is feasible it is considered the most desirable method of sampling, since it is the method most likely to produce a sample that is representative of the population.

Suppose we found that of 500 randomly selected American adults, 28.6% report opposing any form of gun control. This does not mean that exactly 28.6% of American adults oppose gun control. Even in random samples there is chance fluctuation in the statistics we collect, just as tossing a coin six times will not always result in exactly three heads. However, we can be fairly confident that the estimate of 28.6% is not grossly inaccurate. Furthermore, if we could collect a large series of random samples of 500 American adults and average the percent opposing gun control in each sample, we would have a very accurate estimate of the percent of American adults opposed to gun control.

Selecting subjects randomly can be more difficult than it sounds. Suppose you are asked by a college with a population of 7,246 students to administer a survey on student satisfaction to a random sample of 200 students. You might be tempted to choose names "at random" from the student directory. This procedure is unlikely to produce a true random sample. Without intending to you could tend to choose students more often from the first half of the directory than the second half, or males more often than females, or students with interesting sounding names more often than other students. The following are three acceptable procedures you could use to randomly sample 200 students from the population.

Drawing Random Digits. Each student is assigned a different number from 0 to 7,245. Eight slips of paper are placed in a container, representing the digits 0 through 7. Three more containers are created, each containing 10 slips of paper to represent the digits 0 through 9. One slip is drawn from each container to create a 4-digit number such as 0116, which indicates that Student 116 should be asked to participate. The slips are returned and the procedure repeated until 200 students have been selected. Student numbers start at 0 since the combination 0000 is possible. This method is similar to the procedure used by many states to select winning lottery numbers.

Random Digit Lists. A similar procedure can be conducted using a published list of random digits. RAND (1955), for example, generated a list of one million random digits, a small portion of which is provided in Table E–1 of Appendix E. Each student at the university is assigned a different number from 0 to 7,245, and a starting point is arbitrarily selected from Table E–1.

Part of Table E–1 is reprinted in Table 2.1. Suppose you arbitrarily chose to begin at the digit 8 printed in bold in Table 2.1. The goal is to continue through the table from your starting point, identifying subjects to include in the sample by number. For example, the first four digits from the starting point in Table 2.1 are 8011. Since there is no subject

TABLE 2.1   A Portion of Table E–1.

16959	76737	16654	13542	20728	13928	30394	43895	21995	85942
04994	99280	94784	55171	14880	40420	15667	84423	62403	77012
25594	15045	07410	61877	55872	77197	82477	33640	06882	89657
63364	34022	88784	94445	84722	77505	64618	61370	18**8**01	16361
08694	33467	29511	18888	57516	63467	16959	21585	35113	25620
50046	65487	22656	74729	84950	60194	80964	92915	53704	66919
28960	79829	02580	24360	40273	75814	04835	00662	29784	88808
22308	89960	58428	34381	49539	89565	73880	27768	79531	29346
98592	23403	19929	67535	74484	80083	45577	62977	13548	04909
18040	39633	74903	07420	15147	31795	84481	90974	24042	24544

Source: Adapted from RAND. (1955). *A million random digits with 100,000 normal deviates*. New York: The Free Press. Copyright © 1955 by RAND. Reprinted by permission.

8011, the digit 8 can be ignored. The next four digits, 0116, indicate that student 116 will be asked to participate. The selection of subjects proceeds as follows:

> student 3610 is selected
>
> 8 is ignored, since there is no subject 8694
>
> student 6943 is selected
>
> student 3467 is selected.

Note that although the table includes spaces after every five digits and every five lines, these are inserted purely to make reading the table easier. The table is used as if it were a single string of digits with no blank spaces or lines.

The process is repeated until 200 students have been selected. This is just one of many procedures that could be used to select subjects using the RAND list; more sophisticated methods of choosing a starting point and dealing with invalid sequences are described in the original text.

Computerized Random Sampling. Many computer programs are available which can generate numbers in approximately random order. The most efficient method I know to use this tool for random sampling involves generating a random number for each student, and reordering the students from lowest to highest random number. Since the order of the students is now random, the first 200 students on the list represent a random sample.

2.2.2 Stratified Random Sampling

Stratified random sampling is *a variant of random sampling in which the researcher insures that the random sample reflects the population on important variables*. It has been found that women are more likely to agree to participate in research than men (e.g., Range, Turzo, & Ellis, 1990). Suppose that in the first round of surveying on student satisfaction only 28% of students who agreed to participate were male. In choosing additional subjects, you might focus on surveying male students until the proportion of males in the sample is approximately equal to that in the entire student population.

The stratification method can be quite complicated. The researcher may try to match the population simultaneously on several variables such as gender, ethnic status, education, and income. In very large studies it may even be possible to match the population on complex combinations of variables, such as the proportion of white females earning less than $10,000 per year.

2.2.3 Convenience Sampling

Random sampling is an ideal rarely met in practice, since researchers usually do not have access to the entire population of interest. Furthermore, samples of humans are almost never random because they consist of those members of the population willing to participate. In most behavioral studies the sample is selected on the basis of **convenience sampling**, *selecting a sample of subjects because it is a group to which the researcher has ready access*. The extent to which findings can be generalized to the population of interest depends on the extent to which a convenient sample can reasonably be considered representative of that population, which in turn depends partly on how homogeneous the population is.

Homogeneous Populations. For example, the Wistar rat is a strain of rats widely used in animal laboratories. The Wistar rats in all laboratories are genetically similar, and are raised under relatively standardized laboratory conditions. A researcher studying a sample of Wistar rats born in her laboratory can feel fairly comfortable generalizing her results to Wistar rats in laboratories all over the country. A sports physiologist studying pupil dilation in college freshmen at a private midwestern university may feel similarly comfortable generalizing the results of his research to the population of all healthy young adults, since pupil dilation responses are likely to be very similar in all members of that population.

Heterogeneous Populations. In other ways human populations are quite diverse. A political scientist studying political views among students at a private midwestern university should feel much less comfortable about generalizing the findings to all young adults than the sports physiologist. The study would need to be repeated in a variety of settings before the conclusions can be generalized to the population with confidence. *The more heterogeneous the population on the variables of interest, the more questionable is the representativeness of a sample chosen for convenience.*

2.3 THE STRUCTURE OF THIS TEXT

At this point you have been introduced to all the concepts that you need to understand how the rest of this text is structured. Before I begin discussing statistical methods, I think it is important to introduce several concepts related to the design of research studies. This will be the subject of Chapter 3. The information contained there will provide you with the context for understanding the research examples in subsequent chapters.

The subsequent chapters are organized around the two major categories of statistics. **Descriptive statistics** refer to *statistics used to describe characteristics of a sample*. The frequency of dice rolls equal to 7 in a sample of 600 dice rolls, or the number of students in a sample who strongly disagreed with the statement "I feel good about myself," represent descriptive statistics. Descriptive statistics are discussed in Chapters 4–8 of this text.

Inferential statistics refer to *statistics used to draw conclusions about a population on the basis of a sample*. Chapters 9–12 discuss basic issues surrounding inferential statistics and introduce some simple examples. Chapters 13–25 each focuses on a specific inferential statistic.

There are two general categories of inferential statistics: hypothesis testing statistics and interval estimation statistics. Hypothesis testing statistics are introduced beginning with Chapter 10, interval estimation statistics with Chapter 12.

Chapter 26 is designed to help you integrate all the material you have learned. Drawing on information from all preceding chapters, Chapter 26 provides a model for determining the appropriate statistics to use for a specific research project.

KEY TERMS

convenience sampling	random sampling
descriptive statistics	sample
inferential statistics	statistic
parameter	stratified random sampling
population	subject

EXERCISES

Answers to all exercises may be found in Appendix B.

1. For each of the following, indicate whether a *population* or a *sample* is being described, and if it is a sample the population from which it was drawn:
   a. Twenty shoppers at the mall are stopped and asked which stores they prefer.
   b. All voters in the school board election are asked who they voted for.
   c. Voters from three voting sites for the mayoral election are asked who they voted for.
   d. The weight gain of 50 Long-Evans hooded rat pups is measured when they are allowed to feed naturally.
   e. The set of scores on Professor Smith's midterm exam
   f. Those students who attended Professor Smith's class on Thursday completed a teacher evaluation survey.
   g. Arthur took a sip and declared the container of milk had gone sour.
   h. Margaret searched every closet in the house looking for the missing shoes.
   i. Renee flipped the coin 10 times, and claimed the coin was fixed.

2. Identify whether the following are examples of *random sampling*, *stratified random sampling*, or *convenience sampling*:
   a. To compare males and females on a test of mathematical skills, 20 male and 20 female college students are chosen at random from the general student population.
   b. To compare males and females on a test of mathematical skills, 10% of all male students and 10% of all female students are chosen at random from the general student population.
   c. All shoppers at Henderson's store fill out slips, and one is pulled from a box to win a gift certificate.
   d. Professor Smith administers a rating scale on attitudes towards abortion to her Thursday morning statistics class.
   e. To compare two versions of a final exam, the teacher randomly gives one version to half the class and another version to the other half.

   f. The first three students who arrive at school every morning help the teacher prepare the classroom.
   g. The outcome of a coin flip
   h. Since 13% of all students at the university are seniors, the researcher made sure that 13% of students filling out the survey were seniors.

3. Congressman Nash decided to vote for the death penalty because 3 out of every 4 voters who called his office were in favor of the death penalty. What sampling method was he using? What is the problem with this method of sampling?

4. You must randomly sample 10 students from a list of 1000. Each has been assigned a number from 0 to 999. Turn to Table E–1 in Appendix E, and assume you have arbitrarily chosen to start on the 12th line of the table, the 4th block from the left; you will start with the series of digits 71269. What are the numbers for the 10 students you will ask to serve in your sample?

5. You must randomly sample 8 students from a list of 20. Each is assigned a number from 0 to 19. In Table E–1 of Appendix E, you arbitrarily choose to start on the 18th line, the 5th block from the left; you will start with the series of digits 94352. What are the numbers for the 8 students you will ask to serve in your sample?

6. In each of the following cases a sample is gathered and a statistic is computed. Indicate whether each of the following was based on a *descriptive statistic* (which describes the sample) or an *inferential statistic* (which uses sample data to describe the population):
   a. Between 40 and 42% of voters are expected to vote for the Democratic candidate.
   b. For the last three hours I drove at an average speed of 50 mph.
   c. College students we saw ranged in age from 17 to 59 years old.
   d. American college students generally range in age between 17 and 22 years old.
   e. Taking certain vitamins daily reduces the risk of developing certain types of cancer.

CHAPTER 3

Basic Concepts in Research Design

Although the purpose of this text is to discuss statistics rather than research design, an understanding of some basic research concepts will provide the context for understanding the role statistics play in research. This chapter focuses on two topics: the scientific hypothesis and the three types of research study. For those who prefer a more thorough discussion of research design and the role of statistics, the supplement to this chapter briefly outlines the steps involved in designing and conducting research studies.

3.1 THE SCIENTIFIC HYPOTHESIS

Every research study is based on at least one **scientific hypothesis**. This may be defined as *a guess about some variable pattern, or relationship among variables, in a given population which can be tested by a research study.*[1] The next three sections each address a portion of this definition (repeated in italics).

3.1.1 Hypotheses Concerning Patterns

A guess about some variable pattern: Hypotheses sometimes have to do with the pattern of frequencies for the values of a single variable. Suppose we ask a sample of American adults whether they support or oppose restrictions on access to abortions. The responses represent a **dichotomous variable**, *a discrete variable with only two possible values.* Depending on previous research findings, any of the following might be a reasonable hypothesis concerning the pattern of values for this variable:

1. The percentage of American adults supporting such restrictions is greater than the percentage opposing such restrictions.
2. The percentage of American adults supporting such restrictions is less than the percentage opposing such restrictions.
3. The percentage of American adults supporting such restrictions equals the percentage opposing such restrictions.

---

[1]To simplify the discussion, I often imply that a research study tests a single scientific hypothesis. In practice, research studies usually test at least several scientific hypotheses.

In each case, a guess is being made about the pattern of the data, in this case whether one value of the dichotomous variable occurs more frequently than the other.

3.1.2 Hypotheses Concerning Relationships

Or a relationship among variables: In most studies the scientific hypothesis has to do with the relationship between two or more variables. For now I will stick to examples involving two variables, although hypotheses involving three or more variables are possible. Whenever statistics introduced later in this text use the terms *correlation, association, independent* or *dependent,* you can be sure they address whether a relationship exists between two (or more) variables.

In Chapter 2.1 a study was described in which high school students responded to the statement "I feel good about myself" on a scale from 1 (Strongly Disagree) to 5 (Strongly Agree). The higher the score on the self-esteem rating scale, the greater the subject's self-reported level of self-esteem. To demonstrate the concept of relationship, two studies will be described which build on this study. These are followed by a discussion of the nature of variable relationships.

Self-Esteem and Grades. Suppose that we collected students' grade point averages, or GPAs, in addition to asking how they felt about themselves. Depending on previous research, any of the following might be a reasonable hypothesis concerning the relationship between these variables:

1. Students with higher scores on the self-esteem scale are likely to report higher GPAs, while students with lower self-esteem scores are likely to report lower GPAs. This hypothesis would make sense if, for example, the researcher believes that getting higher grades enhances self-esteem.
2. Students with lower scores on the self-esteem scale are likely to report higher GPAs, while students with higher self-esteem scores are likely to report lower GPAs. This hypothesis would make sense if, for example, the researcher believes that better students tend to be more self-critical.
3. There is no relationship between self-esteem and GPA; GPA scores tend to be the same at every level of self-esteem. This hypothesis would make sense if the researcher believes that self-esteem and grades have nothing to do with each other.

Self-Esteem and Peer Counseling. In this study, we are interested in whether level of self-esteem can be affected by a single session with a peer counselor, a student who has been trained in basic counseling skills. Suppose we divide a sample of 100 high school students into two groups of 50. Students in one group meet individually with a peer counselor to discuss a problem of their choice; students in the other group do not receive peer counseling. The treatment received represents a dichotomous variable. Depending on previous research, any of the following might be a reasonable hypothesis for this study:

1. Students who receive peer counseling tend to have higher scores on the self-esteem scale after treatment than students who do not participate. This hypothesis would make sense if the researcher believes that a single session of peer counseling can help students feel better about themselves.
2. Students who receive peer counseling tend to have lower scores on the self-esteem scale after treatment than students who do not participate. This hypothesis would make

sense if, for example, the researcher believes that a single session of peer counseling can stir up negative feelings without providing enough counseling to resolve them.

3. Self-esteem scores for students who participate in peer counseling are on average equal to scores for students who do not participate. This would suggest that no relationship exists between treatment condition and self-esteem after treatment. This hypothesis would make sense if the researcher believes a single session of peer counseling has no impact on self-esteem.

Relationships and Prediction. In each example two variables were collected from the same subjects to study whether a relationship existed between the variables. *A relationship exists between two variables when knowing subjects' outcomes on one variable allows you to make predictions about those subjects' outcomes on the other variable.* Suppose we conducted the study on self-esteem and grades, and found that students with higher grades tended to score higher on the self-esteem variable than students with lower grades. If you were presented with two students from the sample, one of whom had an above average GPA and the other a below average GPA, which would you expect has the higher self-esteem score?

You would probably predict the above average student's self-esteem score was higher than the below average student's. This prediction would not always be correct, since it is unlikely that every above average student in the sample had a higher self-esteem score than every below average student. However, it represents your best bet in this case. When two variables are related, information about one variable also provides information about the other variable.

Reasons Relationships Exist. Why would a relationship exist between the variables self-esteem and grades? There are three possible reasons for a relationship to exist between two variables, X and Y:[2]

1. X has a direct effect on Y. A **direct effect** exists when *differences in one variable produce differences in a second variable.* For example, if research consistently demonstrates that children who feel good about themselves when they begin school do better than students who do not feel good about themselves, this may suggest that self-esteem has a direct effect on school performance. Self-esteem may also be referred to as a *cause* of school performance. This possibility may be symbolized as

$$X \rightarrow Y.$$

2. Y has a direct effect on X. For example, if research consistently demonstrates that children who do well in school subsequently show an increase in self-esteem, this may suggest that school performance has a direct effect on self-esteem. This possibility may be symbolized as

$$Y \rightarrow X.$$

3. Neither variable has a direct effect on the other, and the relationship exists due to a third variable Z. For example, if research consistently demonstrates that supportive parents produce children who both do better in school and feel better about themselves,

---

[2]Italicized letters will be used in this book to represent variables. The letter Y will generally be used to represent outcome variables, while the letter X is generally used to represent variables believed to have a direct effect on Y.

then the relationship between self-esteem and school performance may only exist because a third variable is related to both. This possibility may be symbolized as

$$Z$$
$$\swarrow \quad \searrow$$
$$X \quad \quad Y$$

3.1.3 Testability of the Hypothesis

Which can be tested by a research study: A hypothesis is only scientific if it is possible to test whether it is false. This condition renders a hypothesis such as "God exists" unscientific, since there is no way to design a research study that is capable of testing whether God exists. A hypothesis which is impervious to testing cannot be considered scientific. The purpose of scientific research is the testing of scientific hypotheses; *the purpose of statistics in scientific research is to determine whether the data collected support the existence of a hypothesized pattern or relationship.*

3.2 THE THREE TYPES OF STUDY

Once the hypothesis is identified, a research study is designed to test that hypothesis. Research studies fall into three major categories: true experiments, quasi-experiments, and observational studies. If statistical analysis suggests the existence of a certain relationship in the data, the extent to which you can feel confident about why the relationship exists depends on the type of study conducted.

3.2.1 True Experiments

A research study qualifies as a **true experiment** when (1) *the researcher (or experimenter) randomly assigns subjects their values on an independent variable, and* (2) *the impact of manipulating the independent variable on some other variable, called the dependent variable, is then evaluated.* The self-esteem and peer counseling study described earlier will be used to illustrate the true experiment.

3.2.1.1 Random Assignment to the Independent Variable

The **independent variable** refers to *a variable that is manipulated by the experimenter.* In the peer counseling study the subject's treatment group is an independent variable since the researcher directly controls the conditions of treatment. The experimenter determines what happens to the subjects in each treatment, for example, when and under what circumstances peer counseling takes place. **Random assignment** occurs if *the researcher assigns subjects their independent variable values at random.*

Suppose our sample consists of 100 high school students. The following are three procedures we could use to randomly assign subjects, similar to the random sampling procedures discussed in the last chapter.

Drawing Random Numbers. Each student is assigned a different number from 1 to 100. One hundred slips of paper are placed in a container, each with a unique subject number

TABLE 3.1	A Portion of Table E-2																		
42	30	28	59	4	76	44	87	58	13	97	27	23	47	98	72	33	94	21	1
45	55	3	35	39	38	66	84	70	69	81	24	34	46	77	99	86	96	7	91
2	50	5	17	10	92	57	95	52	32	49	85	40	14	79	29	19	65	60	83
89	88	37	48	90	12	8	6	62	20	75	25	11	22	56	80	9	26	93	36
78	51	82	15	61	63	54	*	68	31	64	53	67	41	74	16	18	73	43	71

Source: Adapted from TABLES OF RANDOM PERMUTATIONS, by Lincoln E. Moses and Robert V. Oakford, with the permission of the publishers, Stanford University Press. Copyright © 1963 by the Board of Trustees of the Leland Stanford Junior University.

Note: The asterisk represents subject 100.

on it, and slips are pulled one at a time. The student whose number is picked first is assigned value 1 of the independent variable (peer counseling), the second student picked is assigned value 2 (no peer counseling), the third student receives peer counseling, the fourth receives no peer counseling, and so forth until all students are assigned.

Random Number Lists. Moses and Oakford (1963) published sets of numbers in random order. Some of their random orderings of the numbers 1 to 100 are provided in Table E-2 of Appendix E. Each student is assigned a different number from 1 to 100, and one set is arbitrarily selected from Table E-2. The numbers in that set are then treated as if they had been picked sequentially from the container in the previous method. For example, suppose you chose the set from Table E-2 that is reprinted in Table 3.1. The first three numbers in the first row of the set are 42, 30, and 28, indicating that subject 42 is assigned to peer counseling, subject 30 is assigned to no peer counseling, and subject 28 is assigned to peer counseling. The process continues until all students are assigned. Moses and Oakford provided random orders for samples ranging in size from 9 to 1000.

Computerized Random Assignment. A computer program is used to generate a random number for each student. Students are then arranged in order from the lowest to the highest random number, a procedure which randomly reorders the subjects. The first subject on the list is assigned to peer counseling, the second to no peer counseling, the third to peer counseling, and so forth until all students are assigned.

Creating Groups. Any of these three methods will produce two randomly assigned groups of 50 subjects. We can refer to 100 as the **sample size**, *the number of subjects in the study*. The **group size** is *the number of subjects at each value of a discrete variable*. I will use N to symbolize sample sizes, and n to symbolize group sizes.

The group of subjects that is exposed to the central treatment in an experiment is often referred to as the **experimental group**. *The group of subjects that serves as a comparison group for the experimental group* is often referred to as the **control group**. Since the central issue in our study is whether peer counseling affects self-esteem, the group of students who receive peer counseling is considered the experimental group. The group of subjects who do not receive peer counseling serves as the control group.

3.2.1.2 Measuring the Dependent Variable

Once all students in the experimental group have completed their peer counseling session, the self-esteem question is administered to all subjects. The self-esteem question represents the **dependent variable**, *a variable which is measured by an experimenter after manipulation of the independent variable*. The purpose of the study is to investigate whether the groups differ in their responses to the self-esteem question after treatment.

3.2.1.3 Explaining the Findings

Suppose our statistics suggest that students who participated in peer counseling tend to report more self-esteem after treatment than students in the control group. This indicates that a relationship exists between the independent variable, treatment group, and the dependent variable, level of self-esteem after treatment. How can we explain this finding? What is the reason this relationship exists?

Alternative Explanations. As you learned earlier in the chapter, two variables X and Y may be related for one of three reasons:

1. X has a direct effect on Y.
2. Y has a direct effect on X.
3. The relationship exists because both X and Y are related to some third variable Z.

If a well-designed true experiment suggests that a relationship exists between an independent variable X and a dependent variable Y, then there is good evidence that X had a direct effect on Y. The true experiment allows the experimenter to rule out most alternative explanations for the relationship.

Ruling Out Y Affects X. The manipulation of the independent variable occurs before the dependent variable is measured. This eliminates the possibility that the relationship exists because Y had a direct effect on X. In our example, this would be equivalent to claiming that self-esteem after treatment had an effect on the treatment group in which a student was placed, clearly an impossible occurrence.

Ruling Out Third Variables. An example of a third variable Z that could account for the relationship between X and Y in our study is level of self-esteem before treatment. Suppose the students who received peer counseling had a higher level of self-esteem even before treatment began than the students who did not receive peer counseling. We could expect they would also have a higher level of self-esteem after treatment, even if peer counseling has no effect on self-esteem. The variable self-esteem before treatment would therefore be related to both treatment condition (since subjects in one treatment condition differed from subjects in the other treatment condition) and self-esteem after treatment (since those with higher self-esteem to start should tend to be higher in self-esteem even after treatment). We may symbolize this as

self-esteem before treatment

↙   ↘

treatment condition   self-esteem after treatment

Subject Confounds. Self-esteem before treatment represents a potential subject confound in our study. A **confound** is an *unmeasured variable that offers an alternative explanation for an observed pattern or relationship to that explanation preferred by the researcher*. A **subject confound** is *a confound having to do with differences between subjects prior to any treatment*, such as level of self-esteem before treatment.

In order for a third variable to confound the relationship between two measured variables, the confounding variable must be related to both measured variables. In the example we have been using, self-esteem before treatment can only confound the relationship between treatment condition and self-esteem after treatment if it is related to both of these variables.

Random Assignment and Subject Confounds. Randomly assigned groups should be equivalent before treatment begins; there should be no differences between groups in level of self-esteem before treatment, intelligence, proportion of the two genders, or any other variable. Successful random assignment means self-esteem before treatment—and any other potential subject confound—is not related to treatment condition, and therefore cannot account for the relationship between treatment condition and self-esteem after treatment.

Summary. To summarize the discussion so far, there are three possible reasons a relationship might exist between two variables: X has a direct effect on Y, Y has a direct effect on X, or both X and Y are related to a third variable Z. In a true experiment, the dependent variable Y is measured after manipulation of the independent variable X, meaning Y could not have had a direct effect on X. Successful random assignment eliminates the impact of potential subject confounds, which represent potential third variables. If a true experiment provides evidence of a relationship between X and Y, there is reasonable evidence that the relationship exists because X had a direct effect on Y.

Remaining Problems. There remain two problems with the interpretation of true experiments. First, random assignment is not always successful; one of the groups may start with a higher level of self-esteem than the other group by chance. The larger the group size, the more likely random assignment will be successful. Hsu (1989) examined the relationship between sample size and the likelihood of successful random assignment, and concluded that random assignment is likely to be effective when the number of subjects in each of two groups is greater than or equal to 40. Smaller group sizes (20–40 subjects per group) are generally acceptable. When the group size is 15 or less, random assignment is likely to fail 10% of the time or more.

Second, there is another class of confounds over which true experiments do not offer any built-in control, called situational confounds. A **situational confound** is *a confound created by differences between groups in the conditions under which a variable is measured.* For example, in the peer counseling study an important situational confound is students' expectations of improvement: a difference may be found between groups just because participation in peer counseling creates the expectation that self-esteem will be enhanced.

It is up to the researcher to build controls over important situational confounds into the research design. Students in the control condition could participate in an unstructured discussion session with a student untrained in counseling skills. This treatment should have little effect on self-esteem, but could produce similar expectations of improvement. If we find a difference in self-esteem after treatment between the two groups, the case is stronger for concluding that peer counseling has a direct effect on level of self-esteem. *A treatment applied to subjects in a control group which is considered relatively ineffective, but which creates expectations similar to those of experimental group subjects* is known as a **placebo condition.**

TABLE 3.2   Random Sampling versus Random Assignment

	Random Sampling	Random Assignment
It is used to:	select subjects from a population.	divide subjects into groups.
It is used in:	any study where it is feasible.	primarily true experiments.
It serves to:	enhance the representativeness of the sample.	help rule out subject confounds.

3.2.1.4 Random Sampling versus Random Assignment

Students often find the distinction between random sampling and random assignment confusing. Table 3.2 offers a list of the differences between the two procedures. Although the methods used to achieve random sampling and random assignment are similar, they serve very different goals.

3.2.2 Quasi-Experiments

A research study qualifies as a **quasi-experiment** when *(1) the researcher (or experimenter) does not randomly assign subjects their values on an independent variable, and (2) the impact of manipulating the independent variable on the dependent variable is then evaluated.*

Quasi-experiments exhibit the same time sequence as true experiments: measurement of the dependent variable occurs after manipulation of the independent variable. For this reason, if a quasi-experiment indicates a relationship exists between the variables, the possibility that Y had a direct effect on X can still be ruled out. However, the absence of random assignment means the control of subject confounds is poorer than in true experiments, and there is again no built-in control over situational confounds.

The peer counseling study could be conducted as a quasi-experiment if students were not randomly assigned to treatment. For example, suppose for practical reasons only students from class 10A received peer counseling, while only students from class 10B were in the control condition. Because students are not randomly assigned, all sorts of subject confounds are possible. If students in class 10A are brighter or more motivated than students in 10B, differences in self-esteem after treatment may not be due to peer counseling.

3.2.3 Observational Studies

A research study qualifies as an **observational study** when *all variables are allowed to vary freely.* The researcher does not assign subjects to variable values or manipulate subjects' exposure to events. The researcher's role is limited to measuring variables. There is no independent or dependent variable, no experimental or control group, and it is inappropriate to call the researcher an experimenter. Studies that test a pattern hypothesis — a hypothesis dealing with only one variable — tend to be observational, since true and quasi-experiments deal with relationships between at least two variables.

Observational studies offer little built-in control over subject or situational confounds. In addition, the possibility that Y had a direct effect on X usually cannot be ruled out. For this reason, observational research tends to offer the weakest basis for drawing conclusions about why a relationship exists.

There are certain situations where an observational study is appropriate, as when a researcher is interested in whether a certain pattern or relationship exists and is unconcerned about the reason it exists. This is true, for example, of surveys concerning attitudes towards social issues, where the goal is simply to examine people's preferences. However, even when the researcher would like to draw conclusions about why a relationship exists there is often no alternative to the observational study.

The peer counseling study could be conducted as an observational study if students who have participated in peer counseling on their own are compared on level of self-esteem to students who have not participated in peer counseling. This study is particularly susceptible to subject confounds, in that the type of student who chooses to participate in peer counseling is likely to be very different than the student who does not. There is also no control over the nature of the peer counseling sessions they received, which may vary drastically in terms of length, amount of training for the peer counselors, and so forth.

3.2.4 Comparing the Types of Studies

When a statistical analysis indicates that two variables are related, the final step in the research process often involves offering some explanation for the existence of this relationship. The degree to which this explanation can be offered with confidence depends on the type of study employed.

A true experiment which indicates X and Y are related provides strong support for concluding that the independent variable X has a direct effect on the dependent variable Y, assuming adequate group sizes and control of situational confounds. The support for concluding that independent variable X directly affects dependent variable Y tends to be weaker in a quasi-experiment because of the potential impact of subject confounds. Observational studies generally offer the weakest basis for ruling out alternative explanations of a relationship.

When we try to address questions such as "What are the causes of poverty," or "What are the best methods for teaching nonviolent methods of confrontation," it is clearly important to be able to rule out alternative explanations for our findings. The extent to which we can draw clear conclusions from our studies depends on the quality of our research designs. While this conclusion implies all studies should be conducted as true experiments, there are many situations where a true experiment is not practical or appropriate, or where an observational study is the only available option. In addition, an observational study is preferred if the goal is simply to investigate whether a certain pattern or relationship exists.

Hopefully, this discussion has made clearer the role statistics serve in the research process. Statistics are used to decide whether we have evidence that a certain pattern or relationship exists. It is the research design which determines how confidently we can conclude why it exists.

KEY TERMS

confound

control group

dependent variable

dichotomous variable

direct effect

experimental group

group size

independent variable

observational study

placebo condition

quasi-experiment

random assignment

research study

sample size

scientific hypothesis

situational confound

subject confound

true experiment

EXERCISES

Answers to all exercises may be found in Appendix B.

1. Which of the following represent scientific hypotheses?
   a. There is life in the next galaxy.
   b. There are creatures all around us we cannot detect because they exist in another dimension.
   c. In 20 years the average American's life will be five years longer.
   d. John is thinking of the color blue right now.

2. Identify each of the following as a hypothesis about a *pattern* or a hypothesis about a *relationship*:
   a. There is life in the next galaxy.
   b. This coin is unfair.
   c. Males tend to be taller than females.
   d. There are more Democrats than Republicans.

3. For the following research ideas, identify the appropriate research design (*true experiment, quasi-experiment,* or *observational study*) for studying the topic:
   a. Drinking patterns in alcoholics at a bar.
   b. Are males or females smarter?
   c. If the students in class 5A get nutritional supplements every morning, will their academic performance improve compared to students in 5B?
   d. Students are randomly assigned to receive either praise of positive behavior or punishment of negative behavior.
   e. Subjects complete mazes after they are administered an amphetamine and again after they are administered a placebo.

4. A researcher is interested in whether a relationship exists between ethnic status and blood pressure. Blood pressure readings are to be taken from a sample of 20 black and 20 white adults. Since blood pressure varies according to time of day, members of the sample are randomly assigned to a morning or afternoon blood pressure reading.
   a. Is this study a *true experiment, quasi-experiment,* or *observational study*?
   b. Provide three possible scientific hypotheses for this study.

5. Suppose a researcher would like to design a study on the impact of heavy metal rock versus soft piano music on blood pressure in college students. Students from his two statistics courses are available to serve as subjects.
   a. For practical reasons, the instructor must place all the students from his morning statistics section in one condition (heavy metal), and all the students from his afternoon statistics section in the other. What type of study is this (*true experiment, quasi-experiment,* or *observational study*)?
   b. Suppose instead, all students listen to heavy metal on Monday and piano music Tuesday. What type of study is this?
   c. Suppose instead, students are assigned at random to listen to heavy metal or piano music. What type of study is this?
   d. Suppose instead, students are asked which type of music they prefer, and the blood pressure of those who prefer heavy metal is compared to that of students who prefer piano music. What type of study is this?

6. You are randomly assigning 100 subjects to 3 groups (the first group will have one more subject than the other two groups). Turn to Table E–2 in Appendix E. Each set of 5 rows represents a block of 100 subjects. Suppose you arbitrarily decide to use the 7th block:

the first row begins with the numbers 42, 30, 28. Moving across the rows, identify the first five subjects in each group.

7. You are randomly assigning 100 subjects to 4 groups. In Table E–2 of Appendix E, you arbitrarily choose to use the 9th block. The first row begins with 80, 74, 69. Moving across the rows, identify the first three subjects in each group.

8. Each of the following represents the statistical finding of a study and a potential interpretation of the finding. Suggest an alternative potential interpretation in each case:

    a. *Finding*: People in red cars get more speeding tickets than people in cars of other colors.
        Interpretation: People in red cars drive faster.

    b. *Finding*: Women are more often diagnosed as depressed than men.
        Interpretation: Depression is biologically related to gender.

    c. *Finding*: More people die in bathtubs than in cars.
        Interpretation: It is safer to drive than to take a bath.

    d. *Finding*: Towns with more churches also have more bars.
        Interpretation: Church-goers drink more.

    e. *Finding*: Cancer patients who take Dr. Smith's snake oil tonic report feeling less nauseous.
        Interpretation: Dr. Smith's snake oil tonic is an effective treatment for nausea associated with cancer.

    f. *Finding*: Five students who were randomly assigned to complete a statistics test administered by computer achieved higher scores than five students randomly assigned to complete the test on paper.
        Interpretation: Computer administration of tests enhance student performance.

Hopefully this chapter has enhanced your understanding of the relationship between statistics and research. This supplement provides a more thorough discussion of the conduct of research projects. Although still meant only as an introduction, it includes all the major steps involved in designing a research study.

Figure S3.1 outlines the research process. The first three steps lead to the development of the scientific hypothesis: selecting a research idea, reviewing the literature, and stating the scientific hypothesis. The next five boxes represent issues to be considered when designing a study: the type of study to be conducted, external validity, construct validity, internal validity, and the ethical treatment of subjects. The final two steps are involved in actually conducting the study: the collection of data, and the analysis and interpretation of the findings. The remainder of this supplement will outline each step in the process. Chapter sections devoted to each topic are provided in parentheses in Figure S3.1.

S3.1 SELECT A RESEARCH IDEA

The original idea for a study can come from at least four sources. First, the idea may grow out of a personal interest. For example, you may want to study learning disabilities because you or an acquaintance are learning disabled, or because you worked in a program that tutored learning disabled students.

Second, the idea may emerge from personal observations. We spend much of our lives observing the behavior of humans and other animals. Almost any of these observations could spark an idea for a study.

Third, the idea may be based on the implications of previous research. Research studies often leave important questions unanswered, or raise new questions to be addressed. Many reports of research studies actually conclude with suggestions for future research.

Finally, the idea may follow from a scientific theory. A **scientific theory** may be defined as *an integrated model describing the occurrence of certain natural events.* You have probably learned about many scientific theories in the courses you have taken. Scientific theories contribute to knowledge by providing a description of how certain types of events occur. Scientific research can be used to evaluate the accuracy of hypotheses derived from theory. Results that contradict the implications of a theory can lead to revision or even rejection of the theory.

The first time students develop a research project, I find they tend to rely on their personal interests or observations as a source of research ideas. While this can lead to a good study, I encourage you to consider the other two sources as well. The most important research studies tend to be those based on previous research or on scientific theories.

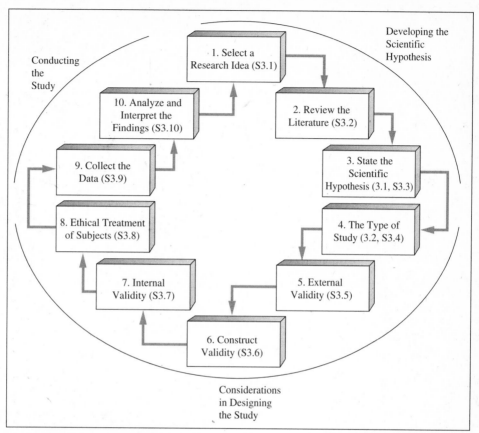

FIGURE S3.1 The research process. Chapter sections discussing each step in the research process are provided in parentheses. For example, the (3.1, S3.3) attached to "State the Scientific Hypothesis" indicates that Section 1 in Chapter 3 and Section S3.3 of the Chapter 3 Supplement are devoted to this topic.

S3.2 REVIEW THE LITERATURE

Publication Indexes. Once you have a research idea in mind, the next step is a review of the literature. Every year thousands of articles describing research studies and scientific theories are published in scientific journals. No matter what your idea, it is likely that someone else has already published research related to the topic.

There are several publication indexes that can help you find articles on your topic. You are probably already familiar with the *Reader's Guide to Periodical Literature*, which indexes magazine and journal articles for the general public. Psychological research studies are indexed in *Psychological Abstracts*, educational research in the *Educational Resources Information Center* (*ERIC*), medical research in *Index Medicus*, and sociological research in *Sociological Abstracts*. Another helpful tool is the *Social Sciences Citation Index* (*SSCI*), which identifies articles that *cited*, or referred to, a given article. If you are interested in finding articles that respond to the conclusions drawn in a publication by Jones and Smith published in 1991, the *SSCI* can be used to locate any articles that referred to Jones and Smith's publication. Many libraries can provide access to these and other indexes by computer. This can be a quick and efficient method of finding research on your topic.

Reasons to Review the Literature. Reviewing the literature is important for at least four reasons. First, it helps you refine your research idea. Your initial idea may be quite vague, for example, that you would like to study alcoholism. Reviewing the literature helps you narrow the topic.

Second, you can determine whether the study you are considering has been done before. If so, you may want to modify your study to make it unique since most scientific journals tend not to publish simple replications of previous research.

Third, it helps you develop your research method. If other researchers have developed procedures that are appropriate for your study, don't waste your time reinventing the wheel. Use established methods whenever possible.

Finally, it introduces you to scientific writing. Good scientific writing sticks to the facts, and presents them in a logical sequence without drama or exaggeration. This does not mean scientific articles need to be boring, just straightforward and honest.

S3.3 STATE THE SCIENTIFIC HYPOTHESIS

The nature of the scientific hypothesis was discussed in detail in Section 1 of this chapter. Upon completing your literature review you should be able to state the scientific hypothesis for your study. In addition, your review will probably give you some sense of the type of study and the methods you will use to evaluate the hypothesis.

S3.4 THE TYPE OF STUDY

This topic was discussed in Section 2 of this chapter. The student who wants a more detailed discussion of the three types of study is strongly encouraged to read two classic works on the topic by Campbell and Stanley (1966) and Cook and Campbell (1979).

S3.5 EXTERNAL VALIDITY

The **external validity** of the study refers to *the extent to which the researcher can generalize the results of a research study to the population of interest*. The external validity of the study is affected by two factors.

First, the more representative the sample is of the population, the better the external validity of the study. As discussed in Chapter 2, the representativeness of the sample tends to vary depending on the sampling method used. Random sampling or stratified random sampling are more likely to produce a representative sample of the population of interest than using a sample of convenience.

Second, the more realistic the conditions in which the study takes place, the better the external validity of the study. A treatment first evaluated under optimal conditions is likely to prove less effective when it is later examined under normal conditions. For example, new drugs are usually first tested on hospitalized patients. When they are later administered to outpatients success rates tend to drop, because it is more difficult to insure that patients take the medication at the appropriate times and in the appropriate amounts. The extent to which the setting where the study takes place is unique or different limits the extent to which the researcher can confidently generalize the results to other members of the population.

S3.6 CONSTRUCT VALIDITY

The **construct validity** of a study refers to *the extent to which the activities and conditions associated with each variable in a research study are likely to represent those variables accurately*. For some variables it is possible to define a procedure which results in a very accurate representation of the variable. Examples include body temperature, blood pressure, or injection with a fixed quantity of a drug. In other cases a variable is only represented in an approximate way. This is particularly true of variables based on rating scales such as self-esteem, where accurate measurement requires that (1) subjects perceive themselves accurately, and (2) they respond honestly.

A full discussion of the issues involved in establishing the construct validity of the variables in a study is beyond the limits of this introduction. Whole books have been devoted to the construct validity of behavioral variables. The interested student is referred to Allen and Yen (1979) or Crocker and Algina (1986) as a starting point.

S3.7 INTERNAL VALIDITY

The *extent to which alternative explanations of research findings can be ruled out* is referred to as the **internal validity** of the study. It was demonstrated in the chapter that true experiments generally are associated with greater internal validity than quasi-experiments, which are generally associated with greater internal validity than observational studies. However, no type of study offers complete control over potential confounds. When designing a study, a researcher should consider whether there are potential alternative interpretations for the desired finding which are not controlled by the type of study used. To the extent possible the research design should incorporate methods for ruling out these alternative interpretations.

One of three methods may be used to enhance the internal validity of a study. **Equalization of group conditions** refers to *a method of enhancing internal validity by insuring equivalence across groups on potential situational confounds*. This method can be used to control situational confounds in any type of study involving groups. Exposing control subjects to a placebo condition, so that their expectations for change equal those of experimental subjects, is an example of equalizing group conditions.

Modified random assignment refers to *a method of enhancing internal validity by modifying the random assignment procedure to insure equivalence across groups on potential subject confounds*. Modified random assignment is used to control subject confounds in true experiments. The most popular modified random assignment procedure is implemented in the **matched groups study**, *a true experiment in which random assignment occurs within blocks of subjects who are approximately equivalent on some* *potential subject confound, to equalize groups on that confound.*[3] This method assures that groups are relatively equal on that subject confound. You will see an example of the matched groups study in Chapter 15.

Statistical equalization refers to *a method of enhancing internal validity by statistically analyzing data as if subjects were equivalent on potential subject confounds.* This method may be used to control subject confounds in any type of study. It requires the use of fairly sophisticated statistical techniques which are beyond the scope of the present discussion.[4]

S3.8 ETHICAL TREATMENT OF SUBJECTS

The federal government and some professional organizations have established guidelines for the ethical treatment of human and animal subjects. According to federal guidelines, institutions that conduct research must establish an Institutional Review Board responsible for reviewing the ethical issues raised by research at that institution. In addition, institutions that conduct animal research are required to establish an Institutional Animal Care and Use Committee whose job it is to oversee the treatment and housing of laboratory animals.

Ethical guidelines for research with humans are particularly extensive. It is important to treat your subjects with dignity and respect. Become familiar with the ethical requirements for research with humans and animals before you attempt to conduct research.

S3.9 COLLECT THE DATA

Prior to collecting the data, you should determine the appropriate sample size. The number of subjects to include in a study largely depends on which inferential statistics will be used. Accordingly, I will delay the discussion of this topic until Chapter 11.

It is very helpful to create a detailed list of every step of the project before you begin: who is responsible for doing what, and how each step will be accomplished. Once you begin the study you will often find that the project does not proceed as planned. Perhaps a piece of equipment breaks down, or subjects do not respond to some task as expected. In such cases a modification of the design may be necessary. For this reason, when the study involves a new or complex procedure it is recommended that you first conduct a **pilot study**, *a trial run of a research study with a small sample to evaluate the adequacy of the design.*

S3.10 ANALYZE AND INTERPRET THE FINDINGS

Data Analysis. During the course of a study a fair amount of data is collected. Statistics are used to organize the information gathered, allowing conclusions to be drawn from the data about the accuracy of the scientific hypothesis. The rest of this book is primarily devoted to the statistical analysis of data, so at this point I will limit myself to some general comments

---

[3]Less popular modified random assignment procedures include *Latin square* and *hierarchical* designs.

[4]The most popular statistical techniques used for statistical equalization include multiple regression (Cohen & Cohen, 1983; Edwards, 1979) and the analysis of covariance (Huitema, 1980).

about the role of statistics in the research process. First, the statistics used to analyze a set of data are determined by two factors: the type of pattern or relationship suggested by the scientific hypothesis, and the types of variables collected. This topic is the focus of Chapter 26.

Second, although much of this book is devoted to the discussion of inferential statistics, these statistics play a very small role in the entire research process. The purpose of inferential statistics is simply to evaluate whether the data suggest that a hypothesized pattern or relationship exists in the population of interest.

Interpreting Findings. Once you have drawn a conclusion about the scientific hypothesis based on your inferential statistics, it is up to you as the researcher to interpret this information. The amount of confidence you can place in your interpretations depends on the construct, external, and internal validity of your study. Specifically:

1. The greater the external validity of your sample, the more confident you can be that the relationships or patterns you found are true for the population of interest.
2. The greater the construct validity of the variables, the more confident you can be that the relationships or patterns you found are true for the variables of interest.
3. The greater the internal validity of your study, the more confident you can be that the relationships or patterns you found exist for the reasons you suggested.

Future Research. An important lesson to learn about scientific research is that few studies are perfect; it is rare that a researcher can draw conclusions with complete confidence. When presenting the results of your study you should be appropriately cautious about drawing grand conclusions on the basis of fallible research.

If you go back to Figure S3.1, you will see there is an arrow from "Analyze and Interpret the Findings" back to "Select a Research Idea." This is because good research tends to spur further research. Your findings may generate new research ideas, reveal problems with the validity of previous studies, or suggest that a scientific theory needs to be modified or even rejected. The research process never ends; reaching the end of one research study leads you to the beginning of the next.

S3.11 SUPPLEMENT KEY TERMS

construct validity
equalization of group conditions
external validity
internal validity
matched groups study

modified random assignment
pilot study
scientific theory
statistical equalization

PART II

Variable Patterns

Descriptive Statistics for One Variable

As defined in Chapter 2, descriptive statistics refer to statistics that describe characteristics of sample data. The descriptive statistics to be discussed in this text can be divided into those which describe the pattern of data for a single variable, and those which describe the relationship in the data for two variables. Notice that this distinction is consistent with that drawn in Section 3.1 of Chapter 3 between hypotheses concerning variable patterns and hypotheses concerning variable relationships.

The next three chapters introduce methods for describing the pattern of scores associated with a single variable. Chapter 4 deals with methods of communicating or presenting an entire data set in an efficient and comprehensible form. Important topics include:

- methods of presenting frequency data
- graphic representations of frequency data

Chapters 5–6 introduce some descriptive statistics used to summarize a variable pattern. Chapter 5 focuses on the most important class of descriptive statistics for describing variable patterns, the measures of central tendency. Important topics include:

- the summation symbol
- the mode, mean, and median

Chapter 6 introduces the remaining topics to be covered under descriptive procedures for a single variable. Important topics include:

- the measures of variability
- transformations of variable data into more directly interpretable scores

CHAPTER 4

Frequency Distributions

A study was described in Chapter 1 that involved asking 600 subjects to rate their support for legalized abortion on the following scale:

    1 = strongly opposed to legalized abortion

    2 = opposed to legalized abortion

    3 = neutral about legalized abortion

    4 = supportive of legalized abortion

    5 = strongly supportive of legalized abortion.

To make these data more informative, I computed the frequency for each value. I then generated a **frequency distribution**, *a summary of the frequency of occurrence for each value of a single variable.* Providing the frequency of values is a simple way to communicate information about the data you have collected.

    The first part of this chapter will describe the most popular methods of presenting a frequency distribution in the form of a table. The second topic to be discussed will be the presentation of frequency data in the form of a graph. The chapter will conclude with a comparison of the two methods.

4.1 FREQUENCY DISTRIBUTION TABLES

A number of methods have been suggested for presenting frequency data in the form of a table, the most popular of which are (1) the ungrouped frequency distribution, (2) the grouped frequency distribution, (3) the cumulative frequency distribution, and (4) the relative frequency distribution.

4.1.1 The Ungrouped Frequency Distribution

The most straightforward method for presenting a frequency distribution is the **ungrouped frequency distribution**, *a table based on the frequency distribution which provides the frequency for each variable value that appears in the sample.* The production of the ungrouped frequency distribution is described in Procedure Box 4.1. The first column of the ungrouped frequency distribution, labeled *V*, lists variable values in size order from lowest to highest. Notice that although it was possible for students to receive a score of 15, this value is

PROCEDURE BOX 4.1

The Ungrouped Frequency Distribution

Goal   25 students completed a set of 15 math problems. The number correctly answered by each student was:

6	3	13	8	7
10	9	5	4	10
7	4	7	5	2
8	9	5	9	7
6	7	8	9	13

Create the ungrouped frequency distribution for these data.

Step 1   *Compute the frequency for each value.* As you come across each new value, add it to your list and put a slash next to it. As you come across additional outcomes of the same value add more slashes:

6	//
10	// ◄——*there are two outcomes equal to 10*
7	///// ◄——*there are five outcomes equal to 7*
8	///
3	/
9	////
4	//
13	//
5	///
2	/

Step 2   *Create the ungrouped frequency distribution.* Arrange values in size order from lowest to highest in the left column, the number of slashes for each in the right, with the N at the bottom:

V	f
2	1
3	1
4	2
5	3
6	2
7	5
8	3
9	4
10	2
13	2
N	25

excluded because none of the students had that score. The ungrouped frequency distribution is limited to those variable values that appear in the sample.

The second column, labeled f, indicates the frequency for each value in the sample. The final line of the distribution indicates the sample size, which should equal the sum of the frequencies. If you compare the raw data in Procedure Box 4.1 (provided under the **Goal**) to the ungrouped frequency distribution, you should see that the frequency distribution communicates information more effectively. For example, a quick review of the ungrouped frequency distribution reveals that scores between 7 and 9 were most common. While you could gather the same information from the raw data, it would probably take longer to draw the same conclusion.

4.1.2 The Grouped Frequency Distribution

An ungrouped frequency distribution is adequate for the presentation of frequency data as long as the number of values represented is small. This is not always the case, particularly if the variable is continuous. Table 4.1 provides part of the ungrouped frequency distribution of grade point averages, or GPAs, achieved by a sample of 615 college students by the end of their second year of college. The line with three dots (called an *ellipsis*) indicates part of the distribution is omitted because the entire table would require several pages. An ungrouped frequency distribution this long is likely to prove almost as confusing and uninformative as the raw data.

In cases where there are many values the presentation may be enhanced by using a **grouped frequency distribution**, *a table based on the frequency distribution in which values are grouped into equal intervals*. The method for creating a grouped frequency distribution is described in Procedure Box 4.2.

Important Points. A couple of points should be made about the grouped frequency distribution. First, in Step 1 of Procedure Box 4.2 I suggested aiming for 15 intervals, but

TABLE 4.1   An Ungrouped Frequency Distribution of Grade Point Averages

V	f
0.00	23
0.05	1
0.10	1
0.20	1
0.25	2
0.28	1
0.30	1
0.33	1
. . .	
3.86	1
3.87	1
3.90	1
3.93	1
3.97	1
4.00	1
N	615

PROCEDURE BOX 4.2

The Grouped Frequency Distribution

Goal   Create the grouped frequency distribution for 615 college students' grade point averages.

Step 1   *Select the number of intervals you want.* Grouped frequency distributions of 10 to 20 intervals tend to make for the best presentation. It is usually safe to aim for approximately 15 intervals to start.

Step 2   *Estimate the interval width.* Use the formula:

$$w = \frac{V_{\text{Max}} - V_{\text{Min}}}{\text{\# of intervals}},$$

where w is the estimated interval width, V_{Max} is the largest value in the sample, and V_{Min} is the smallest value. For 15 GPA intervals this equals

$$w = \frac{4.00 - 0.00}{15} = 0.267.$$

Step 3   *Round w if appropriate.* Some values of w are easier to work with than others. If the estimate of w is less than 10, round the interval width to the nearest multiple of 2, 3, or 5; round an interval width greater than 10 to the nearest multiple of 5 (Spence, Cotton, Underwood, & Duncan, 1990). In the present case w could be rounded from 0.267 to 0.30.

Step 4   *Define the lower limit of the first interval.* The lower limit of the first interval should be a multiple of w. If the lowest value that occurs in the sample is a multiple of w, the lower limit of the first interval is simply set to the lowest value in the sample. If the lowest value in the sample is not a multiple of w, the lower limit of the first interval is set at the next lower multiple of w. The lowest value in our sample is 0.00, a multiple of 0.30 (0.00/0.30 = 0), so our first interval will begin at 0.00.

Suppose instead the lowest value in the sample had been 0.67. Since this is not a multiple of 0.30 the lower limit of the first interval would be set at 0.60, the next lower multiple of 0.30.

Step 5   *Define the lower limit for subsequent intervals.* Each subsequent interval begins with the next multiple of w. The second interval begins at 0.30. This means that the first interval will include all values from 0.00 to 0.29, the second all values from 0.30 to 0.59, and so forth.

Continued

The grouped frequency distribution continued

Step 6   *Create the grouped frequency distribution.* Compute the frequency for each interval:

V	f
0.00–0.29	29
0.30–0.59	15
0.60–0.89	17
0.90–1.19	22
1.20–1.49	32
1.50–1.79	57
1.80–2.09	79
2.10–2.39	79
2.40–2.69	81
2.70–2.99	70
3.00–3.29	64
3.30–3.59	37
3.60–3.89	29
3.90–4.19	4
N	615

ended up with 13 instead. This is because w was rounded from 0.267 to 0.30. The number of intervals is approximated in Step 1; the final number will often be different.

Second, the first and last intervals may include values not found in the sample, values that may not even be able to occur. In Procedure Box 4.2 the last interval includes values greater than 4.00 even though GPAs above 4.00 are impossible. This is not unusual when creating a grouped frequency distribution, because of the equal intervals requirement.

Third, any frequency distribution of a continuous variable is in fact a grouped frequency distribution. When we talk about the continuous variable height for example, remember that the value 65 inches really refers to any value within the interval 64½ inches to 65½ inches. Continuous variables are inherently grouped.

Real Interval Limits. The real limits of a grouped frequency distribution interval differ depending on whether the grouped variable is continuous or discrete. Suppose we created a grouped frequency distribution of subjects' heights and one of our intervals was 63–65 inches. Remember that height represents a continuous variable. A person considered to be 63 inches tall is not *exactly* 63 inches tall; this value indicates a person whose height falls somewhere between 62½ and 63½ inches (see Section 1.3.2). Similarly, the value 65 is applied to any subject whose height falls between 64½ and 65½ inches. The lower real limit of the interval 63–65 is therefore 62½, while the upper real limit is 65½. In the GPA example, the real limits of the interval 0.90–1.19 are 0.895 and 1.195, while the real limits of the interval 1.20–1.49 are 1.195 and 1.495. Notice that the upper real limit of one interval (1.195) is also the lower real limit of the next interval.

In contrast, suppose we created a grouped frequency distribution of dice roll outcomes and one of the intervals was 2–4. Since this is a discrete variable, the lower real limit of the

TABLE 4.2   An Ungrouped Cumulative Frequency Distribution

These data were originally provided in Procedure Box 4.1:

V	f	cum f
2	1	1
3	1	2
4	2	4
5	3	7
6	2	9
7	5	14
8	3	17
9	4	21
10	2	23
13	2	25
N	25	

interval is 2 and the upper real limit is 4. In grouped frequency distributions of discrete variables, the *real* limits of each interval equal the *stated* limits. In grouped frequency distributions of continuous variables, the real limits of each interval are further apart than the stated limits.

Stem and Leaf Plots. Tukey (1977) suggested an alternative to the grouped frequency distribution called the *stem and leaf plot*. The stem and leaf plot has some advantages over the grouped frequency distribution, but is not as generally familiar. The construction of stem and leaf plots is described in the supplement.

4.1.3 The Cumulative Frequency Distribution

The **cumulative frequency distribution** is *a variant of the ungrouped or grouped frequency distribution which uses cumulative frequencies*. The **cumulative frequency** is *the frequency of values or intervals less than or equal to a given value or interval*. The cumulative frequency will be indicated by cum f rather than f.

Table 4.2 provides the ungrouped frequency distribution originally created in Procedure Box 4.1. A third column, labeled cum f, has been added which indicates the cumulative frequency for each value. Since there were seven scores less than or equal to 5, the cumulative frequency for the value 5 is seven. Notice that the cumulative frequency for each value is the frequency for that value, plus the cumulative frequency for the previous value. A cumulative grouped frequency distribution is provided in Table 4.3 for the GPA data. For example, a cumulative frequency of 61 for the interval 0.60–0.89 indicates that 61 of the GPAs were less than or equal to 0.89.

4.1.4 The Relative Frequency Distribution

A **relative frequency distribution** is *a variant of the ungrouped or grouped frequency distribution, cumulative or not, which lists proportions or percentages rather than frequencies*.

The **proportion** (p) is *the frequency of some variable value relative to the total sample size*, and is computed by dividing the frequency associated with each value or interval by N:

$$p = \frac{f}{N}.$$

TABLE 4.3   A Grouped Cumulative Frequency Distribution of Grade Point Averages

V	f	cum f
0.00–0.29	29	29
0.30–0.59	15	44
0.60–0.89	17	61
0.90–1.19	22	83
1.20–1.49	32	115
1.50–1.79	57	172
1.80–2.09	79	251
2.10–2.39	79	330
2.40–2.69	81	411
2.70–2.99	70	481
3.00–3.29	64	545
3.30–3.59	37	582
3.60–3.89	29	611
3.90–4.19	4	615
N	615	

TABLE 4.4   Relative Frequency Distributions of Grade Point Averages

V	f	cum f	p	%	cum p	cum %
0.00–0.29	29	29	.0472	4.72	.047	4.72
0.30–0.59	15	44	.0244	2.44	.072	7.15
0.60–0.89	17	61	.0276	2.76	.099	9.92
0.90–1.19	22	83	.0385	3.85	.135	13.50
1.20–1.49	32	115	.0520	5.20	.187	18.70
1.50–1.79	57	172	.0927	9.27	.280	27.97
1.80–2.09	79	251	.1285	2.85	.408	40.81
2.10–2.39	79	330	.1285	12.85	.537	53.66
2.40–2.69	81	411	.1317	13.17	.668	66.83
2.70–2.99	70	481	.1138	11.38	.782	78.21
3.00–3.29	64	545	.1041	10.41	.886	88.62
3.30–3.59	37	582	.0602	6.02	.946	94.63
3.60–3.89	29	611	.0472	4.72	.994	99.35
3.90–4.19	4	615	.0065	0.65	1.000	100.00
N	615					

Proportions can vary between 0 (indicating a frequency of 0 for that value) and 1.0 (indicating that the frequency for that value equals the sample size). The **percentage** (%) is *the proportion multiplied by 100*. Percentages can vary between 0% (when $f = 0$) and 100% (when $f = N$). Cumulative relative frequencies are computed by dividing the cumulative frequencies by N. Examples of various relative frequency distributions using the proportion and percentage may be found in Table 4.4.

   A note of caution about the use of relative frequencies: these can be misleading statistics when sample or group sizes are small. For example, suppose a college is interested in ethnic differences in graduation rate. If the entering class included only 3 Native Americans, and 2 of them graduated, the percent graduating in this group is a remarkably high 67%. The data are less impressive when one realizes these results are based on 3 subjects. When the sample size is small, the actual frequency should always be provided in addition to the relative frequency, to place the relative frequency in its appropriate context.

4.1.5 Checking Your Work

When creating a frequency distribution, there are several ways to verify that your computations are correct:

1. In an ungrouped or grouped frequency distribution the frequencies should sum to N.
2. In a cumulative ungrouped or grouped frequency distribution, the last cumulative frequency should equal N.
3. In a relative frequency distribution the proportions should sum to 1.00 and the percentages to 100, assuming no rounding error.
4. In a cumulative relative frequency distribution the last cumulative relative frequency should be 1.00 for the proportion or 100 for the percentage.

4.2 GRAPHIC REPRESENTATIONS OF FREQUENCY DISTRIBUTIONS

The methods described so far present a frequency distribution in the form of a table. Frequency distributions can also be presented graphically, in the form of a picture. Methods of graphically representing frequency data for discrete variables will be presented first, followed by a discussion of methods applicable to continuous variables.

4.2.1 Graphic Representations of Discrete Variables

Table 4.5 provides frequency data on the ethnic composition of a sample of 75 college students. The frequency distribution of this discrete variable can be graphically represented by a pie chart or by a bar graph.

The pie chart gets its name because it resembles a pie cut into slices. Each slice represents one of the values of the variable. The **pie chart** is *a representation of the proportion associated with each value of a discrete variable via the relative size of pie slices.*

A pie chart of the ethnicity data is provided in Figure 4.1. Each "slice" of the pie represents one of the ethnic groups, one value of the discrete ethnicity variable. The size of each slice depends on the relative size of the ethnic group. You may remember from geometry there are 360° to a circle. Since there are 27 white students in a sample of $N = 75$, the slice representing white students should comprise

$$360° \left(\frac{27}{75} \right) = 129.60°$$

of the pie. Notice that in Figure 4.1, the angle at the point of the slice representing whites is 129.60°. This procedure is repeated to determine the size of each slice. The relative size

TABLE 4.5   Ethnicity Data for 75 College Students

V	f	p
African-Americans	14	.187
Asians	2	.027
Hispanics	22	.293
Native Americans	10	.133
Whites	27	.360
N	75	

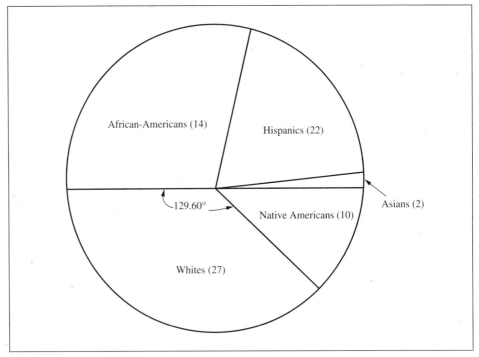

FIGURE 4.1 Pie chart of student ethnicity data from Table 4.5. It is common when creating a pie chart to attach the frequency to the label for each slice.

of the slices communicates to the viewer the relative frequency of the five ethnic groups. The angles for the five slices are as follows:

$$\text{Whites:}\quad 129.60°$$

$$\text{African-Americans:}\quad 360°\left(\frac{14}{75}\right) = 67.20°$$

$$\text{Asians:}\quad 360°\left(\frac{2}{75}\right) = 9.60°$$

$$\text{Hispanics:}\quad 360°\left(\frac{22}{75}\right) = 105.60°$$

$$\text{Native Americans:}\quad 360°\left(\frac{10}{75}\right) = 48.00°$$

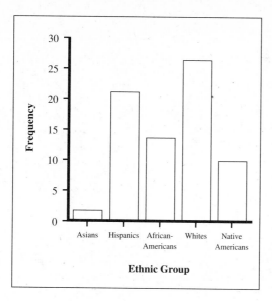

FIGURE 4.2 Bar graph of student ethnicity data from Table 4.5.

The **bar graph** is *a representation of the frequency or relative frequency associated with each value of a discrete variable via the height of bars in a graph*. Information is placed on two axes. Variable values are listed on the horizontal axis, also known as the *X axis* or *abscissa*. Frequencies or proportions are listed on the vertical axis, also known as the *Y axis* or *ordinate*. The height of the bar above each variable value indicates the frequency of that value as listed on the *Y* axis. A bar graph for the ethnicity data may be found in Figure 4.2.

The pie chart and bar graph tend to be used for different purposes. Bar graphs are preferred in scientific reports, since the *Y* axis provides exact information about the frequency or relative frequency. The pie chart tends to be better at attracting the reader's attention, and for this reason is more popular in articles written for the general public. Another difference worth noting is that, while the bar graph is relatively easy to construct by hand, accurate pie charts are more difficult, and best left to computers to produce.

4.2.2 Graphic Representations Appropriate for Continuous Variables

The frequency distribution of a continuous variable can be represented by a histogram or by a frequency polygon, although the latter is also often used for discrete variables. Examples will be based on the grouped GPA data in Procedure Box 4.2. Table 4.6 repeats the stated limits for intervals of the GPA data. The midpoint, the value halfway between the upper and lower limit for each interval, is also provided. These will be used in the development of the graphs that follow.

The **histogram** is *a representation of the frequency or relative frequency associated with each interval of a continuous variable via the height of bars in a graph*. The histogram looks very much like the bar graph. Values of the variable to be graphed are placed on the *X* axis, frequency or relative frequency on the *Y* axis. On both axes the lowest

TABLE 4.6   Upper and Lower Limits and Midpoints for GPA Data Intervals

Upper and Lower Limits	Midpoints	f
0.00–0.29	0.145	29
0.30–0.59	0.445	15
0.60–0.89	0.745	17
0.90–1.19	1.045	22
1.20–1.49	1.345	32
1.50–1.79	1.645	57
1.80–2.09	1.945	79
2.10–2.39	2.245	79
2.40–2.69	2.545	81
2.70–2.99	2.845	70
3.00–3.29	3.145	64
3.30–3.59	3.445	37
3.60–3.89	3.745	29
3.90–4.19	4.045	4

Note. These are the *stated* upper and lower limits, not the *real* upper and lower limits.

values are placed closest to the point of origin (where the two axes meet), the highest value furthest from the point of origin. Values on the X axis may be represented by the endpoints of the interval, or by the midpoint of the interval (see Figure 4.3). Bar height is used to represent frequency, but unlike bar graphs the bars are usually placed adjacent to each other to represent the continuous nature of the variable.

The most common method used to represent continuous variables is the **frequency polygon**, *a representation of the frequency or relative frequency associated with each interval of a continuous variable via the heights of points in a line graph.* The frequency polygon is equivalent to the histogram, except that:

1. Instead of bars, dots are placed where the center of each bar top would be.
2. The dots are connected with straight lines.
3. The left-most dot and right-most dot are connected to the X axis with straight lines. This encloses an area which represents the "polygon" (a figure with many sides) in the term frequency polygon. Connecting the dots to the X axis is frequently recommended, but may be considered an optional step.

The steps involved in creating a frequency polygon are demonstrated in Figure 4.4. Note that by following the above steps, you could also convert a bar graph to a frequency polygon. The frequency polygon is applicable to either discrete or continuous variables, although more commonly used with continuous variables. With discrete variables, it is not appropriate to connect the endpoints of the line to the X axis.

The frequency polygon is used more often than the histogram for several reasons. First, it is very easy to draw a frequency polygon by hand. Second, it is possible to smooth the line for aesthetic purposes. Figure 4.5 illustrates a smoothed version of the frequency polygon in Figure 4.4. Smoothing is accomplished by replacing sharp angles with rounded curves. Although the information in Figure 4.5 is not as accurate as in the original graph,

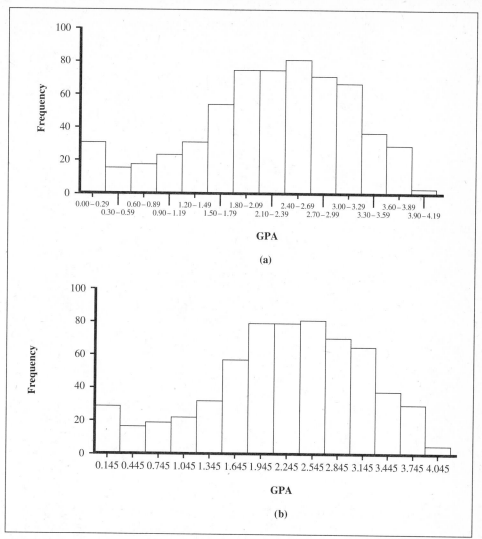

FIGURE 4.3 Two histograms of grade point averages from Table 4.6. X axis values are indicated by the endpoints of the intervals in (a), and by the midpoints of the intervals in (b).

the smoothed figure presents the general pattern in the data effectively. Many computer programs that generate graphs can smooth the frequency polygon automatically.

Finally, the frequency polygon is generally preferred over the histogram for the representation of cumulative frequency distributions. Figure 4.6 provides the cumulative frequency distribution for the GPA data. The Y axis now represents the cumulative frequency. Notice that upper stated limits are used on the X axis instead of midpoints, since the dots now reflect the number of observations less than or equal to the upper limit. When

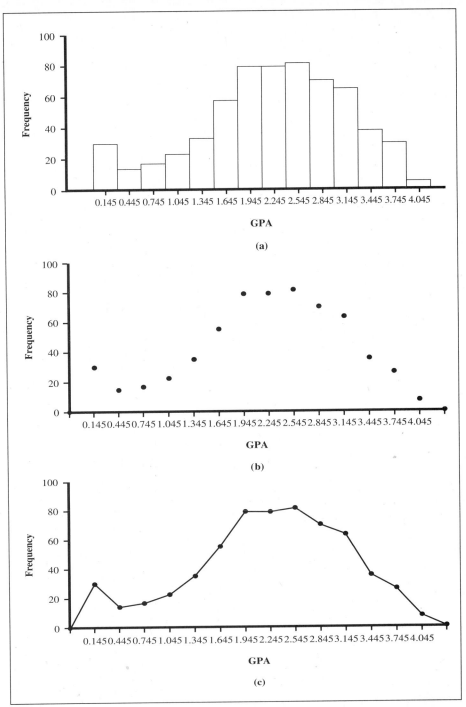

FIGURE 4.4 Transforming a histogram into a frequency polygon. The histogram in Figure 4.3(b) is transformed into a frequency polygon by replacing the bars with dots, connecting the dots with lines, and connecting the first and last dots to the X axis.

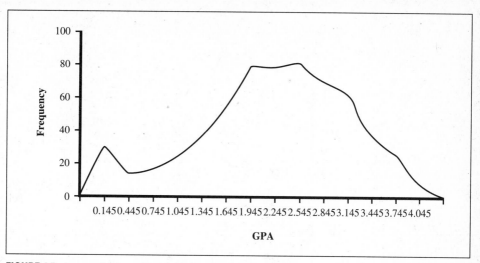

FIGURE 4.5 A smoothed version of the frequency polygon in Figure 4.4.

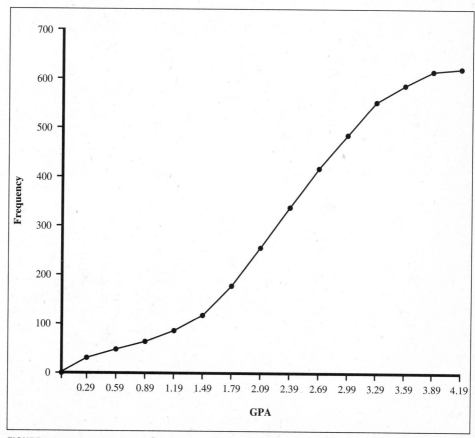

FIGURE 4.6 Cumulative frequency polygon of grade point averages from Procedure Box 4.2.

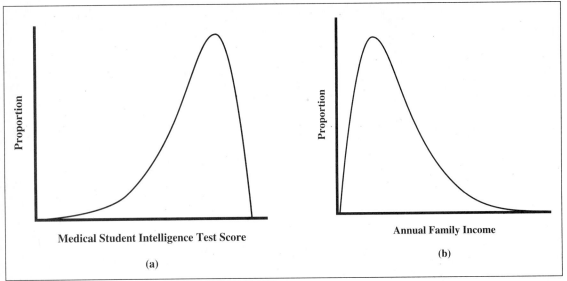

FIGURE 4.7 Skewed distributions. (a) A negatively skewed distribution. This represents the hypothetical distribution of intelligence test scores for a sample of medical students. (b) A positively skewed distribution. This represents the hypothetical distribution of annual incomes for a sample of American families.

representing a cumulative frequency distribution, the right-most dot should not be connected to the *X* axis.

4.2.3 Important Frequency Distribution Patterns

The frequency polygons in Figures 4.7 and 4.8 illustrate some important variable patterns. These are idealized figures; don't expect the frequency polygons you produce from actual data to look as smooth or as simple as these.

Skew. Figure 4.7 demonstrates the concept of *skew*. Suppose you collected intelligence test scores from a very large sample of medical students. Since this represents a relatively bright group of people, you might expect most of the scores to cluster near the high end of the distribution, with a few scores trailing off at the lower end. The smoothed frequency polygon might look much like that in Figure 4.7(a), with a *tail* at the lower end of the distribution. *A distribution for which the frequency polygon has a tail at the lower end* is called a **negatively skewed distribution**.

Suppose you collected yearly income data for a large sample of American families. Since most American families are fairly similar in income and make much less than the very wealthy, you might expect most of the scores to cluster near the low end of the distribution, with a few scores trailing off at the upper end. The smoothed frequency polygon might look much like that in Figure 4.7(b). This is a **positively skewed distribution**, *a distribution for which the frequency polygon has a tail at the upper end.*

I remember these terms by thinking of the X axis as a number line. On the number line, negative values fall to the left of zero, positive numbers to the right:

The tail of the negatively skewed distribution points towards the *negative* numbers on the X axis; the tail of the positively skewed distribution points towards the *positive* numbers on the X axis (see Figure 4.9).

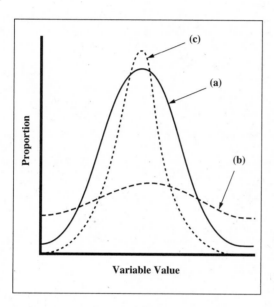

FIGURE 4.8 Some symmetrical distributions. Frequency polygon (a) represents a normal distribution. Frequency polygon (b) represents a platykurtic distribution. Frequency polygon (c) represents a leptokurtic distribution.

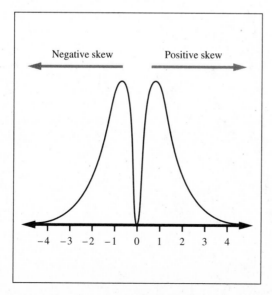

FIGURE 4.9 How to remember positive and negative skew. In a negatively skewed distribution, the distribution tail points in the negative direction on the X axis. In a positively skewed distribution, the distribution tail points in the positive direction on the X axis.

Negatively and positively skewed distributions are common in the variables studied in the behavioral sciences. Positively skewed distributions are particularly common. They tend to occur when the variable has an absolute minimum, or *floor*, but no absolute maximum, or *ceiling*, as with income data.

Symmetrical Distributions. The frequency polygons in Figure 4.8 represent **symmetrical distributions**, *distributions in which the left half of the frequency polygon is a mirror image of the right half*. Figure 4.8(a) is a **normal distribution**, *a theoretical bell-shaped symmetrical distribution of a continuous variable with a specific relationship between the elevation of the tails and the body of the bell.*

Notice the word *theoretical* in the definition. I will not offer an example of a research study that would produce normally distributed data, since it is almost impossible to create conditions under which a normal distribution would occur (see Micceri, 1989). Even so, you will see later that the normal distribution plays a very important role in the theory underlying many inferential statistics. The nature of the relationship between the bell and the tails of the normal distribution will be discussed in Chapter 6. The role of the normal distribution in inferential statistics will be introduced in Chapter 12.

Symmetrical bell-shaped distributions in which the relative frequency of values in the tails is greater than in the normal distribution are called **platykurtic distributions**, an example of which may be found in Figure 4.8(b). *Symmetrical bell-shaped distributions in which the relative frequency of values in the tails is lower than in the normal distribution* are called **leptokurtic distributions**, an example of which may be found in Figure 4.8(c). I remember these terms by using the physical characteristics of the body of the distribution: the body of the platykurtic bell seems *flatter* than the normal distribution bell ("flat" rhymes with *plat*), while the body of the leptokurtic bell seems to have *leapt up* when compared to the normal distribution.

Looking at Figure 4.8, one might be tempted to believe that it is possible to determine whether a symmetrical distribution is normal, platykurtic, or leptokurtic simply by examining the frequency polygon for the distribution. This is not the case, as demonstrated by Figure 4.10. Each graph provides the frequency polygon for the same normal distribution, but by manipulating the values on the X and Y axes, the distribution can be made to look platykurtic or leptokurtic. Visual inspection of the frequency polygon is not a sufficient basis for concluding whether or not a symmetrical distribution is normal.

4.3 FREQUENCY TABLES VERSUS GRAPHIC REPRESENTATIONS

While frequency tables and graphic representations of frequency distributions relay similar information, they tend to be used for different purposes. If the goal of the presentation is to offer a general impression of the pattern of the data, a graphic representation is superior. It allows the viewer to get a general sense of the data without focusing on the details. If the goal is to communicate exact information about the frequency distribution, a table is more useful. However, it can be difficult to get a general impression of the data from a frequency table.

Even in scientific reports the audience is usually more interested in the general pattern than the specifics, so graphic representations tend to be the preferred method of presenting frequency distributions. However, because it is more difficult to focus on details, graphs can be manipulated to bias the viewer's perception of the data. Remember how different

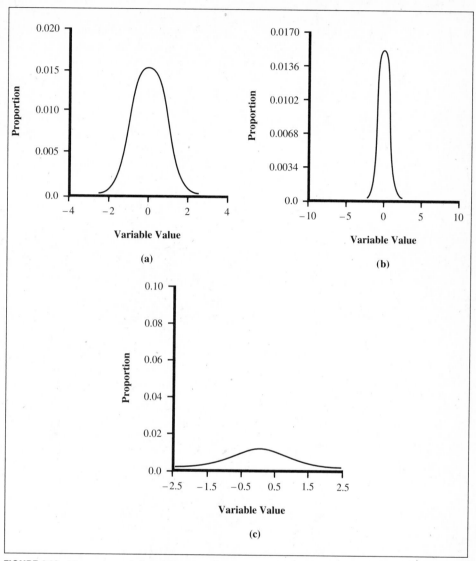

FIGURE 4.10 Alternative graphs of the same distribution. The shape of the frequency polygon for a normal distribution can be manipulated by changing the values for the X and Y axes.

the normal distribution looked when the X and Y axes were modified in Figure 4.10. Figure 4.11 offers another example.

Suppose we were studying the effectiveness of a new treatment for depression, and found that 51% of subjects who received the treatment showed full recovery within 3 months, as opposed to 46% of those who received a placebo treatment. Figure 4.11 contains two bar graphs of these results. Figure 4.11(a) might lead the reader to conclude the new treatment

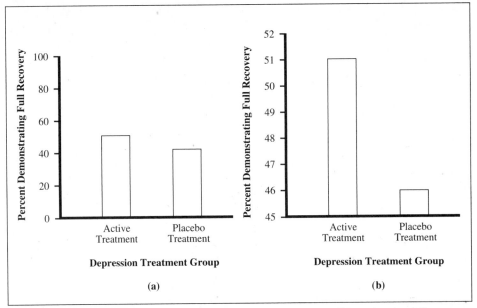

FIGURE 4.11 Two bar graphs representing the percent of depression sufferers showing full recovery within 3 months of receiving an active versus placebo treatment. The two bar graphs may lead to very different conclusions about the effectiveness of this treatment for depression.

is little better than the placebo, while Figure 4.11(b) is more likely to be interpreted as evidence of a dramatic effect.

Both bar graphs in Figure 4.11 are correct. By manipulating the *Y* axis it is possible to minimize or exaggerate differences. You should never rely on a quick impression from a graph to make judgments about the presence or absence of a pattern or relationship. Such determinations should be based upon close inspection of the data. Whenever you are presented with a graph of data results, at the very least you should examine the *Y* axis to see whether your initial impressions are accurate.

KEY TERMS

bar graph
cumulative frequency
cumulative frequency distribution
frequency distribution
frequency polygon
grouped frequency distribution
histogram
interval
leptokurtic distribution
lower real limit
midpoint

negatively skewed distribution
normal distribution
percentage
pie chart
platykurtic distribution
positively skewed distribution
proportion
relative frequency distribution
symmetrical distribution
ungrouped frequency distribution
upper real limit

EXERCISES

Answers to all exercises may be found in Appendix B.

1. Sixty entering college students completed an examination of basic reading skills. The following represent the number of items completed correctly by each student:

12	14	15	10	12
16	20	17	11	11
20	19	14	15	20
20	18	19	14	19
14	16	20	18	16
17	20	16	19	14
18	21	14	17	13
12	19	19	12	15
13	12	17	11	14
16	14	16	10	12
19	10	12	14	19
10	16	11	16	17

a. What type of variable is this: *nominal, ordinal, interval*, or *ratio*; *continuous* or *discrete*?
b. Create an ungrouped frequency distribution, cumulative frequency distribution, relative frequency distribution, and cumulative relative frequency distribution of the data.

2. The length of time in minutes each student took to complete the examination was also recorded:

12.1	14.6	15.4	10.2	12.6
16.4	20.5	17.6	11.1	11.2
20.3	19.3	14.1	15.5	20.1
20.4	18.7	19.9	14.8	19.1
14.2	16.9	20.8	18.3	16.4
17.6	20.2	16.5	19.9	14.5
18.9	21.8	14.7	17.8	13.0
12.3	19.3	19.9	12.6	15.7
13.5	12.0	17.0	11.1	14.8
16.0	14.5	16.4	10.8	12.3
19.1	10.9	12.6	14.0	19.3
10.5	16.3	11.3	16.3	17.2

a. What type of variable is this: *nominal, ordinal, interval*, or *ratio*; *continuous* or *discrete*?
b. Create a grouped frequency distribution for the data. Begin by assuming you would like to aim for 10 intervals.

3. The following is the hair color data for a class of 29 students:

V	f
Brown Hair	11
Red Hair	2
Blonde	7
Black Hair	8
N	28

a. What type of variable is this: *nominal, ordinal, interval*, or *ratio*; *continuous* or *discrete*?
b. If you were to create a pie chart for these data, how many degrees of the circle would be devoted to each hair color?
c. Create a bar graph for these data.

4. Create a histogram and frequency polygon using the data from Question 2. Use the interval limits for the *X* axis. Construct the graphs again using the midpoints.

5. Forty cardiac patients from a local hospital who reported experiencing severe anxiety over their heart problems were randomly assigned to two treatments. Twenty participated in a leaderless support group for five weeks, twenty in a support group led by a trained counselor. Each week they rated their level of anxiety concerning their health on the following scale:

None

Mild

Moderate

Severe.

The number of patients in each group reporting severe anxiety each week were as follows:

Group	Week				
	1	2	3	4-1	5
Led	18	14	11	6	6
Unled	14	13	10	10	9

a. Is this a *random sample, stratified random sample*, or *convenience sample*?
b. Is this study a *true experiment, quasi-experiment*, or *observational study*?
c. Identify the *independent variable* and *dependent variable*. Indicate whether each is a *nominal, ordinal, interval*, or *ratio* variable, and whether it is *continuous* or *discrete*.
d. Construct the frequency polygon for the number of patients reporting severe anxiety in the Led group, using Week for the *X* axis variable and Frequency for the *Y* axis variable.
e. Construct the frequency polygon for the Unled group using the same graph.
f. Examine the two frequency polygons. How might you interpret these data?

6. For each of the following variables, indicate whether you would expect the data to be *positively skewed*, *negatively skewed*, or roughly *symmetrical*. Justify your selection in each case:
   a. Scores on a very easy examination
   b. Length of time it takes to complete a moderately difficult untimed examination
   c. The number of times people report they have seen a UFO
   d. Daily temperatures taken at noon
   e. Heights of adult American males
   f. Age of tenth grade students in a school district where many students are held back
   g. Time it takes to complete a very difficult test with a one-hour time limit

7. When would you more likely use a:
   a. Pie chart than a bar graph?
   b. Bar graph than a pie chart? (Challenge: Try to identify *two* situations in which the bar graph is preferable).
   c. Histogram than a bar graph?
   d. Frequency polygon than a histogram? (Challenge: Try to identify at least *three* situations in which the frequency polygon is preferable).

S4.1 STEM AND LEAF PLOTS

The stem and leaf plot was introduced by Tukey (1977) as a more informative alternative to the grouped frequency distribution. Two examples of stem and leaf plots will be provided.

Example 1.

Table S4.1 provides the time in seconds it took for 50 college students to complete a complex maze. Table S4.2 contains the stem and leaf plot for these data. The plot was generated using the following steps:

Step 1. *Define each subject's stem.* Start with the lowest value in the distribution, in the present example 73 seconds. The stem is the left-most digit in this value; in this case, the stem

TABLE S4.1   Time in Seconds Required by 50 College Students to Complete a Maze

126	139	76	113	92
117	183	109	147	167
93	143	157	184	191
108	133	169	114	97
134	187	163	121	142
136	98	79	164	197
153	83	103	76	134
124	141	112	126	161
143	163	129	99	108
121	196	73	151	103

TABLE S4.2   Stem and Leaf Plot for Data from Table S4.1

Stem	Leaf
7	3669
8	3
9	23789
10	33889
11	2347
12	114669
13	34469
14	12337
15	137
16	133479
17	
18	347
19	167

is 7. Since this digit falls in the tens column for the value 73, the value in each subject's tens column represents that subject's stem. Other stems include 8, 9, 10, and so forth up to 19.

Step 2. *Define each subject's leaf.* The leaf is the digit to the right of the stem. For a subject with a time of 113 seconds the stem is 11 and the leaf is 3.

Step 3. *Create the stem and leaf plot.* Arrange the stems in size order from lowest to highest in the left column. The leaf values associated with that stem are then listed in size order in a row to the right of the stem. Notice that the stem 17 was included even though it is associated with a frequency of 0.

Advantages of the Stem and Leaf Plot. The stem and leaf plot communicates more specific information than the grouped frequency distribution, since at least two digits from each subject's score is reported. At the same time, the length of the rows in the stem and leaf plot serve a similar function to the height of the bars in a histogram or bar graph: longer rows indicate greater frequencies.

This is demonstrated in Figure S4.1. The stem and leaf plot from Table S4.2 has been turned on its side and placed above a histogram for these data. Longer rows in the stem and leaf plot correspond to longer bars in the histogram.

Example 2.

Table S4.3 contains high temperatures for 60 summer days. Note there are very few stems in this data set: the left-most digit is always either 7, 8, or 9. Using the steps for creation of the plot provided in the first example results in the stem and leaf plot found in Table S4.4.

This plot is not nearly as informative as the plot from the first example. This is because of the small number of stems. It is not uncommon when working with stem and leaf plots to find that the simplest method does not always produce a very informative display. In the present circumstance, there are two ways to make a more useful plot:

1. Use the first two digits as the stem. This alternative is demonstrated in Table S4.5.

TABLE S4.3 High Temperatures for 60 Summer Days

74.3	78.5	82.9	85.6	89.3	92.3
74.7	78.6	83.2	86.1	89.3	92.3
75.4	79.4	83.3	86.3	89.6	92.4
76.2	79.7	83.5	86.4	89.7	92.4
76.3	80.5	83.5	86.7	89.9	92.5
76.4	81.1	84.2	86.9	90.2	92.7
76.5	81.4	84.6	87.4	90.6	93.1
76.7	81.7	84.6	87.5	91.1	93.2
76.7	81.9	84.7	87.5	91.2	93.2
78.4	82.3	85.6	89.3	91.2	93.8

TABLE S4.4 Stem and Leaf Plot for Data from Table S4.3

Stem	Leaf
7	44566666688899
8	0111122333344445566666777999999
9	001112222223333

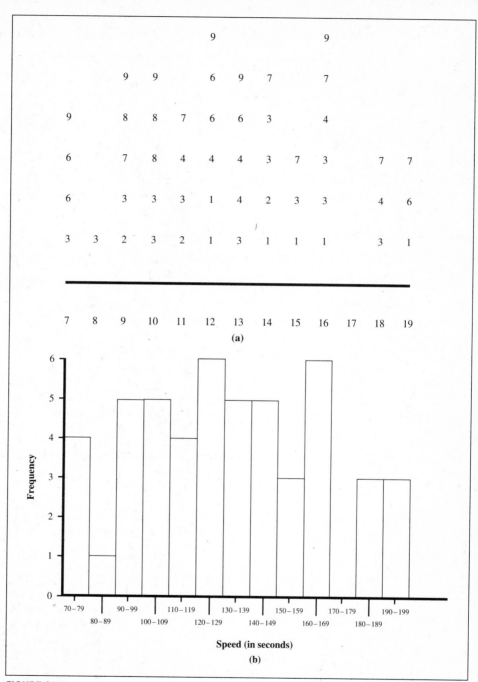

FIGURE S4. 1 A stem and a leaf plot compared to a bar graph. The leaves in a stem and leaf plot serve the same purpose as the bars in a histogram or bar graph; length provides information on relative feedback.

TABLE S4.5   A Second Stem and Leaf Plot for Data from Table S4.3, Using Two-Digit Stems

Stem	Leaf
74	37
75	4
76	234577
77	
78	456
79	47
80	5
81	1479
82	39
83	2355
84	2667
85	66
86	13479
87	455
88	
89	333679
90	26
91	122
92	334457
93	1228

TABLE S4.6   A Third Stem and Leaf Plot for Data from Table S4.3, Using Two Lines Per Stem

Stem	Leaf
7	44
7	566666688899
8	011112233334444
8	5566666777999999
9	001112222223333
9	

2. Increase the number of lines per stem. When using this alternative, the possible leaf values must be equally divided across the lines. The stem and leaf plot in Table S4.6 was created by taking the plot from Table S4.4, but the number of lines per stem has been increased to two. Cases where the leaf value is in the first half of the possible leaf values (0–4) are included in the first line, while cases where the leaf value is in the second half of the possible leaf values (5–9) are included in the second line.

In the present case I find the second alternative more informative. However, one of the drawbacks of the stem and leaf plot is that you may have to try several alternatives before you produce a plot that is acceptable.

Conclusions The stem and leaf plot communicates a general sense of the pattern of data for a variable while still providing more specific information than the grouped frequency distribution. For this reason it is well worth consideration as an alternative to the grouped frequency distribution. However, producing an informative plot may require several attempts. In addition, I have found that stem and leaf plots tend to be most useful with fairly small data sets, such as those with less than 100 observations. For larger data sets the stem and leaf plot can be confusing.

CHAPTER 5

Summation and Measures of Central Tendency

The frequency distribution tables and graphic methods introduced in the last chapter are used to communicate the pattern of data associated with a single variable. Descriptive statistics for a single variable go one step further, by expressing aspects of the variable pattern in a simple numeric form. This chapter begins with a discussion of the summation symbol, which is used in many of the statistical formulas that follow. You will then be introduced to the most important set of one-variable descriptive statistics, the measures of central tendency.

5.1 THE SUMMATION SYMBOL

The **summation symbol** is *a symbol used to indicate the sum of a series of variable values*. It is represented by Σ, the Greek capital letter sigma. Suppose we wanted to sum a set of scores on some variable. Any score in the set can be symbolized by Y_i, where the subscript i represents a unique number for each subject: Y_1 would refer to the score for subject 1, Y_2 to the score for subject 2, and so on to Y_N (the score for the last subject). The sum of all the scores can be symbolized by:

$$\sum_{i=1}^{N} Y_i.$$

This means "sum the scores for the variable Y, starting with the first score (subscript i equal to 1) and continuing until you reach score N, the last score in the data set."

Summing and Squaring. One aspect of summation that many students find confusing is the distinction between squaring scores before summing them, versus summing scores before squaring them. The expression

$$\sum_{i=1}^{N} Y_i^2$$

means "sum the squared scores"; each score is squared before they are added together. In contrast, the expression

---

TABLE 5.1   Summing Squared Scores, versus Squaring Summed Scores

Five students generated the following scores on a pop quiz in their statistics course: 6, 10, 7, 8, and 6. These values will be used to demonstrate the difference between summing squared scores, versus squaring summed scores.

Summing squared scores

$$\sum_{i=1}^{N} Y_i^2 = 6^2 + 10^2 + 7^2 + 8^2 + 6^2 = 285$$

Squaring summed scores

$$\left(\sum_{i=1}^{N} Y_i\right)^2 = (6 + 10 + 7 + 8 + 6)^2 = 1369$$

The result when you square summed scores will always be at least as large as the result of summing squared scores.

$$\left(\sum_{i=1}^{N} Y_i\right)^2$$

means "square the summed scores"; scores are summed and then the sum is squared. The difference between the two expressions is demonstrated in Table 5.1. Make sure you understand this difference, because it will save you from making some serious mistakes when you compute statistics later.

There is some additional information about the summation symbol in the supplement. You may find this information interesting or helpful, particularly if you plan to read the supplements in later chapters, but the information is not necessary to understand the material contained in the chapters themselves.

5.2 MEASURES OF CENTRAL TENDENCY

Measures of central tendency refer to *descriptive statistics which indicate the most representative value in a frequency distribution.* Unfortunately, the concept of "the most representative value" is ambiguous, and can be interpreted several ways: Is it the most common value? Is it the value that falls in the middle of the distribution? I will discuss three measures of central tendency, each of which is based on a different definition of the most representative value in the distribution. The next several sections will be devoted to detailed discussions of each measure of central tendency, followed by a summary of the measures.

5.2.1 The Mode

The **mode** (*Mo*) is *the value or interval in a frequency distribution with the highest frequency.* In an ungrouped frequency distribution the mode is the most commonly occurring value, the value associated with the highest frequency. In a grouped frequency distribution,

TABLE 5.2   A Bimodal Distribution

The following is an ungrouped frequency distribution of scores from a statistics midterm examination:

V	f
79	4
82	7
84	7
85	8
86	9
88	5
89	4
91	3
93	9
94	6
95	2
N	64

the mode is the midpoint of the interval with the highest frequency. The mode may be computed for any of the seven types of variables listed in Table 1.1 of Chapter 1.

Problems with the Mode. The mode is considered the least useful measure of central tendency for several reasons. First, it may not be possible to identify a unique mode. Table 5.2 provides a distribution of scores from Professor Smith's statistics midterm. Two scores, 86 and 93, share the highest frequency. This sort of distribution may be called *bimodal* (two modes) or *multimodal* (multiple modes).

It is also the measure of central tendency that shows the greatest change from sample to sample. If you drew a large series of random samples from the same population and determined the mode for each sample, you would find that the sample mode varies more from sample to sample than the other measures of central tendency. Because of the extent to which the mode fluctuates, the sample mode provides a relatively poor estimate of the most representative value in the population.

Finally, the mode can vary markedly depending on whether the distribution is ungrouped or grouped, and if it is grouped on the interval width selected. Table 5.3 illustrates this problem.

Advantages of the Mode. Despite its drawbacks the mode has its uses. Of the three measures of central tendency to be discussed, it is the only one appropriate for nominal variables. If the variable of interest is ethnicity, the other measures of central tendency cannot be computed, but you can determine the modal ethnic group in a sample.

Also, a bimodal distribution can indicate that two populations have been combined inappropriately in your sample. If for example upon closer inspection you find one mode is the mode for female subjects and the other is the mode for male subjects, it may indicate that females and males in the population differ on the variable of interest.[1] In subsequent analyses of that variable you may want to analyze the results for males and females separately.

---

[1]However, the absence of bimodality in a distribution does not necessarily indicate the sample represents a single population (see Murphy, 1964).

TABLE 5.3   The Effect of Grouping on the Mode

The following data represent the number of minutes required by 50 college students to complete a set of algebraic problems:

25	12	27	24	15	15	16	17	17	25
15	17	21	12	12	8	12	26	27	12
12	21	16	27	25	27	26	15	25	24
11	24	15	17	27	27	17	12	12	17
22	8	7	12	17	6	12	17	26	27

An ungrouped frequency distribution, a grouped frequency distribution with $w = 3$, and a grouped frequency distribution with $w = 4$ were created (the creation of grouped frequency distributions was described in Procedure Box 4.2 in Chapter 4):

ungrouped		$w = 3$		$w = 4$	
V	f	V	f	V	f
6	1	6–8	4	4–7	2
7	1	9–11	1	8–11	3
8	2	12–14	10	12–15	15
11	1	15–17	15	16–19	10
12	10	18–20	0	20–23	3
15	5	21–23	3	24–27	17
16	2	24–26	10		
17	8	27–29	7		
21	2				
22	1				
24	3				
25	4				
26	3				
27	7				

For the ungrouped frequency distribution, $Mo = 12$.
For the grouped frequency distribution with $w = 3$, $Mo = 16$.
For the grouped frequency distribution with $w = 4$, $Mo = 25.5$.

5.2.2 The Mean

The **mean** ($\overline{Y}$) is *the sum of the scores in a distribution divided by N*, and is the most commonly used measure of central tendency. The mean for a set of ungrouped data is computed by summing all the scores and dividing by the sample size:

$$\overline{Y} = \frac{\sum_{i=1}^{N} Y_i}{N}.$$

The mean may be computed for any ordinal, interval, or ratio variable. The formula for computing the mean of a frequency distribution is provided in the supplement, as is the formula for a variation of the mean called the *weighted mean*.

The Balance Point. The mean is sometimes referred to as the *balance point* of the distribution. If we compute the difference between each score in the distribution and the mean, these difference scores will sum to zero, assuming there is no rounding error:

$$\sum_{i=1}^{N}(Y_i - \overline{Y}) = 0.$$

This is proven in the supplement.

As the distribution's balance point, the mean differs from the mode and median in that its value is affected by the exact location of every score in the distribution. Changing the value of any score in the distribution changes the value of the mean, although the impact of any one score on the mean is small when the sample size is large. For example, the mean of the five scores 1, 2, 3, 4, and 4 is

$$\frac{1 + 2 + 3 + 4 + 4}{5} = 2.8,$$

while the mean of the five scores 1, 2, 3, 4 and 26 is

$$\frac{1 + 2 + 3 + 4 + 26}{5} = 7.2.$$

The value of the mean is "pulled" by extreme scores, scores that are divergent from the rest of the scores in the distribution (see Figure 5.1). Procedure Box 5.1 demonstrates the computation of the mean, as well as the concept of the mean as the balance point of the distribution.

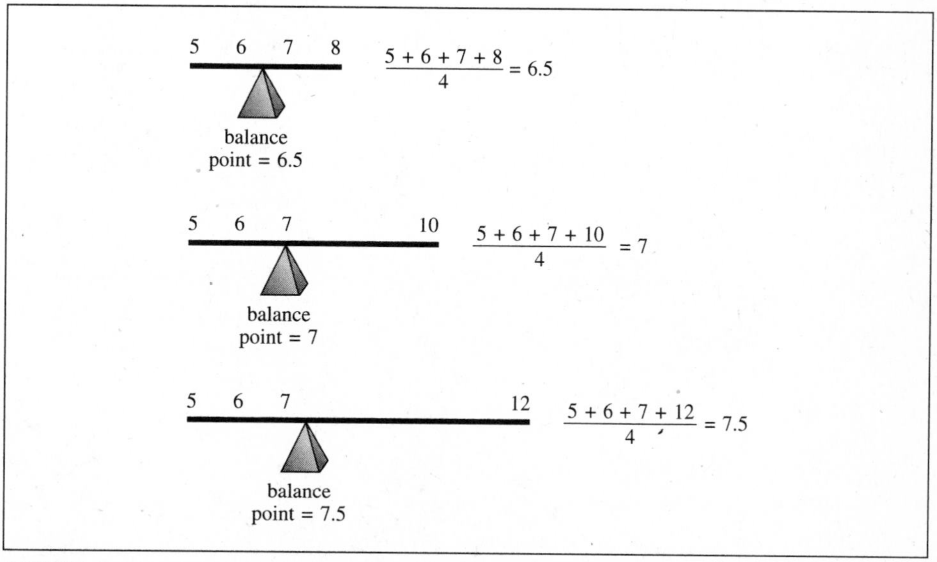

FIGURE 5.1 The mean is "pulled" by extreme scores. As the balance if the distribution, the mean moves as the scores change.

The Mean

Goal   Compute the mean of 5 students' scores on a statistics pop quiz: 6, 10, 7, 8, and 6.

To Compute the Mean:

$$\overline{Y} = \frac{\sum\limits_{i=1}^{N} Y_i}{N}$$

Step 1   *Sum the scores.*

$$6 + 10 + 7 + 8 + 6 = 37$$

Step 2   *Divide the sum by the number of scores.*

$$\overline{Y} = \frac{37}{5} = 7.4$$

Demonstration that the Mean is the Balance Point of the Distribution:

$$\sum\limits_{i=1}^{N} (Y_i - \overline{Y}) = 0$$

Step 1   *Subtract the mean from each score.*

$$6 - 7.4 = -1.4$$
$$10 - 7.4 = 2.6$$
$$7 - 7.4 = -.4$$
$$8 - 7.4 = .6$$
$$6 - 7.4 = -1.4$$

Step 2   *Sum the differences.*

$$(-1.4) + 2.6 + (-.4) + .6 + (-1.4) = 0$$

Advantages of the Mean. The mean is the most popular measure of central tendency for two reasons. First, of the three measures it tends to vary the least from sample to sample. If you drew a large series of random samples from the same population and determined the mean for each sample, you would find that the sample mean changes less than the other measures of central tendency.

The second reason has to do with the relationship between sample means and population means. The mean of a population is symbolized by μ, the Greek letter mu. If a sample is randomly selected from the population, *the mean of the sample is the best single estimate of the corresponding μ.* For example, suppose members of a random sample of 50 high school students complete an intelligence test on which we know the μ for the population from which these students were drawn is 100. Even so, the sample mean may not equal 100: it could equal 98, or 103.7, or any other reasonable value.

However, if we were able to collect an infinite number of random samples with $N = 50$ from this population, and computed the mean test score for each sample, we would find that the mean of these sample means equals 100. Although any one sample mean may not equal μ, $\overline{Y}$ is considered the best estimate of μ in the sample, because across an infinite set of random samples with equal N the mean of the sample means must equal μ.

5.2.3 The Median

The **median** (*Md*) is *the value which separates the lower half of the scores in a frequency distribution from the upper half.* The median is the value that divides the distribution in half: half the scores are less than or equal to the median, and half are greater than or equal to the median. The median may be computed for ordinal, interval, or ratio variables.

The computation of the median for ungrouped data is described in Procedure Box 5.2. The computation of the median in grouped frequency distributions is provided in the supplement. It was explained in Section 1.3.2 that distributions of continuous variables are inherently grouped. Because of this, the method in the supplement technically should be applied to ungrouped data from continuous variables as well. However, the simpler method described in Procedure Box 5.2 is often used in practice.

If you look at the example in Procedure Box 5.2 you will see that the value of the median is not affected by extreme scores. It would not matter if the largest value is 8, 10, or 104; the median would remain the same. Unlike the mean, the median is not influenced by the exact value of each score in the distribution.

Advantages of the Median. Unlike the mean, the median is not affected by a small number of extreme scores in a sample. For this reason, if there are extreme scores in the sample, the median can provide a better sense of what most of the scores are like than the mean.

For example, suppose five people are asked how many cups of coffee they drink per day. The responses are 1, 3, 2, 2, and 27. While the mean (7) provides a measure of central tendency that includes information from all the subjects, the median (2) provides a measure of central tendency that is more representative of most of the sample, although it is unrepresentative of one person in the sample. In circumstances where there are extreme scores, the median adds useful information to the mean.

The Median for Ungrouped Data

Goal   Compute the median of 5 students' scores on a statistics pop quiz: 6, 10, 7, 8, and 6.

To Compute the Median with an Odd Sample Size:

Step 1   *Order the scores from lowest to highest.*

$$6 \quad 6 \quad 7 \quad 8 \quad 10$$

Step 2   *Determine the middle score.* This is the score associated with position $(N+1)/2$ in the ordered distribution. Since $N = 5$, the median equals score number $(5+1)/2 = 3$. The third value in the ordered distribution is 7, so $Md = 7$.

To Compute the Median with an Even Sample Size:

Suppose a sixth student's score of 2 is added.

Step 1   *Order the scores from lowest to highest.*

$$2 \quad 6 \quad 6 \quad 7 \quad 8 \quad 10$$

Step 2   *The median is the mean of the two middle scores.* These are the scores associated with positions $N/2$ and $(N/2) + 1$ in the ordered distribution. Since $N = 6$, these are scores number $6/2 = 3$ and $(6/2) + 1 = 4$. The third score in the ordered distribution is 6, the fourth 7. The median is the mean of these two values:

$$\frac{6+7}{2} = 6.5$$

5.2.4 Summary

Table 5.4 provides a summary of the most important characteristics of the three measures of central tendency.

5.2.5 Skew and Measures of Central Tendency

The differences between the three measures of central tendency are particularly evident when the distribution is skewed. If a distribution is symmetrical and has only one mode then the mean, median, and mode of that distribution will be equal, as illustrated in

TABLE 5.4   Characteristics of Measures of Central Tendency

The **mode** is:
1.   the most commonly occurring value in the distribution.
2.   more variable across samples than the median or mean.
3.   the easiest measure of central tendency to compute.
4.   the only measure of central tendency suitable for nominal as well as non-nominal variables.

The **mean** is:
1.   the balance point of the distribution.
2.   responsive to the exact position of each score in the distribution.
3.   more sensitive to extreme scores than the median or mode.
4.   less sensitive to sampling fluctuations than the median or mode.
5.   appropriate for any non-nominal variable.

The **median** is:
1.   the value that divides the upper half of scores from the lower half.
2.   not responsive to the exact position of scores.
3.   more variable across samples than the mean, but less variable than the mode.
4.   appropriate for any non-nominal variable.

Figure 5.2(a). If the distribution is positively skewed and has only one mode as in Figure 5.2(b), then in general

$$\text{Mean} \geq \text{Median} \geq \text{Mode}.$$

This is because most of the scores are relatively low, so that the mode will be associated with a low value. The mean on the other hand is pulled higher by the extreme scores in the tail at the upper end of the distribution. The median remains at the halfway point in the distribution. To help remember this relationship, notice that when the distribution is positively skewed the three measures fall in positive alphabetical order: mean, then median, then mode.

If the distribution is negatively skewed and has only one mode as in Figure 5.2(c), then in general the measures of central tendency occur in *negative* alphabetical order:

$$\text{Mode} \geq \text{Median} \geq \text{Mean}.$$

Examination of the relative size of the three measures of central tendency can help you determine whether and in which direction the distribution is skewed.

When the distribution is very skewed, the three measures of central tendency can create very different impressions of the distribution. We have already seen that average yearly income is a positively skewed variable, suggesting that the mean will be the highest measure of central tendency, the mode the lowest. A president running for reelection might want yearly incomes to appear as large as possible, and use the mean to represent average yearly income. The challenger could instead choose the mode, which will make average yearly incomes appear low. Both are correct because the ambiguous term *average* may be applied to any measure of central tendency. A good research report never refers to the average unless it is explicit which measure of central tendency is meant. In this book I will only use the word *average* to refer to the mean.

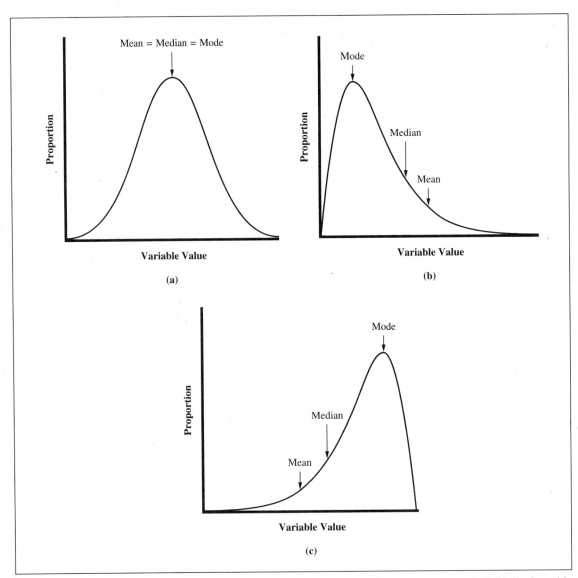

FIGURE 5.2 The relationship between skew and the measures of central tendency. (a) In a symmetrical distribution with one mode, the mean, median, and mode are equal. (b) In a positively skewed distribution with one mode, the mean tends to be greater than the median, which tends to be greater than the mode. (c) In a negatively skewed distribution with one mode, the mean tends to be less than the median, which tends to be less than the mode.

When the distribution is severely skewed, presenting all three measures of central tendency offers the most complete picture, and statisticians recommend the median as the best single measure of central tendency. However, be aware that in practice most researchers continue to limit their discussion of central tendency to the mean, even when it may not be the most appropriate indicator. I would recommend always computing and reporting at least the mean and median.

KEY TERMS

frequency distribution	median
mean	mode
measures of central tendency	summation symbol

EXERCISES

Answers to all exercises may be found in Appendix B.

1. Compute the following values using the data

$$X_1 = 10 \quad X_2 = 6$$
$$X_3 = 14 \quad X_4 = 8$$

   a. $\displaystyle\sum_{i=1}^{N} X_i =$

   b. $\displaystyle\sum_{i=1}^{2} X_i =$

   c. $\displaystyle\sum_{i=2}^{3} X_i =$

   d. $\displaystyle\sum_{i=1}^{N} X_i^2 =$

   e. $\displaystyle\left(\sum_{i=1}^{N} X_i\right)^2 =$

2. Sixty entering college students completed an examination of basic reading skills. The following represent the number of items completed correctly by each student:

12	14	15	10	12
16	20	17	11	11
20	19	15	15	20
20	18	19	14	19
14	16	20	18	16
17	20	16	19	14
18	21	15	17	13
12	19	19	12	15
13	12	17	11	14
16	14	16	10	12
19	10	12	14	19
10	16	11	16	17

   a. What is the mode of this distribution?
   b. On the basis of your answer to a., what concerns might you raise about this distribution?

3. In the following cases, which would be the most appropriate measure of central tendency, and why?
   a. A researcher interested in average length of stay in the hospital for medical patients notices that while most are in the hospital less than 20 days, a few stay as long as half a year.
   b. Subjects are divided according to hair color.
   c. The researcher would like the best possible estimate of the population μ.

4. Name at least one potential advantage of the:
   a. Mode
   b. Mean
   c. Median

5. On a statistics quiz with a maximum possible score of 25, Professor Smith's class of 20 students generated the following set of scores:

12	14	15	8	10
16	20	17	10	11
20	19	14	15	20
20	18	6	14	19

   a. Compute the mean, median, and mode.
   b. Based on these statistics, would Professor Smith conclude the *data is positively skewed, negatively skewed,* or *symmetrical?*

6. A sample of 20 college students is randomly divided into two groups. One group is given a powerful nutritional supplement, the second group an inactive

placebo pill. Both groups then complete a complex maze. The time in seconds it takes them to complete the maze is as follows:

Supplement	Placebo
10.8	11.4
6.9	8.3
9.2	7.4
6.8	9.1
7.1	6.9
9.8	12.2
10.6	9.8
8.3	8.6
12.2	13.6
6.3	9.4

a. What type of study is this: *true experiment, quasi-experiment,* or *observational study?*

b. For each of the variables in the study (type of pill and time), indicate whether it is a *nominal, ordinal, interval,* or *ratio variable,* and whether it is *continuous* or *discrete.* Also, if the study is a true experiment or quasi-experiment, identify which is the *independent variable* and which is the *dependent variable.*

c. Compute the mean time to completion for each group.

d. Examine the means. How might you want to interpret these data? What alternative explanation is possible, given the relatively small sample size?

7. For males in the population of students at College A, the average SAT score is 933. For females the average SAT score is 867.

a. What parameter is probably represented here?

b. How would you interpret this information?

8. In each of the following cases two measures of central tendency are provided. In each case, indicate whether they suggest a *positively skewed distribution, a negatively skewed distribution,* or a *symmetrical distribution.* Then indicate the expected relative position of the third measure. For example, if the following values are provided,

$$Mo = 12, \quad \overline{Y} = 13,$$

these suggest a positively skewed distribution, and Md should fall between 12 and 13.

a. $Mo = 4, Md = 3$

b. $\overline{Y} = 8, Mo = 6$

c. $Md = 8.9, \overline{Y} = 8.9$

S5.1 SUMMATION RULES

There are several rules which apply to the summation symbol when it is used in an algebraic equation. These rules will be important in algebraic proofs found in this and subsequent supplements (where they are referred to by their caption). However, learning about these rules is not required to understand the information contained in subsequent chapters.

1. Summing a Constant

   When a constant is summed N times, the result is equal to multiplying that constant by N:

$$\sum_{i=1}^{N} c_i = N(c). \tag{S5.1}$$

Example:
If the constant value 2 is to be summed across three observations then

$$\sum_{i=1}^{N} c_i = \sum_{i=1}^{3} 2 = 2 + 2 + 2 = 6$$

$$= 3(2)$$

$$= N(c).$$

2. Summing the Product of a Constant and a Variable

   When a set of scores is each multiplied by a constant before being summed, the result is equal to multiplying the sum of the scores by that constant:

$$\sum_{i=1}^{N} c_i X_i = c \sum_{i=1}^{N} X_i. \tag{S5.2}$$

Example:
If $c = 2$ and there are three observations where $X_1 = 3$, $X_2 = 4$, and $X_3 = 1$, then

$$\sum_{i=1}^{N} c_i X_i = \sum_{i=1}^{3} 2(X_i) = 2(3) + 2(4) + 2(1) = 16$$

$$= 2(3 + 4 + 1)$$

$$= c \sum_{i=1}^{N} X_i.$$

3. The Sum of a Sum

When scores from two variables X and Y are summed for each subject, and the sums are then added together, the result is equal to summing all the X scores first, then all the Y scores, then adding the two sums together:

$$\sum_{i=1}^{N}(X_i + Y_i) = \sum_{i=1}^{N} X_i + \sum_{i=1}^{N} Y_i. \qquad (S5.1)$$

Example:
If $X_1 = 3$, $X_2 = 4$, and $X_3 = 1$, and $Y_1 = 6$, $Y_2 = 5$, and $Y_3 = 2$ then

$$\sum_{i=1}^{N}(X_i + Y_i) = (3+6) + (4+5) + (1+2) = 21$$

$$= (3+4+1) + (6+5+2)$$

$$= \sum_{i=1}^{N} X_i + \sum_{i=1}^{N} Y_i.$$

S5.2 FORMULA FOR THE WEIGHTED MEAN

The weighted mean is used if scores are to be differentially weighted. The formula is:

$$\overline{Y} = \frac{\sum\limits_{i=1}^{N} w_i Y_i}{\sum\limits_{i=1}^{N} w_i},$$

where w_i is the weight for a particular value.

Example:
Grade point averages are weighted means in which the weight for each course grade is the number of credits earned. Compute the grade point average based on three courses:

Biology: 4 credits, grade = 3.0

History: 3 credits, grade = 2.0

Phys Ed: 1 credit, grade = 3.5

$$\overline{Y} = \frac{\sum\limits_{i=1}^{N} w_i Y_i}{\sum\limits_{i=1}^{N} w_i}$$

$$= \frac{4(3.0) + 3(2.0) + 1(3.5)}{4 + 3 + 1}$$

$$= \frac{21.5}{8}$$

$$= 2.69.$$

If the weights for all the scores are equal, w_i is a constant and the weighted mean and normal mean formulas will produce the same value. The proof of this statement follows:

$$\frac{\sum_{i=1}^{N} w_i Y_i}{\sum_{i=1}^{N} w_i} = \frac{w \sum_{i=1}^{N} Y_i}{N(w)} \quad \text{(from S5.1 and S5.2)}$$

$$= \frac{\sum_{i=1}^{N} Y_i}{N}. \quad \text{(simplifying a fraction)}$$

S5.3 FORMULA FOR THE FREQUENCY DISTRIBUTION MEAN

The formula for the mean of an ungrouped frequency distribution is:

$$\overline{Y} = \frac{\sum_{i=1}^{k} f_i V_i}{N} = \frac{\sum_{i=1}^{k} f_i V_i}{\sum_{i=1}^{k} f_i},$$

where k is the number of values in the distribution, f_i is the frequency for value i, and V_i is the associated value. N is the total sample size, which is also the sum of the frequencies associated with each interval.

Example:
Compute the mean for the following ungrouped distribution:

V	f
2	8
4	7
7	2
10	5
N	22

$$\overline{Y} = \frac{\sum_{i=1}^{k} f_i V_i}{N}$$

$$= \frac{8(2) + 7(4) + 2(7) + 5(10)}{8 + 7 + 2 + 5}$$

$$= \frac{108}{22}$$

$$= 4.91.$$

The procedure for grouped frequency distributions is the same, except that the midpoint of each interval is used to represent the values.

Example:
Compute the mean of the following grouped distribution:

V	f
0–3	8
4–7	7
8–11	2
12–15	5
N	22

$$\overline{Y} = \frac{\sum\limits_{i=1}^{k} f_i V_i}{N}$$

$$= \frac{8(1.5) + 7(5.5) + 2(9.5) + 5(13.5)}{8 + 7 + 2 + 5}$$

$$= \frac{137}{22}$$

$$= 6.23.$$

The frequency distribution mean can be thought of as a special case of the weighted mean, in which the frequencies associated with each value or interval serve as the weights.

S5.4 PROOF THAT THE MEAN IS THE BALANCE POINT OF THE DISTRIBUTION

$$\sum_{i=1}^{N}(Y_i - \overline{Y}) = \sum_{i=1}^{N} Y_i - \sum_{i=1}^{N} \overline{Y} \quad \text{(from S5.3)}$$

$$= \sum_{i=1}^{N} Y_i - N\overline{Y} \quad \text{(from S5.1)}$$

$$= \sum_{i=1}^{N} Y_i - \sum_{i=1}^{N} Y_i \quad \text{(from the formula for a mean)}$$

$$= 0.$$

S5.5 FORMULA FOR THE GROUPED FREQUENCY DISTRIBUTION MEDIAN

Computing the median of a grouped frequency distribution first entails identifying the interval in which the median falls, the interval which contains the $N/2$th score. The following formula is then used to compute the median:

$$Md = V_{LL} + w\left(\frac{\frac{N}{2}-[\text{cum } f - f]}{f}\right),$$

where V_{LL} is the lower real limit of the interval in which the median falls, w is the interval width based on the real limits, cum f is the cumulative frequency for the interval, and f is the frequency for the interval.

Example:

Compute the median of the following distribution of a continuous variable:

V	f	cum f
0–3	8	8
4–7	7	15
8–11	2	17
12–15	5	22
N	22	

There are 22 scores, so the median is score $22/2 = 11$. The cumulative frequency column indicates that the 11th score from the bottom falls in the second interval, 4–7. The frequency of this interval is 7, and the cumulative frequency is 15. Since this is a continuous variable the lower real limit for this interval is 3.5, and the width is the difference between the upper and lower real limits: $w = 7.5 - 3.5 = 4$. The median is:

$$Md = V_{LL} + w\left(\frac{\frac{N}{2} - [\text{cum } f - f]}{f}\right)$$

$$= 3.5 + 4\left(\frac{\frac{22}{2} - [15 - 7]}{7}\right)$$

$$= 5.21.$$

CHAPTER 6

Measures of Variability and Transformations

6.1 MEASURES OF VARIABILITY

Measures of variability, also called **measures of dispersion**, are *descriptive statistics which describe the amount of variability in a frequency distribution.* For example, the mean score for the adolescent population on the Wechsler Intelligence Scale for Children (Wechsler, 1991), or WISC, is set at 100. If you administer the WISC to a class of high school students and find the mean score is 101.5, it suggests the typical member of the class is of average intelligence. If WISC scores in the class all fall between 98 and 105 as in Figure 6.1(a), then the value 101.5 characterizes all members of the sample quite well. The teacher could expect all the students in the class will learn at about the same rate.

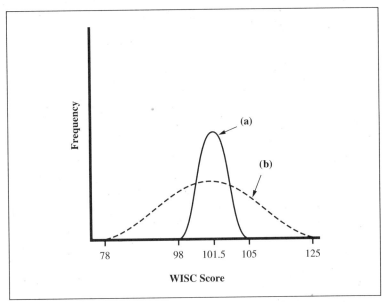

FIGURE 6.1 Two distributions of scores with the same mean but differing in the degree of variability. Frequency polygon (a) represents a distribution of WISC scores in a class where $\overline{Y} = 101.5$ and all scores fall between 98 and 105; frequency polygon (b) represents a distribution of WISC scores in a class where $\overline{Y} = 101.5$ and all scores fall between 78 and 125.

If instead the WISC scores in the class vary between 78 and 125 as in Figure 6.1(b), then the value 101.5 is not that representative of the class as a whole. A teacher who expects all the students in the class to learn at about the same rate will be very disappointed: students with scores well below average will be overwhelmed, while students with very high scores may find the class boring.

This example illustrates the primary purpose of measures of variability: to indicate the amount of spread in a set of scores. This has important implications for the usefulness of an average value. The more diverse a sample, the less representative the "most representative value" is going to be, and predictions made about sample members on the basis of a sample average will tend to be less accurate. The three most commonly used measures of variability will be discussed in this chapter: the range, the variance, and the standard deviation.

6.1.1 The Range

The **range** (*Rn*) is simply *the difference between the highest and lowest value in the distribution*. The range may be computed for any ordinal, interval, or ratio variable. In ungrouped frequency distributions it is computed using the following formula:

$$Rn = V_{\text{Max}} - V_{\text{Min}},$$

where V_{Max} is the largest value in the sample, V_{Min} the smallest.

For example, suppose five students generated the following scores on a pop quiz in their statistics class: 6, 10, 7, 8, and 6. The range would be

$$Rn = 10 - 6 = 4.$$

In grouped frequency distributions, including distributions for continuous variables, the range is computed using the formula

$$Rn = V_{\text{Max}UL} - V_{\text{Min}LL},$$

where $V_{\text{Max}UL}$ is the upper real limit of the highest interval, $V_{\text{Min}LL}$ the lower real limit of the lowest interval. In the example above, the statistics professor might assume scores on the pop quiz reflect an underlying continuous distribution of the degree to which students understand the material. This assumption implies that the data are inherently grouped. The score 10 would then represent the midpoint of an interval for which the upper real limit would be 10.5, while the score 6 would be the midpoint of an interval with a lower real limit of 5.5. The range would be

$$Rn = 10.5 - 5.5 = 5.$$

The range will be slightly larger when the data are considered grouped than when the data are considered ungrouped.

Problems with the Range. While the range is simple to compute, it is not a very stable measure of dispersion. It is more subject to sampling fluctuations than the other measures of variability to be discussed. It is also influenced by extreme scores more than the other measure of variability. The *interquartile range* and *semi-interquartile range* are variants of the range that are more resistant to extreme scores. They are discussed in the supplement.

6.1.2 The Variance

Defining the Variance. The **variance** (s_Y^2) may be defined as *the average squared difference from the mean*. The most commonly used version of the variance may be computed using the formula

$$s_Y^2 = \frac{\sum_{i=1}^{N}(Y_i - \overline{Y})^2}{N - 1}.$$

s_Y^2 represents the best sample estimate of the population variance, σ_Y^2 (σ is the Greek lowercase letter sigma). While the sample s_Y^2 may not equal σ_Y^2, the average of the s_Y^2 values from an infinite series of random samples with equal N drawn from the population will equal σ_Y^2. The variance may be computed for any ordinal, interval, or ratio variable.

Stated in words, the formula for s_Y^2 suggests that the variance of variable Y is computed by first finding the difference between each score and the mean, squaring these differences, and adding them together. *The sum of a set of squared differences from the mean is referred to as a* **sum of squares** (*SS*):

$$SS = \sum_{i=1}^{N}(Y_i - \overline{Y})^2.$$

The sum of squares is then divided by $N-1$ to generate the variance.

Squaring the differences before summing them is required because, as was discussed in the last chapter, the sum of the differences from the mean always equals 0:

$$\sum_{i=1}^{N}(Y_i - \overline{Y}) = 0.$$

Summing the unsquared differences from the mean will always produce a value of zero, not a particularly useful basis for a measure of variability. When a number is squared the result is always a positive number, so squaring the differences from the mean eliminates the negative differences. One consequence of this squaring is that the variance will always be a positive number.

The Computational Formula. Squaring the scores does introduce a new problem. Suppose the sample mean is rounded from 7.3333333 . . . to 7.3. Each time you subtract this mean from a score in the distribution you introduce a small amount of rounding error, which is then compounded by squaring the difference. Across a large series of scores the error introduced by rounding may become substantial.

The computational error created by rounding can be reduced. It is demonstrated in the supplement that the following formula can also be used for the sum of squares:

$$SS = \sum_{i=1}^{N}Y_i^2 - \frac{\left(\sum_{i=1}^{N}Y_i\right)^2}{N}.$$

This suggests an alternative formula for the variance:

$$s_Y^2 = \frac{\sum\limits_{i=1}^{N} Y_i^2 - \dfrac{\left(\sum\limits_{i=1}^{N} Y_i\right)^2}{N}}{N-1}.$$

The original formula provided is sometimes referred to as a **definitional formula,** *a formula which corresponds closely to the definition of a statistic.* The second formula is a **computational formula,** *a formula used for computational purposes.* If you do not have to round the mean, both formulas produce the same value. If the definitional formula would require rounding the mean, the computational formula will give you a value closer to the true variance. Computation of the variance is demonstrated in Procedure Box 6.1. Additional information about the variance — why the denominator is $N-1$ rather than N, for example — may be found in the supplement.

6.1.3 The Standard Deviation

The **standard deviation** (s_Y) is simply *the square root of the variance.* The definitional formula for the standard deviation is

$$s_Y = \sqrt{\frac{\sum\limits_{i=1}^{N} (Y_i - \overline{Y})^2}{N-1}}$$

and the computational formula is

$$s_Y = \sqrt{\frac{\sum\limits_{i=1}^{N} Y_i^2 - \dfrac{\left(\sum\limits_{i=1}^{N} Y_i\right)^2}{N}}{N-1}}.$$

To compute the standard deviation, simply find the square root of the variance (see Procedure Box 6.1).

If the standard deviation is just the square root of the variance, you may wonder why you should bother learning about both. The reason is that both play a role in inferential statistics. Some inferential statistics (the z and t tests) involve the standard deviation, while the most commonly used inferential statistic (the F test) requires the computation of variances.

The standard deviation has one advantage over the variance as a descriptive statistic, in that the unit of measure is the same as the original scores. Suppose you find the mean height in a sample of American males is 69.7 inches with a standard deviation of 2.32. Your results suggest that in the population, you would expect heights to deviate from the

The Variance and Standard Deviation

Goal Compute the variance of 5 students' scores on a statistics pop quiz: 6, 10, 7, 8, and 6.

Using the Definition Formula:

$$s_Y^2 = \frac{\sum_{i=1}^{N}(Y_i - \overline{Y})^2}{N - 1}$$

Step 1 *Compute the mean.* The mean for these data was computed earlier in Procedure Box 5.1.

$$\overline{Y} = 7.4$$

Step 2 *Subtract the mean from each score and square the differences.*

Y	$Y - \overline{Y}$	$(Y - \overline{Y})^2$	
6	$6 - 7.4 = -1.41$	.96	◄——— *These*
10	$10 - 7.4 = 2.6$	6.76	◄——— *numbers*
7	$7 - 7.4 = .4$	.16	◄——— *must*
8	$8 - 7.4 = .6$	.36	◄——— *be*
6	$6 - 7.4 = -1.41$	.96	◄——— *positive*

Step 3 *Sum the squared difference scores.*

$$\sum_{i=1}^{N}(Y_i - \overline{Y})^2 = 1.96 + 6.76 + .16 + .36 + 1.96 = 11.20$$

Step 4 *Divide by* $N - 1$.

$$s_Y^2 = \frac{11.20}{4} = 2.8$$

Using the Computational Formula:

$$s_Y^2 = \frac{\sum_{i=1}^{N} Y_i^2 - \dfrac{\left(\sum_{i=1}^{N} Y_i\right)^2}{N}}{N-1}$$

Continued

The variance and standard deviation continued

Step 1   *Compute the sum of Y and Y^2.*

	Y	Y^2
	6	36
	10	100
	7	49
	8	64
	6	36
Sums:	37	285

Step 2   *Square the sum of the Y scores and divide by N.*

$$\frac{\left(\sum_{i=1}^{N} Y_i\right)^2}{N} = \frac{37^2}{5} = \frac{1369}{5} = 273.8$$

Step 3   *Subtract the result of Step 2 from the sum of the squared Y scores and divide by N–1.*

$$s_Y^2 = \frac{285 - 273.8}{4}$$

$$= \frac{11.2}{4} \leftarrow \textit{This numerator must be positive}$$

$$= 2.8$$

To Compute the Standard Deviation:

Find the square root of the variance.

$$s_Y = \sqrt{2.8} = 1.6733.$$

population μ by 2.32 inches. For this reason, the standard deviation is usually considered more useful than the variance for descriptive purposes. In presenting the results of your study, these results are conventionally reported in the following way:

The mean height was 69.7 inches ($SD = 2.32$).

6.1.4 The Standard Deviation and Normal Distributions

One of the defining characteristics of a normal distribution is that *the percentage of scores at any distance from the mean in standard deviation units is the same in all normal distributions*. To understand the concept of standard deviation units, imagine there existed a

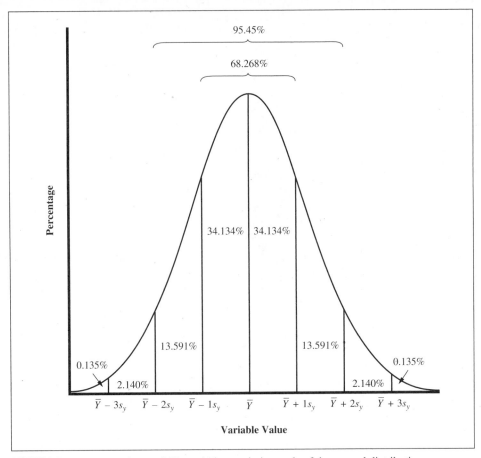

FIGURE 6.2 Percentage of cases falling within certain intervals of the normal distribution.

normally distributed sample with $\overline{Y} = 10$ and $s_Y = 2$. A score of 12 would be 1 standard deviation unit above the mean $(\overline{Y} + 1s_Y)$, while a score of 7 would be 1.5 standard deviation units below the mean $(\overline{Y} - 1.5s_Y)$. A score of 10 would be 0 standard deviation units from the mean.

Figure 6.2 demonstrates the relationship between standard deviation units and the percentage of scores in normal distributions. In any normal distribution, approximately 34.134% of the scores will fall between the mean and one standard deviation above the mean, and approximately 34.134% of the scores will fall between the mean and one standard deviation below the mean. Combining these two groups, we can say that approximately 68.268% of all scores in a normal distribution will fall within one standard deviation of the mean. Approximately 13.591% of the scores fall between one and two standard deviations above the mean, with another 13.591% falling between one and two standard deviations below the mean. Combining these four groups, we can say that approximately 95.45% of the scores in a normal distribution will fall within two standard deviations of the mean. Percentages are always the same for any fraction of a standard deviation as well; for example, 19.146% of the scores will fall within ½ standard deviation above the mean, and 14.988% of the scores will fall between ½ standard deviation and 1 standard deviation above the mean.

This characteristic of the normal distribution will be discussed again in Section 6.3.4. In addition, it will play an important role in an inferential statistic called the z test which is discussed in Chapter 12.

6.2 SKEW AND KURTOSIS

Measures of central tendency and variability do not by themselves capture all characteristics of a frequency distribution. There are many other one-variable descriptive statistics which tell us about the shape of the distribution. The most well-known of these are the measures of skew and kurtosis.

The concept of skew was introduced in Chapter 4, and refers to the extent to which a distribution is asymmetrical. Measures of skew indicate how positively or negatively skewed a distribution is.

Measures of kurtosis indicate the extent to which the relative height of the bell and the tails of a symmetrical distribution is consistent with that of a normal distribution. Measures of kurtosis can be used to evaluate whether a distribution is leptokurtic (there are relatively more cases close to the mean than in a normal distribution) or platykurtic (there are relatively more cases in the tails than in a normal distribution).

These measures are far less commonly used than the measures of central tendency and variability and will not be discussed in detail here. The most important point I want to make here is that, while measures of central tendency and variability are the most important descriptive statistics for describing aspects of a single variable's distribution, there are others. Do not assume that the measures of central tendency and variability capture all the information that is available about a distribution of scores.

6.3 VARIABLE TRANSFORMATIONS

Suppose you receive a grade of 79 on your statistics midterm. Without additional information you would not be able to interpret this grade. How does it compare with other scores in the class? Did you do better or worse relative to the rest of the class than you did on the history test for which you received a 68? A value of 79 by itself is meaningless; it is only within the context of the entire distribution of scores that a given value makes sense.

Many methods have been developed for *transforming* variable values to make them more meaningful, by replacing them with values that indicate relative standing within the distribution of scores. In the following sections I will discuss some commonly used transformations: rank ordering, percentiles, z scores, and other standard scores.

6.3.1 Rank Ordering

Variable values are transformed into ranks (R) by replacing each score with its order in the distribution. Ranks can potentially vary between 1 (indicating the lowest score in the distribution) and N (the sample size, indicating the highest score). Procedure Box 6.2 demonstrates the transformation.

The transformation to ranks is a straightforward process, although slightly more complicated when there are tied scores. Tied scores receive the mean of the ranks they would

PROCEDURE BOX 6.2

Transformation to Ranks

Goal   Transform 5 students' scores on a statistics pop quiz to ranks:

$$Y_1 = 7 \qquad Y_2 = 10 \qquad Y_3 = 7 \qquad Y_4 = 8 \qquad Y_5 = 6$$

Step 1   *Order the values from lowest to highest.*

$$Y_5 = 6$$
$$Y_3 = 7$$
$$Y_1 = 7$$
$$Y_4 = 8$$
$$Y_2 = 10$$

Step 2   *Replace unique values (values with a frequency of 1) with their position in the list.*

$R_5 = 1$ ◄———*The lowest score is replaced with* 1
$Y_1 = 7$ ◄———*This score is not yet replaced*
$Y_3 = 7$ ◄———*This score is not yet replaced*
$R_4 = 4$ ◄———*This score is replaced with* 4
$R_2 = 5$ ◄———*The highest score is replaced with* 5

Step 3   *Replace tied scores with the mean of their positions in the list.*

$R_5 = 1$
$R_1 = 2.5$ ◄———*This score is replaced with the mean of* 2 *and* 3
$R_3 = 2.5$ ◄———*This score is replaced with the mean of* 2 *and* 3
$R_4 = 4$
$R_2 = 5$

receive if they were not tied. For example, in Procedure Box 6.2 scores for students 1 and 3 both equal 7. If they were not tied they would be ranked 2nd and 3rd, so both are ranked 2.5. The next highest score, 8, is transformed to a rank of 4. Rankings also may be numbered from highest to lowest, so that rank 1 goes to the highest score and rank N to the lowest.

Suppose your statistics professor informs you that you ranked 61st in a class of 100. If you also know you ranked 9th out of 25 on your history test and that scores were ranked from highest to lowest, you would know you did better in history than in statistics even though the history score was lower.

6.3.2 Percentiles

Variable values are transformed into percentiles (P) by replacing each score with the percentage of scores in the distribution that are lower. Percentile values can potentially vary between 0 (indicating the lowest score) and 99.999 . . . (indicating the highest score). Procedure Box 6.3 demonstrates the transformation of scores to percentiles in an ungrouped distribution. The correct method for transforming variable values to percentiles for grouped distributions is provided in the supplement.

Suppose your statistics professor informs you that 39% of the scores on the midterm were below 79. The percentile score that corresponds to your score is therefore 39, a number which indicates your relative standing in the class. If the percentile score associated with the 68 you received on your history test was a 64, you know you did better in history than in statistics.

6.3.3 z Scores

The z Transformation. The z score transformation represents the simplest method of transformation to a **standard score,** *a transformation of variable scores into standard deviation units*. Standard deviation units were introduced earlier in the chapter, and indicate the number of standard deviations a value falls from the mean. A score which equals the mean of the distribution would be transformed to a z score of 0, since that score is 0 standard deviation units from the mean. A score 1 standard deviation above the mean is transformed to a z score of $+1$. A score $2\frac{1}{4}$ standard deviations below the mean is transformed to a z score of -2.25. One consequence of converting scores to standard deviation units is that the mean of the z scores is always 0 and the standard deviation 1.0, unless there is rounding error.

Variable values are transformed into z scores using the formula

$$z_i = \frac{Y_i - \overline{Y}}{s_Y}.$$

That is, the mean is subtracted from subject i's score, and the difference is divided by the standard deviation. The computation of z scores is demonstrated in Procedure Box 6.4.

Suppose you receive the following information from your teachers:

	Your Score	$\overline{Y}$	s_Y	z
Statistics	79	85	5.7	-1.05
History	68	53	6.6	$+2.27$

PROCEDURE BOX 6.3

Transformation to Percentiles

Goal: Transform 5 students' scores on a statistics pop quiz to percentiles:

$$Y_1 = 6 \qquad Y_2 = 10 \qquad Y_3 = 7 \qquad Y_4 = 8 \qquad Y_5 = 6$$

Step 1. *Order the values from lowest to highest.*

$$Y_1 = 6$$
$$Y_5 = 6$$
$$Y_3 = 7$$
$$Y_4 = 8$$
$$Y_2 = 10$$

Step 2. *Replace each score with the percentage of scores that are lower than that score.*

$P_1 = 0 \longleftarrow$ ————— 0% of scores are lower than 6

$P_5 = 0 \longleftarrow$ ————— 0% of scores are lower than 6

$P_3 = \dfrac{2}{5}(100) = 40 \longleftarrow$ ——— 40% of scores are lower than 7

$P_4 = \dfrac{3}{5}(100) = 60 \longleftarrow$ ——— 60% of scores are lower than 8

$P_2 = \dfrac{4}{5}(100) = 80 \longleftarrow$ ——— 80% of scores are lower than 10

Now you know your statistics test score is 1.05 standard deviations below the mean, while your history test score is 2.27 standard deviations above the mean. The z scores indicate to you that relative to the test distributions, your 68 on the history test was actually a better score than the 79 you received in statistics.

z **Scores in Normal Distributions.** When I introduced the concept of standard deviation units I pointed out that the percentage of cases falling within any distance from the mean in standard deviation units is fixed in a normal distribution: 34.134% will fall less than one standard deviation below the mean, and so forth. Since z scores represent standard deviation units, if the distribution is normal there will be a fixed percentage of scores falling between

PROCEDURE BOX 6.4

Transformation to z Scores

Goal   Transform the outcomes on 5 students' scores on a statistics pop quiz to z scores:

$$Y_1 = 6 \qquad Y_2 = 10 \qquad Y_3 = 7 \qquad Y_4 = 8 \qquad Y_5 = 6$$

To Compute z Scores:

$$z_i = \frac{Y_i - \overline{Y}}{s_Y}$$

Step 1   *Compute the mean and standard deviation.* The mean for these data was computed earlier in Procedure Box 5.1, the standard deviation in Procedure Box 6.1.

$$\overline{Y} = 7.4$$

$$s_Y = 1.6733$$

Step 2   *Subtract the mean from each score and divide by the standard deviation.*

$$z_1 = (6 \ - 7.4)/1.6733 = -.8367$$

$$z_2 = (10 - 7.4)/1.6733 = \ \ 1.5538$$

$$z_3 = (7 \ - 7.4)/1.6733 = -.2390$$

$$z_4 = (8 \ - 7.4)/1.6733 = \ \ \ .3586$$

$$z_5 = (6 \ - 7.4)/1.6733 = -.8367$$

Demonstration that the Mean of the z Distribution Equals 0:

$$\bar{z} = \frac{(-.8367) + 1.5538 + (-.2390) + .3586 + (-.8367)}{5} = 0$$

Continued

Transformation to z scores continued

Demonstration that the Standard Deviation of the z Distribution Equals 1.0:

Step 1   *Compute the sum of z and z^2.*

z	z^2
−.8367	.7000
1.5538	2.4143
−.2390	.0571
.3586	.1286
−.8367	.7000
Sums: 0	4.0000

Step 2   *Square the sum of the scores and divide by N.*

$$\frac{0^2}{5} = 0$$

Step 3   *Subtract the result of Step 2 from the sum of the squared scores, divide by $N-1$, and find the square root.*

$$s_z = \sqrt{\frac{4-0}{4}} = 1.00$$

the mean and any given z score. Table E–3 in Appendix E can be used to find the percentage of scores which fall between any given z score and the mean in a normal distribution. For any z score in Column (a) of Table E–3, Column (b) indicates the percentage of z scores which will fall between that z value and 0, the mean of the distribution of z scores. Column (c) indicates the percentage of z scores further away from 0. The table only provides positive z values, but since the normal distribution is symmetrical these percentages apply for negative z values as well.

For example, Table 6.1 repeats a portion of Table E–3. Find the z score 1.35 in Column (a) of Table 6.1. Column (b) indicates that 41.149% of the z scores will fall between 0 and −1.35, while Column (c) indicates 8.851% of the z scores will be less than −1.35 (see Figure 6.3).

6.3.4 Comparing Transformations

Ranks, percentiles, and z scores serve similar purposes. Scores in the distribution are transformed into scores that are more directly interpretable. Ranks and percentiles are useful because they are easily understood even by people without statistical training, while an understanding of z scores requires at least some sense of what means and standard deviations are. However, statisticians usually prefer standard scores for several reasons. First, the rank and percentile transformations convert even interval or ratio variables into an

TABLE 6.1 A Portion of Table E–3

z	Percent between 0 and z	Percent beyond z
1.32	40.658	9.342
1.33	40.824	9.176
1.34	40.988	9.012
→1.35	41.149	8.851
1.36	41.309	8.692
1.37	41.466	8.534
1.38	41.621	8.379
1.39	41.774	8.226
1.40	41.924	8.076

Source: Adapted from Tables II, III, IV, and VII of Fisher & Yates; STATISTICAL TABLES FOR BIO-LOGICAL, AGRICULTURAL AND MEDICAL RESEARCH. Published by Longman Group UK Ltd., 1974. I am grateful to the Longman Group UK Ltd., on behalf of the Literary Executor of the late Sir Ronald A. Fisher, F.R.S. and Dr. Frank Yates, F. R. S. for permission to adapt Tables II, III, IV, and VII from *STA-TISTICAL TABLES FOR BIOLOGICAL, AGRICULTURAL AND MEDICAL RESEARCH 6/E* (1974).

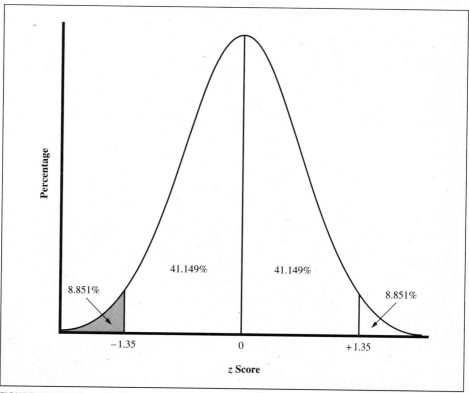

FIGURE 6.3 Percentage of cases in normal distribution associated with a z score less than –1.35. 8.851% of all z scores in a normal distribution will be less than -1.35.

ordinal rank ordering variable. Second, they can change the shape of the distribution. From a statistical perspective these are both considered undesirable characteristics.

Furthermore, if the distribution is normal you can compute the percentiles corresponding to any z value using Table E–3 of Appendix E. This is done using one of the following rules:

1. The percentile score associated with a negative z score is the percentage in Column (c) of Table E–3.
2. The percentile score associated with a positive z score is the percentage in Column (b) of Table E–3 plus 50%.
3. A z score of 0 is associated with the 50th percentile.

Look again at Table 6.1. For the z score −1.35, Column (c) indicates that 8.851% of the z scores will be lower, so the percentile score for a z score of −1.35 is 8.851. For a z score of +1.35, Column (b) indicates 41.149% of the scores fall between +1.35 and the mean. Since another 50% of scores fall below the mean, the percentile score associated with a z score of +1.35 is

$$41.149 + 50 = 91.149.$$

However, remember that this relationship between z scores and percentiles *only holds for normal distributions*.

6.3.5 Other Standard Scores

While z scores are considered preferable to percentiles and ranks, the z transformation introduces the inconvenience of negative numbers. You can generally avoid negative numbers by setting the mean and standard deviation of the standard scores to values other than 0 and 1.0. For example, the T transformation creates standard scores with a mean of 50 and a standard deviation of 10. The T transformation is accomplished using the formula

$$T = \left(\frac{Y - \overline{Y}}{s_Y} \right) 10 + 50.$$

Scores five standard deviations below the mean are extremely unusual, so the T transformation rarely produces a negative value.

Scores on the Scholastic Assessment Tests, or SATs, are also an example of standard scores. SAT scores are transformed so they have a mean of 400 and a standard deviation of 100. A score of 500 on the SAT-Verbal examination represents a score 1 standard deviation above the mean.

You can set the mean and standard deviation of a standard score to any value you want using the general formula:

$$\text{standard score} = \left(\frac{Y - \overline{Y}}{s_Y} \right) SD + M,$$

where SD is the desired standard deviation for the distribution of standard scores and M is the desired mean.

KEY TERMS

computational formula
continuous variable
definitional formula
frequency distribution
interval
lower real limit
measures of variability, measures of
  dispersion

normal distribution
range
standard deviation
standard score
sum of squares
upper real limit
variance

EXERCISES

Answers to all exercises may be found in Appendix B.

1. On a statistics quiz with a maximum possible score of 25, Professor Smith's class of 20 students generated the following set of scores:

12	14	15	8	10
16	20	17	10	11
20	19	14	15	20
20	18	6	14	19

   Compute the range (assuming this is a continuous variable), s_Y^2, and s_Y for these data.

2. When might the range be preferred over the standard deviation or variance?

3. In the exercises for the last chapter, a study was described in which 20 subjects were randomly assigned to receive either a nutritional supplement or a placebo before completing a complex maze. Time in seconds it took to complete the maze for each subject was as follows:

Supplement	Placebo
10.8	11.4
6.9	8.3
9.2	7.4
6.8	9.1
7.1	6.9
9.8	12.2
10.6	9.8
8.3	8.6
12.2	13.6
6.3	9.4

   a. Compute the standard deviation for each group.

   b. How might you interpret these statistics; that is, which group appears to be more variable?

4. After 20 years of collecting data on his statistics midterm, Professor Smith finds that his students' scores are normally distributed, with a mean of 16.2 and a standard deviation of 1.7.

   a. What percentage of the scores fall between 16.2 and 17.9?

   b. What percentage of the scores fall between 16.2 and 19.6?

   c. What percentage of the scores fall between 12.8 and 17.9?

5. Transform the scores in Question 1 to ranks from lowest to highest.

6. Assuming a discrete distribution, transform the scores from Question 1 to percentiles.

7. In the last chapter it was found that the mean for the data in Question 1 is 14.9. Using this mean, and the standard deviation computed for Question 1 in this chapter, transform the scores from Question 1 to z scores.

8. If the following z scores were drawn from a normal distribution, what would be the percentile associated with each?

   a. 1.35

   b. $-.62$

   c. 0

9. When might you prefer percentiles or ranks to z scores?

S6.1 VARIOUS FORMS OF THE RANGE

Since the range is very sensitive to extreme scores, two variants are sometimes used which are more resistant to potential distortion by extreme scores. The *interquartile range* (*IR*) is the range for the middle 50% of the scores. It is computed by finding the difference between the score associated with the 75th percentile and the score associated with the 25th percentile:

$$IR = Y_{75\%} - Y_{25\%}.$$

The semi-interquartile range (SR) is simply the interquartile range divided by 2:

$$SR = \frac{Y_{75\%} - Y_{25\%}}{2}.$$

Either will provide a value that is much more stable across samples than the range.

S6.2 VARIOUS FORMS OF THE VARIANCE

The definition provided for the variance—the average squared deviation from the mean—would imply that the denominator of the variance should be N, as it is for the mean. There is in fact another version of the variance which uses N as the denominator:

$$S_Y^2 = \frac{\sum_{i=1}^{N}(Y_i - \overline{Y})^2}{N}.$$

This statistic is known as the *sample variance*. Notice it is symbolized by a capital S rather than a lowercase s.

Why is there a distinction drawn between the sample variance (S_Y^2), which uses N in the denominator, and the best estimate of the population variance (s_Y^2), which uses $N - 1$ in the denominator? Because unlike the sample mean, the sample variance is not the best sample estimate of the corresponding parameter, the population variance. It can be demonstrated that the sample variance tends to underestimate the population variance as follows.

The formula for a population variance is

$$\sigma_Y^2 = \frac{\sum_{i=1}^{N}(Y_i - \mu)^2}{N},$$

where N now represents the total population size and μ the mean of the population. The best estimate of the population variance should estimate this value.

Suppose we add μ and $-\mu$ to the numerator of the sample variance, an operation which does not change its value:

$$\sum_{i=1}^{N}(Y_i - \overline{Y})^2 = \sum_{i=1}^{N}[(Y_i - \mu) - (\overline{Y} - \mu)]^2$$

$$= \sum_{i=1}^{N}(Y_i - \mu)^2 - \sum_{i=1}^{N}2(Y_i - \mu)(\overline{Y} - \mu) + \sum_{i=1}^{N}(\overline{Y} - \mu)^2$$

(from S1.3 and S5.3)

$$= \sum_{i=1}^{N}(Y_i - \mu)^2 - 2(\overline{Y} - \mu)\left(\sum_{i=1}^{N}Y_i - \sum_{i=1}^{N}\mu\right) + N(\overline{Y} - \mu)^2$$

(from S5.1, S5.2, and S5.3)

$$= \sum_{i=1}^{N}(Y_i - \mu)^2 - 2(\overline{Y} - \mu)(N\overline{Y} - N\mu) + N(\overline{Y} - \mu)^2$$

(from S5.1 and the formula for a mean)

$$= \sum_{i=1}^{N}(Y_i - \mu)^2 - 2N(\overline{Y} - \mu)^2 + N(\overline{Y} - \mu)^2 \quad \text{(from S1.1)}$$

$$= \sum_{i=1}^{N}(Y_i - \mu)^2 - N(\overline{Y} - \mu)^2.$$

This proof demonstrates that the numerator of the sample variance, S_Y^2, underestimates the numerator of σ_Y^2 except in those samples where $N(\overline{Y} - \mu)^2 = 0$, which will only occur when $\overline{Y} = \mu$. Over an infinite series of random samples with equal N, the mean of the sample variances will be less than σ_Y^2. By using $N - 1$ as the denominator rather than N, s_Y^2 corrects for this underestimation. Over an infinite series of random samples with equal N, the mean of the sample s_Y^2 values will equal σ_Y^2.

Since samples are primarily of interest as estimates of population values, this makes s_Y^2 a more useful statistic than S_Y^2. Most computer statistics programs in fact calculate s_Y^2 even when you request the sample variance. The difference is slight except in small samples.

S6.3 PROOF THAT THE DEFINITIONAL AND COMPUTATIONAL FORMULAS FOR THE SUM OF SQUARES ARE EQUIVALENT

$$\sum_{i=1}^{N}(Y_i - \overline{Y})^2 = \sum_{i=1}^{N}(Y_i^2 - 2Y_i\overline{Y} + \overline{Y}^2) \quad \text{(from S1.3)}$$

$$= \sum_{i=1}^{N} Y_i^2 - \sum_{i=1}^{N} 2Y_i\bar{Y} + \sum_{i=1}^{N} \bar{Y}^2 \quad \text{(from S5.3)}$$

$$= \sum_{i=1}^{N} Y_i^2 - 2\bar{Y} \sum_{i=1}^{N} Y_i + N\bar{Y}^2 \quad \text{(from S5.1 and S5.2)}$$

$$= \sum_{i=1}^{N} Y_i^2 - 2 \frac{\sum_{i=1}^{N} Y_i}{N} \sum_{i=1}^{N} Y_i + N \frac{\left(\sum_{i=1}^{N} Y_i\right)^2}{N^2} \quad \text{(from the formula for a mean)}$$

$$= \sum_{i=1}^{N} Y_i^2 - 2 \frac{\left(\sum_{i=1}^{N} Y_i\right)^2}{N} + \frac{\left(\sum_{i=1}^{N} Y_i\right)^2}{N} \quad \text{(simplifying a fraction)}$$

$$= \sum_{i=1}^{N} Y_i^2 - \frac{\left(\sum_{i=1}^{N} Y_i\right)^2}{N}.$$

S6.4 FORMULA FOR GROUPED FREQUENCY DISTRIBUTION PERCENTILES

If you would like to find the score associated with any percentile score, first determine the interval in which the $P_\%(N)/100$th score falls, where $P_\%$ is the desired percentile score. For example, if you would like to find the score associated with the 25th percentile, determine the interval in which the $25(N)/100$th score falls. Once you have found the correct interval, use the following formula to estimate the score associated with that percentile:

$$Y_\% = V_{LL} + w \left(\frac{N\left[\dfrac{P_\%}{100}\right] - [\text{cum } f - f]}{f} \right),$$

where $Y_\%$ is the score associated with a particular percentile, V_{LL} is the lower real limit of the interval in which the score falls, w is the interval width based on real limits, $P_\%$ is the desired percentile score, cum f is the cumulative frequency for the interval, and f is the frequency for the interval.

Example:
Compute the score associated with the 60th percentile for the following distribution of a continuous variable:

V	f	cum f
0–3	8	8
4–7	7	15
8–11	2	17
12–15	5	22
N	22	

Since there are 22 scores, the score associated with the 60th percentile is score $60(22)/100 = 13.2$. The cumulative frequency distribution column indicates that the 13.2th score falls in the second interval, 4–7. The real lower limit of this interval is 3.5, the frequency is 7, $w = 7.5 - 3.5 = 4$, and the cumulative frequency is 15. The score associated with the 60th percentile is:

$$Y_{60\%} = V_{LL} + w \left(\frac{N \left[\dfrac{P_\%}{100} \right] - [\text{cum } f - f]}{f} \right)$$

$$= 3.5 + 4 \left(\frac{22 \left[\dfrac{60}{100} \right] - [15 - 7]}{7} \right)$$

$$= 6.47.$$

The similarity between this formula and the formula for the grouped frequency distribution median (see Section S5.5) is not coincidental; in the grouped frequency distribution, the median is the score associated with the 50th percentile.

To compute the percentile associated with a particular score, use the following formula:

$$P_\% = \frac{100}{N} \left([\text{cum } f - f] + \frac{f[Y_\% - V_{LL}]}{w} \right).$$

Example:
Find the percentile score associated with the value 5 in the following distribution of a continuous variable:

V	f	cum f
0–3	8	8
4–7	7	15
8–11	2	17
12–15	5	22
N	22	

$$P_\% = \frac{100}{N} \left([\text{cum } f - f] + \frac{f[Y_\% - V_{LL}]}{w} \right)$$

$$= \frac{100}{22} \left([15 - 7] + \frac{7[5 - 3.5]}{4} \right)$$

$$= 48.30$$

PART III

Variable Relationships

Descriptive Statistics for
Two Variables

The next two chapters complete the discussion of descriptive statistics by introducing methods for describing relationships between two variables. Chapter 7 introduces the concept of linear relationships between variables. Important topics include:

- the scatterplot
- the Pearson product-moment correlation coefficient
- variations of the Pearson product-moment correlation coefficient

Chapter 8 focuses on simple regression, a method of estimating scores on one variables from scores on another when the variables demonstrate a linear relationship. Important topics include:

- the regression line
- the standard error of estimate
- the relationship between regression and correlation

CHAPTER 7

Scatterplots and the Correlation Coefficient

7.1 LINEAR RELATIONSHIPS

A **linear relationship** refers to *a relationship between two variables which can be approximated using a straight line*. To demonstrate the concept of linear relationship I will return to a study described in Chapter 3.1.2. The study examined the relationship between scores on a self-esteem rating scale and grade point average, or GPA, in high school students. I indicated the researcher might reasonably suggest one of three scientific hypotheses:

1. Students with higher self-esteem scores are likely to report higher GPAs, while students with lower self-esteem scores are likely to report lower GPAs. This hypothesis would make sense if, for example, the researcher believes that getting higher grades enhances self-esteem. This is an example of a **positive linear relationship**, *a linear relationship between two variables X and Y, where higher scores on variable X tend to be associated with higher scores on variable Y, and lower scores on variable X tend to be associated with lower scores on variable Y.*

2. Students with higher self-esteem scores are likely to report lower GPAs, while students with lower self-esteem scores are likely to report higher GPAs. This hypothesis would make sense if for example the researcher believes that better students tend to be more self-critical. This is an example of a **negative linear relationship**, *a linear relationship between two variables X and Y, where higher scores on variable X tend to be associated with lower scores on variable Y, and lower scores on variable X tend to be associated with higher scores on variable Y.*

3. The variables self-esteem and GPA may demonstrate *no linear relationship*. This hypothesis would make sense if the researcher believes that self-esteem and grades have nothing to do with each other. The absence of a linear relationship implies that knowledge of a student's GPA imparts no information about that student's self-esteem score, and knowledge of a student's self-esteem score imparts no information about that student's GPA.

An important point made in Section 3.1.2 about relationships should be repeated here. The existence of a relationship between two variables suggests that knowledge of subjects' scores on one variable provides information about subjects' scores on the other. Knowledge of one variable allows you to make predictions about the other.

The descriptive statistics introduced in this and the next chapter are particularly useful for this type of research study. The present chapter begins with a discussion of the scatterplot, which provides a graphical representation of the relationship between variables, and proceeds to a discussion of the correlation coefficient, a descriptive statistic which provides information about linear relationships.

7.2 THE SCATTERPLOT

The Scatterplot Defined. In Chapter 4 you were introduced to the frequency polygon and other methods of graphically representing the pattern of data for a single variable. The scatterplot can be used to graphically represent relationships between variables. The **scatterplot** is *a graphical representation of the relationship between two variables.*[1] Figure 7.1 provides an example of a typical scatterplot for a sample of 30 subjects. Each subject generated data for two variables. The 30 points in the scatterplot each represent a single subject's scores on the X variable and the Y variable simultaneously. The point that is circled represents a subject who has a score of 26 on the X variable and a score of 4 on the Y variable.

No Relationship. The scatterplots in Figure 7.2 depict typical or important variable relationships. Figure 7.2(a) is an example of a scatterplot where *no relationship* exists between the X and Y variables. Higher X scores are no more likely to be associated with higher Y scores than with lower Y scores, and lower X scores are no more likely to be associated with higher Y scores than with lower Y scores. Notice that the top half of the scatterplot

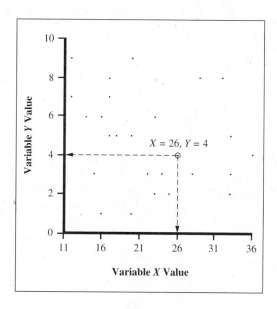

FIGURE 7.1 A typical scatterplot. The circled point indicates a subject whose score on variable X is 26 and whose score on variable Y is 4.

---

[1]Scatterplots representing relationships among three variables are possible but will not be discussed here.

mirrors the bottom half, or the left half mirrors the right half, then the scatterplot suggests the absence of a relationship.

A Perfect Positive Linear Relationship. Figure 7.2(b) is an example of a *perfect positive linear relationship*: higher X scores are consistently associated with higher Y scores, lower X scores with lower Y scores. If you knew a subject's X score, you would be able to predict that subject's Y score perfectly by looking at the scatterplot. You would also be able to predict the subject's X score perfectly from the subject's Y score.

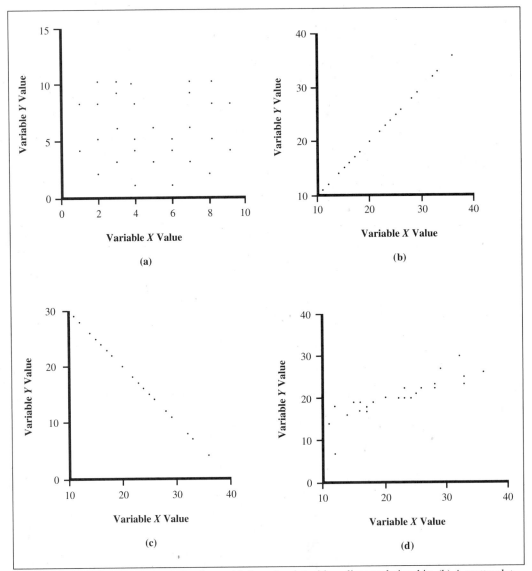

FIGURE 7.2 Some important scatterplot shapes (a) A scatterplot with no linear relationship. (b) A scatterplot with a perfect positive linear relationship. (c) A scatterplot with a perfect negative linear relationship. (d) A scatterplot with a strong positive linear relationship. *(continued on next page)*.

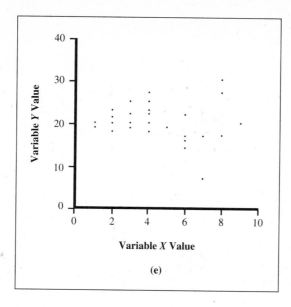

FIGURE 7.2 *(continued)* Some important scatterplot shapes.(e) A scatterplot with a weak negative linear relationship.

An example of two variables with a perfect positive linear relationship would be Fahrenheit and Celsius temperatures. For any Celsius temperature the corresponding Fahrenheit temperature can be computed exactly from the formula

$$°F = \left(\frac{9}{5}\right)°C + 32,$$

and for any Fahrenheit temperature the corresponding Celsius temperature can be computed exactly from the formula

$$°C = \frac{5}{9}(°F - 32).$$

Higher Fahrenheit temperatures are associated with higher Celsius temperatures, lower Fahrenheit temperatures with lower Celsius temperatures. If we created the scatterplot for the peak temperature each day in April using both the Fahrenheit and Celsius scales, the points would form a straight line from the lower left to the upper right of the scatterplot.

A Perfect Negative Linear Relationship. Figure 7.2(c) is an example of a *perfect negative linear relationship*: higher X values are consistently associated with lower Y values, lower X values with higher Y values. The perfectly straight line again indicates that if you knew a subject's X value, you would be able to predict the subject's Y value perfectly by looking at the scatterplot, and vice versa.

An example of two variables with a perfect negative linear relationship is length of nighttime and daytime during each 24-hour period. There are 1440 minutes in a 24-hour day. The number of minutes of nighttime can be perfectly predicted from the number of minutes of daytime by the following formula:

$$\text{Nighttime} = 1440 - \text{Daytime}.$$

Similarly, the number of minutes of daytime can be perfectly predicted from the number of minutes of nighttime using the formula

$$\text{Daytime} = 1440 - \text{Nighttime}.$$

Longer daytime periods are associated with shorter nighttime periods, shorter daytime periods with longer nighttime periods.

If we created the scatterplot for the number of minutes of daytime and nighttime per 24-hour day in April, the points would form a straight line from the upper left to the lower right of the scatterplot.

A Strong Positive Linear Relationship. Cases in which there is a perfect relationship or no relationship between two variables are rare. More common is the case where two variables are related but not perfectly. Figure 7.2(d) depicts a *strong but not perfect positive linear relationship*. Higher X values are generally but not always associated with higher Y values, and lower X values are generally but not always associated with lower Y values. Figure 7.2(d) falls somewhere between the perfect positive linear relationship in Figure 7.2(b), and the perfectly symmetrical scatterplot in Figure 7.2(a).

Scores on two well-designed measures of self-esteem might demonstrate a scatterplot similar to Figure 7.2(d). Subjects who think positively of themselves should tend to score highly on both, while subjects who think badly of themselves should score poorly on both. However, the relationship between the two will be less than perfect unless the test items are extremely similar in content.

A Weak Negative Linear Relationship. Figure 7.2(e) illustrates a *weak negative linear relationship*. Higher X values show a slight tendency to be associated with lower Y values, and lower X values show a slight tendency to be associated with higher Y values. Figure 7.2(e) falls somewhere between the perfect negative linear relationship in Figure 7.2(c), and the perfectly symmetrical scatterplot in Figure 7.2(a).

One might expect a scatterplot similar to Figure 7.2(e) if scores on a self-esteem rating scale are associated with the number of errors made while proofreading written material. Subjects who think badly of themselves may tend to commit more errors, but self-esteem is likely to have little impact on proofreading ability.

7.3 THE CORRELATION COEFFICIENT

Just as measures of central tendency and variability express aspects of a variable pattern in a simple numeric form, measures of linear relationship express aspects of a variable relationship numerically. **Measures of linear relationship** are *descriptive statistics which indicate the strength and direction of a linear relationship between variables*. The most important measure of linear relationship is the correlation coefficient. A second measure of linear relationship, the covariance, is described briefly in the supplement.

7.3.1 The Correlation Coefficient Defined

The **Pearson product-moment correlation coefficient** (r_{XY}), can be defined as *a measure of linear relationship based on the standard scores for two variables*. Although there are other correlation coefficients, the Pearson coefficient is the most commonly used. When the correlation coefficient is mentioned, you can assume it is a Pearson product-moment correlation unless otherwise indicated. The Pearson correlation may be computed for any two variables as long as neither is a nominal variable with more than two values.

The Definitional Formula. One definitional formula for the Pearson statistic is

$$r_{XY} = \frac{\sum_{i=1}^{N} z_{X_i} z_{Y_i}}{N - 1}.$$

Each subject produces a score on the X variable and the Y variable. The X and Y scores are transformed to z scores, creating two sets of z scores from the same sample. We may refer to these as the z_X scores and the z_Y scores. The correlation coefficient is computed by multiplying each subject's z_X score and z_Y score, summing the products, and dividing by $N - 1$.

For example, suppose five high school students rated their level of agreement with the statement "I feel good about myself" from 1 (Strongly Disagree) to 5 (Strongly Agree) and reported their GPAs. The data are as follows:

	Self-Esteem(X)	GPA(Y)
Student 1	4	3.0
Student 2	3	2.5
Student 3	5	2.6
Student 4	3	4.0
Student 5	2	1.8

If we consider self-esteem to be the X variable and GPA to be the Y variable, we can generate the following statistics:

$$\overline{X} = 3.40 \qquad \overline{Y} = 2.78$$
$$s_X = 1.1420 \qquad s_Y = .8075.$$

Using these data we can generate the corresponding z scores and multiply them together:

X	z_X	Y	z_Y	$z_X z_Y$
4	0.5262	3.0	0.2724	0.1434
3	−0.3508	2.5	−0.3467	0.1217
5	1.4033	2.6	−0.2229	−0.3128
3	−0.3508	4.0	1.5108	−0.5301
2	−1.2279	1.8	−1.2136	1.4902

The correlation would be:

$$r_{XY} = \frac{\sum_{i=1}^{N} z_{X_i} z_{Y_i}}{N - 1}$$

$$= \frac{0.1434 + 0.1217 + (-0.3128) + (-0.5301) + 1.4902}{4}$$

$$= +.2281.$$

Positive Correlations. An important characteristic of the correlation coefficient emerges when you examine the column above labeled $z_X z_Y$. Student 1's X score is greater than the mean of X, so Student 1's z_X score is positive. Student 1's Y score is also greater than the mean of Y, so Student 1's z_Y score is also positive. Since both z scores are positive, their product is a positive number.

Student 2's X score is less than the mean of X, so Student 2's z_X score is negative. Student 2's Y score is also less than the mean of Y, so Student 2's z_Y score is also negative. Since both z scores are negative their product is also a positive number.

The point of this exercise is to demonstrate that the $z_X z_Y$ values will tend to be positive if subjects with above average X values tend to have above average Y values, and subjects with below average X values tend to have below average Y values. In other words, *the correlation will be a positive number if there is a positive linear relationship between X and Y.*

Negative Correlations. Student 3's X score is greater than the mean of X, so Student 3's z_X score is positive. Student 3's Y score is less than the mean of Y, so Student 3's z_Y score is negative. Since the product of a positive and a negative number is a negative number, multiplying the two z scores produces a negative number. The $z_X z_Y$ values will tend to be negative if subjects with above average X values tend to have below average Y values, and subjects with below average X values tend to have above average Y values. In other words, *the correlation will be a negative number if there is a negative linear relationship between X and Y.*

Correlations Equalling Zero. If the positive $z_X z_Y$ values exactly equal the negative $z_X z_Y$ values, then these values will sum to zero. In other words, *the correlation will equal zero if there is no linear relationship between X and Y.*

The Computational Formula. In practice the following computational formula is more commonly used:

$$r_{XY} = \frac{\sum\limits_{i=1}^{N} X_i Y_i - \frac{\left(\sum\limits_{i=1}^{N} X_i\right)\left(\sum\limits_{i=1}^{N} Y_i\right)}{N}}{\sqrt{\left[\sum\limits_{i=1}^{N} X_i^2 - \frac{\left(\sum\limits_{i=1}^{N} X_i\right)^2}{N}\right]\left[\sum\limits_{i=1}^{N} Y_i^2 - \frac{\left(\sum\limits_{i=1}^{N} Y_i\right)^2}{N}\right]}}.$$

Believe it or not, this formula is simpler to use because you do not have to compute means, standard deviations, and z scores. Computation of the correlation coefficient using this formula is demonstrated in Procedure Box 7.1.

Characteristics of the Correlation Coefficient. The correlation coefficient has several desirable characteristics. First, the sample correlation coefficient provides the best sample estimate of the population correlation coefficient ρ_{XY} (the Greek letter rho). Second, correlation coefficient values can only vary between $+1.0$ (suggesting a perfect positive linear relationship) and -1.0 (suggesting a perfect negative linear relationship).

7.3 The Correlation Coefficient 113

The Pearson Product-Moment Correlation Coefficient

Goal Five high school students rated their level of agreement with the statement "I feel good about myself" from 1 (Strongly Disagree) to 5 (Strongly Agree) and reported their GPAs. Compute the correlation for the following data:

	Self-Esteem	*GPA*
Student 1	4	3.0
Student 2	3	2.5
Student 3	5	2.6
Student 4	3	4.0
Student 5	2	1.8

$$r_{XY} = \frac{\sum\limits_{i=1}^{N} X_i Y_i - \dfrac{\left(\sum\limits_{i=1}^{N} X_i\right)\left(\sum\limits_{i=1}^{N} Y_i\right)}{N}}{\sqrt{\left[\sum\limits_{i=1}^{N} X_i^2 - \dfrac{\left(\sum\limits_{i=1}^{N} X_i\right)^2}{N}\right]\left[\sum\limits_{i=1}^{N} Y_i^2 - \dfrac{\left(\sum\limits_{i=1}^{N} Y_i\right)^2}{N}\right]}}.$$

Step 1 *Sum the values for X, Y, X times Y, X^2, and Y^2.*

	X	Y	XY	X^2	Y^2
	4	3.0	12.0	16	9.00
	3	2.5	7.5	9	6.25
	5	2.6	13.0	25	6.76
	3	4.0	12.0	9	16.00
	2	1.8	3.6	4	3.24
Sums:	17	13.9	48.1(a)	63(b)	41.25(c)

Step 2 *Multiply (a) the sum of the X values by the sum of the Y values, (b) the sum of the X values by itself, and (c) the sum of the Y values by itself, and divide each by N.*

Continued

The Pearson product-moment correlation coefficient continued

(a) $\dfrac{\left(\sum\limits_{i=1}^{N} X_i\right)\left(\sum\limits_{i=1}^{N} Y_i\right)}{N} = \dfrac{17(13.9)}{5} = 47.26$

(b) $\dfrac{\left(\sum\limits_{i=1}^{N} X_i\right)^2}{N} = \dfrac{17^2}{5} = 57.8$

(c) $\dfrac{\left(\sum\limits_{i=1}^{N} Y_i\right)^2}{N} = \dfrac{13.9^2}{5} = 38.642$

Step 3   *Subtract the results of Step 2 from the corresponding sum in Step 1.*

(a) $\sum\limits_{i=1}^{N} X_i Y_i - \dfrac{\left(\sum\limits_{i=1}^{N} X_i\right)\left(\sum\limits_{i=1}^{N} Y_i\right)}{N} = 48.1 - 47.26 = .84$

(b) $\sum\limits_{i=1}^{N} X_i^2 - \dfrac{\left(\sum\limits_{i=1}^{N} X_i\right)^2}{N} = 63 - 57.8 = 5.2$ ◀—— *This number must be positive.*

(c) $\sum\limits_{i=1}^{N} Y_i^2 - \dfrac{\left(\sum\limits_{i=1}^{N} Y_i\right)^2}{N} = 41.25 - 38.642 = 2.608$ ◀—— *This number must be positive.*

Step 4   *Multiply the results from Steps 3(b) and 3(c) and find the square root.*

$$\sqrt{5.2(2.608)} = 3.6826$$

Step 5   *Divide the result from Step 3(a) by the result from Step 4.*

$$r_{XY} = \dfrac{.84}{3.6826} = +.2281 \quad ◀—— \textit{This number must fall between } -1 \textit{ and } +1.$$

A positive correlation suggests that higher scores on the self-esteem question (greater self-esteem) tend to be associated with higher GPAs.

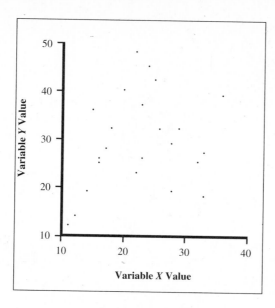

FIGURE 7.3 A scatterplot of two variables where $r_{XY} = +.354$

Look again at the relatively strong positive linear relationship in Figure 7.2(d). The correlation coefficient associated with these data is $+.861$. The scatterplot in Figure 7.2(e) was described as a relatively weak negative linear relationship. The correlation coefficient associated with these data is $-.068$. A correlation coefficient of $+1.0$ or -1.0 suggests every point falls exactly on a straight line, as in Figures 7.2(b) and 7.2(c), while a correlation of 0 indicates no linear relationship as in Figure 7.2(a).

I noted earlier that perfect linear relationships rarely occur in the behavioral sciences. In some cases fairly high correlations are to be expected. For example, the correlation between scores on two well-developed tests of reading speed should exceed .80. In most cases where a high correlation is not to be expected, correlations in the behavioral sciences rarely surpass .50, and usually equal .35 or less. Figure 7.3 is a typical scatterplot for two variables which correlate $+.354$. As you can see, it is not easy to detect a linear relationship of this magnitude just from the scatterplot.

7.3.2 Interpreting Correlation Coefficients

There are several issues to keep in mind when interpreting correlations, as the next three sections demonstrate.

7.3.2.1 The Strength of a Relationship

Correlation coefficient values comprise an ordinal scale. Suppose variables X and Y correlate .20, while variables X and Z correlate .40. While this information suggests the linear relationship between X and Z is stronger than the linear relationship between X and Y, it should not be interpreted as suggesting that the linear relationship between X and Z is twice as strong as the linear relationship between X and Y.

The Index of Association. The square of the correlation coefficient, r_{XY}^2, is sometimes referred to as the **index of association**, and is defined as *the proportion of the variance of one* *variable accounted for by another variable.* For example, suppose we are interested in why students differ in terms of their academic performance. This is a question about variability: why does academic performance vary among students; why do they not all perform the same? One hypothesis would suggest that to some extent grades vary because of general intellectual ability.

The variance, introduced in Chapter 6, is a descriptive statistic that measures the amount of variability in a set of scores. Suppose we find the correlation between intelligence test scores and GPA is $+.40$ in a sample of high school students. The index of association is therefore

$$.40^2 = .16.$$

This means that 16% of the variance in high school GPA can be accounted for by intellectual ability as defined by the intelligence test. While this is not trivial (remember that in the behavioral sciences correlations rarely surpass .35), it suggests that $100\% - 16\% = 84\%$ of the difference in students' high school grades in our sample is *not* accounted for by intellectual ability. The remaining variability probably is accounted for by a combination of many other factors: amount of time spent studying, difficulty of the school, likability of the student, whether the student cheats on tests, errors in the measurement of variables, etc.

Comparing Indexes of Association. The index of association represents a ratio variable of the strength of the relationship between two variables. If variables X and Y correlate .40 and variables X and Z correlate .20, then $r_{XY}^2 = .16$ and $r_{XZ}^2 = .04$. We can say that variable X accounts for four times as much of the variance of variable Y as it does of variable Z, or that the relationship between X and Y is four times as strong as the relationship between X and Z. For this reason, the index of association is often considered a more useful indicator of the strength of the relationship between two variables than the correlation coefficient. Statements such as "variable X accounts for 36% of the variance of variable Y" seems to say more than "variable X and variable Y correlate .60."

An important characteristic of the index of association is that it works both ways. If variable X accounts for 36% of the variance of variable Y, variable Y also accounts for 36% of the variance of variable X. A second method for interpreting the strength of a relationship based on the correlation coefficient, called the *binomial effect size display*, is described in the supplement.

7.3.2.2 Restriction of Range

The Scholastic Assessment Tests, or SATs, are used by many colleges and universities to evaluate applicants for admission. Scores on the combined verbal and quantitative portions of the test typically range between 400 and 1600 points. Suppose College A practices open admissions, so students are accepted regardless of their SAT scores. College B only accepts students with a combined SAT score above 1100. The correlation between SAT combined scores and students' GPAs at the end of the first year of classes should be higher at College A than at College B.

Why is this so? Imagine we could arrange for a random sample of the population of college applicants to apply to and attend College A. The scatterplot in Figure 7.4 gives you an idea of what the relationship between SAT combined scores and GPA after the first year of college might look like for these students (ignore the dotted line for now). I hope you can see there is a reasonable positive linear relationship between SAT scores and college performance; the correlation here is $+.599$.

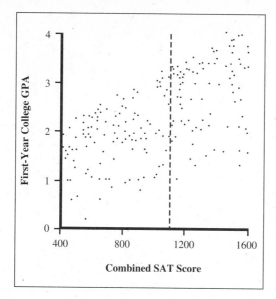

FIGURE 7.4 A hypothetical scatterplot for SAT scores and first-year college GPA. While the data as a whole suggest a positive relationship between SAT scores and GPA, when the range of SAT scores is restricted to those scoring over 1100 (points to the right of the dotted line) the scatterplot becomes more symmetrical, suggesting a weak relationship.

Now suppose we had arranged for our random sample to apply to College B instead. Since College B only accepts students with combined SATs above 1100, the sample on which we would be able to compute the correlation between SAT scores and first-year GPA would be limited to those students to the right of the dotted line in Figure 7.4. Within this restricted range of SAT scores the linear relationship between SAT score and first-year GPA is not as strong. When only the students with SAT scores above 1100 are included, the correlation drops to $+.181$.

Although the sample correlation coefficient is the best estimate of the population correlation coefficient, r_{XY} tends to underestimate ρ_{XY} if the range of scores in the sample is restricted on either variable. College B's error in estimating ρ_{XY} will not balance out over a series of random samples; any college that restricts the range of SAT scores among its students will consistently tend to underestimate the true strength of the linear relationship between SAT scores and college performance.

7.3.2.3 Non-Linear Relationships

I have tried to stress that the Pearson correlation coefficient only indicates the strength of the *linear* relationship between X and Y. Examine the scatterplot in Figure 7.5. The relationship between X and Y is very strong; I can predict Y values from X values with almost perfect accuracy. However, in this case a straight line does not reflect the relationship well. This is an example of a primarily non-linear relationship. The Pearson correlation coefficient will underestimate the strength of the relationship between X and Y, since it only indicates the strength of the linear relationship. In this case $r_{XY} = +.038$. If another version of the correlation coefficient is used which also takes into account the non-linear relationship between X and Y, the correlation increases to $+.794$.

It is common practice for researchers to compute correlation coefficients without reviewing the associated scatterplots. This is done for the sake of efficiency; it is not unusual for a researcher to generate hundreds of correlation coefficients when analyzing the data from a

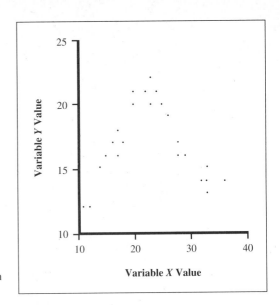

FIGURE 7.5 Scatterplot of a relationship with both linear and nonlinear components.

study, and reviewing all the associated scatterplots would be a grueling effort. I must caution you against this practice. Without reviewing the scatterplots you will miss non-linear relationships, and can underestimate the strength of the relationship between two variables.

7.3.3 Variations of the Correlation Coefficient

Although the Pearson formula is the most commonly used formula for the correlation coefficient, in large data sets it is not an easy statistic to compute by hand. There are conditions under which simpler computational formulas are available. The **point-biserial correlation coefficient** (r_{pb}) is *a computational formula for the correlation coefficient which may be used when one variable is a dichotomous variable and the other is an ordinal, interval, or ratio variable*. The **phi coefficient** (r_ϕ) is *a computational formula for the correlation coefficient which may be used when both variables are dichotomous variables*. The **Spearman rank-order correlation coefficient** (r_s) is *a computational formula for the correlation coefficient which may be used when both variables represent rank orders without tied ranks*.

Any of these correlations could be computed using the Pearson formula as long as all variables are recorded using numeric values. For example, the dichotomous variable gender could be recorded numerically if males are assigned a value of 1 on the gender variable and females are assigned a value of 2 (or any other pair of arbitrarily chosen numbers).

In fact, some computer programs that calculate correlation coefficients only use the Pearson formula. Even if the Pearson formula is used, the names used here may still be applied. A correlation coefficient between a dichotomous variable and an ordinal, interval or ratio variable is usually called a point-biserial correlation coefficient even if it is computed using the Pearson formula, for example. If you must compute correlations by hand, in some circumstances these computational formulas will make your computations easier. Additional discussion of the three variations is provided in the supplement.

KEY TERMS

dichotomous variable

index of association

linear relationship

measures of linear relationship

negative linear relationship

Pearson product-moment correlation coefficient

phi coefficient

point-biserial correlation coefficient

positive linear relationship

scatterplot

Spearman rank-order correlation coefficient

EXERCISES

Answers to all exercises may be found in Appendix B.

1. Two very different rating scales of self-esteem have been developed. On each a high score is supposed to indicate a high level of self-esteem. A researcher is interested in whether they are in fact measuring the same variable. A researcher administers the two rating scales to 10 college students, producing the following data:

	X	Y
Student 1	1	5
Student 2	3	7
Student 3	6	9
Student 4	4	3
Student 5	4	5
Student 6	5	7
Student 7	4	9
Student 8	9	8
Student 9	8	4
Student 10	7	3

   a. Indicate whether this is a *true experiment, quasi-experiment,* or *observational study*.
   b. Indicate whether the two variables being studied are *nominal, ordinal, interval,* or *ratio*, and whether they are *continuous* or *discrete*.
   c. Construct the scatterplot for the data.
   d. Compute r_{XY}.
   e. Do the two scales seem to be measuring the same variable? What sort of correlation would you expect in this situation?

2. What would you expect the scatterplot for variables X and Y to look like if the correlation suggests there is:
   a. a strong negative relationship between X and Y?
   b. a weak positive relationship between X and Y?
   c. no relationship between X and Y?

3. Subjects participated in one of two reading enhancement programs. Assignment was based on which group the subject could attend. Variable X indicates which program a subject received. Variable Y is a measure of improvement in number of words read per minute. Compute the correlation coefficient using the following data:

X	Y
1	5
1	7
1	2
1	3
1	5
2	7
2	9
2	8
2	4
2	3

   a. What type of study is this: a *true experiment, quasi-experiment,* or *observational study*?
   b. Indicate whether the two variables being studied are *nominal, ordinal, interval,* or *ratio*, and whether they are *continuous* or *discrete*.
   c. What type of correlation coefficient is this: a *Pearson product-moment correlation coefficient, point-biserial, phi coefficient,* or *Spearman*?
   d. Construct the scatterplot for these data.
   e. Compute r_{XY}.
   f. Interpret this correlation coefficient.

4. Subjects suffering from chronic back pain were randomly chosen to receive either placebo or ibuprofen daily. After one week they were asked whether their pain was improved. Variable X represents treatment,

where 1 indicates placebo, 2 ibuprofen. Variable Y indicates response, where a 1 indicates unimproved, a 2 improved. Compute the correlation coefficient using the following data:

X	Y
1	1
1	1
1	1
1	1
1	1
2	1
2	2
2	2
2	2
2	2

a. What type of study is this: a *true experiment, quasi-experiment*, or *observational study*?
b. Indicate whether the two variables being studied are *nominal, ordinal, interval*, or *ratio*, and whether they are *continuous* or *discrete*.
c. What type of correlation coefficient is this: *Pearson, point-biserial, phi coefficient*, or *Spearman*?
d. Compute r_{XY}.
e. Interpret this correlation coefficient.

5. In a sample of students who participated in honors history classes in high school, the index of association between score on the advanced placement examination in history and performance in college history courses is $+.12$. Discuss what this means about the relationship between these two variables, and identify at least two issues related to the interpretation of this finding.

6. Students are asked to estimate in seconds how much time it will take to complete a simple maze (X). Their performance is then timed (Y):

X	Y
4	4
3	2
6	6
4	3
4	2
5	2
4	3
9	6
8	5
7	6

a. What type of study is this: a *true experiment, quasi-experiment*, or *observational study*?

b. Indicate whether the two variables being studied are *nominal, ordinal, interval*, or *ratio*, and whether they are *continuous* or *discrete*.
c. Compute r_{XY}.
d. Interpret this correlation coefficient.
e. Construct the scatterplot for these data. How would you modify your interpretation in light of the scatterplot?

7. Students complete two simple mazes. The time it took them to complete each maze (within one-half second) was as follows:

X	Y
4.0	4.0
3.0	2.0
6.0	6.0
4.5	3.0
6.5	2.5
5.0	3.5
5.5	5.5
9.0	7.5
8.5	5.0
7.0	6.5

a. What type of study is this: a *true experiment, quasi-experiment*, or *observational study*?
b. Are these *nominal, ordinal, interval*, or *ratio* variables; are they *continuous* or *discrete*?
c. When a time is recorded as 4.0 seconds, what are the upper and lower real limits of this interval? What is its midpoint?
d. Compute r_{XY}. Is this a *Pearson product-moment correlation coefficient*, point-biserial correlation coefficient, *phi coefficient*, or *Spearman rank-order correlation coefficient*?
e. Convert both sets of scores to rank orders. In other words, take the set of X values and convert them to rank orders (from lowest to highest), then do the same for the set of Y values. What types of variables are rank orders?
f. Compute r_{XY} using the ranks. Is this a *Pearson product-moment correlation coefficient, point-biserial correlation coefficient, phi coefficient*, or *Spearman rank-order correlation coefficient*?
g. Suppose the first X value had been 6.0 seconds instead of 4.0, so that there were two X values of 6.0. Which formula would then provide a more accurate estimate of the correlation between the two sets of ranks: the Pearson formula, or the Spearman rank-order formula?

S7.1 THE COVARIANCE

The covariance is also a measure of linear relationship, but unlike the correlation coefficient it is not based on standard scores. The formula for the best estimate of the population covariance is

$$s_{XY} = \frac{\sum\limits_{i=1}^{N}(X_i - \overline{X})(Y_i - \overline{Y})}{N - 1}$$

$$= \frac{\sum\limits_{i=1}^{N} X_i Y_i - \dfrac{\left(\sum\limits_{i=1}^{N} X_i\right)\left(\sum\limits_{i=1}^{N} Y_i\right)}{N}}{N - 1}$$

The second is the best computational formula. The formula for the sample covariance, S_{XY} (capital S rather than lowercase s), is the same except that the denominator is N rather than $N - 1$. Like the sample variance (see Section S6.2), the sample covariance tends to underestimate the population covariance.

Like the correlation coefficient, positive covariance values suggest a positive linear relationship, negative values suggest a negative linear relationship, and a value of zero indicates no relationship. However, the value of the covariance is influenced not only by the strength of the linear relationship between X and Y, but by the size of s_X and s_Y as well. The larger the standard deviations of X and Y, the larger the absolute value of the covariance will be. If $s_X = 20$ and $s_Y = 15$, the absolute value of the covariance can vary between 0 (if there is no linear relationship between X and Y) and $20(15) = 300$ (if there is a perfect linear relationship). If $s_X = 2$ and $s_Y = 1.5$, the absolute value of the covariance can only vary between 0 (if there is no linear relationship) and $2(1.5) = 3$ (if the linear relationship is perfect). A covariance of 2.9 in the second case actually indicates a stronger linear relationship than a covariance of 50 in the first case. It is for this reason that the correlation coefficient is generally preferred as a descriptive statistic.

S7.2 THE BINOMIAL EFFECT SIZE DISPLAY

The index of association was offered in the chapter as a method of using the correlation coefficient to understand the strength of the relationship between two variables. A second method, called the binomial effect size display (BESD), was first suggested by Rosenthal and Rubin (1982).

A Research Example. Imagine a study in which men in their 50s receive either a new medication that is believed will reduce the risk of heart attacks, or a placebo alternative, for

5 years. The sample is then divided into those who suffered a heart attack during those 5 years and those who did not.

This study focuses on the relationship between two dichotomous variables: treatment condition (active versus placebo treatment), and whether or not the subject suffered a heart attack. After five years the heart attack rate is indeed determined to be lower among those who received the active treatment than among those who received placebo. The phi coefficient is computed and found equal to .20. The index of association, $.20^2 = .04$, indicates that 4% of the variance in heart attacks is accounted for by treatment. The BESD offers a second method of understanding this finding.

The BESD. Assume that (1) half of the subjects were in each treatment condition, and (2) half of the subjects suffered heart attacks. If the phi coefficient had equalled 0 it would mean that exactly half the subjects in the active treatment had heart attacks and half the subjects in the placebo treatment had heart attacks. We can symbolize this as

| | | Suffered a Heart Attack | |
		Yes	No
Treatment	Active	.50	.50
Condition	Placebo	.50	.50

In this table the number in each box indicates the proportion of subjects in that row who either did or did not suffer a heart attack.

However, we know that the heart attack rate was lower among subjects who received active treatment, and this difference was associated with a phi coefficient of .20. If the two assumptions listed above are true, the proportions in each row of the table that would produce a phi coefficient of .20 would be

| | | Suffered a Heart Attack | |
		Yes	No
Treatment	Active	.40	.60
Condition	Placebo	.60	.40

In other words, if the two assumptions were true, the proportion of subjects receiving active treatment who did not suffer heart attacks (.60) minus the proportion who suffered heart attacks (.40) would equal the correlation coefficient:

$$.60 - .40 = .20.$$

The proportion would be reversed for the placebo condition. The BESD offers a method of interpreting the strength of a relationship in terms of the potential difference in the proportion of subjects achieving different outcomes.

BESD versus Index of Association. The BESD can make the strength of the linear relationship seem much larger than does the index of association. Finding that a treatment accounts for 4% of the variance in heart attacks sounds much less impressive than a potential improvement in success rate of 20% over placebo. However, two points should be kept in mind concerning the BESD. First, it is really only appropriate to use the BESD when it makes sense to think of the two variables in dichotomous terms. Second, it is rare that the two assumptions listed will be met. For example, the proportion of males in their 50s who will suffer a heart attack during a given 5-year period is likely to be far less than 50%. The further the true proportions vary from .50, the less dramatic the effect appears. The BESD indicates a *potential* difference in proportions, not necessarily the true difference.

S7.3 THE POINT-BISERIAL CORRELATION COEFFICIENT

Computing the Correlation. The point-biserial correlation coefficient formula may be used to calculate the correlation when one variable is dichotomous and the second is an ordinal, interval, or ratio variable. If variable X is a dichotomous variable, there are two groups of subjects defined by variable X. An example is gender, which defines a group of male subjects (Group 1) and a group of female subjects (Group 2). The computational formula for the point-biserial correlation is

$$ r_{pb} = \frac{(\overline{Y}_1 - \overline{Y}_2)\sqrt{\dfrac{n_1 n_2}{N - 1}}}{s_Y}, $$

where $\overline{Y}_1$ is the mean score on variable Y among subjects in Group 1, $\overline{Y}_2$ is the mean score on variable Y among subjects in Group 2, n_1 is the number of subjects in Group 1, n_2 is the number of subjects in Group 2, and s_Y is the standard deviation of all the Y scores.

You can also use the Pearson formula to compute the point-biserial correlation if you numerically code the dichotomous variable. To code gender numerically, males are assigned one numeric value and females are assigned another. Since these numbers represent values of a nominal variable the choice is arbitrary: males could be 1 and females 0, or males could be 12 and females 316. If you then compute the Pearson correlation coefficient between the gender and self-esteem variables, the resulting value would be the same value generated using the point-biserial correlation coefficient formula, and it is still appropriate to refer to this value as a point-biserial correlation.

Interpreting the Correlation. The point-biserial correlation between gender and self-esteem will equal 0 (suggesting no relationship between X and Y) if the mean self-esteem score for females exactly equals the mean self-esteem score for males. This would suggest that knowing a subject's gender provides you no information about that subject's level of self-esteem and vice versa.

The point-biserial correlation can only equal 1.0 if every male has the same score on the self-esteem scale, if every female has the same score, and if males and females have different scores. This would mean that knowing a subject's gender would allow perfect prediction of that subject's level of self-esteem.

The direction of the point-biserial correlation (negative or positive) is arbitrary. It will vary depending on which gender is called Group 1 and which Group 2 (if you are using the point-biserial computational formula), or on which gender is coded with the higher number (if you are using the Pearson formula).

S7.4 THE PHI COEFFICIENT

Computing the Correlation. The phi coefficient formula may be used to calculate the correlation when both variables are dichotomous. If both variables X and Y are dichotomous variables, there are two groups of subjects defined by variable X and by variable Y. If variable X is gender and variable Y is treatment condition (peer counseling or placebo), the data may be structured as follows:

Treatment (Y)

		Peer Counseling	Placebo	
Gender (X)	Male	$n_{11} = 23$	$n_{12} = 14$	$n_{\text{row }1} = 37$
	Female	$n_{21} = 17$	$n_{22} = 32$	$n_{\text{row }2} = 49$
		$n_{\text{column }1} = 40$	$n_{\text{column }2} = 46$	$N = 86$

In each case n refers to the group size. For example, n_{12} is the group size for males who did not receive peer counseling (first X value, second Y value). $n_{\text{column }2}$ refers to the number of subjects who received placebo (the second Y value); it is the n for the second column of the table. Using these symbols, the computational formula for the phi coefficient is

$$r_\phi = \frac{(n_{11})(n_{22}) - (n_{21})(n_{12})}{\sqrt{(n_{\text{row }1})(n_{\text{row }2})(n_{\text{column }1})(n_{\text{column }2})}}$$

You can also use the Pearson formula to compute the phi coefficient if you numerically code both variables. The choice of numbers to associate with each value is again arbitrary. If you then compute the Pearson correlation coefficient between the gender and peer counseling variables, the resulting value would be the same value generated using the phi coefficient formula, and it is still appropriate to refer to this value as a phi coefficient.

Interpreting the Correlation. The phi coefficient between gender and treatment condition will equal 0 (suggesting no relationship between X and Y) if the proportion of males (and females) is the same in the two conditions. This would mean that knowing a subject's gender provides no information about that person's treatment condition and vice versa.

The phi coefficient can only equal 1.0 if every male is in one treatment condition and every female is in the other treatment condition. This would mean that knowing a subject's gender allows perfect prediction of that subject's treatment condition and vice versa.

The direction of the phi coefficient (negative or positive) is arbitrary. It is determined by your choice of which groups to consider 1 and 2 (if you are using the phi coefficient computational formula), or which groups are coded with the higher numbers (if you use the Pearson formula).

S7.5 THE SPEARMAN RANK-ORDER CORRELATION COEFFICIENT

The Spearman formula may be used to calculate the correlation when both variables represent rank orders without tied ranks. Suppose we are interested in whether popularity in school is related to class rank among third-graders. Our sample consists of a class of 33 third-grade students. To measure popularity, students are asked to list everyone in the class they consider to be their friend. Subjects are then rank ordered based on the number of lists in which they were included. If variable X (popularity) has been transformed into ranks R_X, and variable Y (class rank) into ranks R_Y, then the correlation can be computed using the following formula:

$$r_s = 1 - \frac{6 \sum_{i=1}^{N} (R_{X_i} - R_{Y_i})^2}{N(N^2 - 1)}.$$

This formula is mathematically equivalent to the Pearson formula only if there are no tied ranks. When ties occur the Pearson formula should always be used. For this reason, the Spearman formula is of limited usefulness.

CHAPTER 8

Simple Regression

8.1 REGRESSION ANALYSIS

The correlation coefficient estimates the strength of the linear relationship between two variables. Remember that the existence of a linear relationship between X and Y means it is possible to make a prediction about subjects' Y scores based on their X scores, and vice versa. The stronger the relationship, the more accurate these predictions will be. **Regression analysis** refers to *statistical procedures for which the primary purpose is the estimation of scores on one variable from scores on other variables.* Regression analysis can be applied to any combination of variables so long as all the variables are either dichotomous or at least ordinal; only nominal variables with more than two values are excluded.[1]

Uses of Regression Analysis. Such estimates may be useful in several ways. The Wechsler Intelligence Scale for Children (Wechsler, 1991), or WISC, is the most commonly used method of measuring intelligence in children. However, it can require 90 minutes with a trained test administrator, an expensive method of testing. Suppose I develop a new test which can be completed in fifteen minutes, and I find that scores on my new test correlate +.93 with WISC scores. The relationship is clearly a strong one. I could then use regression statistics to estimate what a person's score would be on the WISC based on that person's score on the new test. My estimates would not be perfect, since the correlation between the two tests is not perfect. However, the high Pearson product-moment correlation suggests my estimates would be very accurate on average, and I might recommend using my new test when administering the WISC is impractical.

Regression analysis can also be used to make predictions about the future. Suppose we know that height at age 12 correlates +.85 with height at age 21. If this is true, we can estimate how tall a person will be as an adult based on height at age 12. Again, it is not likely to be a perfect estimate in any one case since the correlation is not perfect, but the correlation is high enough that on average the estimates should be fairly accurate.

Predictor and Criterion Variables. To summarize, regression analysis can be used to estimate values of one variable based on other variables. The stronger the relationship

---

[1]Actually, there is a form of regression analysis, sometimes called ANOVA via regression, that even allows for the use of nominal variables with more than two values (Cohen & Cohen, 1983; Huitema, 1980). The statement above is correct for the form of regression analysis discussed in this text.

between the variables, the more accurate these estimates will be. *Variables used to estimate values on another variable* are called **predictor variables,** while *the variable to be estimated from predictor variables* is called the **criterion variable.** In the first example above, the score on the new intelligence test is the predictor variable, and the WISC score is the criterion variable. In the second example, height at age 12 is the predictor, height at age 21 the criterion. Predictor variables will generally by symbolized by X, criterion variables by Y.

A regression analysis can only include one criterion variable, but can include one or more predictor variables. **Simple regression** refers to *a regression analysis involving a single predictor variable*. The two studies described so far involved a single predictor variable, score on the new intelligence test in the first example and height at age 12 in the second.

Multiple regression refers to *a regression analysis involving more than one predictor variable*. For example, weight is strongly related to height, but is also influenced by diet. To estimate weight, a multiple regression using both subjects' heights and subjects' average daily caloric intake as predictor variables will produce better estimates than either predictor variable by itself. Although multiple regression is a very important and useful statistical procedure, it is a complex one. The discussion here will be limited to simple regression.[2]

8.2 THE REGRESSION LINE

The Geometric Line. At some point in studying mathematics you probably learned the geometric formula for a line:

$$Y = bX + a, \text{ where } b = \frac{\Delta Y}{\Delta X} = \frac{Y_1 - Y_2}{X_1 - X_2}.$$

b represents the *slope* of the line. It is computed by finding the difference between any two Y values on the line, and dividing by the difference between the corresponding X values. For example, one of the points on the line in Figure 8.1 falls at $X = 2$, $Y = 4$. Another point falls at $X = 4, Y = 7$. The slope of the line in Figure 8.1 equals

$$b = \frac{4 - 7}{2 - 4} = +1.5.$$

The result would be the same no matter which two points on the line you use to compute the slope.

The slope is defined as *the change in Y per unit change in X*. A slope of $+1.5$ means that when X changes by 1 unit, Y changes by 1.5 units in the same direction. For example, as X increases from 2 to 3 (a change of 1 unit), Y increases from 4 to 5.5 (a change of 1.5 units). As X decreases from 4 to 3, Y decreases from 7 to 5.5. Notice that the linear pattern of lower left to upper right in Figure 8.1 is the same pattern you see in the scatterplot of two variables that are positively related.

The slope of the line in Figure 8.2 is -0.80. A negative slope means X and Y change in opposite directions. As X increases by 1 unit, Y decreases by 0.8 units; as X decreases

---

[2]If you are interested in learning more about multiple regression I would recommend the book by Edwards (1979).

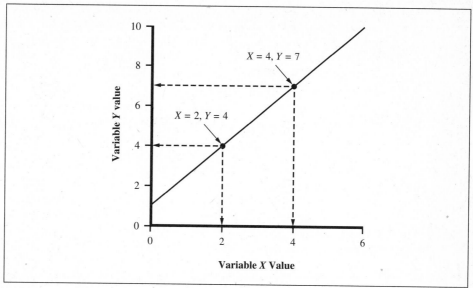

FIGURE 8.1 The geometric line with $b = +1.5$ and $a = +1.0$.

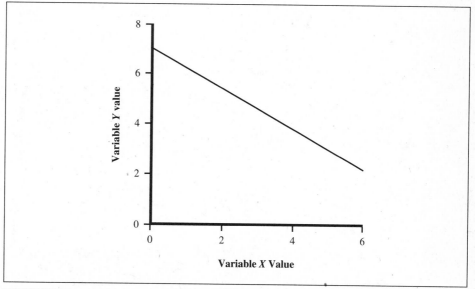

FIGURE 8.2 The geometric line with $b = -0.8$ and $a = +7.0$.

by 1 unit, Y increases by 0.8 units. Notice that the linear pattern of upper left to lower right in Figure 8.2 is the same pattern you see in the scatterplot of two variables that are negatively related.

The a in the formula for a geometric line is called the *y-intercept*. This is the Y value on the line that corresponds to an X value of 0. It is called the y-intercept because it is the value at which the line intercepts, or crosses, the Y axis. In Figure 8.1 the y-intercept is 1; in Figure 8.2 it is 7.

Determining Y from X. A geometric line can be used to determine the Y value that corresponds to any X value. Using the line in Figure 8.1, the Y value that corresponds to an X value of 23 can be computed even though the X axis in the figure does not extend that far:

$$Y = 1.5(23) + 1 = 35.5.$$

If two variables such as self-esteem and grade point average (GPA) demonstrated a perfect linear relationship, it would be possible to compute the geometric line using the data from any two subjects in the sample. This line could then be used to determine the Y value that corresponds with any X value. If you knew any subject's self-esteem score, you could perfectly predict that subject's GPA, and vice versa.

The Regression Line. Unfortunately real life is rarely perfect, and the data points in behavioral science scatterplots usually do not form straight lines. However, if two variables are linearly related it is possible to generate a **regression line**, *a line that is used to estimate criterion variable values from predictor variable values*. The regression line can be distinguished from the geometric line in that a regression line can be defined even when the relationship between the two variables is less than perfect, although the estimates produced using this line will not be perfect unless the relationship is perfect. The **regression equation** is *the formula for the regression line*, and may be stated as follows:

$$\hat{Y}_i = b_{Y \cdot X} X_i + a_{Y \cdot X}.$$

$b_{Y \cdot X}$ represents the **regression coefficient**, *the slope of the regression line*. $a_{Y \cdot X}$ is the **regression constant**, the *y-intercept for the regression line*. X_i is subject i's X score, and $\hat{Y}_i$ is the estimate of subject i's Y score based on the regression equation. The *caret* ($\wedge$) is a mathematical symbol that means "best estimate of," so $\hat{Y}_i$ is "the best estimate of Y_i."

The subscript $Y \cdot X$ indicates that Y is the criterion variable to be estimated on the basis of X scores. This is referred to as "regressing Y onto X."

Estimating Y from X. Figure 8.3 provides the scatterplot of the data in Table 8.1. A regression line has been added to the scatterplot which may be used to estimate Y values from X values. The derivation of this line will be discussed after I have introduced some issues surrounding the use of the regression line.

Student 1's self-esteem score is 4. Following the dotted line up from 4 on the X axis to the regression line, and over to the Y axis, we can see that Student 1's $\hat{Y}$ (our best estimate of Student 1's GPA given the student's self-esteem score) is approximately 2.88. However, student 1's true GPA is 3.0. *The difference between a criterion variable score and the estimated criterion variable score,*

$$Y_i - \hat{Y}_i,$$

is called the **error of estimate**. For Student 1 the error of estimate is approximately

$$3.00 - 2.88 = 0.12,$$

indicating that this regression line underestimated this student's GPA by approximately 0.12 points. The estimates and errors of estimate for each subject are:

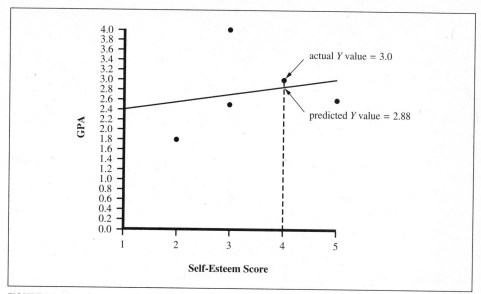

FIGURE 8.3 Scatterplot of self-esteem and GPA data from Table 8.1 with a regression line added. The regression line underestimates this subject's GPA by approximately .12 points.

TABLE 8.1   Sample Data for the Self-Esteem and GPA Study

Five high school students rated their level of agreement with the statement "I feel good about myself" on a scale from 1 (Strongly Disagree) to 5 (Strongly Agree). They also reported their GPAs:

	Self-Esteem	GPA
Student 1	4	3.0
Student 2	3	2.5
Student 3	5	2.6
Student 4	3	4.0
Student 5	2	1.8

The correlation between self-esteem and GPA was found in Procedure Box 7.1 to be $+.2281$.

	Self-Esteem (X)	GPA (Y)	$\hat{Y}$	Error
Student 1	4	3.0	2.8769	0.1231
Student 2	3	2.5	2.7154	−0.2154
Student 3	5	2.6	3.0384	−0.4384
Student 4	3	4.0	2.7154	1.2846
Student 5	2	1.8	2.5539	−0.7539

As you might expect, the errors of estimate all equal zero when the relationship is perfect.

Alternative Regression Lines. If the relationship between X and Y is less than perfect, there may be several different lines that generate reasonable estimates of Y based on X. For example, Figure 8.4 is the same scatterplot found in Figure 8.3, but now it contains

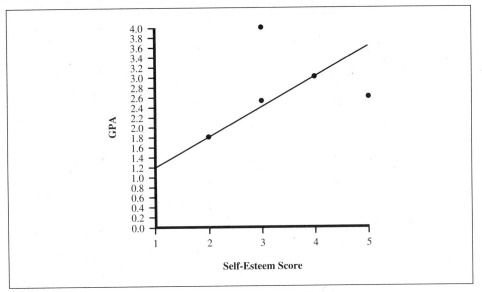

FIGURE 8.4   Another possible regression line for the data from Table 8.1.

a line that runs through the data points for Subjects 1 and 5. Using this line, the estimates and errors of estimate are:

	Self-Esteem (X)	GPA (Y)	$\hat{Y}$	Error
Student 1	4	3.0	3.0	0.00
Student 2	3	2.5	2.4	0.10
Student 3	5	2.6	3.6	−1.00
Student 4	3	4.0	2.4	1.60
Student 5	2	1.8	1.8	0.00

These estimates may seem no better or worse than those generated by the line in Figure 8.3: some are smaller, and some larger. How does one select the "best" regression line?

   The Method of Least Squares. Several criteria have been suggested for selecting what would be the "best" regression line. The most commonly used method for defining the regression line is called the **method of least squares**, which refers to *a procedure for computing the regression coefficient and constant that minimizes the sum of the squared errors of estimate.* Suppose we computed the error of estimate for each subject, and squared and summed these errors:

$$\sum_{i=1}^{N}(Y_i - \hat{Y}_i)^2.$$

No other line you could use to predict Y values from X values would produce a smaller value for this quantity than the line generated by using the method of least squares. For example, the regression line in Figure 8.3 was actually generated using the method of least squares. The sum of the squared errors of estimate equals

$$0.1231^2 + (-0.2154)^2 + (-0.4834)^2 + 1.2846^2 + (-0.7539)^2 = 2.47.$$

In contrast, the sum of the squared errors from the regression line in Figure 8.4 is

$$0^2 + 0.10^2 + (-1.0)^2 + 1.6^2 + 0^2 = 3.57.$$

According to the method of least squares, the regression line in Figure 8.3 is superior to the regression line in Figure 8.4.

The method of least squares regression coefficient can be computed from either of the following formulas:

$$b_{Y \cdot X} = r_{XY} \left(\frac{s_Y}{s_X} \right)$$

$$= \frac{\displaystyle\sum_{i=1}^{N} X_i Y_i - \frac{\left(\displaystyle\sum_{i=1}^{N} X_i \right) \left(\displaystyle\sum_{i=1}^{N} Y_i \right)}{N}}{\displaystyle\sum_{i=1}^{N} X_i^2 - \frac{\left(\displaystyle\sum_{i=1}^{N} X_i \right)^2}{N}}$$

The second represents a computational formula for the regression coefficient.

The method of least squares regression constant can be computed from the following formula:

$$a_{Y \cdot X} = \overline{Y} - b_{Y \cdot X} \overline{X}.$$

The computation of the regression line for the self-esteem and GPA study is demonstrated in Procedure Box 8.1.

8.3 THE STANDARD ERROR OF ESTIMATE

The **standard error of estimate** is the *standard deviation of the errors of estimate*, and is computed from either of the following formulas:

$$s_{Y \cdot X} = \sqrt{\frac{\displaystyle\sum_{i=1}^{N} (Y_i - \hat{Y}_i)^2}{N - 2}} = s_Y \sqrt{\frac{N - 1}{N - 2} (1 - r_{XY}^2)}.$$

In the study of grades and self-esteem, we found the errors when we estimated GPA from self-esteem to be:

	Self-Esteem (X)	GPA (Y)	$\hat{Y}$	Error
Student 1	4	3.0	2.8769	0.1231
Student 2	3	2.5	2.7154	−0.2154
Student 3	5	2.6	3.0384	−0.4384
Student 4	3	4.0	2.7154	1.2846
Student 5	2	1.8	2.5539	−0.7539

The Regression Line

Goal   Compute the regression line for regressing GPA onto self-esteem using the data from Table 8.1:

	Self-Esteem	GPA
Student 1	4	3.0
Student 2	3	2.5
Student 3	5	2.6
Student 4	3	4.0
Student 5	2	1.8

To Compute the Regression Coefficient

$$b_{Y \cdot X} = \frac{\displaystyle\sum_{i=1}^{N} X_i Y_i - \frac{\left(\displaystyle\sum_{i=1}^{N} X_i\right)\left(\displaystyle\sum_{i=1}^{N} Y_i\right)}{N}}{\displaystyle\sum_{i=1}^{N} X_i^2 - \frac{\left(\displaystyle\sum_{i=1}^{N} X_i\right)^2}{N}}$$

Step 1   *Compute the sum of* X, Y, X *times* Y, *and* X^2.

	X	Y	XY	X^2
	4	3.0	12.0	16
	3	2.5	7.5	9
	5	2.6	13.0	25
	3	4.0	12.0	9
	2	1.8	3.6	4
Sums:	17	13.9	48.1(a)	63(b)

Step 2   *Multiply the sum of the* X *values (a) by the sum of the* Y *values and (b) by itself, and divide by* N.

$$\text{(a)} \quad \frac{\left(\displaystyle\sum_{i=1}^{N} X_i\right)\left(\displaystyle\sum_{i=1}^{N} Y_i\right)}{N} = \frac{17(13.9)}{5} = 47.26$$

Continued

The regression line continued

(b) $\dfrac{\left(\sum\limits_{i=1}^{N} X_i\right)^2}{N} = \dfrac{17^2}{5} = 57.8$

Step 3   *Subtract the results from Step 2 from the corresponding sum in Step 1.*

(a) $\sum\limits_{i=1}^{N} X_i Y_i - \dfrac{\left(\sum\limits_{i=1}^{N} X_i\right)\left(\sum\limits_{i=1}^{N} Y_i\right)}{N} = 48.1 - 47.26 = .84$

(b) $\sum\limits_{i=1}^{N} X_i^2 - \dfrac{\left(\sum\limits_{i=1}^{N} X_i\right)^2}{N} = 63 - 57.8 = 5.2 \longleftarrow$ *This number must be positive.*

Step 4   *Divide the result from 3(a) by the result from 3(b).*

$$b_{Y \cdot X} = \dfrac{.84}{5.2} = +.1615$$

To Compute the Regression Constant

$$a_{Y \cdot X} = \overline{Y} - b_{Y \cdot X} \overline{X}$$

Step 1   *Compute the mean of X and Y.*

	X	Y
	4.0	3.0
	3.0	2.5
	5.0	2.6
	3.0	4.0
	2.0	1.8
Means:	3.4	2.78

Step 2   *Multiply the mean of X by the regression coefficient.*

$$.1615(3.4) = .5491$$

Step 3   *Subtract the result of Step 2 from the mean of Y.*

$$a_{Y \cdot X} = 2.78 - .5491 = 2.2309$$

Like deviations from the mean, the errors of estimate always sum to 0, so they must be squared before they are summed. The standard error of estimate in this case is

$$s_{Y \cdot X} = \sqrt{\frac{\sum_{i=1}^{N}(Y_i - \hat{Y}_i)^2}{N-2}}$$

$$= \sqrt{\frac{.1231^2 + (-.2154)^2 + (-.4384)^2 + 1.2846^2 + (-.7539)^2}{3}}$$

$$= 0.9078.$$

The standard error of estimate is useful because it indicates the amount of error to expect in your predicted Y values. In the present example, we can say the expected difference between our $\hat{Y}$ values and the true values is 0.91 points. In other words, the estimates of GPA based on self-esteem tend to be incorrect by about 1 point. Given that GPAs have a very limited possible range (0 to 4), this is not particularly good. However, given that the correlation between self-esteem and GPA was a not very strong .2281, this is not a surprising finding.

It should be obvious from the discussion that the larger the absolute value of the correlation coefficient (the stronger the relationship between the two variables), the smaller the standard error of estimate will be relative to the size of the Y values. Remember that when the correlation is perfect, the errors of estimate will equal zero, so the standard error of estimate equals zero. Some additional information about the standard error of estimate may be found in the supplement.

8.4 REGRESSION AND CORRELATION

Regression analysis and the correlation coefficient are interrelated statistical procedures, in a number of ways. In this section I will briefly summarize two of the important relationships between regression and correlation.

8.4.1 The Sign of r_{XY} and the Sign of $b_{Y \cdot X}$

One of the formulas offered for the regression coefficient is

$$b_{Y \cdot X} = r_{XY}\left(\frac{s_Y}{s_X}\right).$$

Standard deviations are always positive numbers, so if r_{XY} is a positive number then $b_{Y \cdot X}$ will also be a positive number. If r_{XY} is a negative number $b_{Y \cdot X}$ will also be a negative number.

8.4.2 The Absence of a Relationship

If $r_{XY} = 0$ then

$$b_{Y \cdot X} = r_{XY} \left(\frac{s_Y}{s_X} \right)$$

$$= 0.$$

A slope of zero means that as X changes the best estimate of Y neither increases nor decreases; the regression line is a horizontal line. If $b_{Y \cdot X}$ equals zero, then

$$a_{Y \cdot X} = \overline{Y} - b_{Y \cdot X} \overline{X}$$

$$= \overline{Y} - (0) \overline{X}$$

$$= \overline{Y}.$$

So when $r_{XY} = 0$ the regression line is a horizontal line at the mean of Y (see Figure 8.5). No matter what a subject's X value, your best estimate of that subject's Y value is the mean of Y. Knowledge of a subject's X value offers no additional information about the subject's Y value, which is what you would expect when there is no relationship between two variables.

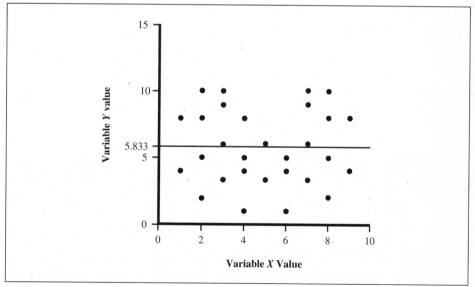

FIGURE 8.5 The regression line when $r_{XY} = 0$ and $\overline{Y} = 5.833$. The horizontal registration line falls at 5.833, the mean of variable Y in this example.

8.5 REGRESSING X ONTO Y

So far the discussion has focused on regressing the variable identified as Y onto the variable identified as X. There is no reason why you could not also regress the X variable onto the Y variable. It was noted in the last chapter that Celsius temperatures can be computed from Fahrenheit temperatures, and Fahrenheit temperatures can also be computed from Celsius temperatures. Similarly, you can estimate level of self-esteem from GPA instead of estimating GPA from level of self-esteem. The formulas for the regression line would then be

$$b_{X \cdot Y} = r_{XY} \left(\frac{s_X}{s_Y} \right)$$

$$= \frac{\displaystyle\sum_{i=1}^{N} X_i Y_i - \frac{\left(\displaystyle\sum_{i=1}^{N} X_i \right) \left(\displaystyle\sum_{i=1}^{N} Y_i \right)}{N}}{\displaystyle\sum_{i=1}^{N} Y_i^2 - \frac{\left(\displaystyle\sum_{i=1}^{N} Y_i \right)^2}{N}}$$

and

$$a_{X \cdot Y} = \overline{X} - b_{X \cdot Y} \overline{Y}.$$

Note that $b_{X \cdot Y}$ will not equal $b_{Y \cdot X}$ unless $s_X = s_Y$, and $a_{Y \cdot X}$ rarely equals $a_{X \cdot Y}$. When we regressed GPA onto self-esteem earlier in the chapter, the least squares statistics were $b_{Y \cdot X} = .1615$ and $a_{Y \cdot X} = 2.2309$. If we instead regress self-esteem onto GPA, the corresponding statistics equal $b_{X \cdot Y} = .3221$ and $a_{X \cdot Y} = 2.5046$. The difference in the two regression lines is illustrated in Figure 8.6. The standard error of estimate also changes unless $s_X = s_Y$:

$$s_{X \cdot Y} = \sqrt{\frac{\displaystyle\sum_{i=1}^{N} (X_i - \hat{X}_i)^2}{N - 2}}$$

$$= s_X \sqrt{\frac{N-1}{N-2}(1 - r_{XY}^2)}.$$

However, the correlation coefficient and index of association are unaffected when X is considered the criterion variable rather than the predictor. The proportion of the variance of Y accounted for by X is the same as the proportion of the variance of X accounted for by Y.

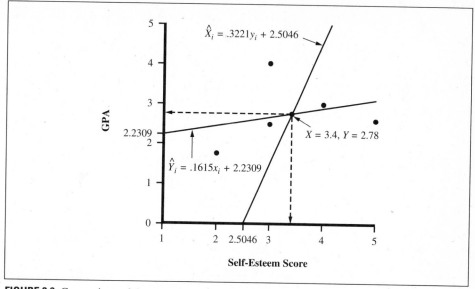

FIGURE 8.6 Comparison of the regression lines that results from regressing GPA (*Y*) onto self-esteem (*X*) and self-esteem (*X*) onto GPA (*Y*), from data in Table 7.1. The two lines cross where the mean of *X* (3.4) and the mean of *Y* (2.78) meet.

To summarize, when you regress *X* onto *Y* instead of regressing *Y* onto *X*, the following statistics may be expected to change:

1. the regression coefficient
2. the regression constant
3. the standard error of estimate

The following statistics will remain the same:

1. the correlation coefficient
2. the index of association

Which variable is considered the predictor and which the criterion affects the value of regression statistics, but not of the correlational statistics introduced in the last chapter.

KEY TERMS

criterion variable
error of estimate
method of least squares
multiple regression
Pearson product-moment correlation
    coefficient
predictor variable

regression analysis
regression coefficient
regression constant
regression equation
regression line
simple regression
standard error of estimate

EXERCISES

Answers to all exercises may be found in Appendix B.

1. In which of the following cases would simple regression not be applicable?
   a. A researcher would like to estimate people's age of death based on how long they expect to live when they are 21 years old.
   b. A researcher would like to estimate lifespan based on whether or not subjects lost a parent before the age of 12.
   c. A researcher would like to estimate people's age of death based on how long they expect to live when they are 21 years old, as well as a general rating of health collected at age 21.
   d. A researcher categorizes subjects into those who lost a mother before age 12, those who lost a father before age 12, and those who lost neither parent before age 12. The researcher would like to estimate lifespan using this variable.
   e. A researcher is interested in the strength of the relationship between a general rating of health at age 21 and lifespan.

2. Name at least two ways in which the geometric line and the regression line differ.

3. Identify the following symbols:
   a. $\hat{Y}_i$
   b. $b_{Y \cdot X}$
   c. $b_{X \cdot Y}$
   d. $a_{Y \cdot X}$
   e. $Y_i - \hat{Y}_i$
   f. $s_{Y \cdot X}$
   g. $s_{X \cdot Y}$

4. In the exercises for the last chapter, a study was described in which two scales of self-esteem were correlated. The correlation was only found to be $+.04$. The data were as follows:

X	Y	X	Y
1	5	5	7
3	7	4	9
6	9	9	8
4	3	8	4
4	5	7	3

a. Construct the regression line using the method of least squares to predict Y scores from X scores.
   b. Compute the predicted Y value and error of estimate for each subject.
   c. Compute and interpret the standard error of estimate.

5. Using the data from Question 4:
   a. Regress X onto Y.
   b. Compute the predicted X value and error of estimate for each subject.
   c. Compute and interpret the standard error of estimate.

6. a. The formula for transforming Celsius temperatures to Fahrenheit temperatures is:

$$^{\circ}F = \left(\frac{18}{10}\right)^{\circ}C + 32.$$

From the perspective of regression analysis, what is the slope of the regression line for predicting Fahrenheit temperatures from Celsius temperatures? What is the regression constant?

   b. The formula for transforming Fahrenheit temperatures to Celsius temperatures is:

$$^{\circ}C = \frac{10}{18}(^{\circ}F - 32).$$

From the perspective of regression analysis, what is the slope of the regression line for predicting Celsius temperatures from Fahrenheit temperatures? What is the regression constant?

7. The correlation between variables X and Y is -1.0.
   a. What can you say about the $\hat{Y}$ values?
   b. If $s_X = 3$ and $s_Y = 6$, what will $b_{Y \cdot X}$ equal? What will $b_{X \cdot Y}$ equal?
   c. If $\overline{Y} = 5$ and $\overline{X} = 10$, what will $a_{Y \cdot X}$ equal? What will $a_{X \cdot Y}$ equal?
   d. If $N = 100$, what will $s_{X \cdot Y}$ equal? What will $s_{Y \cdot X}$ equal?

S8.1 MORE ON THE STANDARD ERROR OF ESTIMATE

The formulas provided in the chapter are for the best estimate of the population standard error of estimate. The sample standard error is provided by one of the following formulas:

$$S_{Y \cdot X} = \sqrt{\frac{\sum\limits_{i=1}^{N}(Y_i - \hat{Y}_i)^2}{N}}$$

$$= S_Y \sqrt{1 - r_{XY}^2}.$$

See the supplement to Chapter 6 for more about S_Y, the sample standard deviation.

When X and Y are unrelated, the sample standard error of estimate equals the standard deviation of Y,

$$S_{Y \cdot X} = S\sqrt{1 - r_{XY}^2}$$

$$= S_Y \sqrt{1 - 0}$$

$$= S_Y.$$

At the opposite extreme, when the correlation between X and Y reaches 1.0 or -1.0 the sample standard error of estimate will equal zero:

$$S_{Y \cdot X} = S_Y \sqrt{1 - r_{XY}^2}$$

$$= S_Y \sqrt{1 - 1}$$

$$= 0.$$

So the sample standard error of estimate can vary between 0 (when X and Y are perfectly related) and S_Y (when X and Y are unrelated). You can use this information to help interpret the standard error of estimate. The closer the standard error of estimate comes to 0, the stronger the relationship between X and Y; the closer it comes to the standard deviation of Y, the weaker the relationship between X and Y, and the poorer the estimates of Y based on the regression line.

PART IV
Understanding Inferential Statistics

The remainder of this text is devoted to the study of inferential statistics. First defined in Chapter 2, these are statistics used to draw conclusions about a population based on sample data. The next four chapters introduce the concepts you will need to understand the inferential statistics discussed in subsequent chapters.

Chapter 9 introduces some statistical concepts which underlie all inferential statistics. Important topics include:

- probability
- sampling distributions

The inferential statistics to be discussed in this text fall into two categories: hypothesis testing statistics and interval estimation statistics. Chapters 10 and 11 provide an introduction to the logic of hypothesis testing using an inferential statistic called the binomial test. The discussion begins in Chapter 10, where important topics include:

- the role of inferential statistics in the research process
- statistical hypotheses
- statistical decision-making
- controlling Type I error rates

Chapter 11 focuses primarily on issues that are essential to setting the sample size for a study. Important topics include:

- controlling Type II error rates
- power
- estimating effect size
- power and sample size

Chapter 12 introduces a second hypothesis testing statistic and provides the logic for interval estimation statistics. Important topics include:

- the one-group z test
- the logic of interval estimation

CHAPTER 9

Concepts Underlying
Inferential Statistics

All the inferential statistics to be discussed in this text rely upon the concepts of probability and sampling distributions. The present chapter provides an introduction to these concepts. This will serve as the basis for the discussion of inferential statistics which begins in the next chapter.

9.1 PROBABILITY

Probability Defined. The **probability** may be defined as *the expected proportion associated with each value of a variable*. The proportion was defined in Chapter 4 as the frequency of a variable value relative to the total sample size. If flipping a coin 50 times results in 39 heads, the proportion of heads in this sample equals

$$p = \frac{f}{N} = \frac{39}{50} = .78,$$

p in this case referring to the proportion of coin flips where the outcome was a head.

Suppose we are interested in the proportion of heads in the entire population of coin flips for a certain dime. It is impossible to observe the entire population of coin flips, but if we assume it is a fair coin, and that fair coins produce heads and tails at an equal rate, then the proportion of heads in the population should equal .50.

This proportion represents a probability. It is based not on the observation of coin flips, but on an expectation derived from a general understanding of the coin. To distinguish them from proportions, probabilities will be symbolized by $p(V)$, where V is a given variable value. If we believe the probability of a head in the population is .50, this may be symbolized by

$$p(H) = .50.$$

Probabilities versus Confidence. The word probability is also sometimes used to refer to one's subjective level of confidence. Consider the statement

I would say the probability that Elvis Presley is alive is about .10.

Based on the definition of probability provided above, this statement is inaccurate. If probability refers to the expected relative frequency of some outcome, the statement would only make sense if there were a large population of Elvis Presleys, only 10% of whom are alive.

The word probability in the statement above is used to refer to the speaker's subjective confidence in the truth of the statement. To avoid confusion I will only use the term probability to refer to expected relative frequencies. This is consistent with the concept of probability as applied in both hypothesis testing and interval estimation.[1]

9.1.1 Mutually Exhaustive and Mutually Exclusive Outcomes

Mutually Exhaustive Outcomes. Imagine a study in which college students are asked to report how much time they spend on average doing schoolwork each day using the following scale:

1 = 0 hours

2 = 1 hour

3 = 2 hours

4 = 3 hours

5 = more than 3 hours.

It is possible for subjects not to fall in any of the categories provided, for example a person who works $1\frac{1}{2}$ hours per day. These outcomes are not mutually exhaustive. **Mutually exhaustive outcomes** refer to *the set of all possible variable outcomes*. The values in this scale could be made mutually exhaustive as follows:

1 = 0–1 hour

2 = 1–2 hours

3 = 2–3 hours

4 = more than 3 hours.

Now all possibilities are included.

Mutually Exclusive Outcomes. There is a second problem with this revised rating scale: it is possible for subjects to fall in more than one category, for example a student who works exactly 2 hours per day. These are not **mutually exclusive outcomes**, *variable outcomes which cannot occur simultaneously*. The values in the scale could be made mutually exclusive as follows:

1 = less than 1 hour

2 = at least 1 but less than 2 hours

3 = at least 2 but less than 3 hours

4 = more than 3 hours.

Now one and only one value will apply to any subject. The choices available in a well-developed rating scale should always be both mutually exhaustive and mutually exclusive.

The concepts of mutually exclusive and mutually exhaustive outcomes will come up later when the addition rule for probabilities is discussed. In addition, they play an important role in the development of statistical hypotheses, a topic addressed in the next chapter.

---

[1] I should note that when using another class of inferential statistics called Bayesian statistics the distinction between probability and confidence is not so firmly drawn.

9.1.2 Dependent versus Independent Outcomes

Dependent Outcomes. Two possible outcomes are said to be **dependent outcomes** when the *probability for one possible outcome depends upon the outcome of another event*. For example, life insurance companies are very interested in determining the probability that a customer will die within the next year. This probability in part depends on the customer's age. A 40 year old customer has a .0025 (2.5 in a thousand) probability of dying in the next year, while an 80 year old customer has a .0750 chance (75 in a thousand), so a life insurance company will charge an 80 year old more than they would a 40 year old for the same policy (Tobias, 1982).

The two probabilities for dying in the next year may be written

$$p(\text{dying} \mid 40) = .0025$$

$$p(\text{dying} \mid 80) = .0750.$$

Another way of stating the first is "the probability of dying in the next year *given* that the person's age is 40 is .0025." The second probability may be stated as "the probability of dying in the next year *given* that the person's age is 80 is .0750." The probability of dying within the next year is *dependent* upon the variable age.

These examples demonstrate the concept of **conditional probability**, *the probability of some outcome given that some other outcome has occurred*. If two outcomes are dependent, then the conditional probability of outcome Y given that some other outcome X has occurred will differ from the overall probability for outcome Y. For example, the conditional probability of dying in the next year, given the person is 80 years old, is .0750; whereas the overall probability of dying in the next year for the entire American population is approximately .004, or 4 in a thousand.

Independent Outcomes. Two outcomes are **independent outcomes** when *the probability for one possible outcome does not depend upon the outcome of the other event*. Let's assume the probability of dying in the next year is unrelated to whether a person is right-handed or left-handed; for both, the probability of dying in the next year would then be approximately .004. The conditional probabilities are:

$$p(\text{dying} \mid \text{left-handed}) = p(\text{dying} \mid \text{right-handed}) = p(\text{dying}) = .004.$$

The conditional probabilities given the preferred hand are equal, and equal to the overall probability, suggesting independent outcomes.

9.1.3 Probability Rules

Probabilities exhibit certain characteristics which can be summarized as a series of rules. This section introduces five of the basic rules governing probabilities.

Proportions and Probabilities. Within any sample the proportion associated with some value of a variable need not match the expected proportion. Even if the probability of a head in the population of all coin flips is .50, the proportion of heads in any one sample will vary. However, as the size of the sample increases the proportion associated with any value will approach the probability.

For example, in a sample of 2 coin flips it would not be surprising to find the proportion of heads equals 1.0 even if the probability of a head for this coin is .50. As the number of coin flips is increased, the proportion of heads should come closer to .50. If it were possible to collect a sample consisting of an infinite number of coin flips, the sample proportion of heads would equal the population probability for a head.

This provides the basis for the first rule of probability:

Rule #1: The observed proportion will approach the probability as the number of observations in the sample increases.

Addition Rules. Suppose we are rolling a regular pair of six-sided dice. If the dice are fair, the following are the standard probabilities associated with each possible outcome:

Outcome	p(Outcome)	Outcome	p(Outcome)
2	1/36	8	5/36
3	2/36	9	4/36
4	3/36	10	3/36
5	4/36	11	2/36
6	5/36	12	1/36
7	6/36		

Suppose we are interested in the probability of an outcome greater than 10 (an 11 or 12). If the probability of an 11 is 2/36, and the probability of a 12 is 1/36, then the probability of an outcome greater than 10 is

$$p(11 \text{ or } 12) = \frac{2}{36} + \frac{1}{36} = \frac{3}{36} = \frac{1}{12}.$$

That is, if the dice are rolled 12 times, we would only expect one roll to result in an outcome greater than 10.

Now suppose we wanted to choose one student from a class of 100 students in which we know 56% of the students are female and 12% are left-handed. The previous example would suggest the probability that the student we choose is either female or left-handed is

$$p(F \text{ or } L) = p(F) + p(L) = .56 + .12 = .68.$$

This answer is incorrect. Since left-handed females are included in both groups, they have been counted twice. We have overestimated the probability of choosing a left-handed student or a female.

If 7% of the students are left-handed females, this 7% is included in both the 56% that are females and the 12% that are left-handed. The correct probability of choosing either a female or a left-handed student is

$$p(F \text{ or } L) = (.56 + .12) - .07 = .61.$$

Subtraction was not necessary in the dice example because the possible outcomes for a single dice roll are mutually exclusive; they cannot occur together.

Probabilities are summed when we are interested in determining the probability of either of two outcomes occurring. The following rules govern the addition of probabilities:

Rule #2: The probability of either of two outcomes occurring equals the sum of their probabilities, minus the probability of both outcomes occurring simultaneously:

$$p(V_1 \text{ or } V_2) = p(V_1) + p(V_2) - p(V_1 \text{ and } V_2).$$

Rule #3: The probability of either of two mutually exclusive outcomes occurring equals the sum of their probabilities:

$$p(V_1 \text{ or } V_2) = p(V_1) + p(V_2).$$

If you think about these rules for a minute, it should be obvious that the probabilities associated with a set of mutually exclusive and mutually exhaustive outcomes must sum to 1.0.

Multiplication Rules. Returning to the dice example, what is the probability that a roll of 7 will be followed immediately by a 6? The answer is provided by multiplying the probabilities for the two outcomes provided above:

$$p(7 \text{ and } 6) = \frac{6}{36}\left(\frac{5}{36}\right) = \frac{30}{1296} = \frac{5}{216}.$$

That is, if the dice are rolled 216 times, we would only expect the combination of 7 followed by 6 to occur five times.

Now let's return to the class of 100 students. We know that 56% of the students are female. Suppose we also learn that 3 (5.36%) of the females and 4 (9.09%) of the males are classified for special education, so that overall 7.00% of the class is classified. We can state these probabilities as follows:

$$p(SE \mid F) = .0536$$
$$p(SE \mid M) = .0909$$
$$p(SE) = .0700.$$

If we choose one student at random from the class, what is the probability this student is a female receiving special education?

The previous example would suggest the probability is provided by the formula

$$p(F)p(SE) = .56(.07) = .0392.$$

This is incorrect, however, since the probability of receiving special education services is dependent upon gender. The correct solution is

$$p(F \text{ and } SE) = p(F)p(SE \mid F) = .56(.0536) = .0300.$$

Use of a conditional probability is not necessary in the dice example because the probability for the second outcome (6) was not dependent on the outcome of the first dice roll, so the conditional probability of a 6 equalled the overall probability of a 6.

Probabilities are multiplied when we are interested in determining the probability of both of two outcomes occurring. The following rules govern the multiplication of probabilities:

Rule #4: The probability of two outcomes both occurring equals the probability of the first, multiplied by the conditional probability of the second given the first:

$$p(V_1 \text{ and } V_2) = p(V_1)p(V_2 \mid V_1).$$

Rule #5: The probability of two outcomes both occurring when the outcomes are independent equals the probability of the first, multiplied by the probability of the second:

$$p(V_1 \text{ and } V_2) = p(V_1)p(V_2).$$

9.2 SAMPLING DISTRIBUTIONS

9.2.1 Probabilities for Sample Statistics

We know that for a fair coin the probability of a head is approximately .50. John bets Ted that if Ted flips a fair coin 10 times the number of heads will equal exactly 5. How would Ted decide whether or not he should take this bet?

Remember that the frequency of heads in a sample of 10 coin flips represents a sample statistic. Until now we have been discussing the probability of some outcome for one or two events. Now we are asking a question about the probability of some outcome for the entire set of events in a sample. Answering such questions require the use of sampling distributions.

9.2.2 The Sampling Distribution

The $N = 2$ Case. Suppose we flipped John's coin twice and recorded the number of heads. This would represent a sample of $N = 2$ randomly drawn from the population of coin flips. There are four possible sets of data which could be associated with this sample:

two heads (HH),

a head followed by a tail (HT),

a tail followed by a head (TH), or

two tails (TT).

If the probability of a head is .50, then each of these four sets of data is equally likely to occur. In samples of two coin flips, the probability that the outcome will equal 0 heads (a data set of TT) is .25, the probability of 1 head (a data set either of HT or TH) is .50, and the probability of 2 heads (a data set of HH) is .25. These probabilities are illustrated by the bar graph in Figure 9.1(a). If $p(H) = .50$ and we were in a position to collect a very large number of samples of 2 coin flips using this coin, we would expect the proportion of samples with 0, 1, or 2 heads to look very much like the bar graph in Figure 9.1(a).

The bar graph in Figure 9.1(a) is very different from the relative frequency distributions you have seen until now. It is not the relative frequency distribution of a *variable* in a *sample*; it is also not the relative frequency distribution of a *variable* in a *population*. This distribution is the *expected relative frequency* distribution, or probability distribution, of a *statistic across a series of samples of equal N*. The statistic here is the frequency of heads in each sample, which has the possible values 0, 1, or 2 in samples where $N = 2$. The Y axis represents the probability that a given number of heads will occur in any one sample. This type of distribution is referred to as a **sampling distribution**, *the probability distribution of a sample statistic*

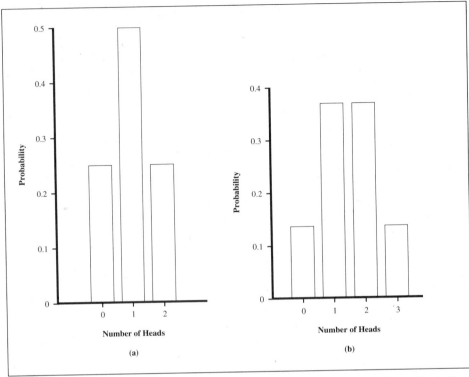

FIGURE 9.1 Binomial distributions for the number of heads in samples of $N = 2$ and $N = 3$ coin flips. The number of heads in a sample represents a discrete ratio variable. The bar graph may be used to present the probabilities.

for all random samples of a given size from some population. Table 9.1 summarizes differences between a sample distribution, a sampling distribution, and a population distribution.

Coin flipping is associated with a sampling distribution called the **binomial distribution**, *a sampling distribution of a dichotomous variable* (a variable with only two values). Since flipping a coin only allows two possible outcomes, the binomial distribution can be used to answer questions about the probability of a certain number of heads in a sample.

The $N = 3$ Case. Suppose we flipped Ted's coin three times instead of twice. Now there are eight possible data sets which could be associated with this sample:

$$HHH \quad HHT \quad HTH \quad HTT$$
$$THH \quad THT \quad TTH \quad TTT.$$

If we assume $p(H) = .50$, we can compute the probability of 0, 1, 2, or 3 heads:

$$p(0H) = 1/8 = .125$$
$$p(1H) = 3/8 = .375$$

TABLE 9.1   Differences between Sample Distributions, Sampling Distributions, and Population Distributions

	Sample Distribution	Sampling Distribution	Population Distribution
It is an:	observed frequency distribution	expected probability distribution	expected probability distribution
Of a:	variable	statistic	variable
In a:	sample	series of samples	population

$$p(2H) = 3/8 = .375$$

$$p(3H) = 1/8 = .125.$$

This defines the sampling distribution for $N = 3$ found in Figure 9.1(b).

9.2.3 Characteristics of Sampling Distributions

The discussion so far demonstrates two important characteristics of sampling distributions. First, the shape of the sampling distribution generally changes as the sample size changes. Figure 9.2 provides examples of binomial distributions for some other sample sizes, and when $p(H)$ is varied.

Second, we can define characteristics of the sampling distribution without ever collecting data if we make some assumptions. By assuming the probability of a head equals .50 we generated the sampling distribution for samples of $N = 2$ and $N = 3$.

There even exists a formula, called the *binomial formula*, which can be used to compute the probability associated with each value in the binomial distribution. The binomial formula is discussed in the supplement. To determine the probability of exactly 5 heads in a sample of 10 coin flips, we could either list every possible outcome from a set of 10 coin flips as we did for the $N = 2$ and $N = 3$ cases, or use the binomial formula. Either way, we would find the probability of exactly 5 heads in a sample of 10 coin flips is $p(5H) = .2461$. Only about 25% of samples of 10 coin flips should result in exactly 5 heads. Ted should take the bet, since his chances of winning are pretty good.

9.2.4 Uses of Sampling Distributions

Whenever the question of interest is the probability of some outcome in an entire sample of data, sampling distributions provide the mechanism for answering the question. In the coming chapters you will be introduced to a number of sampling distributions for various sample statistics. As you will see, sampling distributions are used extensively to find the probability of sample outcomes in hypothesis testing, or to estimate parameters based on sample statistics in interval estimation.

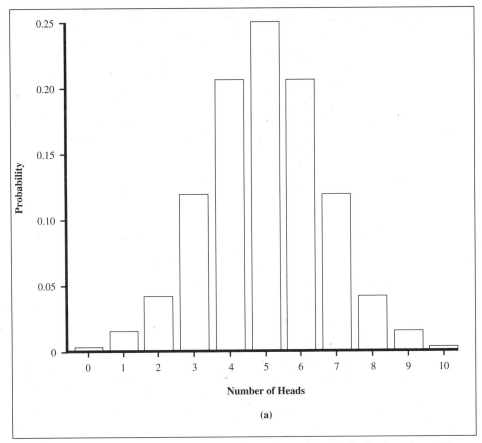

FIGURE 9.2 Other examples of binomial distributions. (a) The binomial distribution when $p(H) =$ .50 and $N = 10$. *(continued on next page)*

KEY TERMS

binomial distribution
conditional probability
dependent outcomes
dichotomous variable
independent outcomes
mutually exclusive outcomes
mutually exhaustive outcomes

parameter
probability
proportion
sample size
sampling distribution
statistic

EXERCISES

Answers to all exercises may be found in Appendix B.

1. According to the chapter, are the following acceptable uses of the term *probability*?
   a. The probability that life exists on earth is 1.0.

   b. The probability that a student will fail Professor Smith's statistics course is .09.

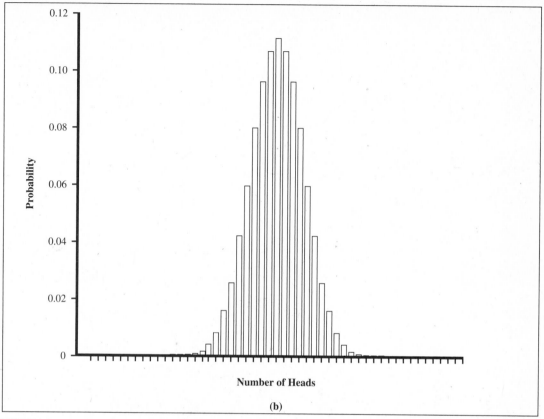

FIGURE 9.2 (*continued*) Other examples of binomial distributions. (b) The binomial distribution when $p(H) = .50$ and $N = 50$.

(*continued on next page*)

c. The probability that a certain population mean (μ) falls between 87 and 92 is about .95.

d. The probability that a sample mean will fall within 5 points of the population μ is about .95.

e. The probability that this particular candidate will win the election is .65.

f. The probability that a voter will vote for this particular candidate is .65.

g. The probability that a sitting member of congress will win re-election is .65.

2. In each of the following cases, a variable is followed by two possible values of that variable. Which pairs of values are *mutually exclusive*; which are *mutually exhaustive*?

a. Rolling a pair of dice: a value less than 7 versus a value greater than 7.

b. Gender: males versus females.

c. Weather: rainy versus cloudy.

d. Time of day: morning versus afternoon.

e. Rolling a pair of dice: a value less than 8 versus a value greater than 7.

f. Emotional state: happy versus sad.

g. Type of variable according to the mathematical model: continuous versus discrete.

3. For each of the following, indicate whether *independent outcomes* or *dependent outcomes* are indicated:

a. A job applicant's gender has no effect on whether or not the applicant receives the job.

b. Blondes have more fun.

c. The preference for candidate Jones is consistent across all age groups of voters.

d. The bigger they are, the harder they fall.

e. Whether you like it or not, fall must eventually make way for winter.

f. Certain forms of cactus tend to bloom only when they are placed in the dark for long periods of time.

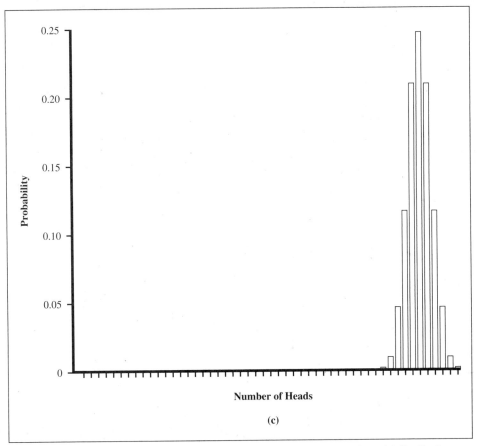

FIGURE 9.2 *(continued)* Other examples of binomial distributions. (c) The binomial distribution when $p\,(H) = .70$ and $N = 50$. Notice that when the probability of one head changes, the histogram shifts along the X axis.

4. Human immunodeficiency virus (HIV) is the virus believed to be responsible for AIDS. It has been estimated that if an HIV-infected male has unprotected genital sex with an uninfected female one time, the probability she will be infected is .002 (Michael, Gagnon, Laumann, & Kolata, 1994); in other words, the probability of not getting infected is .998. If this couple has unprotected genital sex two times, what is the probability she will get infected?

   a. Some students answer this question with .002(.002) = .000004. Why is this answer incorrect?

   b. Some students answer this question with .002 + .002 = .004. Why is this answer incorrect?

   c. Now that you have thought about it a bit, what is the probability of infection? (Challenge: There are two ways to compute the correct answer. See if you can figure out both.)

5. This problem addresses some of the common errors one sees in the use of probabilities. In the movie *The Pagemaster*, McCauley Culkin refuses to climb a ladder to a treehouse on the grounds that "8% of all household accidents involve ladders; another 3% involve trees. We're looking at an 11% probability here" of an accident. There are two reasons why the probability of his getting hurt is less than .11. One has to do with the overall probability of an accident. The second has to do with whether accidents and falling off a ladder are mutually

exclusive outcomes. Can you explain McCauley's errors?

6. Of 500 recently unemployed participants in a career counseling program, 260 were referred for additional training in their chosen career. Another 42 were advised to change their career goals. The remaining 148 were referred for immediate job placement in their chosen career. Of the 500 participants, 460 are receiving unemployment benefits, including 220 of those referred for additional training. Answer each of the following using an addition or multiplication rule:

a. If a new person enters the program, what is the probability that person will be referred for additional training or a career change?

b. What is the probability that a new participant will either be referred for additional training or will be receiving unemployment benefits?

c. What is the probability that a new participant will receive unemployment benefits and will be referred for additional job training?

7. Indicate whether the following statements are *true* or *false*:

a. The larger the random sample, the more representative it will be of the population.

b. If a coin is fair, the proportion of heads in any reasonably large sample of coin flips will equal 50.

c. Sampling distributions are used to answer questions about the probability of a certain value for a parameter.

d. Sampling distributions are used to answer questions about the probability of a certain variable value occurring in a sample.

e. Sampling distributions are used to answer questions about the probability of a certain value for a statistic.

f. In a sample of two coin flips, the probability of at least one tail is .75 if the coin is tossed fairly.

S9.1 THE BINOMIAL FORMULA

If we refer to the two values of a dichotomous variable as V_1 and V_2, the probability of getting f outcomes equal to V_1 in a sample of size N equals

$$p(f\,V_1) = \frac{N!}{f!\,(N-f)!}\,p(V_1)^{\,f}\,p(V_2)^{(N-f)}.$$

This formula is called the *binomial formula*, a formula for computing the probability that a certain value of a dichotomous variable will occur with frequency f in a sample of size N. The ! indicates the factorial, a mathematical operation where all the numbers from 1 to N are multiplied together:

$$N! = N \times (N-1) \times (N-2) \times \ldots 1.$$

If the probability of a head in a single coin flip is .50, then the probability of 0 heads in a sample of 2 coin flips is

$$p(OH) = \frac{2!}{0!\,(2-0)!}(.5)^0(.5)^{(2-0)}$$

$$= \frac{2 \times 1}{1(2 \times 1)}(1)(.25)$$

$$= .25.$$

This is the same probability indicated in Figure 9.1(a).

The example in the chapter requires determining the probability of getting 5 heads in a sample of 10 coin flips where the probability of one head is .50. Using the binomial formula, we can determine this probability to be

$$p(5H) = \frac{10!}{5!\,(10-5)!}(.5)^5(.5)^{(10-5)}$$

$$= \frac{10(9)(8)(7)\ldots 1}{5(4)(3)(2)(1)(5)(4)(3)(2)(1)}(.5)^{10}$$

$$= .2461.$$

CHAPTER 10

The Logic of Hypothesis Testing

10.1 INFERENTIAL STATISTICS AND THE RESEARCH PROCESS

Democrat Don Douglas is running for president against Republican Ron Richards. Douglas hires our polling firm to conduct a telephone survey of eligible voters. We randomly sample 30 eligible voters, of whom 22 (73% of the sample) report they would vote for Douglas and 8 (27%) report they would vote for Richards. Do the results suggest that most eligible voters support Douglas, or did we happen to choose a very unusual sample? Addressing this question requires the use of hypothesis testing statistics.

Hypothesis testing statistics are *inferential statistics that are used to evaluate the accuracy of a statistical hypothesis.* A **statistical hypothesis** is *a guess concerning the value of a parameter.* The process of hypothesis testing can be divided into three steps:

1. defining the null and alternative hypotheses,
2. testing the null hypothesis, and
3. making a decision about the null hypothesis.

An inferential statistic called the binomial test, because it is based on the binomial distribution, will be used to demonstrate the use of hypothesis testing in the present example.

10.2 DEFINING THE NULL AND ALTERNATIVE HYPOTHESES

The Scientific Hypothesis. The Democrats' hypothesis that most voters support Douglas meets all the requirements for a scientific hypothesis as defined in Chapter 3.1:

1. The population of interest may be defined as the opinion of all voters.
2. The hypothesis has to do with a variable pattern, in this case the pattern of support for the two candidates.
3. It is possible to conduct a study that will help evaluate whether the scientific hypothesis is true.

The first step in the process of hypothesis testing involves translating the scientific hypothesis into a pair of statistical hypotheses, called the null and alternative hypotheses.

Statistical Hypotheses. We can translate the scientific hypothesis into a statistical statement concerning the probability that a member of the population will support Douglas:

$$p(D) > .50.$$

This will serve as the alternative hypothesis for the study. The **alternative hypothesis** is symbolized H_1, and may be defined as *a guess concerning the value of a parameter which suggests the presence of some pattern or relationship of interest*.

A second statistical hypothesis can be defined which represents the contradictory position:

$$p(D) \leq .50.$$

This will serve as the null hypothesis for the study. The **null hypothesis** is symbolized H_0, and may be defined for our purposes as *a guess concerning the value of a parameter which suggests the absence of some pattern or relationship of interest*. Notice that the null hypothesis includes an exact value for $p(D)$: if $p(D)$ exactly equals .50, then the null hypothesis is true. In contrast, the alternative hypothesis offers only a range of values. This is an important and universal characteristic of null and alternative hypotheses: *null hypotheses always include an equal sign, alternative hypotheses do not*.

If you examine the null and alternative hypotheses for the study,

$$H_0: p(D) \leq .50$$

$$H_1: p(D) > .50,$$

you will find that the two statements are mutually exclusive and mutually exhaustive (see Section 9.1.1). You may find it helpful to think of the research study as a contest between two competing statistical hypotheses, in which either the null hypothesis or the alternative hypothesis will be supported by the data. Since the statistical hypotheses are based on the scientific hypothesis, the results of this contest have implications for the existence of the pattern or relationship suggested by the scientific hypothesis.

10.3 TESTING THE NULL HYPOTHESIS

From the perspective of hypothesis testing, the null hypothesis is the more important of the two statistical hypotheses. When we refer to *hypothesis testing* it is the accuracy of the null hypothesis that is being directly tested. We begin this test by assuming the null hypothesis is true. If the null hypothesis is true, the probability that a voter supports Douglas is $\leq .50$. For now, we will deal only with the case in which we assume that the probability equals .50.

Based on this assumption, it is possible to generate a binomial distribution where the dichotomous variable of interest is the preferred candidate. Information provided by this distribution will be used to make a decision concerning the accuracy of the null hypothesis.

Using the binomial distribution for $N = 30$ when 50% of eligible voters support Douglas (Figure 10.1), it can be determined that the probability of 22 out of 30 sample members supporting Douglas is

$$p(22D) = .00545.$$

In other words, if the null hypothesis is true then the probability of exactly 22 out of 30 voters supporting Douglas is about 5 in 1000.

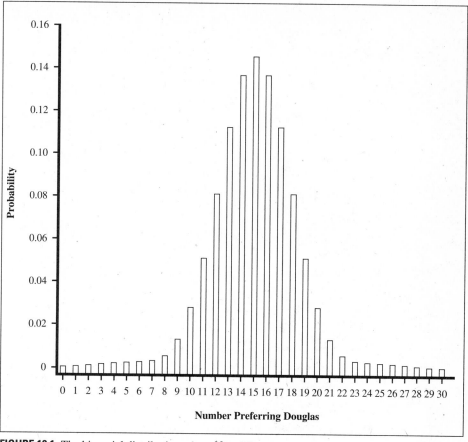

FIGURE 10.1 The binomial distribution when $N = 30$.

Random Samples. Remember that the binomial distribution is based on an infinite series of random samples. In Chapter 2 it was noted that samples of humans are rarely random: people may refuse to participate in the poll, and some people will not be home when we call them. It would seem inappropriate to apply a sampling distribution based on the assumption of a random sample to the present situation.

This dilemma is resolved by assuming the sample is a random subset of some hypothetical population. It may be the sample is more accurately considered a random subset of the population of eligible voters willing to participate in a survey who tend to be at home between 6 and 8 PM, for example. It is always possible to define a hypothetical population for which the sample may be considered a random subset. The question for the researcher is then whether the results of a study may reasonably be applied to the original population of interest as well: do findings based on the population of eligible voters willing to participate in a survey who tend to be at home between 6 and 8 PM provide us with useful information about the entire population of eligible voters?[1] If not, then the value of the study is questionable.

---

[1]This question reflects the importance of *external validity*, which is discussed in Section S3.6.

10.4 MAKING A DECISION ABOUT THE NULL HYPOTHESIS

Rejecting the Null Hypothesis. An outcome associated with a .00545 probability of occurrence seems very unlikely, and it seems safe to decide that assuming the null hypothesis is true is an unreasonable assumption. This decision is known as *rejecting the null hypothesis*. Rejecting the null hypothesis lends support for the accuracy of the alternative hypothesis and therefore the original scientific hypothesis that most voters support Douglas. Had the sample outcome been one more likely to occur if the null hypothesis were true (for example, if only 15 or 16 out of 30 subjects had supported Douglas), it would be inappropriate to reject the null hypothesis.

However, there is still the possibility of an error; perhaps the null hypothesis is true but we happened by chance to get one of those 5 in 1,000 samples where 22 out of 30 subjects would support Douglas. Whenever a researcher decides to reject or not reject the null hypothesis, the researcher runs the risk of an incorrect decision.

Possible Outcomes. The decision to reject or not to reject the null hypothesis results in one of four possible outcomes:

Fact

		H_0 is True	H_1 is True
Statistical Decision	Reject H_0	incorrect rejection (Type I error) p (incorrect rejection) $= \alpha$	correct rejection p (correct rejection) $= 1 - \beta$ (power)
	Do Not Reject H_0	correct non-rejection p (correct non-rejection) $= 1 - \alpha$	incorrect non-rejection (Type II error) p (incorrect non-rejection) $= \beta$

The thick line running down the middle of the table indicates that either the null hypothesis or the alternative hypothesis is factually correct, since they are mutually exclusive and exhaustive hypotheses. In any study only the outcomes in the first column can occur, or only the outcomes in the second column can occur. Unfortunately, since you do not know which column applies to your study, you should plan for all four possible outcomes. After all, if Douglas already knew the preferred candidate he would not need the poll.

If the null hypothesis is true, then one of two outcomes can occur:

1. the decision to reject the null hypothesis is an error. This error is referred to as an *incorrect rejection of the null hypothesis*, or more commonly as a **Type I error**.
2. the decision not to reject the null hypothesis is a correct decision, and is referred to as a *correct non-rejection of the null hypothesis*.

If the alternative hypothesis is true, then one of two outcomes can occur:

1. the decision to reject the null hypothesis is a correct decision, and is referred to as a *correct rejection of the null hypothesis*.
2. the decision not to reject the null hypothesis is an error. This error is referred to as an *incorrect non-rejection of the null hypothesis*, or more commonly as a **Type II error**.

The probabilities associated with each possible outcome are addressed in the next section.

A Comparison. The concepts just introduced can be confusing at first, so I will pause here to draw a comparison you may find helpful. The logic of hypothesis testing is very similar to the logic of the English/American criminal justice system:

1. The defendant is either guilty or not guilty. These are mutually exclusive and exhaustive factual possibilities.
2. At first, the defendant is assumed to be innocent. This is similar to the assumption that the null hypothesis is true.
3. The jury must make a decision to reject or not reject this assumption. The decision to reject results in conviction, the decision not to reject in acquittal.
4. In theory, the jury may not reject this assumption so long as there is a *reasonable doubt* concerning guilt. The criterion of reasonable doubt is similar to the requirement that the null hypothesis can be rejected only if the sample outcome is unlikely to occur were the null hypothesis true.

Any criminal trial can therefore result in one of four outcomes:

		Fact	
		Innocent	Guilty
Jury	Convict	incorrect rejection	correct rejection
Decision	Acquit	correct non-rejection	incorrect nonrejection

The line running down the middle of the table indicates that in fact, either the defendant is innocent or guilty. In any trial only the outcomes in the first column or the outcomes in the second column can occur. Unfortunately, since the guilt or innocence of the defendant is unknown, all four possibilities must be considered.

10.5 CONTROLLING THE TYPE I ERROR PROBABILITY

One of the weaknesses of the criminal justice system is the ambiguity of the term "reasonable doubt." Different juries may come to different decisions based on exactly the same evidence, because they disagree on whether their doubts can be considered reasonable. In contrast, statisticians offer very specific guidelines for the conditions under which rejection of the null hypothesis is acceptable, and for controlling the probability of Type I and Type II errors. The rest of this chapter focuses primarily on the control of Type I errors; Chapter 11 deals primarily with the control of Type II errors.

Setting the Alpha Level. It is impossible to eliminate the risk of a Type I error, unless you decide never to reject the null hypothesis. However, if you can establish an acceptable risk of a Type I error, it is possible to insure that the probability of a Type I error does not exceed that level. *The acceptable probability of a Type I error* is symbolized by α, the Greek letter alpha, and is often referred to as the **alpha level** or as the **level of significance**. Most researchers in the behavioral sciences consider a Type I error probability of .05 (5 in 100) an acceptable risk. To understand what this means, imagine we conducted the same study many, many times in circumstances where the null hypothesis is true. If α is set at .05, we would incorrectly reject the null hypothesis 5% of the time and correctly not reject the null hypothesis 95% of the time; 95% of our decisions would be correct.

Determining the Critical Value. Suppose we want to limit the risk of a Type I error in our study to .05. If $p(D) = .50$ (the null hypothesis is true) and $N = 30$, then:

$$p(20D) = .027981600$$

$$p(21D) = .013324572$$

$$p(22D) = .005450961$$

$$p(23D) = .001895987$$

$$p(24D) = .000552996$$

$$p(25D) = .000132719$$

$$p(26D) = .000025523$$

$$p(27D) = .000003781$$

$$p(28D) = .000000405$$

$$p(29D) = .000000028$$

$$p(30D) = .000000001$$

These probabilities sum to .0494. This means that any sample of 30 subjects in which 20 or more subjects support Douglas is associated with a total Type I error probability of less than .05. To insure the risk of a Type I error does not exceed .05, we cannot reject the null hypothesis unless at least 20 subjects report they would vote for Douglas.

The value 20 is referred to as the **critical value**, *the value in the sampling distribution that represents the dividing line between rejection and non-rejection of the null hypothesis at a desired alpha level.* The set of values 20–30 represents the **critical region**, *the set of values in the sampling distribution which would allow rejection of the null hypothesis at a desired alpha level.* To insure a Type I error probability of .05, we would reject the null hypothesis if 20 or more subjects support Douglas, and not reject the null hypothesis if less than 20 subjects support Douglas.

Our decision to reject the null hypothesis when we found 22 subjects would vote for Douglas is consistent with conventional policy, since 22 falls within the critical region. If we were to publish our study as a research article the notation

$$p < .05$$

would be used to indicate that this decision is associated with a Type I error probability of less than .05. *A statistical result which allows one to reject the null hypothesis at a desired alpha level* is called a **significant result**.

What Rejecting the Null Hypothesis Means. You may be tempted to assume that rejecting the null hypothesis when $\alpha = .05$ implies there is only a .05 probability that the null hypothesis is true. This would be an incorrect assumption, just as it would be incorrect to say that I believe the probability Elvis Presley is alive is .10. Elvis is either alive or dead, the defendant is either guilty or innocent, and the null hypothesis is either true or false. These are factual statements. The $\alpha = .05$ indicates only that a certain sample finding would occur 5% of the time or less if the null hypothesis is true, and based on this information a decision is made to reject the null hypothesis.

It would be more appropriate to say that when the null hypothesis is rejected at $\alpha = .05$ the researcher has 95% confidence in the decision to reject the null hypothesis. This is similar to deciding to believe that Elvis is dead or that a defendant is guilty on the basis of the evidence: one cannot be sure that the decision is correct, but the decision is made with a certain degree of confidence.

Even so, no decision to reject or not reject the null hypothesis can be made with complete confidence. For that reason, *any important hypothesis should be tested in several different studies before a final decision is made about whether the evidence supports or does not support the hypothesis.*

Changing the Alpha Level. Using a different alpha level than .05 means changing the critical value (see Figure 10.2). Setting $\alpha = .001$ would mean the researcher is very conservative, only willing to accept a 1 in 1000 probability of a Type I error. If we wanted to set $\alpha = .001$ we would not be able to reject the null hypothesis unless 24 or more subjects in the sample would vote for Douglas. Since there were only 22 Douglas supporters in the

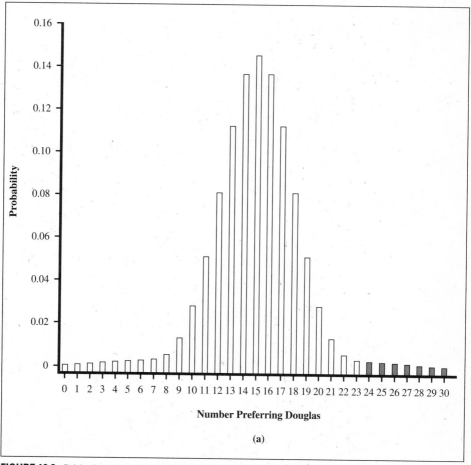

(a)

FIGURE 10.2 Critical regions for various values of alpha. (a) If the probability that a member of the population will support Douglas is .50, the probability of 24 or more voters supporting Douglas in a sample of 30 is < .001. (*continued on next page*)

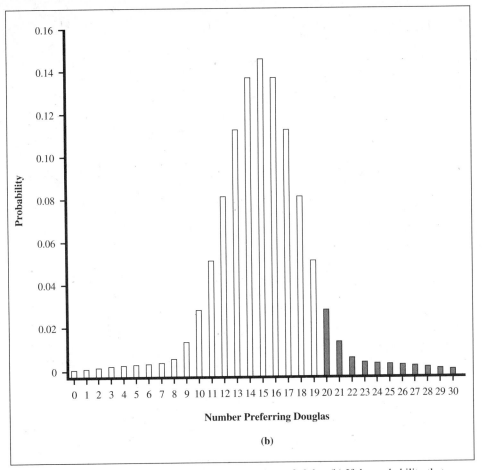

FIGURE 10.2 (*continued*) Critical regions for various values of alpha. (b) If the probability that a member of the population will support Douglas is .50, the probability of 20 or more voters supporting Douglas in a sample of 30 is < .05. (*continued on next page*)

sample, we would not have been able to reject the null hypothesis. If instead we wanted to set $\alpha = .10$ the critical value would be 19. The smaller the desired alpha level (the more confident you want to feel about the accuracy of your decision), the more extreme the sample statistic must be before you can reject the null hypothesis.

10.6 DIRECTIONAL AND NONDIRECTIONAL HYPOTHESES

The statistical hypotheses

$$H_0: p(\text{D}) \leq .50$$

$$H_1: p(\text{D}) > .50$$

are examples of directional hypotheses. A **directional hypothesis** is *a statistical hypothesis that suggests a direction for the hypothesized pattern or relationship*. It is also possible to test a **nondirectional hypothesis**, *a statistical hypothesis that does not suggest the*

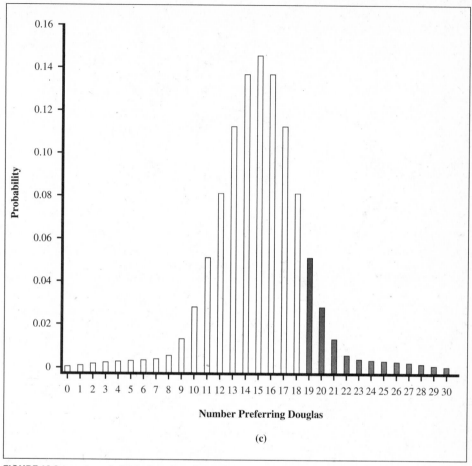

FIGURE 10.2 (*continued*) Critical regions for various values of alpha. (c) If the probability that a member of the population will support Douglas is .50, the probability of 19 or more voters supporting Douglas in a sample of 30 is < .10.

direction of a hypothesized pattern or relationship. The nondirectional statistical hypotheses for the voter preference study would be

$$H_0\colon p(\mathrm{D}) = .50$$

$$H_1\colon p(\mathrm{D}) \neq .50.$$

In this case the nondirectional alternative hypothesis is true if the probability of supporting Douglas is greater than or less than .50. The null hypothesis is only true if the probability of supporting Douglas is exactly equal to .50. Again, notice that the null hypothesis includes an equal sign, the alternative hypothesis does not.

Scientific hypotheses usually suggest a direction: the coin is fixed to produce too many heads, adolescents with higher grade point averages report more self-esteem, females report more self-esteem than males. You might therefore expect that statistical hypotheses are usually directional. In fact, nondirectional hypotheses are generally preferred, for several reasons. Results opposite in direction from the researcher's expectations frequently have important implications. The researcher may hypothesize that females report more self-esteem than males, but it would also be interesting to learn that males report more self-esteem than females. A directional hypothesis would not allow the researcher to detect patterns or relationships contrary to expectation. In addition, examples will be provided later in this text of hypothesis tests where directional hypotheses are not possible. Despite the preference for nondirectional hypotheses, I will continue to use the directional null and alternative hypotheses in the present example.

One-Tailed Tests. If we use the directional statistical hypotheses

$$H_0: p(D) \leq .50$$
$$H_1: p(D) > .50,$$

rejection of the null hypothesis can only occur if the results suggest the probability that a voter supports Douglas is greater than .50. For this reason, the critical region consists of the values 20–30, which are in the upper tail of the sampling distribution that was created by assuming the null hypothesis is true. Figure 10.3(a) again illustrates the critical region for

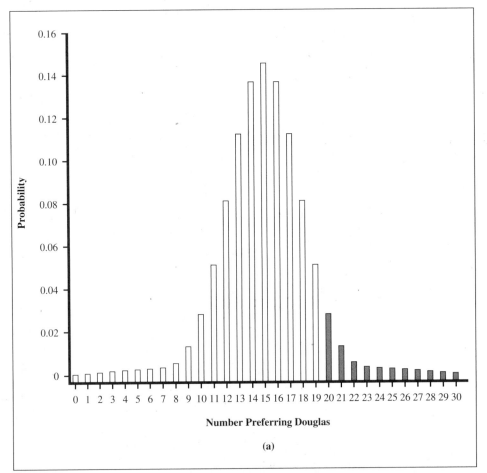

FIGURE 10.3 One- versus two-tailed critical regions for the sampling distribution of coin flips when $N = 30$. (a) If the probability that a member of the population will support Douglas is .50, the probability of 20 or more voters supporting Douglas in a sample of 30 is $< .05$. (*continued on next page*)

testing this null hypothesis in a sample of $N = 30$ assuming that $p(D) = .50$. This is an example of a **one-tailed test**, *a test of the null hypothesis in which the critical region falls in one tail of the sampling distribution created by assuming the null hypothesis is true.*

A different one-tailed test would be required if our scientific hypothesis suggested that the probability a voter would support Douglas was less than .50 (the scientific hypothesis we would have adopted if the Republicans had hired us instead of the Democrats). In this case the null and alternative hypotheses would be

$$H_0: p(D) \geq .50$$

$$H_1: p(D) < .50.$$

Notice again that only the null hypothesis indicates an exact value for $p(D)$. The critical region would lie in the lower tail of the sampling distribution, and include the values 0–10. Figure 10.3(b) illustrates the critical region for testing this null hypothesis in a sample of $N = 30$ assuming that $p(D) = .50$.

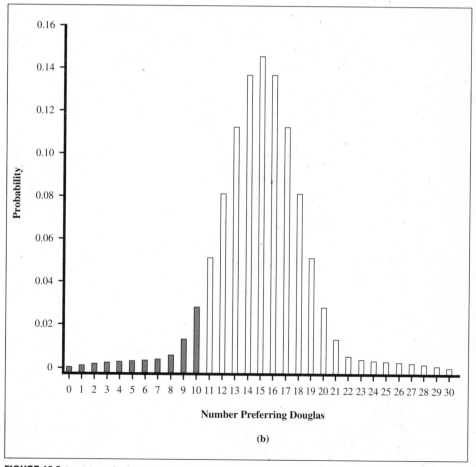

(b)

FIGURE 10.3 (*continued*) One- versus two-tailed critical regions for the sampling distribution of coin flips when $N = 30$. (b) If the probability that a member of the population will support Douglas is .50, the probability of 10 or less voters supporting Douglas in a sample of 30 is $< .05$. (*continued on next page*)

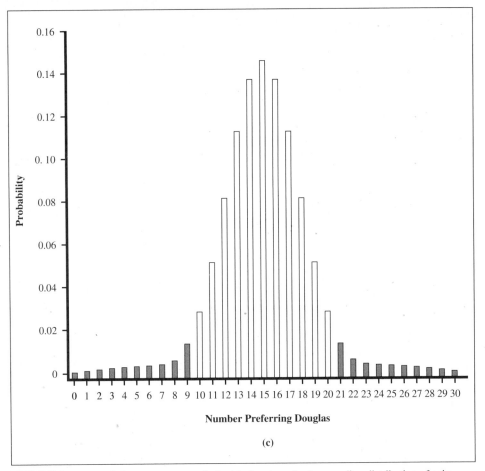

FIGURE 10.3 (*continued*) One- versus two-tailed critical regions for the sampling distribution of coin flips when $N = 30$. (c) If the probability that a member of the population will support Douglas is .50, the probability of 21 voters or more, or 9 voters or less, supporting Douglas in a sample of 30 is < .05.

Two-Tailed Tests. Suppose we instead used the nondirectional hypotheses for our study:

$$H_0: p(D) = .50$$

$$H_1: p(D) \neq .50.$$

These might have been our preferred scientific hypotheses if we were hired by some neutral organization such as a newspaper to investigate who is the favored candidate. This null hypothesis should be rejected if the data suggest the probability a voter supports Douglas is greater than .50 or is less than .50. Testing this null hypothesis would require a critical region in each tail of the sampling distribution, and would represent a **two-tailed test**, *a test of the null hypothesis in which a critical region is defined in each tail of the sampling distribution created by assuming the null hypothesis is true.*

To maintain the alpha level for the two-tailed test at .05, the critical region for each tail must be associated with a Type I error probability no greater than .025. In our study this

TABLE 10.1   Selected Aspects of the Binomial Test

Type of Statistical Hypotheses	General Form of Statistical Hypotheses	Type of Test	Symbol for Alpha	Critical Region in
nondirectional	$H_0: p(V) = ?$ $H_1: p(V) \neq ?$	two-tailed	α	both tails
directional	$H_0: p(V) \leq ?$ $H_1: p(V) > ?$	one-tailed	$\alpha(D)$	upper tail
directional	$H_0: p(V) \geq ?$ $H_1: p(V) < ?$	one-tailed	$\alpha(D)$	lower tail

would require setting the critical value for the upper tail of the sampling distribution to 21, and the critical value for the lower tail to 9 as in Figure 10.3(c). When the probability of a Type I error is added together for all the values of 9 or less and 21 or more, they sum to .043, so the alpha level is still less than .05.

Critical Values. To summarize, a one-tailed binomial test is appropriate when the statistical hypotheses are directional. A single critical value is defined for either the upper or lower tail of the null hypothesis sampling distribution, depending on the direction of the alternative hypothesis.

A two-tailed binomial test is used when the alternative hypothesis is nondirectional. A critical value is defined for each tail of the null hypothesis sampling distribution. This critical value will be further out on the tail than the critical value for the one-tailed test. In the rest of this text, the symbol α will be used to refer to the alpha level for a test of a nondirectional null hypothesis. The symbol $\alpha(D)$ will be used to refer to the alpha level for the test of a directional null hypothesis.

Critical values are therefore determined by two factors: the alpha level and whether the test is one-tailed or two-tailed. The alternative hypothesis can be used to determine where the critical value falls. In the case of the binomial test, an alternative hypothesis containing the symbol $\neq$ indicates a two-tailed test is appropriate. The symbol $>$ in the alternative hypothesis indicates a one-tailed test with the critical value in the upper tail. The symbol $<$ in the alternative hypothesis indicates a one-tailed test with the critical value in the lower tail (see Figure 10.3). This and other aspects of the binomial test are summarized in Table 10.1.

KEY TERMS

alpha level, level of significance
alternative hypothesis
critical region
critical value
directional hypothesis
hypothesis testing statistics
nondirectional hypothesis
null hypothesis
one-tailed test

probability
random sampling
scientific hypothesis
significant result
statistical hypothesis
two-tailed test
Type I error
Type II error

EXERCISES

Answers to all exercises may be found in Appendix B.

1. State the relationship between the scientific hypothesis and the statistical hypothesis. What does the null hypothesis suggest about the pattern or relationship discussed in the scientific hypothesis? What does the alternative hypothesis suggest about the pattern or relationship discussed in the scientific hypothesis? Finally, why does the null hypothesis always include an equal sign?

2. Suggest both a directional and nondirectional alternative and null hypotheses for the following scientific hypotheses. Remember that μ refers to a population mean, ρ_{XY} to a population correlation coefficient, σ to a population standard deviation, and σ^2 to a population variance.
   a. Pitching speed is much more variable in the American League East than the American League West.
   b. As pitching speed increases, accuracy (measured as distance from a target) decreases.
   c. Pitching speed is higher in the American League than the National League.
   d. The proportion of players with batting averages over .300 is greater in the National League than in the American League.

3. Which of the following are unacceptable as a pair of null and alternative hypotheses? If the pair is unacceptable, indicate why. Remember that μ refers to a population mean, ρ_{XY} to a population correlation coefficient.
   a. $H_0: p(D) > p(R)$
      $H_1: p(D) \leq p(R)$
   b. $H_0: \mu > 30$
      $H_1: \mu < 30$.
   c. $H_0: \rho_{XY} \geq 0$
      $H_1: \rho_{XY} < 0$.
   d. $H_0: \mu > 30$
      $H_1: \mu \leq 31$.

4. For each of the following sets of statistical hypotheses, indicate which is the null hypothesis and which is the alternative hypothesis.

   a. $\rho_{XY} < .10$
      $\rho_{XY} \geq .10$.
   b. $\mu \leq 10$
      $\mu > 10$.
   c. $\rho_{XY} \neq .10$
      $\rho_{XY} = .10$.
   d. $\sigma = 3.5$
      $\sigma \neq 3.5$.

5. Indicate whether the following statements are true or false. If false, indicate why.
   a. A Type I error can only occur if the alternative hypothesis is true.
   b. A jury's decision to convict is much like a researcher's decision to reject the null hypothesis.
   c. Depending on whether the null or alternative hypothesis is actually true, the decision to reject the null hypothesis results in either a correct rejection or an incorrect rejection.
   d. If the alternative hypothesis is true, then the only possible outcomes for a study are correct rejection or incorrect rejection.
   e. If the null hypothesis is true, then the only possible outcomes for a study are incorrect rejection or correct non-rejection.
   f. $1 - \alpha$ is used to symbolize the probability of a correct rejection if the null hypothesis is true.
   g. If the jury convicts, but the defendant is actually innocent, the jury has committed a case of incorrect rejection, or a Type II error.
   h. If the null hypothesis is true, and a study is repeated many times with α set at .01, then the null hypothesis should be rejected in 99% of the studies.

6. Which is more conservative, an alpha level of .10 or an alpha level of .01? Why?

7. It was indicated in the chapter that the only way to eliminate the possibility of a Type I error is to decide never to reject the null hypothesis. Why is this an unacceptable option?

CHAPTER 11

Type II Error and Power

11.1 CONTROLLING THE TYPE II ERROR PROBABILITY

A study was described in the last chapter in which 30 voters were asked which of two candidates they preferred: Democrat Don Douglas or Republican Ron Richards. The decision was made to reject the null hypothesis

$$H_0:\ p(\text{D}) \le .50.$$

It was indicated in Chapter 10 that any study can result in one of four outcomes:

		Fact	
		H_0 is True	H_1 is True
Statistical Decision	Reject H_0	incorrect rejection (Type I error) p (incorrect rejection) $= \alpha$	correct rejection p (correct rejection) $= 1 - \beta$ (power)
	Do Not Reject H_0	correct non-rejection p (correct non-rejection) $= 1 - \alpha$	incorrect non-rejection (Type II error) p (incorrect non-rejection) $= \beta$

The last chapter discussed the control of Type I error, or incorrect rejection of the null hypothesis when the null hypothesis is true. This chapter focuses on issues surrounding the control of Type II errors, the incorrect non-rejection of the null hypothesis when the null hypothesis is false.

Setting the Beta Level. If the alternative hypothesis is true, then the researcher will either correctly reject the null hypothesis or incorrectly not reject the null hypothesis (a Type II error). It is impossible to eliminate the risk of a Type II error, unless you decide to always reject the null hypothesis. However, if you can establish an acceptable risk of a Type II error, it is possible to insure that the probability of a Type II error does not exceed that level. *The acceptable probability of a Type II error* is symbolized by β, the Greek letter beta, and may be referred to as the **beta level.** Cohen (1988) has recommended a Type II error probability of .20 as a standard. To understand what this means, imagine we conducted the same study many, many times in circumstances where the alternative hypothesis is true. If β is set at .20, we would correctly reject the null hypothesis 80%

80% of the time, and incorrectly not reject the null hypothesis 20% of the time; 80% of our decisions would be correct.

The probability of correctly rejecting the null hypothesis when the alternative hypothesis is true is called the **power** of the study, symbolized by $1-\beta$. If the alternative hypothesis is true, increasing the power of the study means that the probability of a Type II error decreases.

Factors Affecting Power. Controlling the probability of a Type II error is not as simple as controlling the probability of a Type I error. Any factor that increases the probability of rejecting the null hypothesis also increases the power of the study. There are three factors in our study that influence the probability of rejecting the null hypothesis: the alpha level, the effect size, and the sample size. The next three sections will describe the impact of each on the power of the study.

11.1.1 The Alpha Level

As the alpha level increases, power increases. I noted in the last chapter that if we set $\alpha = .10$ the critical value would be 19 rather than 20. This would increase the probability of rejecting the null hypothesis, and if the alternative hypothesis is true then the power of the study would be greater. However, this strategy has its risks. If the null hypothesis is true rather than the alternative hypothesis, then increasing the alpha level increases the probability of a Type I error. Since increasing the alpha level has undesirable consequences if the null hypothesis is true, this is not commonly used as a method for increasing power.

11.1.2 The Effect Size

Effect Size Defined. An **effect size** is *a measure of the true size, or strength, of a pattern or relationship in the population.* This definition indicates that the effect size represents a parameter. You have already been introduced to one effect size measure in Chapter 7, the population correlation coefficient ρ_{XY}. The larger ρ_{XY} is, the stronger the relationship in the population between the variables X and Y. The population correlation coefficient is an indicator of the size of the relationship between two variables in a population.

In the case of a probability from a dichotomous variable, the absolute value of the difference between the true probability that a voter will support Douglas and .50 is a measure of the effect size. If the null hypothesis is true, and the probability that a voter supports Douglas really is .50, then the effect size is

$$|.50 - .50| = 0.$$

If the true probability that a voter supports Douglas is .80, then the effect size is

$$|.80 - .50| = .30.$$

Similarly, if the true probability that a voter supports Douglas is .23, then the effect size is

$$|.23 - .50| = .27.$$

The larger the effect size, the stronger the pattern of support for one candidate over the other in the population.

Effect Size and Power. *As the effect size increases, power increases.* With alpha set at .05, the critical value is 20. Suppose the alternative hypothesis is true, and the true probability that a voter supports Douglas is .60. The effect size equals

$$|.60 - .50| = .10.$$

and according to the binomial formula, 29% of random samples with $N = 30$ will include 20 or more voters who support Douglas, as indicated in Figure 11.1(a). The probability of correctly rejecting the null hypothesis is only .29.

Suppose the alternative hypothesis is true, but the true probability that a voter supports Douglas is .80. The effect size now equals

$$|.80 - .50| = .30,$$

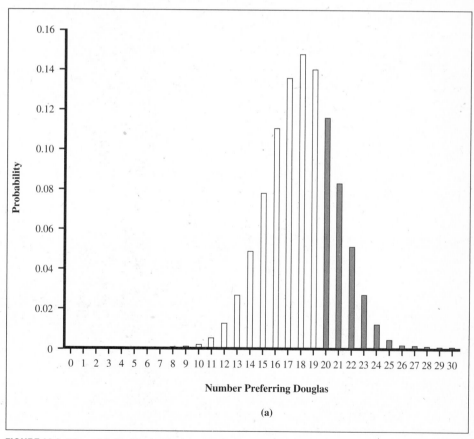

Number Preferring Douglas

(a)

FIGURE 11.1 Binomial distributions when $p(H) = .60$ and $p(H) = .80$. (a) If the probability that a voter supports Douglas is .60, 20 or more voters will support Douglas in about 29% of random samples with N = 30 (*continued on next page*).

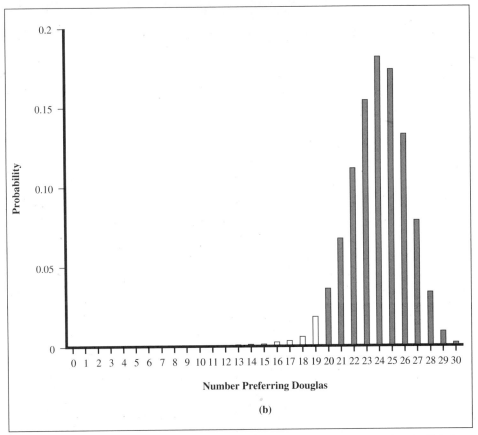

FIGURE 11.1 (*continued*) Binomial distributions when $p(H) = .60$ and $p(H) = .80$. (b) If the probability that a voters supports Douglas is .80, 20 or more voters will support Douglas in about 97% of random samples with $N = 30$.

and the binomial distribution for this case indicates that 20 or more voters will support Douglas in 97% of random samples of 30 voters, as indicated in Figure 11.1(b). The probability of correctly rejecting the null hypothesis is .97.

These examples demonstrate the impact of effect size on power. In both cases the alpha level was set to .05 by using 20 as the critical value. However, in the case where the effect size equaled .10 the power of the study was only .29. If the effect size is actually .30 the power of the study is .97.

Unfortunately, the true effect size is not always a factor that is easily manipulated. Our polling firm cannot make more people support Douglas to increase our chances of rejecting the null hypothesis. Furthermore, the true effect size is rarely known: remember that if the exact probability of a voter supporting Douglas were known the study would be unnecessary. For these reasons, increasing the effect size is generally not a practical method of increasing power.[1]

---

[1]However, in some studies the effect size can be increased to some extent by using a homogeneous sample, by studying the sample under homogeneous conditions, or by increasing the intensity of the treatment.

11.1.3 The Sample Size

As the sample size increases, power increases. If alpha is set at .05, the following table indicates the critical values for various sample sizes for our study, and the critical value as a percentage of the sample size:

N	Critical Value	Critical Value as a Percentage of N
5	5	100%
10	9	90%
20	15	75%
30	20	66%

If our sample consisted of 5 voters, 100% of subjects would have to support Douglas before we could reject the null hypothesis. In a sample of 30, only $2/3$ of the subjects need to support Douglas to reject the null hypothesis. As the sample size increases it becomes relatively easier to reject the null hypothesis.

Of the three factors which influence power (alpha level, effect size, and sample size), sample size is the one most open to control by the researcher. The probability of a Type II error is most easily controlled by manipulating the sample size. The next section describes the selection of a sample size that insures an acceptable level of power.

11.2 SELECTING THE SAMPLE SIZE

Setting Alpha and Beta. You now have all the information you need to determine the appropriate sample size for controlling the Type II error probability in our study. The first step requires choosing the desired alpha and beta levels. Under most circumstances the desired alpha level will be set to .05 (two-tailed) and the beta level to .20.

Estimating the Effect Size. The next step requires estimating the true effect size in the population. If the alternative hypothesis is true, the effect size (the true probability of supporting Douglas minus .50) can be any value greater than 0 up to .50. The discussion will be limited to three possible effect sizes, which will be referred to as *small*, *medium*, and *large* effect sizes.[2] Cohen (1988) has suggested that when testing whether a probability significantly differs from .50, .05 should generally be considered a small effect size, .15 should be considered a medium effect size, and .25 should be considered a large effect size. In our study, an effect size of .05 would mean the probability a voter supports Douglas is .55 (or .45), an effect size of .15 would mean the probability is .65 (or .35), and an effect size of .25 would mean it is .75 (or .25).

Using Table 11.1. Table 11.1 provides some guidelines for deciding whether you should expect a small, medium, or large effect size. Familiarize yourself with this table; the information will be of use many times in the coming chapters. The table includes a number of guidelines, but they can be essentially summarized as follows:

---

[2]Cohen (1988), whose book provides the basis for Table 11.2 and the tables in Appendix C, and Kraemer and Thiemann (1987) provide sample size information for a wide range of effect sizes.

TABLE 11.1 Guidelines for Estimating Effect Sizes

The best effect size estimate is based on previous research. For example, Lipsey and Wilson (1993) reviewed a large number of studies summarizing effect sizes associated with psychological, educational, and behavioral treatment programs. On average, the results suggest such programs are associated with a medium to large effect size. Additional information was provided concerning effect sizes to expect for specific types of treatment.

It is usually impossible to base your estimate on previous studies. Even if previous research is available, differences in the population sampled or in the variables measured can invalidate previous effect size estimates. In addition, the statistical procedures required for computing and combining effect size information from previous studies are too complicated to introduce here.

A less accurate but often more useful approach involves basing your effect size estimate on the *smallest meaningful* effect size: the smallest effect size which would suggest a nontrivial difference from the null hypothesis. Some guidelines for using this method follow:

Assume a small effect size when:

1. The effect is important or meaningful but difficult to detect with the naked eye.
    Example: Data from the National Center of Health Statistics (NCHS), Najjar, and Rowland (1987) suggest that the difference in mean height for 16 and 17 year old boys represents a small effect.
2. You are investigating a previously unexplored research area, or are working in circumstances where there is little control over subjects.
    Example: A long-term psychotherapy program is attempted for very resistant patients.
3. You are studying the effectiveness of some treatment for which the potential benefits clearly outweigh the risks or costs.
    Examples: Willard, Lange, and Hillis (1992) examined whether aspirin taken once every two days effectively reduces the rate of heart attacks. J. S. Terman, M. Terman, Schlager, et al. (1990) studied whether $\frac{1}{2}$ hour of exposure to bright light in the morning was an effective treatment for recurrent wintertime depression.
4. You are studying the impact of a single element in a series of events with a cumulative effect (Abelson, 1985).
    Example: The effect of a single radio advertisement on buying patterns may be small, but the cumulative effect of hearing the advertisement many times may be much greater. Note that this assumes the effect adds up over the series. If after hearing the ad six times people tend to buy the item less or buying levels out, this assumption is not met.
5. Even small effects can translate into large numerical differences.
    Example: This is often a consideration in public opinion polls. If only 55% of the adult American population supports a reduction in taxes, this means about 7 million more eligible voters support the reduction than oppose it.

Assume a medium effect size when:

1. The effect should be visible to the naked eye.
    Example: The difference in mean height for 16 and 18 year old boys represents a medium effect (NCHS et al., 1987).
2. You are studying the effectiveness of some treatment which demonstrates both marked risks or costs and marked potential benefits.
    Example: Drugs used for the control of depression are often associated with minor side effects, and are occasionally associated with serious side effects such as sexual dysfunction and high blood pressure (Dewan & Koss, 1989).

(Continued)

TABLE 11.1 (*continued*)   Guidelines for Estimating Effect Sizes

---

3.   You are not sure into which category your research topic falls, in which case assuming a medium effect size is a safe bet.
     Example: Cohen (1992) reported that medium-sized effects are typical in a variety of research areas (see also Lipsey & Wilson, 1993).

Assume a large effect size when:
1.   The effect should be "grossly perceptible" to the naked eye (Cohen, 1988, p. 27).
     Example: The difference in mean height for 14 and 16 year old boys, when most adolescent growth occurs, represents a large effect (NCHS et al., 1987).
2.   You are studying the effectiveness of some treatment where there is controversy over whether the potential benefits outweigh the risks or costs.
     Example: Electroconvulsive therapy is a treatment for depression which causes convulsions, and has been associated with memory loss.

The true effect size may differ from the smallest meaningful effect size. For example, psychotherapy is associated with relatively low risks and costs (time commitment, expense). This suggests that in studies comparing psychotherapy to placebo treatment even a small to medium effect size would be meaningful, and sample sizes could be set under this assumption. In fact, most studies examining the effectiveness of psychotherapy suggest the true effect size is medium to large (Lipsey & Wilson, 1993), suggesting that psychotherapy may be more effective than it needs to be to consider it worthwhile.

---

1. If possible, use previous research to estimate the effect size.
2. When Rule 1 is not feasible, use one of the following rules to estimate the smallest meaningful effect size:
   a. If even a small, barely noticeable difference from the value suggested for a parameter by the null hypothesis could be considered important, then assume a small effect size.
   b. If a difference from the value suggested by the null hypothesis would not be considered important until the difference is visible to the naked eye, then assume a medium effect size.
   c. If a difference from the value suggested by the null hypothesis would not be considered important until the effect is grossly obvious, then assume a large effect size.

Let's consider the implications of the guidelines in Table 11.1 for our study. The best way to estimate effect size is on the basis of previous findings. Suppose previous polls generally found 75% of voters support Douglas. This would suggest the effect size is

$$|.75 - .50| = .25,$$

a large effect size. This is the most accurate method of estimating the effect size.

If ours is to be the first poll comparing the candidates, or if we have reason to believe opinions have changed markedly since the last poll was completed, we will have to base our effect size estimate on the *smallest meaningful* effect size: the smallest effect size that would provide evidence of a meaningful difference in preference for the two candidates. This judgment could be based on several considerations.

TABLE 11.2   A Portion of Table C–1

Power	two-tailed .05 / one-tailed .025			two-tailed .10 / one-tailed .05		
	Estimated Effect Size					
	Small	Medium	Large	Small	Medium	Large
.80	783	85	30	616	67	**23**
.90	1047	113	40	853	91	33

Cohen (1988) reported that the winner received more than 55% of the popular vote in fewer than half of presidential elections since 1872. A small effect size (.05) would then be meaningful, since a .55 probability that a voter supports Douglas would indicate a strong likelihood that he will be elected.

On the other hand, unless the support for Douglas is very strong, events occurring before the election could still place the results in doubt. This argues for considering a large effect size (.25) the smallest important effect size, particularly if the poll is taken early in the campaign.

The example highlights the problem with using the smallest meaningful effect size as one's effect size estimate. It is a subjective decision, and one might be able to argue for several different choices. The selection of the smallest meaningful effect size should be made with a great deal of thought.

Setting the Sample Size.   Table C–1 in Appendix C provides the sample size necessary to achieve a power of .80 or .90 in the voter selection study for the most common alpha levels. Part of that table is repeated here as Table 11.2. Suppose you would like to set the alpha and beta levels to $\alpha(D) = .05$ and $\beta = .20$, and you believe the smallest meaningful effect size would be a large one. Table 11.2 indicates the appropriate sample size is 23. If the probability that a voter supports Douglas is .75, and if we collected many, many random samples of 23 voters, we would reject the null hypothesis 80% of the time. Our sample size of 30 is more than enough to insure a Type II error probability of .20 given the assumption of a large effect size. If we instead assumed a small effect size was meaningful, we should sample at least 616 voters if we wanted to insure a .20 probability of a Type II error.

This exercise demonstrates the important relationship between sample size and effect size: the smaller the estimated effect, the larger the sample necessary to detect it. Detecting small effect sizes generally requires sample sizes which are practical only for well-financed researchers. This should be a consideration when you choose a research topic: avoid research areas where small effects matter greatly unless you have the resources necessary to gather the required sample.

11.3 ANOTHER LOOK AT DIRECTIONAL HYPOTHESES

Directional Null Hypotheses.   The concept of effect size can be used to help improve your understanding of directional hypotheses. Remember that the null hypothesis for our study is

$$H_0: \ p(D) \leq .50.$$

The directional null hypothesis suggests the probability a voter will support Douglas can fall anywhere in the interval 0 to .50. So far the discussion of the null hypothesis has been limited to the case where we assumed $p(D) = .50$. What about all the other possible null hypothesis values?

Suppose the true probability of a preference for Douglas is .60. We should be able to reject the null hypothesis, assuming sufficient power. If the null hypothesis value .50 is used as the basis for computing the binomial distribution, the effect size is

$$|.60 - .50| = .10,$$

and I determined earlier that the power of the study for a sample with $N = 30$ is .29, as indicated in Figure 11.1(a).

Suppose we assumed that the probability of a preference for Douglas is .20 rather than .50, an assumption that is still consistent with the null hypothesis. The effect size for this test of the null hypothesis is

$$|.60 - .20| = .40,^3$$

and the power of the study has increased to over .99 (Cohen, 1988).

This example illustrates why we can safely ignore all the null hypothesis values less than .50. The value .50 falls right at the border between the range of values associated with the null hypothesis, and the range of values associated with the alternative hypothesis. If the null hypothesis is false, the binomial test based on assuming $p(D) = .50$ is true will be less powerful than the test based on any other null hypothesis value. If we can reject the null hypothesis when we assume the probability a voter supports Douglas is .50, then we can reject the null hypothesis if we assume the probability a voter supports Douglas is any value less than .50.

Summary. To summarize, whether your hypothesis is directional (so the null hypothesis includes a range of values) or nondirectional (so the null hypothesis includes a single value), you only need to conduct one hypothesis test. For one-tailed tests, use the null hypothesis value that is closest to the range of values associated with the alternative hypothesis. In our study, assuming the null hypothesis value of .50 is true provides the least powerful test of the null hypothesis. Rejection of the null hypothesis when the probability a voter supports Douglas is assumed to be .50 means that the null hypothesis can be rejected if the probability a voter supports Douglas is assumed to be any value less than .50.

KEY TERMS

alpha level	one-tailed test
beta level	power
critical value	probability
directional hypothesis	sample size
effect size	two-tailed test

---

[3] Technically, the computation of the effect size is more complicated for null hypothesis values other than .50, but the value provided is close enough for our purposes.

EXERCISES

Answers to all exercises may be found in Appendix B.

1. It was indicated in the chapter that the only way to eliminate the possibility of a Type II error is to decide to always reject the null hypothesis. Why is this an unacceptable option?

2. Which of the following would increase the power of a study on candidate support if the alternative hypothesis is true?
   a. Increasing the number of candidates from which subjects can choose.
   b. Increasing the alpha level.
   c. Increasing the heterogeneity of subjects.
   d. Increasing the sample size.
   e. Increasing the beta level.

3. Explain why increasing the alpha level is generally considered unacceptable as a method of enhancing power.

4. For each of the following studies, indicate what you would consider the smallest meaningful effect size:
   a. Bipolar disorder is a severely damaging mental disorder, involving dramatic shifts between depression and mania. You would like to evaluate the use of lithium as a treatment for the disorder. Lithium is a fairly toxic drug and frequent blood tests are required to protect against overdosing.
   b. Sigmund Freud hypothesized that all males pass through an oedipal stage at the age of 5 or 6, one sign of which is attempts to separate the mother from the father. A researcher would like to observe 5–6 year old and 8–9 year old boys at random intervals to study whether they differ in the frequency of behaviors meant to separate the parents.
   c. A computer program has been designed to enhance math skills over a series of 25 hour-long sessions. An educational researcher is interested in the effect of a single session with the computer on math skills.
   d. A researcher investigates differences in verbal skills among 10- and 18-year olds.

   e. A researcher is interested in the difference between males and females in whether they blame the husband or the wife more when a husband physically abuses his wife.
   f. A teacher administers a course satisfaction survey to the students in her classes.
   g. A researcher is interested in whether or not Americans oppose the death penalty. The researcher guesses on the basis of preliminary surveying that only about 35% of Americans are completely opposed to the death penalty, while 65% would not be opposed at least under certain circumstances.

5. For the given alpha level, beta level, and effect size, provide the appropriate sample size:
   a. $\alpha(D) = .05$, $\beta = .10$, small effect size.
   b. $\alpha = .20$, $\beta = .20$, large effect size.
   c. $\alpha(D) = .025$, $\beta = .20$, medium effect size.

6. Challenge question: A study is conducted to test the following directional hypotheses about a population correlation coefficient:

$$H_0: \rho_{XY} \leq .45$$

$$H_1: \rho_{XY} > .45.$$

Review the following statements, and (a) determine which we could potentially assume to be true if we are assuming the null hypothesis above is true. Of those, determine (b) which would lead to the most powerful test of the null hypothesis if the alternative hypothesis is true, and (c) which would lead to the least powerful test of the null hypothesis if the alternative hypothesis is true. (d) Of all the values for ρ_{XY} associated with the null hypothesis, which would result in the least powerful test of the null hypothesis if the alternative hypothesis is true?

1. $\rho_{XY} = .50$ 2. $\rho_{XY} = 0$
3. $\rho_{XY} = -1.0$ 4. $\rho_{XY} = 1.0$
5. $\rho_{XY} = .01$ 6. $\rho_{XY} = .20$

CHAPTER 12

The One-Group *z* Test and Interval Estimation

The first portion of this chapter introduces the one-group *z* test, an inferential statistic that can be used for purposes of hypothesis testing under certain conditions. The example provided to illustrate the one-group *z* test will then be used to explain the logic of interval estimation, the second class of inferential statistics.

12.1 THE ONE-GROUP Z TEST

12.1.1 Introduction

Suppose we would like to evaluate the scientific hypothesis that college professors are more anxious than the average adult. To do so we go to three colleges and administer the Minnesota Multiphasic Personality Inventory (Butcher, Dahlstrom, Graham, Tellegen, & Kaemmer, 1989), or MMPI, to a sample of $N = 100$ randomly drawn from a population of college professors.

The MMPI is a rating scale that consists of 567 statements such as "I like mechanics magazines." The subject responds to each item by indicating whether the statement is personally true or false. Because of the large number of items, the MMPI can be used to score the individual on a variety of personal characteristics. For example, the Psychasthenia scale provides an indication of how anxious the person is.

The Psychasthenia scale consists of 48 items. Because of the method used to score the scale, possible scores range between 0 and 78. Based on a random sample of 2600 American adults, it has been estimated that the mean score in the general adult population is 26.43 for males ($\sigma_Y = 5.00$), 27.70 for females ($\sigma_Y = 5.10$).

Using these population means and standard deviations, scores on MMPI scales are transformed into T scores. The T score was described in Chapter 6, and refers to a standard score for which the mean is 50 and the standard deviation is 10. MMPI Psychasthenia scale T scores represent a continuous ordinal variable. The scientific hypothesis that college professors are more anxious than the average adult therefore implies that the mean T score should be greater than 50 in the population of college professors from which our sample was drawn.

As with the election poll described in the last chapter, three steps are involved in testing the scientific hypothesis that college professors are more anxious than the average adult: defining the null and alternative hypotheses, testing the null hypothesis, and making a decision about the null hypothesis

12.1.2 Defining the Null and Alternative Hypotheses

The scientific hypothesis that college professors are more anxious than the average adult can be translated into the nondirectional alternative hypothesis

$$H_1: \mu \neq 50,$$

where the μ refers to the mean Psychasthenia T score for the population of college professors. Like the binomial test, the presence of the symbol $\neq$ in the alternative hypothesis for the one-group z test indicates a two-tailed test will be used. I have chosen to use a nondirectional hypothesis for two reasons. First, it is consistent with standard practice. Second, even though the scientific hypothesis suggests college professors are more anxious than the average adult, it would also be interesting if the data suggest college professors are less anxious than the average adult.

The corresponding null hypothesis is

$$H_0: \mu = 50.$$

The null and alternative hypotheses are mutually exclusive and mutually exhaustive; one or the other must be true.

12.1.3 Testing the Null Hypothesis

The Sampling Distribution of the Mean. Testing the null hypothesis begins by assuming the null hypothesis is true. If we assume the mean Psychasthenia T score for college professors is 50, we should be able to generate a sampling distribution that will indicate the probability for the mean of our sample.

When the population standard deviation is known, you can use the sampling distribution of the mean to find the probability of a given sample mean. The **sampling distribution of the mean** is *a sampling distribution of means for all random samples of a given size from some population.* Just as the binomial distribution provides information such as the probability that 5 out of 10 coin flips will result in heads, the sampling distribution of the mean can be used to determine such information as the probability that a sample mean will fall between 50 and 52.5.

Characteristics of the Sampling Distribution. The sampling distribution of the mean demonstrates several important characteristics:

1. If subjects are randomly and independently sampled, and the population distribution for variable Y is normally distributed, then the sampling distribution of the mean for $\overline{Y}$ is also normally distributed. The concept of random sampling was discussed in Chapter 2. The independent sampling requirement would be violated if, for example, one professor influenced another professor's responses to the MMPI.

2. Even if the population from which the sample is drawn is not normally distributed, the sampling distribution may still look very much like a normal distribution. The **Central Limit Theorem** is *a theorem which states that as the sample size increases, the sampling distribution of the mean increasingly resembles a normal distribution.* If each sample were infinitely large, the sampling distribution would be a normal distribution regardless of how nonnormal the population distribution is.
3. The mean of the sampling distribution of the mean will equal the population μ. If we assume the null hypothesis is true, we are assuming that the mean Psychasthenia score for the population of college professors is 50, and therefore that the mean of the sampling distribution of the mean will also equal 50.
4. The standard deviation of the sampling distribution of the mean is equal to the population standard deviation for variable Y, σ_Y, divided by the square root of the sample size for the samples in the distribution. If we use $\sigma_{\overline{Y}}$ to symbolize the standard deviation of the sampling distribution of the mean, then

$$\sigma_{\overline{Y}} = \frac{\sigma_Y}{\sqrt{N}}.$$

Standard deviations of sampling distributions are called **standard errors**, so *the standard deviation of a sampling distribution of the mean* is called a **standard error of the mean**. Since we know the standard deviation of Psychasthenia T scores is 10, we know that the standard error of our sampling distribution is

$$\sigma_{\overline{Y}} = \frac{\sigma_Y}{\sqrt{N}}$$

$$= \frac{10}{\sqrt{100}}$$

$$= \frac{10}{10} = 1.0.$$

So, if we assume that (1) the population is normally distributed, (2) subjects were randomly and independently sampled from some population, and (3) the null hypothesis is true, we can conclude that the sampling distribution of the mean associated with our study:

1. is normally distributed,
2. has a mean value of 50, and
3. has a standard error of 1.0.

This sampling distribution is pictured in Figure 12.1.

Computing the One-Group z Test. Suppose we took the sample means from our sampling distribution and converted each to a z score. The formula for doing this would be

$$z_{\overline{Y}} = \frac{\overline{Y} - \mu_0}{\sigma_{\overline{Y}}},$$

where μ_0 is the mean of the population (and the sampling distribution) suggested by the null hypothesis, and $\sigma_{\overline{Y}}$ is the standard error of the sampling distribution. The symbol $z_{\overline{Y}}$ is used to indicate that these are z scores from a sampling distribution of sample means.

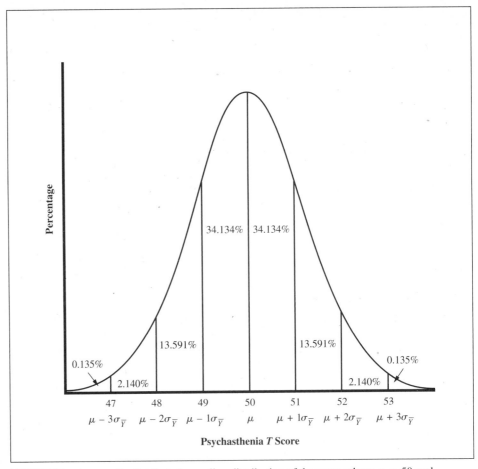

FIGURE 12.1   A normally distributed sampling distribution of the mean where $\mu = 50$ and $\sigma_{\bar{Y}} = 1.0$. In a normal distribution 34.134% of scores will fall between the mean and 1 standard deviation above the mean, 13.591% between 1 and 2 standard deviations above the mean, and so forth. This is also true for standard deviation units below the mean. This was originally discussed in Section 6.1.4.

Based on our three assumptions, for any mean in the sampling distribution based on samples of college professors, the corresponding $z_{\bar{Y}}$ score would be

$$z_{\bar{Y}} = \frac{\bar{Y} - 50}{1.0}.$$

A sample mean of 51 is one standard error higher than μ_0, so the corresponding $z_{\bar{Y}}$ score is $+1.0$; a sample mean of 48 is two standard errors below μ_0, so the corresponding $z_{\bar{Y}}$ score is -2.0. If the null hypothesis is true, the mean $z_{\bar{Y}}$ value would be 0, since the mean of the sample means equals μ_0. Figure 12.2 repeats the sampling distribution in Figure 12.1, this time including the $z_{\bar{Y}}$ scores corresponding to certain sample means. Suppose our sample of 100 college professors produces a mean Psychasthenia *T* score of 51.7. Procedure Box 12.1 describes the computation of $z_{\bar{Y}}$ for this sample. The

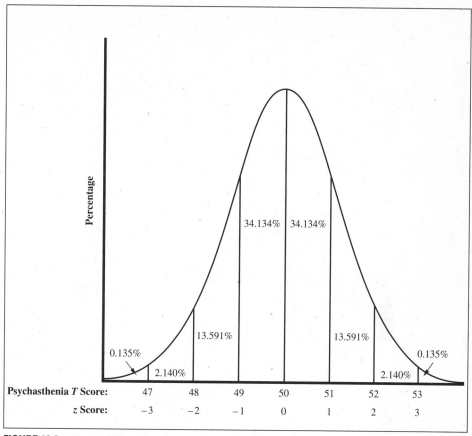

FIGURE 12.2   The sampling distribution of the mean where $\mu = 50$ and $\sigma_{\bar{y}} = 1.0$ with corresponding *z* scores.

resulting $z_{\bar{Y}}$ value is $+1.7$. What is the probability of this outcome if the null hypothesis is true?

We know from Chapter 6 that in a normal distribution the proportion of scores higher or lower than a certain *z* score is fixed. These percentages are provided in Table E–3 of Appendix E. We know for example that 34.134% of *z* values will fall between 0 and $+1.0$, and another 15.866% will be greater than $+1.0$. The information in Table E–3 can be used to find the critical values required for making a decision about the null hypothesis.

12.1.4 Making a Decision about the Null Hypothesis

The use of a two-tailed test means that a critical region must be defined for each tail of the sampling distribution. Using the traditional .05 alpha level, the critical value for each region must be the *z* value that separates the highest 2.5% and the lowest 2.5% of the sample means from the rest of the distribution. Table E–3 in Appendix E indicates that this *z* value is 1.96.

Let's apply this information to the present study. Suppose the null hypothesis is true, and we collect many samples of 100 college professors from our population. If we then

The One-Group *z* Test

Goal   Compute the value of $z_{\overline{Y}}$ for the sample of college professors where $\overline{Y} = 51.7$.

$$z_{\overline{Y}} = \frac{\overline{Y} - \mu_0}{\sigma_{\overline{Y}}}$$

Step 1   *Subtract the value for μ suggested by the null hypothesis from the sample mean.*

$$\overline{Y} - \mu_0 = 51.7 - 50 = 1.7$$

Step 2   *Divide the population standard deviation by the square root of N.*

$$\frac{\sigma_Y}{\sqrt{N}} = \frac{10}{\sqrt{100}} = 1.0$$

Step 3   *Divide the result of Step 1 by the result of Step 2.*

$$z_{51.7} = \frac{1.7}{1.0} = +1.7$$

compute the $z_{\overline{Y}}$ score for each sample mean, only 2.5% of these $z_{\overline{Y}}$ values would be greater than or equal to $+1.96$, and only 2.5% would be less than or equal to -1.96. If a sample mean is associated with a $z_{\overline{Y}}$ value $\geq +1.96$ or ≤ -1.96, we can reject the null hypothesis with less than a .05 probability of a Type I error. In other words, the critical value for an alpha level of .05 is $z_{\alpha=.05} = \pm 1.96$, and the critical region includes any z value greater than or equal to $+1.96$ or less than or equal to -1.96 (see Figure 12.3). If

$$|z_{\overline{Y}}| \geq 1.96,$$

we can reject the null hypothesis. Since the sample $z_{\overline{Y}}$ score computed in Procedure Box 12.1 is $+1.7$, we cannot reject the null hypothesis. If the mean Psychasthenia *T* score for this population is 50, a sample mean of 51.7 when $N = 100$ is not unusual enough to justify rejecting the null hypothesis, at least if we want to keep the probability of a Type I error below .05.

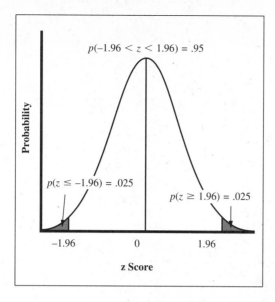

FIGURE 12.3 Probability of a *z* score ≥ 1.96 or ≤ -1.96 in a normal distribution. If the null hypothesus is true, 95% of sample *z* scores will fall between -1.96 and $+1.96$ in a normal distribution; only 5% will fall outside the range -1.96 to $+1.96$.

Interpreting the Results. In an article, we might include a sentence such as the following to summarize our findings:

> The results of our study do not provide evidence that the average Psychasthenia score for college professors is higher than that for the average adult, $z = +1.7$, ns.

The *ns* stands for "not significant," and indicates a nonsignificant result. The evidence was not sufficient to justify rejecting the null hypothesis. The scientific hypothesis that college professors are more anxious than the average adult was not supported by the data from our research study.

Had the results been significant, the sign of $z_{\overline{Y}}$ would indicate the direction of the difference. A significant positive $z_{\overline{Y}}$ value would indicate the sample mean was greater than μ_0, the μ suggested by the null hypothesis. This would suggest that the average Psychasthenia score for college professors is greater than the average for adults in general, providing support for the scientific hypothesis. A significant negative $z_{\overline{Y}}$ value would indicate the sample mean was less than μ_0, suggesting college professors are less anxious than the average adult.

12.1.5 Conditions for Using the Test

Conditions. The one-group *z* test may be used when (1) members of the sample produce a **quantitative variable**, *a variable that is either a ratio, interval, or continuous ordinal variable* (Davison & Sharma, 1988); (2) the null hypothesis has to do with the value of the parameter μ; and (3) the population standard deviation for the variable is known. These conditions are generally only met in observational studies where the goal is to evaluate whether there is a difference between some special group and a population with a known mean and standard deviation.

Assumptions. The test requires the following statistical assumptions:

1. Subjects are randomly and independently sampled from some population.
2. *The population from which the sample was drawn is normally distributed* (called the **normality assumption**).

The second assumption is called a **parametric assumption**, *an assumption about the distribution of scores for the population from which a sample was drawn.* You probably will never know if this assumption is true, since you do not have access to the entire population. *A hypothesis testing statistic which requires parametric assumptions* is called a **parametric test**. The one-group *z* test can be contrasted with the binomial test briefly introduced in Chapter 10, which did not require any information about the shape of the population distribution other than that provided by assuming the null hypothesis is true. The binomial test is an example of a **nonparametric test**, *an inferential statistic which requires no assumptions about the shape of the population distribution.*

Failure to Meet the Assumptions. If these assumptions are not met, the alpha level associated with the critical value ±1.96 may be different than .05. For example, if the population distribution of Psychasthenia scores among college professors is severely skewed, then the sampling distribution of the mean for samples from this population will also be skewed, at least if *N* is small. This means that the probability associated with the critical value ±1.96 may be something different than .05. Unless you know the shape of the population distribution, you cannot be sure about the shape of the sampling distribution if *N* is small.

Robustness. This is why the Central Limit Theorem is important. As the sample size increases, the sampling distribution of the mean will approach a normal distribution. Even if the population is not normally distributed, the critical value associated with a .05 alpha level will still be approximately ±1.96 if the sample is sufficiently large. A good rule of thumb for the one-group *z* test is that once $N \geq 30$ the sampling distribution will usually look very much like a normal distribution, and the values in Table E–3 of Appendix E can be considered correct even if the population is not normally distributed. However, if the population distribution is extremely nonnormal, sample sizes as large a 100 may be necessary before the sampling distribution of the mean looks like a normal distribution.

A parametric test is considered **robust** when *under certain conditions, violation of a parametric assumption does not affect the probability of a Type I error associated with the critical value.* The one-group *z* test is generally considered robust against violation of the normality assumption when $N \geq 30$. This is fortunate, because research suggests that populations are rarely normally distributed. Micceri (1989) examined over 400 cases in which researchers had sampled a large portion of a population, and did not find a single case in which the data suggested the population was normally distributed. When a significance test is based on the assumption that a population is normally distributed you should always insure you are robust against violating the normality assumption, since this assumption is usually questionable.

12.1.6 Directional versus Nondirectional Hypotheses

If we had decided to use directional hypotheses, the null and alternative hypotheses for our study would be

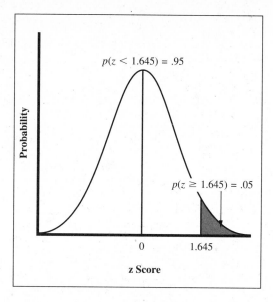

FIGURE 12.4   Probability of a *z* score ≥ 1.645 in a normal distribution. If the null hypothesis is true, 95% of sample *z* scores will be less than $+1.645$; only 5% will equal or exceed $+1.645$.

$$H_0: \mu \leq 50$$

$$H_1: \mu > 50.$$

Just like the binomial test, the presence of the "greater than" sign in the alternative hypothesis indicates that the critical region is in the upper tail of the sampling distribution. Looking at Table E–3 again, the critical value for the test of this directional hypothesis would be $z_{\alpha(D)=.05} = +1.645$. Only 5% of sample $z_{\overline{Y}}$ values would equal $+1.645$ or more if the null hypothesis is true (see Figure 12.4). Since $z_{\overline{Y}}$ for our sample was $+1.7$, we would have been able to reject the null hypothesis had a one-tailed test been used rather than a two-tailed test.

Suppose our scientific hypothesis suggested that college professors tend to be less anxious than the average adult. In this case the null and alternative hypotheses would be

$$H_0: \mu \geq 50$$

$$H_1: \mu < 50.$$

The "less than" sign suggests the critical region is in the lower tail of the sampling distribution based on the null hypothesis; the critical value would be $z_{\alpha(D)=.05} = -1.645$. The sample $z_{\overline{Y}}$ would have to be ≤ -1.645 in order to reject the null hypothesis. We would not have been able to reject the null hypothesis because our $z_{\overline{Y}}$ value was positive. This and other aspects of the one-group *z* test are summarized in Table 12.1.

12.1.7 Power and Sample Size Issues

In the last chapter I identified three factors that affect the power of the study: the alpha level, the effect size, and the sample size. The effect size for the one-group *z* test is in turn determined by two factors. The larger the difference between the true μ and μ_0, the larger the effect size. In addition, the smaller the standard deviation of the population (σ_Y), the

TABLE 12.1   Selected Aspects of the One-Group *z* Test

Test Symbol	Type of Statistical Hypotheses	General Form of Statistical Hypotheses	Type of Test	Symbol for Alpha	Critical Region in
$z_{\bar{Y}}$	nondirectional	$H_0: \mu =?$ $H_1: \mu \neq?$	two-tailed	α	both tails (both positive and negative critical values)
	directional	$H_0: \mu \leq?$ $H_1: \mu >?$	one-tailed	$\alpha(D)$	upper tail (critical value is positive)
	directional	$H_0: \mu \geq?$ $H_1: \mu <?$	one-tailed	$\alpha(D)$	lower tail (critical value is negative)

Note. The ? in the statistical hypotheses refer to some value defined by the researcher.

larger the effect size. Table C–2 in Appendix C provides the sample sizes necessary with small, medium, and large effect sizes to achieve .80 and .90 power. It seems reasonable to assume a medium effect size in this case. If the difference between the μ for college professors and adults in general is so small that it is difficult to observe, it probably does not matter very much; on the other hand, it does not seem reasonable to suggest the effect is worthwhile identifying only if it is grossly obvious. The sample size necessary for a medium effect with $\alpha = .05$ and $\beta = .10$ (power $= .90$) is 44. A sample size of 100 demonstrates more than the acceptable level of power.

12.2 THE LOGIC OF INTERVAL ESTIMATION

This section deals with interval estimation, the second category of inferential statistic to be discussed in this text. **Interval estimation statistics** are *inferential statistics that use sample statistics to estimate an interval of scores in which a parameter is likely to fall.* The goal of hypothesis testing is to make a decision about whether a null hypothesis concerning a parameter is true; the goal of interval estimation is to provide an estimate of the value of a parameter.

   We know that the sample mean is the best single sample estimate of the population μ. However, we also know that sample means will vary. It would be helpful if we could define an interval of scores within which we could be fairly confident the μ falls. This interval is called the **confidence interval**, *an interval of values associated with an established level of confidence of including some parameter.* The next section will describe the computation of the confidence interval for our sample of college professors.

12.2.1 The Confidence Interval for μ when σ_Y is Known

A sample of 100 college professors was used to evaluate the null hypothesis that college professors are as anxious as the average adult. Based on the sample mean of 51.7, it was determined that this null hypothesis could not be rejected. This same sample will be used to estimate the mean Psychasthenia score in the population of college professors represented by this sample.

We know that if the population of college professor Psychasthenia scores is normally distributed, or if $N \geq 30$, then the sampling distribution of the mean may be treated as a normal distribution. If the sampling distribution is normally distributed, 95% of the sample means will fall within 1.96 standard errors of the mean of the sampling distribution, which equals μ. This also implies that for 95% of random samples of 100 college professors, the mean of the sampling distribution (and therefore μ) falls within 1.96 standard errors of the sample mean.

If we subtract 1.96 standard errors from the sample mean, and add 1.96 standard errors to the sample mean, we will have defined the lower and upper endpoints of an interval of values. In 95% of the samples, the mean of the sampling distribution (and therefore μ) will fall within this interval. For our sample of 100 college professors, where $\overline{Y} = 51.7$ and $\sigma_Y = 10$,

$$LL_{.95} = 51.7 - 1.96 \left(\frac{10}{\sqrt{100}} \right) = 51.7 - 1.96 = 49.74,$$

$$UL_{.95} = 51.7 + 1.96 \left(\frac{10}{\sqrt{100}} \right) = 51.7 + 1.96 = 53.66.$$

$LL_{.95} = 49.74$ represents the lower limit of the confidence interval, $UL_{.95} = 53.66$ the upper limit.

Since for 95% of sample means this interval would include μ, we can be *95% confident* that the confidence interval for this particular sample includes μ.[1] This interval is therefore known as the 95% confidence interval. We can state with 95% confidence that the μ for Psychasthenia scores in the population of college professors falls between 49.74 and 53.66.

The formula for the confidence interval for μ when σ_Y is known can be stated in the following general form:

$$LL_{(1-\alpha)} = \overline{Y} - z_\alpha (\sigma_{\overline{Y}}) = \overline{Y} - z_\alpha \left(\frac{\sigma_Y}{\sqrt{N}} \right),$$

$$UL_{(1-\alpha)} = \overline{Y} + z_\alpha (\sigma_{\overline{Y}}) = \overline{Y} + z_\alpha \left(\frac{\sigma_Y}{\sqrt{N}} \right).$$

For example, suppose we wanted to define the confidence interval in which μ is expected to fall 80% of the time. Table E–3 in Appendix E indicates that $z_{\alpha=.20} = 1.28$: 20% of z scores will be greater than $+1.28$ or less than -1.28 in a normal distribution. The 80% confidence interval for our sample would equal

$$LL_{.80} = 51.7 - 1.28 \left(\frac{10}{\sqrt{100}} \right) = 51.7 - 1.28 = 50.42,$$

$$UL_{.80} = 51.7 + 1.28 \left(\frac{10}{\sqrt{100}} \right) = 51.7 + 1.28 = 52.98.$$

---

[1] See the discussion of confidence in Section 9.1.

Notice that the range of scores associated with the 80% confidence interval (52.98 −50.42 = 2.56) is smaller than the range associated with the 95% confidence interval (53.66–49.74 = 3.92). *The higher the desired level of confidence that the parameter is included in the interval, the wider the confidence interval has to be.*

Use of this formula requires conditions similar to those for the one-group z test: (1) Members of the sample produce a quantitative variable, (2) you are interested in estimating the value of μ, and (3) the population standard deviation for the variable is known. Use of the formula requires the random and independent sampling and normality assumptions. However, the formula is generally considered robust against violation of the normality assumption if $N \geq 30$.

12.2.2 Confidence Intervals versus Hypothesis Testing

There is an interesting relationship between the confidence interval and the corresponding hypothesis test. Using the one-group z test I was not able to reject the null hypothesis that $\mu = 50$ with $\alpha = .05$. Notice that the value 50 falls within the 95% confidence interval for our sample of behavioral science majors. This is no coincidence. *If you are not able to reject the null hypothesis at $\alpha = .05$, then the null hypothesis value for the parameter will fall within the 95% confidence interval; if you are able to reject the null hypothesis at $\alpha = .05$, then the null hypothesis value for the parameter will not fall within the 95% confidence interval.* This relationship is true at any alpha level. However, it is only true for two-tailed tests, since the confidence interval as described here uses both tails of the distribution.

This has led many people to suggest that confidence intervals are preferable to hypothesis tests. Confidence intervals not only let you draw a conclusion about the null hypothesis, but give you an estimate of the parametric value as well. In practice, hypothesis testing statistics remain more popular. This is partly because corresponding confidence intervals are not readily available for every hypothesis test, and partly because of greater familiarity and comfort with hypothesis tests among behavioral researchers. For this reason, the emphasis in the remainder of this book is on hypothesis testing rather than on interval estimation.

KEY TERMS

Central Limit Theorem

confidence interval

directional hypothesis

interval estimation statistics

nondirectional hypothesis

nonparametric test

normal distribution

normality assumption

parametric assumption

parametric test

power

quantitative variable

robust

sample size

sampling distribution of the mean

significant result

standard deviation

standard error

standard error of the mean

standard score

EXERCISES

Answers to all exercises may be found in Appendix B.

1. Indicate whether the conditions for using the one-group z test are met in each of the following cases:
   a. Males are compared to females on responses to an attitude survey with known standard deviation.
   b. Adolescents respond to the statement "I feel good about myself" on a 5-point scale from Strongly Disagree (1) to Strongly Agree (5). The scientific hypothesis suggests that the population mean score differs from the neutral point (3) on this scale. To the researcher's knowledge, self-esteem has never been measured using this rating scale before.
   c. The variance of a certain children's test of creative thinking is known to equal 5.3. A researcher is interested in whether the capacity for creativity is different in children who do not have siblings than it is in the population in general.

2. A researcher is interested in whether applicants to medical schools tend to be brighter than the general population of college graduates. Suppose that on the Wechsler Adult Intelligence Scale (Wechsler, 1981), or WAIS, the mean score among college graduates is known to equal 112.73 with a standard deviation of 13.27.
   a. State the non-directional statistical hypotheses for this study.
   b. Is this a *true experiment*, *quasi-experiment*, or *observational study*?
   c. Assuming a large effect size is considered the smallest important effect, and the researcher would like to use $\alpha = .01$, $\beta = .10$, what is the appropriate sample size for this study?
   d. The researcher is able to gather a sample of 15 medical school applicants and administer the WAIS. Use the following scores to compute the one-group z test:

112	123	132	121	115
118	110	108	109	126
111	114	110	123	118

   e. What is the critical value for $\alpha = .01$? What is the appropriate decision concerning rejection of the null hypothesis?
   f. How might these results be interpreted?

3. Indicate whether the following statements about the sampling distribution of the mean are *true* or *false*.
   a. The sampling distribution of the mean is always normally distributed.
   b. The larger the sample sizes, the greater the variability in a sampling distribution of sample means.
   c. In a single sampling distribution, all samples must be of equal sample size.
   d. A sampling distribution is based on an infinite set of random samples.
   e. The larger the sample size, the better any one sample mean will approximate the population μ.

4. It is found that sixth graders on average spend 1.2 hours doing homework each weeknight, with a standard deviation of .4 hours. The distribution is normal. If we could collect an infinite number of random samples containing 100 sixth graders, and compute the mean time spent on homework for each sample:
   a. What would be the average of these sample means?
   b. On average, how much would sample means vary from the distribution mean?
   c. What is the probability that a random sample of 100 students would produce a sample mean of 1.12 hours or less?

5. a. Compute the 99% confidence interval associated with the data from Question 2d.
   b. Are the results of the interval estimation consistent with the results of the hypothesis test? If so, in what way? If not, why not?

6. Explain why failure to reject the null hypothesis using a two-tailed test suggests that the null hypothesis value will fall within the corresponding confidence interval.

PART V

Population Patterns
Inferential Statistics for One Variable

The remaining chapters are devoted primarily to the description of various inferential statistics. Each chapter focuses on a single inferential statistic, which means they are shorter than previous chapters. For each statistic the description will follow the same general pattern, although some topics may be omitted:

- an introduction to the statistic
- developing the null and alternative hypotheses
- testing the null hypothesis
- making a decision about the null hypothesis (including a discussion of interpreting the results)
- conditions for using the test
- directional versus nondirectional hypotheses
- power and sample size issues
- corresponding confidence intervals

To maintain consistency with the discussions of scientific hypotheses and descriptive statistics, inferential statistics will be divided into those used to evaluate hypotheses concerning the pattern of population data for a single variable, and those used to evaluate hypotheses concerning relationships between variables in the population. The two inferential statistics introduced so far, the binomial test and the one-group z test, are used to evaluate hypothesized population patterns: whether a certain pattern exists in the frequency data from a single variable. Two more such tests are introduced in Chapters 13 and 14. Chapter 13 focuses on the one-group t test, a test similar in purpose to the one-group z test. Chapter 14 introduces the chi-square goodness of fit test.

CHAPTER 13

The One-Group *t* Test

13.1 INTRODUCTION

The one-group z test was introduced in the last chapter as a hypothesis testing statistic which can be used when (1) members of the sample produce a quantitative variable, (2) the null hypothesis has to do with the value of the parameter μ, and (3) the population standard deviation for the variable is known. This last condition is rarely met. I have indicated it is unusual to have information about the value of a parameter. The one-group t test is a statistic which is used under circumstances similar to those for the one-group z test, except that the t test does not require knowledge of σ_Y. The trade-off is that the computation of the one-group t test and determination of the critical value are more complicated.

13.2 DEFINING THE NULL AND ALTERNATIVE HYPOTHESES

In the last chapter the MMPI was administered to a sample of 100 college professors. If college professors are more anxious than the average adult, it was suggested that the mean Psychasthenia t score for the population of college professors is greater than 50.

The null and alternative hypotheses for the one-group t test are the same as those for the one-group z test. The nondirectional statistical hypotheses are

$$H_0: \mu = 50$$
$$H_1: \mu \neq 50.$$

The directional versions would be

$$H_0: \mu \leq 50$$
$$H_1: \mu > 50.$$

To be consistent with the last chapter I will use the nondirectional hypotheses.

13.3 TESTING THE NULL HYPOTHESIS

The formula for the one-group z test is

$$z_{\bar{Y}} = \frac{\bar{Y} - \mu_0}{\sigma_{\bar{Y}}} = \frac{\bar{Y} - \mu_0}{\dfrac{\sigma_Y}{\sqrt{N}}},$$

a formula that requires knowledge of the standard deviation for the population. The one-group t test formula uses the best sample estimate of σ_Y instead, s_Y (introduced in Chapter 6):

$$t_{\bar{y}} = \frac{\bar{Y} - \mu_0}{s_{\bar{Y}}} = \frac{\bar{Y} - \mu_0}{\dfrac{s_Y}{\sqrt{N}}}$$

$$= \frac{\bar{Y} - \mu_0}{\sqrt{\dfrac{\sum\limits_{i=1}^{N} Y_i^2 - \dfrac{\left(\sum\limits_{i=1}^{N} Y_i\right)^2}{N}}{N(N-1)}}}$$

The symbol $t_{\bar{Y}}$ indicates this is a t test for a single group mean. The last formula represents a computational formula for t based on the computational formula for s_Y. Procedure Box 13.1 demonstrates the computation of the one-group t test.

It is important to be clear about the distinction between s_Y and $s_{\bar{Y}}$. s_Y is the best sample estimate of the population standard deviation. If we could compute a standard deviation using the Y score for each member of the population, s_Y would be the best sample estimate of this value. $s_{\bar{Y}}$ is the best sample estimate of the standard error of the sampling distribution of the mean. If we could compute the means for an infinite number of random samples drawn from the population, and compute the standard deviation of these means, $s_{\bar{Y}}$ would be the best sample estimate of this value.

Our sample of 100 college professors produced a sample mean of 51.7. Suppose that for this sample we find $s_Y = 12.32$. Then

$$t_{\bar{Y}} = \frac{51.7 - 50}{\dfrac{12.32}{\sqrt{100}}}$$

$$= +1.38.$$

13.4 MAKING A DECISION ABOUT THE NULL HYPOTHESIS

The t Distribution. If we collected many samples of 100 college professors and computed a t value for each sample, we could generate a t **distribution**: *a sampling distribution of t values for all random samples of a given size from some population.* As

The One-Group *t* Test

Goal   Five high school students rated their level of agreement with the statement "I feel good about myself" on a 5-point scale:

>   1 = Strongly Disagree
>
>   2 = Disagree
>
>   3 = Unsure or Neutral
>
>   4 = Agree
>
>   5 = Strongly Agree

Compute the *t* value associated with the null hypothesis that the mean response in the population would be "Unsure or Neutral" (3) from the following data:

>   Student 1: 4
>
>   Student 2: 3
>
>   Student 3: 5
>
>   Student 4: 3
>
>   Student 5: 2

$$t_{\overline{y}} = \frac{\overline{Y} - \mu_0}{\sqrt{\dfrac{\displaystyle\sum_{i=1}^{N} Y_i^2 - \dfrac{\left(\displaystyle\sum_{i=1}^{N} Y_i\right)^2}{N}}{N(N-1)}}}$$

Step 1   *Compute the sum of Y and Y^2 and the mean of Y.*

	Y	Y^2
	4	16
	3	9
	5	25
	3	9
	2	4
Sums:	17	63
Mean:	3.4	

Continued

The one-group t test continued

Step 2   *Square the sum of the scores and divide by N.*

$$\frac{\left(\sum_{i=1}^{N} Y_i\right)^2}{N} = \frac{17^2}{5} = 57.8$$

Step 3   *Subtract the result of Step 2 from the sum of the squared scores, divide by $N(N-1)$, and find the square root.*

$$\frac{s_Y}{\sqrt{N}} = \sqrt{\frac{63 - 57.8}{5(5-1)}} = .5099 \longleftarrow \textit{This number must be positive}$$

Step 4   *Subtract the null hypothesis μ from $\overline{Y}$.*

$$\overline{Y} - \mu_0 = 3.4 - 3.0 = .4$$

Step 5   *Divide the result of Step 4 by the result of Step 3.*

$$t_{\overline{Y}} = \frac{.4}{.5099} = .785$$

with other sampling distributions it is possible to define the characteristics of the t distribution:

1. Assuming random and independent sampling and a normal population distribution, the shape of the t distribution for the one-group t test depends on the degrees of freedom, which for the one group t test equals $N-1$.
2. If the null hypothesis is true then the mean of the t distribution will equal zero, since on average $\overline{Y}$ will equal μ_0 and $\overline{Y} - \mu_0$ will equal zero.

Degrees of Freedom. The first characteristic represents an important difference between the t distribution and the sampling distribution of the mean. If we assume the population is normally distributed, then the sampling distribution of the mean is also normally distributed. The critical value is the same regardless of the sample size. In contrast, if we assume the population is normally distributed, the shape of the t distribution still varies depending on $N-1$. This means that the critical value will change as $N-1$ changes. Figure 13.1 provides the t distributions when $N-1 = 1$, 5, and 20 if the population is normally distributed and the null hypothesis is true. A normal distribution is placed alongside so you can see the difference between the t and normal distributions. Notice that all three t distributions are symmetrical. When $N-1$ is small, the t distribution is platykurtic: the relative frequency of values in the tails is greater than in the normal distribution, so the

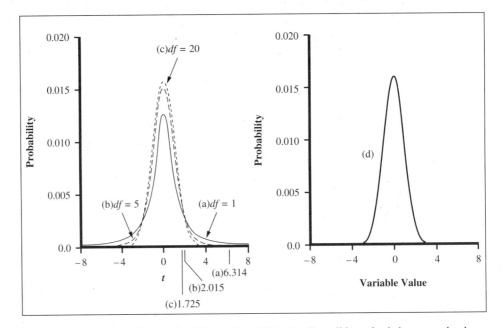

FIGURE 13.1 The *t* distribution for $df = 1, 5$, and 20 when the null hypothesis is assumed to be true. (a) The *t* distributions for $df = 1$ if the null hypothesis is true; the critical value at a $\alpha(d) = .05$ is 6.314. (b) The *t* distribution for $df = 5$ if the null hypothesis is true; the critical value a $\alpha(D) = .05$ is 2.015. (c) The *t* distribution for $df = 20$ if the null hypothesis is true; the critical value at $\alpha(D) = .05$ is 1.725. A normal distribution (d) is placed next to the *t* distributions for purposes of comparison. Notice that as the degrees of freedom increase, the *t* distribution looks more like the normal distribution.

body of the bell looks flatter. However, the *t* distribution looks more like the normal distribution as $N - 1$ increases.

$N - 1$ is referred to as the degrees of freedom (df). For our purposes, I will define the **degrees of freedom** as *a variable which determines the shape of a sampling distribution*. A more detailed explanation of degrees of freedom is offered in the supplement.

The Critical Value. A table of critical values for the *t* distribution for various values of df and α is provided in Table D-1 of Appendix D. Critical *t* values will be indicated by the symbol $t_{\alpha, df}$. Part of Table D-1 is repeated here as Table 13.1. To read Tables 13.1 and D-1, move down the column which corresponds to the desired alpha level until you come to the row that corresponds to the degrees of freedom from your sample. For example, if $N = 41$, then $df = 40$, and Table 13.1 indicates that the two-tailed critical value for the test of the nondirectional null hypothesis is $t_{\alpha=0.5, df=40} = \pm 2.021$. We can reject the null hypothesis if

$$|t_{\bar{Y}}| \geq 2.021.$$

The degrees of freedom for our sample of college professors equal $N - 1 = 99$. This value is not included in Table D-1. The closest values provided are 60 ($t_{\alpha=.05, df=60} = \pm 2.000$)

TABLE 13.1   A Portion of Table D-1

	Alpha Level				
	two-tailed				
			↓		
	.20	.10	.05	.02	.01
	one-tailed				
df	.10	.05	.025	.01	.005
30	1.310	1.697	2.042	2.457	2.750
→ 40	1.303	1.684	**2.021**	2.423	2.704
60	1.296	1.671	2.000	2.390	2.660
120	1.289	1.658	1.980	2.358	2.617
∞	1.282	1.645	1.960	2.326	2.576

Source: Adapted from Tables II, III, IV, and VII of Fisher & Yates; STATISTICAL TABLES FOR BIOLOGICAL, AGRICULTURAL AND MEDICAL RESEARCH. Published by Longman Group UK Ltd., 1974. I am grateful to the Longman Group UK Ltd., on behalf of the Literary Executor of the late Sir Ronald A. Fisher, F. R. S. and Dr. Frank Yates, F. R. S. for permission to adapt Tables II, III, IV, and VII from *Statistical Tables for Biological, Agricultural and Medical Research 6/E* (1974).

and 120 ($t_{\alpha=.05,\,df=120} = \pm 1.980$). Table 13.2 provides guidelines for determining whether a result is significant for nontabled degrees of freedom. Based on these guidelines, in the present case we cannot reject the null hypothesis since $t_{\bar{Y}} < 1.980$. Using the interpolation formula from Table 13.2, the correct critical value is estimated to be ± 1.987. Once again, we do not have sufficient evidence to suggest college professors are any different than the general adult population in terms of anxiety.

Interpreting the Results. The one-group t test is interpreted in the same way as the one-group z test. If the t test is not significant, you do not have evidence that the population μ differs from the null hypothesis μ. If the result is significant, the sign of $t_{\bar{Y}}$ indicates the direction of the difference. A significant positive $t_{\bar{Y}}$ value suggests the population μ is greater than μ_0; a significant negative $t_{\bar{Y}}$ value suggests the population μ is less than μ_0.

13.5 CONDITIONS FOR USING THE TEST

Conditions. The one-group t test may be used when (1) members of the sample produce a quantitative variable, and (2) the null hypothesis has to do with the value of the parameter μ. Rejection of the null hypothesis suggests the existence of a proposed pattern for scores in the population.

Examples of other studies in which the one-group t test could be used include:

1. an observational study to investigate whether police officers differ from the general adult population on some rating scale where the mean for the general adult population is known
2. a quasi-experiment in which subjects exposed to some treatment are compared to their original population to see if the treatment changed their mean score
3. an observational study to investigate whether scores differ from some neutral point (see Procedure Box 13.1 for an example)

Assumptions. The test requires the following statistical assumptions:

1. random and independent sampling
2. the normality assumption. As with the sampling distribution of the mean, recommended critical values are incorrect if this assumption is not met, but the one-group *t*

TABLE 13.2 Determining Significance for Nontabled Degrees of Freedom

1. If the desired degrees of freedom are larger than the largest value in the table, use the critical value associated with infinity (∞). The largest tabled degrees of freedom value in Table D-1 is 120. For any larger degrees of freedom, use the critical value for ∞ degrees of freedom.

2. In many cases the desired degrees of freedom fall between two tabled values. Determining whether the result is significant requires the following variables:

   df_D refers to the desired degrees of freedom
   df_L is the next larger degrees of freedom in the table
   df_S is the next smaller degrees of freedom in the table
   t_L is the next larger critical value in the table
   t_S is the next smaller critical value in the table

   To determine whether $t_{\bar{Y}}$ is significant proceed as follows:
   a. If $t_{\bar{Y}} \geq t_L$ you can reject the null hypothesis at the desired alpha level; estimation of the critical value is not necessary.
   b. If $t_{\bar{Y}} < t_S$ you cannot reject the null hypothesis at the desired alpha level; estimation of the critical value is not necessary.
   c. If $t_S \leq t_{\bar{Y}} < t_L$ you must estimate the critical value using the *interpolation formula*:

$$t_{\alpha, df_D} = t_s + \frac{df_L - df_D}{df_L - df_S}(t_L - t_S).$$

Example:

If $df_D = 99$ and $\alpha = .05$:

$$df_L = 120$$
$$df_s = 60$$
$$t_L = 2.000$$
$$t_s = 1.980.$$

If $t_{\bar{Y}} = 2.000$ you can reject the null hypothesis at $\alpha = .05$. If $t_{\bar{Y}} < 1.980$ you cannot reject the null hypothesis at $\alpha = .05$. If $t_{\bar{Y}} = 1.99$, you must estimate the critical value using the interpolation formula:

$$t_{\alpha=.05, df=99} = 1.980 + \frac{120 - 99}{120 - 60}(2.000 - 1.980)$$
$$= 1.987.$$

Although the method is stated here in terms of the *t* statistic, it is applicable to any other inferential statistic for which the critical value is determined by degrees of freedom.

test is generally considered robust against violation of the normality assumption once $N \geq 30$.

13.6 DIRECTIONAL VERSUS NONDIRECTIONAL HYPOTHESES

The directional alternative and null hypotheses for a one-group t test are the same as those for a one-group z test. For the test of the scientific hypothesis that college professors are more anxious than the average adult:

$$H_0: \mu \leq 50$$
$$H_1: \mu > 50.$$

As with the binomial test, the symbol $>$ in the alternative hypothesis indicates that a one-tailed test with a critical region in the upper tail of the sampling distribution would be appropriate. Critical values for one-tailed tests are provided in Table D-1 of Appendix D. For example, if the sample size is 41, then $df = 40$, and $t_{\alpha(D)=.05,\, df=40} = 1.684$. As you can see from Table 13.1, you can reject the null hypothesis if

$$t_{\bar{Y}} \geq +1.684.$$

For the scientific hypothesis that college professors are less anxious than the average adult, the directional alternative and corresponding null hypotheses would be

$$H_0: \mu \geq 50$$
$$H_1: \mu < 50,$$

and for $N = 41$ you can reject the null hypothesis if

$$t_{\bar{Y}} \leq -1.684.$$

This and other aspects of the one-group t test are summarized in Table 13.3. Again, nondirectional hypotheses (which require a two-tailed test with critical regions in each tail of the sampling distribution) are generally preferred because they allow achieving significance even if the results are contrary to expectation.

TABLE 13.3   Selected Aspects of the One-Group t Test

Symbol Used	Degrees of Freedom	Type of Statistical Hypotheses	General Form of Statistical Hypotheses	Type of Test	Symbol for Alpha	Critical Region in
$t_{\bar{Y}}$	$N - 1$	nondirectional	$H_0: \mu = ?$ $H_1: \mu \neq ?$	two-tailed	α	both tails (both positive and negative critical values)
		directional	$H_0: \mu \leq ?$ $H_1: \mu > ?$	one-tailed	$\alpha\,(D)$	upper tail (critical value is positive)
		directional	$H_0: \mu \geq ?$ $H_1: \mu < ?$	one-tailed	$\alpha\,(D)$	lower tail (critical value is negative)

Note: The ? in the statistical hypotheses refer to some value defined by the researcher.

13.7 POWER AND SAMPLE SIZE ISSUES

Like the one-group z test, the power of the one-group t test is determined by three factors: the alpha level, the sample size, and the effect size. The effect size is a function of the difference between the true μ and μ_0, and the size of σ_Y. As the difference between μ and μ_0 increases, the effect size increases; as the size of σ_Y increases, the effect size decreases.

Table C-2 in Appendix C provides the sample size necessary with small, medium, and large effect sizes to achieve .80 and .90 power for the one-group t test as well as for the one-group z test. In Chapter 9 I suggested a medium effect size might be considered the smallest important effect for this study. For $\alpha = .05$, $\beta = .10$, and a medium effect size the desired sample size is 44. A study with $N = 100$ demonstrates a very high level of power.

13.8 CONFIDENCE INTERVALS

The formula for computing the confidence interval for μ when σ is unknown is

$$LL_{(1-\alpha)} = \overline{Y} - t_{\alpha,df}(s_{\overline{Y}}) = \overline{Y} - t_{\alpha,df}\left(\frac{s_Y}{\sqrt{N}}\right),$$

$$UL_{(1-\alpha)} = \overline{Y} + t_{\alpha,df}(s_{\overline{Y}}) = \overline{Y} + t_{\alpha,df}\left(\frac{s_Y}{\sqrt{N}}\right).$$

If your sample of 100 college professors produced a mean Psychasthenia score of 51.7 with $s_Y = 12.32$, the 95% confidence interval would be

$$LL_{.95} = 51.7 - 1.987\left(\frac{12.32}{\sqrt{100}}\right) = 49.25,$$

$$UL_{.95} = 51.7 + 1.987\left(\frac{12.32}{\sqrt{100}}\right) = 54.15.$$

The value 1.987 was determined to be the critical value for $t_{\alpha=.05,\,df=99}$ in Table 13.2. The presence of the null hypothesis value of 50 in the 95% confidence interval is consistent with the failure to reject the null hypothesis at $\alpha = .05$. The results suggest we can be 95% confident that the mean Psychasthenia score in our population of college professors falls between 49.25 and 54.15.

Use of this formula requires conditions similar to those for the one-group t test: (1) members of the sample produce a quantitative variable, and (2) you are interested in estimating the value of μ. The formula requires the random and independent sampling and normality assumptions. Like the one-group t test, the confidence interval formula is robust against violation of the normality assumption if $N \geq 30$.

KEY TERMS

alternative hypothesis
confidence interval
degrees of freedom
directional hypothesis
nondirectional hypothesis
normality assumption
null hypothesis

platykurtic distribution
power
quantitative variable
robust
sample size
sampling distribution
t distribution

EXERCISES

Answers to all exercises may be found in Appendix B.

1. Indicate whether the conditions for using the one-group *t* test are met in each of the following cases:
   a. Males are compared to females on responses to an attitude survey with known standard deviation.
   b. Adolescents respond to the statement "I feel good about myself" on a 5-point scale from Strongly Disagree (1) to Strongly Agree (5). The scientific hypothesis suggests that the population mean score differs from the neutral point (3) on this scale. To the researcher's knowledge, self-esteem has never been measured using this rating scale before.
   c. The variance of a certain children's test of creative thinking is known to equal 5.3. A researcher is interested in whether the capacity for creativity is different in children who do not have siblings than it is in the population in general.

2. A researcher is interested in whether applicants to medical schools tend to be brighter than the general population of college graduates. Suppose that on the Wechsler Adult Intelligence Scale (Wechsler, 1981), or WAIS, the mean score among college graduates is known to equal 112.73.
   a. State the directional statistical hypotheses for this study.
   b. Assuming a medium effect size is considered the smallest important effect, and the researcher would like to use $\alpha(D) = .05$, $\beta = .20$, what is the appropriate sample size for this study?
   c. The researcher is able to gather a sample of 15 medical school applicants and administer the WAIS. Use the following scores to compute the one-group *t* test.

112	123	132	121	115
118	110	108	109	126
111	114	110	123	118

   d. What is the critical value for $\alpha(D) = .05$? Can the researcher reject the null hypothesis?
   e. How might these results be interpreted? Be as detailed as possible.

3. Subjects are asked to indicate their support for placing restrictions on the types of music record stores can sell to minors on the following scale:

   1 = Completely in Support of Restrictions
   2 = Mainly in Support of Restrictions
   3 = More in Support than Opposed
   4 = Neutral
   5 = More Opposed than in Support
   6 = Mainly Opposed to Restrictions
   7 = Completely Opposed to Restrictions.

   a. Explain why nondirectional statistical hypotheses would clearly be more appropriate in this study than directional hypotheses.
   b. State the nondirectional hypotheses. Explain your reasoning.
   c. What type of study is this: a *true experiment*, *quasi-experiment*, or *observational study*? Explain your choice.
   d. This is a case where, since the general American population is so large, even a small difference in the percentage of voters can impact on lawmakers' decisions. Given this, what would be the desirable sample size for $\alpha = .05$ and $\beta = .20$?
   e. The researcher instead gathers the self-ratings of 20 adult Americans. Use the following scores to compute the one-group *t* test.

5	6	4	3	2
7	4	6	3	4
6	3	2	5	4
1	7	6	2	6

f. What is the critical value for $\alpha = .05$? Can the researcher reject the null hypothesis?

g. How might these results be interpreted? Be as detailed as possible.

4. A researcher is interested in whether nutritional supplements administered to adults can increase intelligence as measured by scores on the Wechsler Adult Intelligence Scale (WAIS). The researcher identifies a sample of adults who are willing to participate in a study on the impact of nutritional supplements on intelligence, and administers a supplement treatment for six months. At the end of six months, all subjects are administered the WAIS.

a. Explain why nondirectional statistical hypotheses would be more appropriate in this study than directional hypotheses.

b. It is known that the mean score on the WAIS in adults is 100. State the nondirectional hypotheses. Explain your reasoning.

c. What type of study is this: a *true experiment*, *quasi-experiment*, or *observational study*? Explain your choice.

d. The nutritional supplement treatment is one that is not known to have any significant side effects; there are occasional mild negative reactions which disappear shortly after discontinuing the supplement. However, the long-term effects of using the supplement are not completely understood, although the available research has not found any long-term negative effects. In terms of changes in intelligence, differences of a few points on the WAIS would not have any real effects on a person's life. Given these considerations, what would you suggest as the smallest meaningful effect size?

e. Suppose you decide to assume a large effect size. For $\alpha = .02$, $\beta = .10$, what is the smallest desirable sample size?

f. The researcher only has 12 people who complete the treatment. Use the following WAIS scores to compute the one-group *t* test.

106	104	108	112
119	122	98	103
108	116	101	95

g. What is the critical value for $\alpha = .05$? Can the researcher reject the null hypothesis?

h. How might these results be interpreted? Be as detailed as possible. In particular, focus on problems with the validity of the study: what are the problems in this study, and how might the study be improved?

5.a. Compute the 99% confidence interval associated with the data from Question 1c. Is it appropriate to use the critical value you used to answer Question 1d to compute the confidence interval?

b. Are the results of the interval estimation consistent with the results of the hypothesis test? If so, in what way? If not, why not?

6.a. Compute the 95% confidence interval associated with the data from Question 2e. Is it appropriate to use the critical value you used to answer Question 2f to compute the confidence interval?

b. Are the results of the interval estimation consistent with the results of the hypothesis test? If so, in what way? If not, why not?

7.a. Compute the 99% confidence interval associated with the data from Question 3f. Is it appropriate to use the critical value you used to answer Question 3g to compute the confidence interval?

b. Are the results of the interval estimation consistent with the results of the hypothesis test? If so, in what way? If not, why not?

8. If the values in the sampling distribution of the mean are converted to z scores, the sampling distribution of the mean serves the same purpose for the one-group z test that the t distribution serves for the one-group t test. Answer the following questions about the z and t distributions.

a. If the null hypothesis is true, what will be the mean of the sampling distribution of z scores? What will be the mean of the sampling distribution of t scores?

b. If samples are drawn from a normally distributed population, under what conditions will the sampling distribution of z scores be normal? Under what conditions will the sampling distribution of t scores be normal?

c. For which distribution are the critical values generally larger? At what point is the same critical value used for both tests?

S13.1 MORE ON DEGREES OF FREEDOM

Suppose we have a set of N scores. The degrees of freedom refer to *the number of these scores that can vary freely*. The best estimate of a population standard deviation will be used to demonstrate this concept.

The definitional formula for s_Y is

$$s_Y = \sqrt{\frac{\sum_{i=1}^{N}(Y_i - \overline{Y})^2}{N-1}}.$$

The sample mean is subtracted from each score in the sample. In Chapter 5 the mean was referred to as the balance point of the distribution, indicating that differences from the mean must sum to zero:

$$\sum_{i=1}^{N}(Y_i - \overline{Y}) = 0.$$

For a set of N differences from the mean, only $N-1$ differences may vary freely; the Nth difference score must equal the value that results in the sum of the difference scores equaling zero. That is, the value of the last difference score is restricted by the requirement that the difference scores sum to zero. For the best sample estimate of the population standard deviation (s_Y), the number of differences from the mean that can vary freely is one less than the number of scores, or $N-1$. Since s_Y is incorporated into the formula for the one-group t test, the degrees of freedom for the one-group t test also equal $N-1$.

Critical values for the t, F, and χ^2 tests depend in part on the degrees of freedom. The mathematical restrictions on the number of scores that can vary freely differ for different statistical tests, so the method of computing the degrees of freedom will also differ. In all cases, though, the degrees of freedom reflect the number of data points that can vary freely.

CHAPTER 14

The Chi-Square Goodness of Fit Test

14.1 INTRODUCTION

The z and t tests introduced so far are used to test hypotheses concerning the value of μ for some quantitative variable. The chi-square (χ^2) goodness of fit test is used to evaluate questions concerning the probabilities associated with each value of a variable. Such questions are usually raised about variables with a relatively small number of values. A study on changes in the pattern of political views among American adults will be used to demonstrate the test.

14.2 DEFINING THE NULL AND ALTERNATIVE HYPOTHESES

Suppose that in 1969 a survey was conducted which found that 31.7% of American adults considered themselves liberal, 36.1% considered themselves conservative, and 32.2% considered themselves moderate in their political views. We suspect that the proportion of people who describe themselves as conservatives has increased since 1969. This scientific hypothesis has implications for the pattern of frequencies for the nominal variable political view. The 1969 survey will be replicated to test our scientific hypothesis.

The chi-square test evaluates whether a series of probabilities are accurate for a population. The null hypothesis for the present example may be stated as

H_0: p(liberal) $= .317$ and

   p(conservative) $= .361$ and

   p(moderate) $= .322$.

The alternative hypothesis may be stated as

H_1: p(liberal) $\neq .317$ and/or

   p(conservative) $\neq .361$ and/or

   p(moderate) $= .322$.

The alternative hypothesis may be stated more straightforwardly as

H_1: One or more of the null hypothesis probabilities is incorrect.

The chi-square goodness of fit test evaluates whether an entire set of probabilities suggested by the null hypothesis is accurate.

14.3 TESTING THE NULL HYPOTHESIS

If we assume the null hypothesis is true, we would expect the following frequencies in a sample of 1000 American adults:

liberal: .317(1000) = 317

conservative: .361(1000) = 361

moderate: .322(1000) = 322

Suppose we collect a sample of $N = 1000$, and find the sample frequencies to be:

liberal: 246

conservative: 349

moderate: 405

Are the differences between the observed frequencies and the expected frequencies due to chance, or do they reflect a true change in the population?

The chi-square goodness of fit statistic is computed using the formula

$$\chi^2 = \sum_{j=1}^{k} \frac{(f_{0_j} - f_{E_j})^2}{f_{E_j}},$$

where f_{0_j} refers to the observed frequency for value j of the variable, and f_{E_j} to the expected frequency. There are k values of the variable; in our study $k = 3$. Since the variable is nominal the order of the values is arbitrary. I will use $j = 1$ to refer to liberals, $j = 2$ to refer to conservatives, and $j = 3$ to refer to moderates. f_{0_1} refers to the observed frequency of value $j = 1$ (246). f_{E_1} refers to the expected frequency of value $j = 1$ (317). Procedure Box 14.1 illustrates the computation of χ^2 for the present example.

14.4 MAKING A DECISION ABOUT THE NULL HYPOTHESIS

The **chi-square distribution** is *a sampling distribution of chi-square values for all random samples of a given size from some population.* The shape of the χ^2 distribution depends solely on the degrees of freedom, where $df = k - 1$. Figure 14.1 provides examples of χ^2 distributions associated with 1, 5, and 20 degrees of freedom under the assumption that the null hypothesis is true. Unlike the sampling distribution of the mean and the t distribution, the χ^2 distribution is always positively skewed when the degrees of freedom are small. This is because differences between observed and expected frequencies are squared before they are added together, so χ^2 must be a positive value.

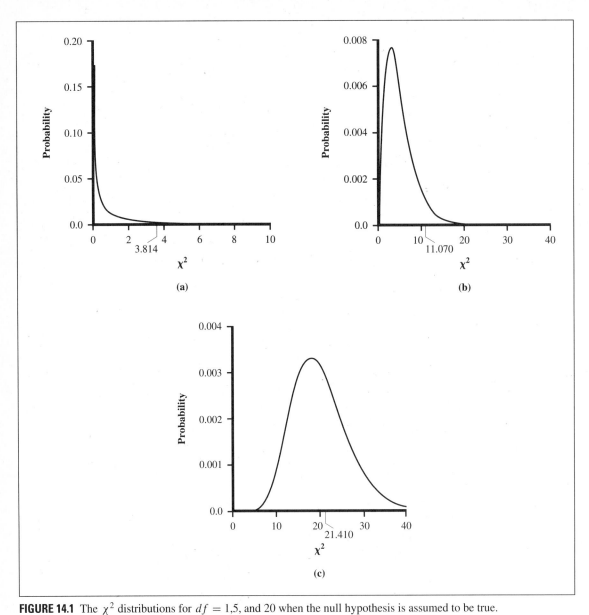

FIGURE 14.1 The χ^2 distributions for $df = 1, 5,$ and 20 when the null hypothesis is assumed to be true.
(a) The χ^2 distribution for $df = 1$ if the null hypothesis is true; the critical value at $\alpha = .05$ is 3.841.
(b) The χ^2 distribution for $df = 5$ if the null hypothesis is true; the critical value at $\alpha = .05$ is 11.070.
(c) The χ^2 distribution for $df = 20$ if the null hypothesis is true; the critical value at $\alpha = .05$ is 21.410.

There is a floor (0) but no ceiling, a situation that tends to produce positively skewed distributions.

The χ^2 distribution becomes less skewed as the degrees of freedom increase. Even if the null hypothesis is true, you can expect small differences between observed and expected frequencies to occur by chance. The larger the degrees of freedom, the more

PROCEDURE BOX 14.1

The Chi-Square Goodness of Fit Test

Goal   Use the following data on political view to compute the chi-square statistic:

	Observed	Expected
liberal	246	317
conservative	349	361
moderate	405	322

$$\chi^2 = \sum_{j=1}^{k} \frac{(f_{0_j} - f_{E_j})^2}{f_{E_j}}$$

Step 1   *Subtract the expected from observed frequencies, square the differences, and divide by the expected frequency.*

	Observed	Expected	Difference	Squared	Divided	
liberal	246	317	−71	5041	15.902	◄——*These numbers*
conservative	349	361	−12	144	0.399	◄——*must be*
moderate	405	322	83	6889	21.394	◄——*positive*

Step 2   *Sum the values in the last column of Step 1.*

$$\chi^2 = 15.902 + .399 + 21.394 = 37.695$$

squared differences are summed, and the larger the average chi-square value will be even if the null hypothesis is true. This characteristic of the chi-square statistic affects the sampling distribution in several ways:

1. The χ^2 test is always one-tailed. Negative z and t values occur when the sample mean is less than μ_0, so the lower tail of the distribution can be used to identify cases where μ seems to be less than μ_0. In the χ^2 distribution, values in the lower tail simply indicate small discrepancies between the observed and expected frequencies, a situation which should lead to non-rejection of the null hypothesis. Only χ^2 values in the upper tail of the distribution provide evidence of a significant result.
2. As the degrees of freedom increase, the critical value also increases. This contrasts with the t test, where the critical value decreases as the degrees of freedom increase.
3. Even though the χ^2 distribution based on the null hypothesis is extremely skewed when the degrees of freedom are small, with greater degrees of freedom the sampling distribution becomes less skewed.

Critical values associated with various degrees of freedom and alpha levels are provided in Table D–2 from Appendix D. For $df = k - 1 = 2$ and $\alpha = .05$, the one-tailed critical value of the nondirectional null hypothesis is $\chi^2_{\alpha=.05, df=2} = 5.991$; we can reject the null hypothesis if

$$\chi^2 \geq 5.991.$$

The computed value of 37.695 allows us to reject the null hypothesis that the population frequencies are the same as those found in 1969.

Interpreting the Results. If $k = 2$ (a study involving a dichotomous variable), interpretation of a significant χ^2 value would be straightforward: the frequencies suggest one population probability is greater than expected, and one probability is less than expected. It is clear in what ways the data are inconsistent with the null hypothesis expectation.

When $k > 2$ the interpretation is more complicated. In our example we have evidence of a change in political views since 1969, but is the change associated with the probability of being a liberal, a conservative, or a moderate; or does the change involve more than one political view?

There are formal procedures for determining where the changes have occurred (Marascuilo & McSweeney, 1977), but we can get a sense of where the differences lie from inspecting the relative contributions to the χ^2 value. Procedure Box 14.1 indicates the following values for $(f_{0_j} - f_{E_j})^2 / f_{E_j}$:

liberal: 15.902

conservative: .399

moderate: 21.394.

The largest value was for moderates. Inspection of the observed and expected frequencies indicates the proportion of sample subjects describing themselves as moderate is markedly greater than was expected. The next largest value results from the decrease in the proportion describing themselves as liberal. Compared to these, the change in the proportion describing themselves as conservative is fairly trivial. The scientific hypothesis that the adult population has become more conservative is only partially supported by these data. Although the results suggest fewer people are willing to describe themselves as liberal, we found little change in the proportion willing to describe themselves as conservative. However, these conclusions must be considered tentative in the absence of hypothesis tests to determine where the differences lie.

14.5 CONDITIONS FOR USING THE TEST

Other Examples. The chi-square goodness of fit test can be used when the scientific hypothesis has to do with the probability of occurrence of values of a variable. Such questions are most commonly of interest for variables with a relatively small number of possible values.

Other examples of studies which could use the chi-square goodness of fit test include the following:

1. A researcher is interested in whether the proportion of males and females among learning disabled students differs from the proportion in the general population of elementary school students.

2. High school students rate their level of agreement with the statement "I feel good about myself" on a scale from 1 (Strongly Disagree) to 5 (Strongly Agree). The researcher believes the most common response will be "Strongly Agree."

Two comments are in order about this second example. First, I used the same example to demonstrate the computation of the one-group t test in Procedure Box 13.1 in the last chapter. Either test is applicable depending on whether the researcher is interested in the population mean or population probabilities. When there is a choice, most researchers opt for the t test, which usually requires a smaller sample size to achieve a desired level of power.

Second, unlike the researcher studying political views, the researcher studying adolescent self-esteem has no preconceived notion of the population probabilities for each variable value; the scientific hypothesis suggests simply that the probability associated with choice 5 will be greater than the proportion associated with any of the other choices. For this study a "generic" null hypothesis is required that assumes all the probabilities are equal:

$$H_0\colon p(1) = p(2) = p(3) = p(4) = p(5) = .20.$$

Statistical Conditions. The test requires the following statistical conditions:

1. Random and independent sampling.
2. The sample size must be sufficiently large. This not a very stringent requirement: Delucchi (1993) concluded that if all expected frequencies are 5 or greater the sample size is more than sufficient.
3. Values of the variable are mutually exclusive and exhaustive. Every subject must fall in only one category. For example, suppose we want to divide drivers involved in accidents during an altered state of consciousness into those who had been drinking, or those who had used illegal drugs. Since many accidents involve a driver who had used both alcohol and illegal drugs, these values are not mutually exclusive. The problem could be resolved by dividing them into three groups: those who had used alcohol only, those who had used illegal drugs only, and those who had used both.

If these conditions are not met, the critical values in Table D–2 are not necessarily correct. Note that none of these conditions require any assumptions about the distribution of the population from which the sample is drawn. Like the binomial test, the chi-square test is a nonparametric test.

14.6 DIRECTIONAL VERSUS NONDIRECTIONAL HYPOTHESES

The chi-square test is always a one-tailed test. Since the differences between observed and expected frequencies are squared, each becomes a positive number regardless of whether the observed frequency is greater or less than the expected frequency. A chi-square value equaling or exceeding the critical value suggests the null hypothesis probabilities are incorrect, but not which ones are incorrect. This and other aspects of the chi square goodness of fit test are summarized in Table 14.1.

This characteristic of the χ^2 test has an advantage and a disadvantage. The advantage is that a single χ^2 test can evaluate the accuracy of a large set of probabilities simultaneously. Contrast this with the binomial test, which can only evaluate the accuracy of the probabilities associated with a dichotomous variable.

TABLE 14.1 Selected Aspects of the Chi-Square Goodness of Fit Test

Symbol Used	Degrees of Freedom	Type of Statistical Hypotheses	General Form of Statistical Hypotheses	Type of Test	Symbol for Alpha	Critical Region in
χ^2	$k - 1$	nondirectional	H_0: all probabilities equal expected values H_1: all probabilities do not equal expected values	one-tailed	α	upper tail

As mentioned previously, the disadvantage is that rejecting the null hypothesis only indicates that not all the null hypothesis probabilities are accurate; it does not indicate which expected probabilities are inaccurate. The only exception to this rule occurs when the chi-square goodness of fit test is applied to a dichotomous variable. Then the chi-square test is essentially equivalent to the binomial test, and can be interpreted straightforwardly (this was mentioned previously under "Interpreting the Results").

We can draw a distinction here between the χ^2 test and the binomial, z, and t tests. For those tests, directional hypotheses could be evaluated using one-tailed tests, while nondirectional hypotheses were evaluated using two-tailed tests. The χ^2 test is always one-tailed, yet only nondirectional hypotheses can be tested.

14.7 POWER AND SAMPLE SIZE ISSUES

The power of the chi-square test depends upon the alpha level, the sample size, the degrees of freedom, and the effect size. The effect size for the chi-square goodness of fit test is based on the size of the differences between the true probabilities and the probabilities suggested by the null hypothesis: the larger these differences, the larger the effect size. Table C–3 in Appendix C provides sample sizes necessary for .80 and .90 power for small, medium, and large effect sizes.

Notice that the necessary sample sizes are generally much larger than those required for the one-group z and t tests. In general, nonparametric tests are less powerful than parametric tests. For this reason, researchers tend to prefer the use of parametric tests when possible.

In the study on political view, I would recommend using a small effect size. Given the size of the adult American population, even a slight change in political views can represent a shift in the attitudes of hundreds of thousands of potential voters. For $\alpha = .05$, $\beta = .20$, $df = 2$ the desired sample size is 964. The sample we used is sufficient to insure a .80 probability of correct rejection if the null hypothesis is false even if the effect size is small.

KEY TERMS

χ^2 distribution
degrees of freedom
dichotomous variable
directional hypothesis
discrete variable
frequency
nondirectional hypothesis

nonparametric test
one-tailed test
power
probability
sample size
sampling distribution

EXERCISES

Answers to all exercises may be found in Appendix B.

1. Indicate whether the conditions for using the chi-square goodness of fit test are met in each of the following cases:
   a. Males are compared to females on rate of left-versus right-handedness
   b. Adolescents respond to the statement "I feel good about myself" on a 5-point scale from Strongly Disagree (1) to Strongly Agree (5). The scientific hypothesis suggests that the population mean score differs from the neutral point (3).
   c. Adolescents respond to the statement "I feel good about myself" on a 5-point scale from Strongly Disagree (1) to Strongly Agree (5). The scientific hypothesis suggests that the neutral point (3) is endorsed more frequently than other options in this population.
   d. A study is done to investigate whether the proportion of females in the population of learning disabled elementary school students has changed since it was first determined in the 1960s.
   e. A medical researcher examines the effectiveness of a new surgical procedure for back pain by classifying patients three months after surgery as either improved, unchanged, or deteriorated.

2. A rat maze is constructed that is shaped like a plus sign, with four alleys connected at a central point. Rats placed in the center of the maze may choose to run into any one of the four alleys. Food is placed in the alley that faces east. This is repeated daily until they choose the east alley 20 times in a row. They are then removed from the maze for 6 months. After 6 months they are returned to the maze to see whether they remember their earlier training.

   a. Is this a *true experiment*, a *quasi-experiment*, or an *observational study*?
   b. What type of variable is alley choice (north, south, east, or west): *nominal*, *ordinal*, *interval*, or *ratio*; *continuous* or *discrete*?
   c. State the null and alternative hypotheses for this study. *Hint:* since differences between the north, south, and west alleys do not matter in this study, they should be grouped together.
   d. What effect size would you consider the smallest meaningful effect size in this situation?
   e. Assuming a medium effect size, $\alpha = .01$, and $\beta = .20$, what is the minimum desired sample size?
   f. Out of 100 rats in the sample, 63 choose the east alley, 15 choose the west alley, 7 choose the north alley, and 15 choose the south alley. Compute the chi-square statistic.
   g. What is the critical value for $\alpha = .05$? Can the researcher reject the null hypothesis?
   h. How might these results be interpreted?

3. A market researcher is studying which of three colas is preferred in a sample of mall shoppers. Subjects taste cola 1, then cola 2, then cola 3, and indicate which they prefer.
   a. Is this a *true experiment*, *quasi-experiment*, or *observational study*?
   b. State the null and alternative hypotheses for this study.
   c. Assuming a medium effect size is considered the smallest important effect, and the researcher would like to use $\alpha = .10$, $\beta = .20$, what is the appropriate sample size for this study?
   d. The researcher is able to gather a sample of 15 shoppers to taste all three colas. She finds that 8

prefer cola 1, 5 prefer cola 2, and 2 prefer cola 3. Compute the chi-square goodness of fit value.
e. What is the critical value for $\alpha = .10$? Can the researcher reject the null hypothesis?
f. How might these results be interpreted?

4. A medical researcher examines the effectiveness of a new surgical procedure for back pain by classifying patients three months after surgery as either improved, unchanged, or deteriorated.
  a. Is this a *true experiment, quasi-experiment,* or *observational study*?
  b. What type of variable is the outcome variable in this study: *nominal, ordinal, interval,* or *ratio*; *continuous* or *discrete*?
  c. State the null and alternative hypotheses for this study.
  d. The operation is an extremely expensive one, and occasionally can result in death. What effect size would you consider the smallest meaningful effect size?
  e. What is the smallest appropriate sample size for each of the following conditions:
    (1) $\alpha = .01$, $\beta = .10$, small effect size
    (2) $\alpha = .05$, $\beta = .20$, large effect size
    (3) $\alpha = .05$, $\beta = .10$, medium effect size
  f. Suppose the researcher finds that out of 300 patients who receive the surgery, 98 are improved, 103 are unchanged, and 99 are deteriorated. Compute the chi-square goodness of fit test.

g. What is the critical value for $\alpha = .10$? Can the researcher reject the null hypothesis?
h. How might these results be interpreted?

5. Another medical researcher objects to the conclusions of the researcher in question 4. Previous research suggests that when back pain sufferers reach the level of severity where surgery is recommended, 75% will deteriorate further in the next three months, 14% will remain unchanged, and only 11% show improvement if surgery is not performed. This researcher reanalyzes the data from question 4 using this information.
  a. State the new null and alternative hypotheses.
  b. Reanalyze the data from part f of question 4 in light of these new statistical hypotheses.
  c. Can the researcher reject the null hypothesis at $\alpha = .10$?
  d. How might the researcher interpret these results?

6. Assuming the null hypothesis is true, compare the χ^2 distribution to the sampling distribution of z and t on the following:
  a. the expected value.
  b. whether the distribution is symmetrical.
  c. the use of one-tailed versus two-tailed tests.
  d. the use of directional versus nondirectional hypotheses.

PART VI

Population Relationships

Inferential Statistics for Two or Three Variables

Most of the remaining chapters introduce inferential statistics used to evaluate whether a relationship exists between two or, in the case of the two-way independent groups analysis of variance in Chapter 21, three population variables. The larger number of inferential statistics in Part 6 when compared to Part 5 reflects the preference in scientific research for hypotheses concerning relationships. The format used in the previous two chapters will apply here as well, although some topics are at times omitted:

- an introduction to the statistic
- developing the null and alternative hypotheses
- testing the null hypothesis
- making a decision about the null hypothesis (including a discussion of interpreting the results)
- conditions for using the test
- directional versus nondirectional hypotheses
- power and sample size issues
- corresponding confidence intervals

Chapters 15–21 focus on parametric tests, tests which require assumptions about the distributions for the populations from which samples are drawn. Chapters 22–25 focus on the most popular nonparametric alternatives.

The final chapter integrates many of the topics raised throughout the text, by providing a model for determining which statistics to use under what circumstances. Chapter 26 is included to help you see how the concepts of scientific hypotheses, statistical analysis, and research design are integrated to meet the goals of scientific research. The supplement to that chapter provides a description of a research project, following it from beginning to end. This may give you a better sense of how all the elements of the research process fit together.

CHAPTER 15

The Dependent Groups *t* Test

15.1 INTRODUCTION

The next two chapters introduce *t* statistics used to evaluate whether a relationship exists between a dichotomous variable and a quantitative variable. The sample is divided into two groups on the basis of the dichotomous variable. The dependent groups *t* test, the focus of the present chapter, is used when these two groups are dependent. The independent groups *t* test, the focus of the next chapter, is used when the two groups are independent.

Dependent groups refer to *groups for which each subject in the first group is in some way associated with a subject in the second group.* One example of a study in which groups are dependent is the matched groups study.

Suppose a researcher is interested in comparing the effectiveness of two weight loss programs. An important potential subject confound in this study is initial weight. Suppose subjects in Group 1 are, on average, less overweight than subjects in Group 2 before treatment begins. The Group 1 subjects are likely to be less overweight than the Group 2 subjects after treatment as well, even if the treatment received by Group 2 is actually more effective. The researcher may choose to randomly assign subjects to groups, but we know that random assignment can sometimes fail. Another alternative is the **matched groups study**, *a true experiment in which random assignment occurs within blocks of subjects who are approximately equivalent on some potential subject confound, to equalize groups on that confound.* The design requires the following steps:

1. *Measure the confound to be controlled.* Using a commonly available chart of ideal body weights, the researcher computes the percent overweight for each subject. For example, a male subject whose weight is 19% greater than the ideal body weight for his height is considered 19% overweight.

2. *Rank order subjects from highest to lowest. Tied subjects are randomly ordered.*

3. *Divide subjects into blocks.* A **block** may be defined as *a set of associated scores across all groups.* The number of subjects per block equals the number of groups.

4. *Randomly assign one member from each block to each group.*

Table 15.1 illustrates the process. The procedure insures the two groups are roughly equal in percent of weight to be lost before treatment begins. It also associates each subject in the first group with a matched subject in the second group.

TABLE 15.1   Subject Assignment in a Matched Groups Study

A researcher wishes to conduct a study comparing the effectiveness of two weight loss programs. The goal is to insure the groups are equal in terms of the amount of weight they need to lose before treatment begins. Ten subjects are available for the study.

Step 1.

Measure the confound to be controlled. Percent overweight for the 10 subjects proves to be:

18	26	32	21	23	31	29	24	19	26

Step 2.

Rank order subjects from highest to lowest. Tied subjects are randomly ordered.

18	19	21	23	24	26	26	29	31	32

Step 3.

Divide subjects into blocks. The number of subjects in each block equals the number of groups to be formed.

Block 1:	18	19	← *The two subjects with the lowest scores comprise block 1.*
Block 2:	21	23	
Block 3:	24	26	
Block 4:	26	29	
Block 5:	31	32	← *The two subjects with the highest scores comprise block 5.*

Step 4.

Randomly assign one member from each block to each group.

	Group 1	Group 2
Block 1:	18	19
Block 2:	23	21
Block 3:	26	24
Block 4:	29	26
Block 5:	31	32

The mean percent overweight for Group 1 is 25.4; the mean percent overweight for Group 2 is 24.4. The procedure has insured that the two groups are essentially equated on percent overweight prior to beginning treatment. This rules out percent overweight as a potential subject confound, since it is unrelated to the treatment group variable.

A second design in which groups are considered dependent is the **repeated measures study**, or **within-subjects study**. This is *a quasi-experimental study in which the same subjects experience all values of the independent variable.* Suppose a researcher is interested in the impact of an AIDS awareness presentation on the frequency of behaviors that increase the risk of infection. The self-reported frequency of risk behaviors in a group of college students is measured before and after listening to the presentation. The dichotomous variable in this case is time of measurement: before versus after the presentation. Each subject is measured at both times; the same students serve as subjects in both groups.

These examples should give a sense of the concept of dependent groups: each subject in one group is associated with a subject in the other group. In a matched groups study this association occurs because the subjects are matched as a block on some potential subject confound. In a repeated measures study the association occurs because the block includes repeated measurements of the same subject. If a matched groups study or repeated measures study only involves two groups, the dependent groups *t* test can be an appropriate inferential statistic.

The dependent groups *t* test is actually a special case of the one-group *t* test using difference scores from each pair of dependent subjects. To demonstrate the statistic I will describe the AIDS awareness study mentioned above in more detail.

15.2 DEFINING THE NULL AND ALTERNATIVE HYPOTHESES

AIDS is believed to occur after infection by the human immunodeficiency virus, or HIV. Certain behaviors are in turn believed to increase the risk of HIV infection such as unprotected sex and intravenous drug use with an unsterilized needle.

We would like to examine whether a presentation for college students on the dangers of AIDS and methods for preventing HIV infection actually leads to a reduction in the frequency of self-reported risk behaviors. A group of 10 college students complete a rating scale indicating the frequency of risk behaviors for HIV infection over the last two weeks. This scale is scored so that higher scores indicate a greater frequency of risk behaviors. The students then attend a 5-hour presentation in which statistics concerning the frequency of AIDS in the general population are discussed, as are methods for reducing the risk of HIV infection. Two weeks later they complete the rating scale again. This represents a quasi-experimental study, in which time of measurement (before versus after the presentation) represents a dichotomous independent variable, and rating scale score represents a continuous ordinal dependent variable.

The nondirectional null and alternative hypotheses are:

$$H_0: \mu_1 = \mu_2$$

$$H_1: \mu_1 \neq \mu_2.$$

μ_1 represents the μ for the first population, the population represented by the college students before the presentation. μ_2 represents the μ for the second population, the population represented by the college students after the presentation. Which population you decide to identify as 1 and which you identify as 2 is arbitrary, although you will see that it affects whether the resulting *t* value is positive or negative.

Suppose we had access to every college student in the population, and could subtract each student's score on the rating scale after the presentation from his or her score before the presentation:

$$D = Y_{\text{before}} - Y_{\text{after}}.$$

This procedure produces a set of difference scores for each member of the population. If the null hypothesis is true then μ_D, the population μ for these difference scores, should equal zero. The null and alternative hypotheses may be restated as

$$H_0: \mu_D = 0$$

$$H_1: \mu_D \neq 0.$$

Note that these are essentially the same hypotheses as those used for the one-group t test. This is no coincidence. The dependent groups t test is actually the one-group t test applied to a group of difference scores.

15.3 TESTING THE NULL HYPOTHESIS

The formula for the dependent groups t test is

$$t_{\overline{D}} = \frac{\overline{D} - \mu_0}{s_{\overline{D}}} = \frac{\overline{D} - \mu_0}{\dfrac{s_D}{\sqrt{N_D}}}$$

$$= \frac{\overline{D} - \mu_0}{\sqrt{\dfrac{\displaystyle\sum_{i=1}^{N_D} D_i^2 - \dfrac{\left(\displaystyle\sum_{i=1}^{N_D} D_i\right)^2}{N_D}}{N_D(N_D - 1)}}}.$$

The symbol $t_{\overline{D}}$ indicates this is a t test for the mean of a group of difference scores.

These are the same formulas provided for the one-group t test, with D substituted for Y to reflect the use of difference scores as data. $s_{\overline{D}}$ is the best estimate of the standard error for the sampling distribution of the mean, where the means are the mean difference scores from an infinite number of samples of equal N. s_D is the best estimate of the standard deviation for the population of difference scores. N_D is the number of *difference scores*, not the number of original scores. In our example we started with 20 scores: ten scores from before the presentation and ten from after. However, from these 20 scores 10 difference scores were computed, so $N_D = 10$.

For the dependent groups t test μ_0 is always 0. The computation of the dependent group's t test for this study is demonstrated in Procedure Box 15.1.

15.4 MAKING A DECISION ABOUT THE NULL HYPOTHESIS

The critical t values are provided in Table D−1 of Appendix D. In this case the degrees of freedom equal $N_D - 1$, so $df = 9$. The two-tailed critical value for testing the non-directional null hypothesis is $t_{\alpha=.05,\, df=9} = \pm 2.262$; we can reject the null hypothesis if

$$|t_{\overline{D}}| \geq 2.262.$$

Our computed $t_{\overline{D}}$ value from Procedure Box 15.1 is $+2.299$, which allows us to reject the null hypothesis at the desired alpha level. There is evidence of a relationship in the population from which these students were drawn between the variables time of measurement and self-reported frequency of risk behaviors.

The Dependent Groups *t* Test

Goal   Ten students completed a rating scale concerning the frequency of risk behaviors before and after an AIDS awareness presentation:

	Before	After
Student 1	15	9
Student 2	22	16
Student 3	18	15
Student 4	16	3
Student 5	9	10
Student 6	8	6
Student 7	17	9
Student 8	11	5
Student 9	4	6
Student 10	10	10

Compute the one-group *t* test using these data.

$$t_{\overline{D}} = \frac{\overline{D} - \mu_0}{\sqrt{\dfrac{\displaystyle\sum_{i=1}^{N_D} D_i^2 - \dfrac{\left(\displaystyle\sum_{i=1}^{N_D} D_i\right)^2}{N_D}}{N_D(N_D - 1)}}}$$

Step 1   *For each pair of dependent scores, subtract the second from the first, and find the sum and mean for the difference scores.*

	Before	After	D
Student 1	15	9	6
Student 2	22	16	6
Student 3	18	15	3
Student 4	16	3	13
Student 5	9	10	−1
Student 6	8	6	2
Student 7	17	9	8
Student 8	11	5	6
Student 9	4	6	−2
Student 10	10	10	0
Sum:			41
Mean:			4.1

Continued

The dependent groups t test continued

Step 2   *Find the sum of the squared difference scores.*

	D	D^2
Student 1	6	36
Student 2	6	36
Student 3	3	9
Student 4	13	169
Student 5	−1	1
Student 6	2	4
Student 7	8	64
Student 8	6	36
Student 9	−2	4
Student 10	0	0
Sum:		359

Step 3   *Find the square of the summed difference scores, and divide by N.*

$$\frac{\sum_{i=1}^{N_D} D^2}{N} = \frac{41^2}{10} = 168.1$$

Step 4   *Subtract the result of Step 3 from the sum of the squared scores, divide by $N_D(N_D - 1)$ and find the square root.*

$$\frac{s_D}{\sqrt{N_D}} = \sqrt{\frac{359 - 168.1}{10(10 - 1)}} = 1.7837 \longleftarrow \text{This number must be positive}$$

Step 5   *Divide the mean of D by the result of Step 4.*

$$t_{\overline{D}} = \frac{4.1}{1.7837} = +2.2986$$

Interpreting the Results. We arbitrarily decided to subtract scores after the presentation from scores before the presentation. Since the computed $t_{\overline{D}}$ value is positive, it indicates that scores before the presentation were on average higher than scores after the presentation. Rejecting the null hypothesis means we have evidence that if members of the population from which this sample was drawn listened to this AIDS presentation, they would subsequently tend to report lower frequencies of risk behaviors. We might therefore recommend offering this presentation to other members of the population.

Although the results were in the desired direction, the results cannot be interpreted with a high degree of confidence. It is questionable to what extent self-reported frequencies of risk behaviors may be considered accurate. In particular, students who have recently heard an AIDS awareness presentation may be embarrassed to admit how frequently they are engaging in risk behaviors. These problems suggest the results of the study must be interpreted with caution.

15.5 CONDITIONS FOR USING THE TEST

Conditions. The dependent groups _t_ test may be used when (1) members of the sample fall into two groups based on a dichotomous variable, (2) the two groups are dependent, (3) members of the sample produce a quantitative variable, and (4) the null hypothesis has to do with whether the μs for the quantitative variable are equal for the populations represented by the two groups. A difference would suggest the existence of a population relationship between the variables.

If the study is a quasi-experiment or true experiment, the dichotomous variable generally represents the independent variable and the quantitative variable the dependent variable. Examples of other studies in which the dependent groups _t_ test may be appropriate include:

1. an observational study examining whether first-born twins tend to be more intelligent at age 10 than the associated second-born twins.
2. a matched subjects true experiment in which subjects are matched on level of depression, then randomly assigned to psychotherapy versus drug therapy for depression

Assumptions. The test requires the same statistical assumptions as the one-group _t_ test:

1. random and independent sampling: For this test, blocks of subjects must be randomly and independently sampled.
2. the normality assumption: For this test, the normality assumption applies to the population of difference scores. The dependent groups _t_ test is generally considered robust against violation of this assumption if $N_D \geq 30$.

15.6 DIRECTIONAL VERSUS NONDIRECTIONAL HYPOTHESES

Remember that with _t_ tests, nondirectional hypotheses are evaluated by a two-tailed test, directional hypotheses by a one-tailed test. Directional hypotheses for the AIDS awareness study would be:

$$H_0: \mu_D \leq 0$$

$$H_1: \mu_D > 0.$$

Since we are subtracting scores after the presentation from scores before the presentation, the alternative hypothesis suggests difference scores will tend to be positive. In this case the critical value would be $t_{\alpha(D)=.05, df=9} = +1.833$. A computed $t_{\bar{D}}$ value ≥ 1.833 would allow us to reject the null hypothesis.

Some have argued that discussing sexual practices or intravenous drug use openly could actually increase the frequency of risk behaviors in some populations. If we

TABLE 15.2 Selected Aspects of the Dependent Groups t Test

Symbol Used	Degrees of Freedom	Type of Statistical Hypotheses	General Form of Statistical Hypotheses	Type of Test	Symbol for Alpha	Critical Region in
$t_{\overline{D}}$	$N_D - 1$	nondirectional	$H_0: \mu_1 - \mu_2 = 0$ $H_1: \mu_1 - \mu_2 \neq 0$	two-tailed	α	both tails (both positive and negative critical values)
		directional	$H_0: \mu_1 - \mu_2 \leq 0$ $H_1: \mu_1 - \mu_2 > 0$	one-tailed	$\alpha(D)$	upper tail (critical value is positive)
		directional	$H_0: \mu_1 - \mu_2 \geq 0$ $H_1: \mu_1 - \mu_2 < 0$	one-tailed	$\alpha(D)$	lower tail (critical value is negative)

believed the frequency of risk behaviors would be greater for college students after the presentation, the directional null and alternative hypotheses would be

$$H_0: \mu_D \geq 0$$

$$H_1: \mu_D < 0.$$

In this case the critical value would be $t_{\alpha(D)=.05, df=9} = -1.833$; to reject the null hypothesis, $t_{\overline{D}}$ must be ≤ -1.833. This and other aspects of the dependent groups t test are summarized in Table 15.2. We would not have been able to reject this null hypothesis, since the computed $t_{\overline{D}}$ value was positive.

When scores are higher after the treatment than before treatment, the researcher may choose to compute the difference scores using the formula

$$D = Y_{\text{after}} - Y_{\text{before}}.$$

This way the computed t value will always be a positive number, which people tend to prefer. The choice of which group's score to subtract when computing difference scores is up to the researcher.

15.7 POWER AND SAMPLE SIZE ISSUES

Since the dependent groups t test is a special case of the one-group t test, Table C−2 can also be used to determine the appropriate sample size for the dependent groups t test. However, remember that the sample size here refers to the number of *difference scores*, not the number of subjects. If you are conducting a matched subjects study, where two subjects are required to produce each difference score, you will need twice as many subjects as the number provided in Table C−2 would suggest.

In the AIDS presentation study the treatment has very little cost and a great deal of potential benefit; even a small effect size may be considered meaningful. For $\alpha = .05$, $\beta = .20$, and a small effect size, the desired N_D is 198. Our sample is obviously much smaller. The fact that we achieved significance anyway may suggest that the presentation is associated with a far larger effect size than needed to consider it a worthwhile program.

15.8 CONFIDENCE INTERVALS

The formula for computing the confidence interval for the difference between two μs when the populations are dependent is

$$LL_{(1-\alpha)} = \overline{D} - t_{\alpha,df}(s_{\overline{D}}) = \overline{D} - t_{\alpha,df}\left(\frac{s_D}{\sqrt{N_D}}\right),$$

$$UL_{(1-\alpha)} = \overline{D} + t_{\alpha,df}(s_{\overline{D}}) = \overline{D} + t_{\alpha,df}\left(\frac{s_D}{\sqrt{N_D}}\right).$$

$\overline{D}$ comes from Step 1 in Procedure Box 15.1, s_D from Step 4. In the AIDS awareness study, the 95% confidence interval would equal

$$LL_{.95} = 4.1 - 2.262(1.7837) = 0.0653,$$

$$UL_{.95} = 4.1 + 2.262(1.7837) = 8.1347.$$

We can be 95% confident that in the population the average drop in score on the risk behavior scale after the presentation is between 0.0653 and 8.1347 points.

Notice that the value for μ_D suggested by the null hypothesis of the dependent groups _t_ test, 0, does not fall within the 95% confidence interval. This finding is consistent with the decision to reject the null hypothesis for the _t_ test at $\alpha = .05$.

Use of this formula requires conditions similar to those for the dependent groups _t_ test: (1) members of the sample must fall into two groups based on a dichotomous variable, (2) the two groups are dependent, (3) members of the sample produce a quantitative variable, and (4) you are interested in estimating the difference between the two quantitative variable μs for the populations represented by the two groups.

The assumption that the population of difference scores is normally distributed is required, although the confidence interval formula is robust against violation of the normality assumption if $N_D \geq 30$. In addition, blocks of subjects must be randomly and independently sampled from the population.

KEY TERMS

block
confidence intervals
degrees of freedom
dependent groups
dependent variable
dichotomous variable
directional hypothesis
independent variable
matched groups study
nondirectional hypothesis
normality assumption

one-tailed test
power
quantitative variable
random assignment
repeated measures study, within-subjects study
robust
sample size
subject confound
_t_ distribution
two-tailed test

EXERCISES

Answers to all exercises may be found in Appendix B.

1. For which of the following studies would the dependent groups *t* test be appropriate?
   a. Subjects are randomly assigned to two different programs aimed at eliminating cigarette smoking.
   b. Subjects are divided into blocks of two on the basis of number of cigarettes smoked per day, and randomly assigned within blocks to two programs to stop cigarette smoking.
   c. For a sample of 100 dogs, number of drops of saliva in the mouth are counted before and after hearing a bell that has previously been associated with receiving food.
   d. Rats are placed at the center of a maze which allows the rat to run in one of three directions. The number of rats out of 100 who choose to turn left instead of right or going straight is recorded before and after placing food in the alley to the left of the rat.

2. *Statistical regression* refers to the tendency for individuals with extreme scores on some scale to move towards the mean over time. For example, people with the lowest scores on a rating scale should tend to show an increase in scores over time, and those with the highest scores should tend to show a decrease. To demonstrate this phenomenon, a researcher administers a measure of self-esteem to 300 college students. One month later she administers the scale again to those 10 students who had the lowest scores on the first administration.
   a. Is this a *true experiment, quasi-experiment, or observational study?*
   b. State the directional statistical hypotheses for this study. Consider the first set of measurements as Group 1, the second set as Group 2.
   c. Assuming a small effect size is considered the smallest meaningful effect, and the researcher would like to use $\alpha(D) = .01$, $\beta = .20$, what is the appropriate sample size for this study?
   d. Compute the dependent groups *t* test using the following data:

Time 1	Time 2	Time 1	Time 2
2	8	5	3
3	10	6	7
3	4	6	12
4	7	6	6
4	9	7	8

   e. What is the critical value for $\alpha(D) = .01$? Can the researcher reject the null hypothesis?
   f. How might these results be interpreted?

3. The number of words correctly defined in a vocabulary test by high school students is measured before and after participation in a 3-hour language skills workshop, to see whether the workshop enhances performance on the test.
   a. Is this a *true experiment, quasi-experiment, or observational study?*
   b. What types of variables are time of testing (before versus after the workshop) and vocabulary skill: *nominal, ordinal, interval,* or *ratio; continuous* or *discrete?*
   c. State the nondirectional null and alternative hypotheses.
   d. The workshop requires little time and effort from the participants. However, if the impact on performance is minor, the expenditure of time probably still is not worthwhile. What would you consider the smallest meaningful effect size?
   e. How many subjects would be desirable for the following conditions?
      (1) $\alpha = .01$, $\beta = .20$, large effect size
      (2) $\alpha(D) = .10$, $\beta = .10$, small effect size
      (3) $\alpha(D) = .05$, $\beta = .20$, medium effect size
   f. Use the following data to compute the dependent groups *t* test:

Before	After
12	14
14	16
16	20
10	14
9	10
7	5

   g. What is the critical value for $\alpha = .05$? Can the researcher reject the null hypothesis?
   h. How might these results be interpreted?

4. a. Compute the 99% confidence interval for the data in Question 2d. Is the critical value used to answer Question 2e appropriate for the computation of the confidence interval?
   b. Are the results for the interval estimation consistent with the results of the hypothesis test? If so, in what way? If not, why not?

5. a. Compute the 95% confidence interval for the data in Question 3f. Is the critical value used to answer Question 3g appropriate for the computation of the confidence interval?

   b. Are the results for the interval estimation consistent with the results of the hypothesis test? If so, in what way? If not, why not?

6. In a matched groups study, how is the sample size provided by Table C – 2 in Appendix C adjusted?

CHAPTER 16

The Independent Groups t Test

16.1 INTRODUCTION

In most studies where two groups of subjects are to be compared on a quantitative variable the groups are not dependent. For example, suppose a true experiment is conducted in which subjects are randomly assigned to two weight control programs (see Section 3.2.1.1 for a discussion of random assignment procedures). Subjects in the first group are not associated with specific subjects in the second group; the groups are independent.

The conditions required for using the independent groups t test are the same as those for the dependent groups t test, except that the two groups must be independent. **Independent groups** are *groups for which the subjects in one group are not associated with subjects in the other group.*

I used a study investigating whether college professors are more anxious than the average adult to demonstrate the one-group z and t tests. In neither case were we able to reject the null hypothesis. Perhaps this is because college professors in different disciplines are not equally anxious. Perhaps some types of college professors are more anxious than the average person, while others are less anxious. To explore this possibility, we will examine whether professors teaching liberal arts courses are more anxious than professors teaching behavioral science courses.

Sample data will be gathered on two variables, type of professor and level of anxiety. In this study type of professor is a dichotomous nominal variable, the two possible values being liberal arts or behavioral science. Level of anxiety is a continuous ordinal variable, represented by scores on the MMPI Psychasthenia scale. The goal of the study will be to examine whether a relationship exists between these two variables: Can knowledge of whether a person teaches liberal arts or behavioral science courses be used to make a prediction about that person's level of anxiety?

16.2 DEFINING THE NULL AND ALTERNATIVE HYPOTHESES

The nondirectional null and alternative hypotheses can be stated as follows:

$$H_0: \mu_1 = \mu_2$$

$$H_1: \mu_1 \neq \mu_2.$$

These could also be stated as

$$H_0: \mu_1 - \mu_2 = 0$$

$$H_1: \mu_1 - \mu_2 \neq 0.$$

The statistical hypotheses are similar but not equivalent to the statistical hypotheses for the dependent groups *t* test:

$$H_0: \mu_D = 0$$

$$H_1: \mu_D \neq 0.$$

The statistical hypotheses for the dependent groups *t* test referred to the mean for a population of differences between dependent scores. In the case of the independent groups *t* test there are no dependent scores, so the statistical hypotheses refer instead to the difference between the means for two independent populations: μ_1 (the mean Psychasthenia score for all liberal arts professors) and μ_2 (the mean Psychasthenia score for all behavioral science professors). The null hypothesis suggests that this difference equals zero.

16.3 TESTING THE NULL HYPOTHESIS

You may remember the formula for the one-group *t* test is:

$$t_{\overline{Y}} = \frac{\overline{Y} - \mu_0}{s_{\overline{Y}}}.$$

This formula consists of three components:

1. the parameter value suggested by the null hypothesis, μ_0, is subtracted from
2. the best sample estimate of that parameter, $\overline{Y}$, and is divided by
3. the best sample estimate of the standard error for the sampling distribution of $\overline{Y}$.

The formula for the independent groups *t* test follows the same format,

$$t_{\overline{Y}_1 - \overline{Y}_2} = \frac{(\overline{Y}_1 - \overline{Y}_2) - (\mu_1 - \mu_2)_0}{s_{\overline{Y}_1 - \overline{Y}}}:$$

1. the parameter value suggested by the null hypothesis, $(\mu_1 - \mu_2)_0$, is subtracted from
2. the best sample estimate of that parameter, $\overline{Y}_1 - \overline{Y}_2$, and is divided by
3. the best estimate of the standard error for the sampling distribution of $\overline{Y}_1 - \overline{Y}_2$.

The symbol $t_{\overline{Y}_1 - \overline{Y}_2}$ indicates this is a *t* test for the difference between two means from independent groups.

Think about what a sampling distribution of $\overline{Y}_1 - \overline{Y}_2$ would be. Suppose we drew an infinite number of random samples, each sample comprised of a group of liberal arts professors randomly sampled from a population of liberal arts professors, and a group of behavioral science professors randomly sampled from a population of behavioral science professors. If we compute the mean anxiety score for each group and find the difference between these means, we would have available the value $\overline{Y}_1 - \overline{Y}_2$ for each sample. The sampling distribution of $\overline{Y}_1 - \overline{Y}_2$ would be the sampling distribution of these mean differences, and $\sigma_{\overline{Y}_1 - \overline{Y}_2}$ represents the standard error of the sampling distribution. $s_{\overline{Y}_1 - \overline{Y}_2}$ is the best sample estimate of this standard error.

It is demonstrated in the supplement that if the variances of the two populations happen to be equal, then the best estimate of the standard error for the sampling distribution of $\overline{Y}_1 - \overline{Y}_2$ is generated by combining, or "pooling," data from the two groups:

$$s_{\overline{Y}_1 - \overline{Y}_2} = \sqrt{\frac{SS_1 + SS_2}{N - 2}\left(\frac{1}{n_1} + \frac{1}{n_2}\right)}$$

$$= \sqrt{\frac{\displaystyle\sum_{i=1}^{n_1} Y_i^2 + \sum_{i=1}^{n_2} Y_i^2 - \frac{\left(\displaystyle\sum_{i=1}^{n_1} Y_i\right)^2}{n_1} - \frac{\left(\displaystyle\sum_{i=1}^{n_2} Y_i\right)^2}{n_2}}{N - 2}\left(\frac{1}{n_1} + \frac{1}{n_2}\right)}.$$

The case in which the population variances are not equal will be discussed later in the chapter.

The symbol SS was introduced in Section 6.1.2. It refers to the sum of squares, the numerator of a variance. Here it refers to the numerator of the variance for Group 1 (SS_1) or Group 2 (SS_2). The last formula is a computational formula, based on the computational formula for SS. $\sum_{i=1}^{n_1} Y_i^2$ refers to the sum of the squared Y scores for Group 1, $\sum_{i=1}^{n_2} Y_i^2$ to the sum of the squared Y scores for Group 2. $\left(\sum_{i=1}^{n_1} Y_i\right)^2$ refers to the square of the summed Y scores for Group 1, $\left(\sum_{i=1}^{n_2} Y_i\right)^2$ to the square of the summed Y scores for Group 2.[1]

The formulas above for $s_{\overline{Y}_1 - \overline{Y}_2}$ are called **pooled variance formulas**, *formulas that pool variance estimates from multiple groups under the assumption that variances for the populations represented by the groups are equal.* If the variances of the two populations are equal, sums of squares for the two groups can be pooled together to get a better estimate of population variability than is provided by either sum of squares alone. In the present example, this would mean we assume that the variance for the population of liberal arts professors equals the variance for the population of behavioral science professors:

$$\sigma_1^2 = \sigma_2^2.$$

Based on this discussion, the following formula can be offered for the independent groups t test:

$$t_{\overline{Y}_1 - \overline{Y}_2} = \frac{(\overline{Y}_1 - \overline{Y}_2) - (\mu_1 - \mu_2)_0}{\sqrt{\dfrac{\displaystyle\sum_{i=1}^{n_1} Y_i^2 + \sum_{i=1}^{n_2} Y_i^2 - \dfrac{\left(\displaystyle\sum_{i=1}^{n_1} Y_i\right)^2}{n_1} - \dfrac{\left(\displaystyle\sum_{i=1}^{n_2} Y_i\right)^2}{n_2}}{N - 2}\left(\dfrac{1}{n_1} + \dfrac{1}{n_2}\right)}}.$$

---

[1]See Section 5.1 for a discussion of the summation symbol, and of squaring summed scores versus summing squared scores.

$-(\mu_1 - \mu_2)_0$ is often eliminated from the formula since in practice the null hypothesis always suggests this quantity equals zero. The choice of which group to consider 1 and which to consider 2 is arbitrary. However, your choice will have an effect on whether $t_{\overline{Y}_1 - \overline{Y}_2}$ is positive or negative.

Suppose a group of 10 liberal arts professors and a group of 10 behavioral science professors completed the MMPI Psychasthenia scale. The computation of *t* for this sample is demonstrated in Procedure Box 16.1.

16.4 MAKING A DECISION ABOUT THE NULL HYPOTHESIS

If the population of liberal arts professors and the population of behavioral science professors from which these samples were randomly drawn are both normally distributed, the shape of the *t* distribution (and therefore the critical value) depends purely on the degrees of freedom. For the independent groups *t* test, the degrees of freedom equal $N - 2$.

The table of critical values for the *t* distribution is provided in Table D–1 of Appendix D. The two-tailed critical value for testing the nondirectional null hypothesis is $t_{\alpha=.05, df=18} = \pm 2.101$; we can reject the null hypothesis if

$$|t_{\overline{Y}_1 - \overline{Y}_2}| \geq 2.101.$$

Since our computed $t_{\overline{Y}_1 - \overline{Y}_2} = -2.54$, we can reject the null hypothesis with $\alpha = .05$.

Interpreting the Results. Inspection of the group means reveals an unexpected finding. The mean for liberal arts professors (55.7) is actually lower than the mean for behavioral science professors (63.4), which is why $t_{\overline{Y}_1 - \overline{Y}_2}$ was a negative value. This outcome is in the opposite direction from what the scientific hypothesis proposed. This is a case in which conducting a two-tailed test allowed us to draw conclusions about the population that are the opposite of what we had expected. Had we conducted a one-tailed hypothesis test, we would not have been able to reject the null hypothesis, and would have missed the presence of a relationship opposite in direction to the one predicted.

16.5 CONDITIONS FOR USING THE TEST

Conditions. The independent groups *t* test may be used when (1) members of the sample fall into two groups based on a dichotomous variable, (2) the two groups are independent, (3) members of the sample produce a quantitative variable, and (4) the null hypothesis has to do with whether the μs for the quantitative variable are equal for the populations represented by the two groups. A difference would suggest the existence of a population relationship between the variables.

The college professor example represents an observational study, since variables were allowed to vary freely. The independent groups *t* test can also be used in studies where subjects are assigned either to an experimental or control condition without blocking. This can occur in true experiments or in quasi-experiments.

PROCEDURE BOX 16.1

The Independent Groups *t* Test

Goal

Ten liberal arts and ten behavioral science professors produce the following MMPI Psychasthenia scores:

Group 1 Liberal Arts	Group 2 Behavioral Science
45	58
63	59
62	63
51	68
54	74
63	68
52	52
54	66
64	69
49	57

Compute the independent groups *t* value for these data.

$$t_{\overline{Y}_1 - \overline{Y}_2} = \frac{(\overline{Y}_1 - \overline{Y}_2) - (\mu_1 - \mu_2)_0}{\sqrt{\dfrac{\displaystyle\sum_{i=1}^{n_1} Y_i^2 + \sum_{i=1}^{n_2} Y_i^2 - \dfrac{\left(\sum_{i=1}^{n_1} Y_i\right)^2}{n_1} - \dfrac{\left(\sum_{i=1}^{n_2} Y_i\right)^2}{n_2}}{N-2} \left(\dfrac{1}{n_1} + \dfrac{1}{n_2}\right)}}.$$

Step 1   *Compute the sum of Y and Y^2, and the mean of Y for each group.*

	Group 1 Liberal Arts		Group 2 Behavioral Science
Y_i	Y_i^2	Y_i	Y_i^2
45	2025	58	3364
63	3969	59	3481
62	3844	63	3969
51	2601	68	4624
54	2916	74	5476
63	3969	68	4624
52	2704	52	2704
54	2916	66	4356
64	4096	69	4761
49	2401	57	3249
Sums: 557	31441	634	40608
Means: 55.7		63.4	

Continued

The independent groups t test continued

Step 2   *Square the sums of the scores and divide by the group n.*

$$\text{Group 1:}\quad \frac{\left(\sum_{i=1}^{n_1} Y_i\right)^2}{n_1} = \frac{557^2}{10} = 31024.9$$

$$\text{Group 2:}\quad \frac{\left(\sum_{i=1}^{n_2} Y_i\right)^2}{n_2} = \frac{634^2}{10} = 40195.6$$

Step 3   *Add together the sums of the squared scores, subtract the two results from Step 2, and divide by N − 2.*

$$\frac{\sum_{i=1}^{n_1} Y_i^2 + \sum_{i=1}^{n_2} Y_i^2 - \frac{\left(\sum_{i=1}^{n_1} Y_i\right)^2}{n_1} - \frac{\left(\sum_{i=1}^{n_2} Y_i\right)^2}{n_2}}{N-2} = \frac{31441 + 40608 - 31024.9 - 40195.6}{20-2}$$

$$= 46.0278 \leftarrow \textit{This number must be positive}$$

Step 4   *Multiply the result from Step 3 by $(1/n_1 + 1/n_2)$ and find the square root.*

$$s_{\overline{Y}_1 - \overline{Y}_2} = \sqrt{46.0278 \left(\frac{1}{10} + \frac{1}{10}\right)} = 3.0341$$

Step 5   *Divide the difference between the means by the result from Step 4.*

$$t_{\overline{Y}_1 - \overline{Y}_2} = \frac{55.7 - 63.4}{3.0341} = -2.54$$

Assumptions. The test requires the following statistical assumptions:

1. Random and independent sampling
2. Normality: both populations are normally distributed. The independent groups *t* test is generally considered robust against violation of this assumption if $n \geq 30$ for both groups.
3. The **homogeneity of variance assumption**: *a parametric assumption that the variances of the populations are equal.* This assumption was used to develop the pooled variance formula for the best estimate of the standard error for the sampling distribution of $\overline{Y}_1 - \overline{Y}_2$.

We have already seen that the normality assumption is rarely met. The homogeneity of variance assumption appears equally unrealistic; there is no reason to expect the two population variances will be equal. In observational studies and many quasi-experiments, the two groups are sampled from different populations. Even in true experiments, where the subjects in the two groups originally came from the same population, they receive different treatments which are likely to affect the variability of the scores.

Fortunately, the pooled variance formula for the independent groups t test is generally considered robust against violation of the homogeneity of variance assumption if n_1 is approximately equal to n_2 (as demonstrated in the supplement): when the group sizes are equal, the pooled variance formula provides the best estimate of $s_{\bar{Y}_1 - \bar{Y}_2}$ regardless of whether or not the population variances are equal. Whenever you plan to use the pooled variance formula for the independent groups t test, n_1 and n_2 should be approximately equal, and greater than or equal to 30. If it proves impractical to generate samples of approximately equal size, many computer statistics programs offer a version of the independent groups t test which does not require the homogeneity of variance assumption. This is often called the **unpooled variance formula,** *a formula for computing a statistic that does not assume population variances are equal.*

16.6 DIRECTIONAL VERSUS NONDIRECTIONAL HYPOTHESES

The null and alternative hypotheses for the college professors study called for a two-tailed test:

$$H_0: \mu_1 - \mu_2 = 0$$

$$H_1: \mu_1 - \mu_2 \neq 0.$$

Suppose we wanted to test the directional hypothesis that liberal arts professors are more anxious than behavioral science professors. If liberal arts professors make up the first population and behavioral science professors the second population, then the null and alternative hypotheses would be

$$H_0: \mu_1 - \mu_2 \leq 0$$

$$H_1: \mu_1 - \mu_2 > 0.$$

Table D–1 in Appendix D indicates the one-tailed critical value is $t_{\alpha(D)=.05, df=18} = +1.734$. Notice that although the critical value in this case is smaller than it was for the two-tailed test, we would not have been able to reject the null hypothesis because our computed $t_{\bar{Y}_1 - \bar{Y}_2}$ value was negative.

If we had wanted to test the scientific hypothesis that liberal arts professors are less anxious than behavioral science professors using directional hypotheses, the null and alternative hypotheses would be

$$H_0: \mu_1 - \mu_2 \geq 0$$

$$H_1: \mu_1 - \mu_2 < 0.$$

TABLE 16.1   Selected Aspects of the Independent Groups _t_ Test

Symbol Used	Degrees of Freedom	Type of Statistical Hypotheses	General Form of Statistical Hypotheses	Type of Test	Symbol for Alpha	Critical Region in
$t_{\bar{Y}_1 - \bar{Y}_2}$	$N - 2$	nondirectional	$H_0: \mu_1 - \mu_2 = 0$ $H_1: \mu_1 - \mu_2 \neq 0$	two-tailed	α	both tails (both positive and negative critical values)
		directional	$H_0: \mu_1 - \mu_2 \leq 0$ $H_1: \mu_1 - \mu_2 > 0$	one-tailed	$\alpha(D)$	upper tail (critical value is positive)
		directional	$H_0: \mu_1 - \mu_2 \geq 0$ $H_1: \mu_1 - \mu_2 < 0$	one-tailed	$\alpha(D)$	lower tail (critical value is negative)

The one-tailed critical value would then be $t_{\alpha(D)=.05, df=18} = -1.734$, and we would have been able to reject the null hypothesis. This and other aspects of the independent groups _t_ test are summarized in Table 16.1.

16.7 POWER AND SAMPLE SIZE ISSUES

The power of the independent groups _t_ test is affected by the same factors that affect the power of the one-group _t_ test: alpha level, sample size, and effect size. Table C–4 in Appendix C provides the group size table for the independent groups _t_ test. There are some important points to make about this table. First, values provided are for _n_, not _N_; this is a _group_ size table, not a _sample_ size table. The desired sample size would be twice that in the table. Second, these values assume that $n_1 = n_2$. If n_1 and n_2 are going to be markedly different a larger mean group size is required to achieve the same level of power (Cohen, 1988).

In Chapter 13 I suggested that a medium effect is a reasonable value for the smallest meaningful effect in this type of study. According to Table C-4, the desired group size for $\alpha = .05$, $\beta = .20$, and a medium effect size is 64. The group sizes were in fact much smaller, so the fact that we still achieved significance suggests the population effect size may be much larger than a medium effect.

Dependent versus Independent Groups Tests. Chapter 15 described the dependent groups _t_ test, which is frequently used to analyze the data from matched groups and repeated measures studies. It should be noted that the independent groups _t_ test could also be computed when two dependent groups are to be compared, and in some circumstances may be the preferred test for reasons of power. When groups are dependent, each score in Group 1 is associated with a score in Group 2. If the correlation between the two sets of scores is relatively high and positive, then the dependent groups _t_ test is more powerful than the independent groups _t_ test.[2] If the correlation between the two sets of scores is relatively low or negative, then the dependent groups _t_ test is less powerful than the independent groups _t_ test.

---

[2] Refer to Chapter 7 for a discussion of correlation coefficients.

The example provided in Chapter 15 involved scores on a rating scale concerning the frequency of risk behaviors before and after an AIDS awareness presentation:

	Before	After
Student 1	15	9
Student 2	22	16
Student 3	18	15
Student 4	16	3
Student 5	9	10
Student 6	8	6
Student 7	17	9
Student 8	11	5
Student 9	4	6
Student 10	10	10

The correlation between these two sets of scores is $+.573$.

In the case of the data from the AIDS study, the independent groups t test formula would produce a value of 1.883. With a two-tailed critical value of $t_{\alpha=.05, df=18} = \pm 2.101$, we would not be able to reject the null hypothesis. The dependent groups t test computed in Chapter 15 was $+2.2986$, which was significant. The independent groups t test is less powerful than the dependent groups t test because the correlation between the two sets of scores is fairly high.

In general, matched groups studies where subjects are matched on the same variable used as the dependent variable, and repeated measures studies where the same subjects serve in both independent variable groups, are associated with relatively high correlations between the two sets of scores. In such cases the dependent groups t test is appropriate. If circumstances occur in which subjects are associated on some variable which is likely to have little or no relationship to the dependent variable, it is probably more appropriate to treat them as independent groups.

16.8 CONFIDENCE INTERVALS

The parameter of interest in the college professor study is the difference between μ_1 and μ_2. The formula for computing the confidence interval for $\mu_1 - \mu_2$ is

$$LL_{(1-\alpha)} = (\overline{Y}_1 - \overline{Y}_2) - t_{\alpha, df}(s_{\overline{Y}_1 - \overline{Y}_2}),$$
$$UL_{(1-\alpha)} = (\overline{Y}_1 - \overline{Y}_2) - t_{\alpha, df}(s_{\overline{Y}_1 - \overline{Y}_2}),$$

where $s_{\overline{Y}_1 - \overline{Y}_2}$ is the denominator of the t test. According to Step 4 in Procedure Box 16.1 for the computation of the t test, $s_{\overline{Y}_1 - \overline{Y}_2} = 3.0341$. The 80% confidence interval would be

$$LL_{.80} = (\overline{Y}_1 - \overline{Y}_2) - t_{\alpha=.20, df=18}(s_{\overline{Y}_1 - \overline{Y}_2}),$$
$$= (55.7 - 63.4) - 1.330(3.0341) = -11.74,$$

$$UL_{.80} = (\overline{Y}_1 - \overline{Y}_2) + t_{\alpha=.20, df=18}(s_{\overline{Y}_1 - \overline{Y}_2})$$
$$= (55.7 - 63.4) + 1.330(3.0341) = -3.66.$$

We can be 80% confident that the difference between the μs falls between −3.66 and −11.74. Another way of saying this: we can be 80% confident that the mean Psychasthenia score in the population of liberal arts professors is between 3.66 and 11.74 points lower than the mean Psychasthenia score in the population of behavioral science professors.

Use of this formula requires conditions similar to those for the independent groups _t_ test: (1) members of the sample fall into two groups based on a dichotomous variable, (2) the two groups are independent, (3) members of the sample produce a quantitative variable, and (4) you are interested in estimating the difference between the quantitative variable μs for the populations represented by the two groups. The random and independent sampling, normality, and homogeneity of variance assumptions are required, although the confidence interval formula is robust against violation of the normality assumption if group sizes are at least 30, and is robust against violation of the homogeneity of variance assumptions if the group sizes are approximately equal.

KEY TERMS

confidence intervals
dichotomous variable
directional hypothesis
homogeneity of variance assumption
independent groups
nondirectional hypothesis
normality assumption
one-tailed test
pooled variance formula

power
quantitative variable
robust
sample size
sampling distribution
sum of squares
_t_ distribution
two-tailed test
unpooled variance formula

EXERCISES

Answers to all exercises may be found in Appendix B.

1. For which of the following studies is the independent groups _t_ test an appropriate analysis:
   a. A researcher randomly assigns subjects to receive either medication or placebo for the treatment of a rash.
   b. A researcher divides subjects into blocks based on the severity of rash, and randomly assigns within blocks to receive either medication or placebo.

   c. Catholics and Muslims are compared on the frequency with which they attend religious services.
   d. Subjects are randomly assigned to one of three weight loss programs. Percent over desired body weight is measured before and after treatment. The difference between percent overweight before and after treatment serves as the dependent variable. The researcher would like to compute

three independent groups t tests, one for each of the possible pairs of groups.

e. For each of the 50 states, the number of speeding tickets distributed in 1995 is divided by the state population, to compute the average number of tickets written per resident. The number of tickets per resident is compared for states that forbid the use of radar detectors to those that allow their use.

2. A researcher is interested in comparing the appetite suppression effects of two drugs, fenfluramine and amphetamine, in rat pups. Five-day-old pups are randomly assigned to be injected with one of the two drugs. After injection, pups are allowed to eat for two hours. Percent weight gain is then measured.

a. Is this a *true experiment*, *quasi-experiment*, or *observational study*?

b. State the nondirectional statistical hypotheses for this study.

c. Assuming a large effect size is considered the smallest meaningful effect, and the researcher would like to use $\alpha = .05$, $\beta = .20$, what is the appropriate *sample* size for this study?

d. Compute the independent groups t test using the following data:

Fenfluramine	Amphetamine
2	8
3	10
3	4
4	7
4	9
5	3
6	7
6	12
6	6
7	8

e. What is the critical value for $\alpha = .05$? Can the researcher reject the null hypothesis?

f. How might these results be interpreted?

3. A researcher is interested in whether political liberals or conservatives tend to be better informed. A 75-item multiple choice test is composed using questions drawn from recent national and international news stories to test political knowledge.

a. Is this study a *true experiment*, *quasi-experiment*, or *observational study*?

b. What types of variables are political position and political knowledge: *nominal*, *ordinal*, *interval*, or *ratio*; *continuous* or *discrete*?

c. (1) State the directional null and alternative hypotheses based on the research hypothesis that liberals are more knowledgeable than conservatives.

(2) State the directional null and alternative hypotheses based on the research hypothesis that liberals are less knowledgeable than conservatives.

(3) State the nondirectional null and alternative hypotheses based on the research hypothesis that liberals differ in level of knowledge from conservatives.

(4) Which of the above three alternatives do you consider most appropriate for this study?

d. What would be the smallest meaningful effect size in this study?

e. What would be the desired minimum *sample* size under the following conditions:

(1) $\alpha = .10$, $\beta = .10$, large effect size

(2) $\alpha(D) = .01$, $\beta = .20$, medium effect size

(3) $\alpha = .20$, $\beta = .20$, small effect size

f. The following data are gathered from 30 college students. Higher scores suggest better performance on the test. Compute the independent groups t test:

Liberal	Conservative
26	18
32	25
18	32
42	53
15	27
16	26
23	19
45	35
53	42
47	51
32	26
23	63
51	42
62	40
19	36

g. Assume the researcher has decided to evaluate the directional null hypothesis based on the scientific hypothesis that liberals are more politically knowledgeable than conservatives. What is the critical value for $\alpha(D) = .01$? Can you reject the null hypothesis?

h. Again, assuming the researcher has decided to evaluate the directional null hypothesis based on the scientific hypothesis that liberals are more politically knowledgeable than conservatives, how would you interpret these results? Is the direction of the results consistent with the direction suggested by the scientific hypothesis?

4. a. Compute the 80% confidence interval associated with the data in question 2d. Is the critical value used for the hypothesis test in question 2e appropriate for the computation of this confidence interval?

   b. Are the results of the interval estimation consistent with those of the hypothesis test? If so, in what way? If not, why not?

5. a. Compute the 95% confidence interval associated with the data in question 3f. Is the critical value used for the hypothesis test in question 3g appropriate for the computation of this confidence interval?

   b. Are the results of the interval estimation consistent with those of the hypothesis test? If so, in what way? If not, why not?

6. A sample of 15 first graders is compared to a sample of 36 second graders on ability to read three-letter words. An independent groups _t_ test is used to determine whether a significant difference exists between first and second graders in reading level. In terms of the assumptions of the test, what are your concerns?

S16.1 COMPUTING THE DENOMINATOR OF THE INDEPENDENT GROUPS t TEST

Remember that the standard error of the mean equals

$$\sigma_{\overline{Y}} = \frac{\sigma_Y}{\sqrt{N}},$$

the population standard deviation divided by the square root of N. Since the standard deviation is the square root of the variance, this formula could also be stated as follows:

$$\sigma_{\overline{Y}} = \sqrt{\frac{\sigma_Y^2}{N}}.$$

Similarly, the best sample estimate for the standard error of the mean is

$$s_{\overline{Y}} = \sqrt{\frac{s_Y^2}{N}}.$$

This is used as the denominator for the one-group t test.

The standard error for the sampling distribution of $\overline{Y}_1 - \overline{Y}_2$ equals

$$\sigma_{\overline{Y}_1 - \overline{Y}_2} = \sqrt{\frac{\sigma_1^2}{n_1} + \frac{\sigma_2^2}{n_2}}.$$

That is, each population variance is divided by the n for the corresponding group. These are then summed and square rooted. This suggests that the best estimate of the standard error is provided by the formula

$$s_{\overline{Y}_1 - \overline{Y}_2} = \sqrt{\frac{s_1^2}{n_1} + \frac{s_2^2}{n_2}}.$$

So far, the computation of $s_{\overline{Y}_1 - \overline{Y}_2}$ is straightforward. However, the best sample estimate for the variances of the two populations differs depending on whether or not these population variances are equal.

Assume the variances of the two populations are equal, that is, the variance of the Psychasthenia scores in the population of liberal arts professors equals the variance of the Psychasthenia scores in the population of behavioral science professors:

$$\sigma_1^2 = \sigma_2^2.$$

If I use σ_Y^2 to refer to the variance of either population, the formula for the standard error may be restated as

$$\sigma_{\overline{Y}_1 - \overline{Y}_2} = \sqrt{\frac{\sigma_Y^2}{n_1} + \frac{\sigma_Y^2}{n_2}}$$

$$= \sqrt{\sigma_Y^2 \left(\frac{1}{n_1} + \frac{1}{n_2} \right)},$$

and data from both groups can be pooled together to estimate σ_Y^2.

The best formula for pooling information from the two groups to estimate σ_Y^2 would be

$$s_y^2 = \frac{(n_1 - 1)s_1^2 + (n_2 - 1)s_2^2}{(n_1 - 1) + (n_2 - 1)}$$

$$= \frac{SS_1 + SS_2}{n_1 + n_2 - 2}$$

$$= \frac{\sum\limits_{i=1}^{n_1} Y_i^2 + \sum\limits_{i=1}^{n_2} Y_i^2 - \frac{\left(\sum\limits_{i=1}^{n_1} Y_i \right)^2}{n_1} - \frac{\left(\sum\limits_{i=1}^{n_2} Y_i \right)^2}{n_2}}{N - 2}.$$

This formula is an example of a *weighted mean*, a concept introduced in Section S5.2 in the Chapter 5 supplement. If $n_1 = n_2$ then the variance estimates for the two groups are weighted equally in estimating the variance. If $n_1 \neq n_2$, the group with the larger n is weighted more heavily, on the grounds that the larger group produces a better estimate of the population variance.

If the two population variances are equal, the best sample estimate of the standard error for the sampling distribution of $\overline{Y}_1 - \overline{Y}_2$ is therefore

$$s_{\overline{Y}_1 - \overline{Y}_2} = \sqrt{\frac{SS_1 + SS_2}{N - 2} \left(\frac{1}{n_1} + \frac{1}{n_2} \right)}$$

$$= \sqrt{\frac{\sum\limits_{i=1}^{n_1} Y_i^2 + \sum\limits_{i=1}^{n_2} Y_i^2 - \frac{\left(\sum\limits_{i=1}^{n_1} Y_i \right)^2}{n_1} - \frac{\left(\sum\limits_{i=1}^{n_2} Y_i \right)^2}{n_2}}{N - 2} \left(\frac{1}{n_1} + \frac{1}{n_2} \right)}.$$

S16.2 THE UNEQUAL VARIANCES CASE

What if $\sigma_1^2 \neq \sigma_2^2$? This means pooling the data from the two groups is not appropriate, and a better estimate of the standard error is provided by the formula suggested earlier:

$$s_{\overline{Y}_1 - \overline{Y}_2} = \sqrt{\frac{s_1^2}{n_1} + \frac{s_2^2}{n_2}}.$$

Unfortunately, you never know if the two population variances are equal. This means that either formula may or may not provide the best estimate of the standard error.

The safest policy is to make sure that $n_1 = n_2$. When the group sizes are equal the pooled and unpooled formulas produce the same value. If $n_1 = n_2$, and n is used to represent either group size, the following proof demonstrates that the pooled variance formula will produce the same value for $s_{\overline{Y}_1 - \overline{Y}_2}$ as the unpooled formula:

$$\sqrt{\frac{(n-1)s_1^2 + (n-1)s_2^2}{(n-1) + (n-1)}\left(\frac{1}{n} + \frac{1}{n}\right)} = \sqrt{\frac{(n-1)(s_1^2 + s_2^2)}{2(n-1)}\left(\frac{2}{n}\right)} \quad \text{(from S1.1)}$$

$$= \sqrt{(s_1^2 + s_2^2)\left(\frac{1}{n}\right)} \quad \text{(simplifying a fraction)}$$

$$= \sqrt{\frac{s_1^2}{n} + \frac{s_2^2}{n}} \quad \text{(from S1.1)}.$$

CHAPTER 17

The *t* Test for a Correlation Coefficient

17.1 INTRODUCTION

The Pearson product-moment correlation coefficient, r_{XY}, was introduced in Chapter 7. This descriptive statistic can be used to describe the direction and strength of a linear relationship between any two variables, as long as neither is a nominal variable with more than two values. The correlation coefficient can vary between $+1.0$, which suggests a perfect positive linear relationship, and -1.0, which suggests a perfect negative linear relationship. A value of 0 indicates no linear relationship exists between the two variables.

The *t* test for a correlation coefficient can be used to evaluate whether the corresponding population correlation, ρ_{XY}, equals zero. If sample data suggest the population correlation is not equal to zero, there is evidence of a linear relationship between the two variables in the population.

The *t* test for a correlation coefficient r_{XY} is also the test of whether the population regression coefficients $b_{Y \cdot X}$ (the regression coefficient when X is used as a predictor of Y) and $b_{X \cdot Y}$ (the regression coefficient when Y is used as a predictor of X) are equal to zero in the population. If $\rho_{XY} = 0$, then $b_{Y \cdot X}$ and $b_{X \cdot Y}$ must equal zero; if $\rho_{XY} \neq 0$, then $b_{Y \cdot X}$ and $b_{X \cdot Y}$ do not equal zero.

17.2 DEFINING THE NULL AND ALTERNATIVE HYPOTHESES

The example that was used to illustrate the correlation coefficient in Chapter 7 involved asking five high school students to rate their level of agreement with the statement "I feel good about myself" on a scale from 1 (Strongly Disagree) to 5 (Strongly Agree). Students' self-esteem scores were then correlated with grade point average, or GPA. The data were as follows:

	Self-Esteem	GPA
Student 1	4	3.0
Student 2	3	2.5
Student 3	5	2.6
Student 4	3	4.0
Student 5	2	1.8

The correlation was found to be $+.2281$ (see Procedure Box 7.1 in Chapter 7). A positive correlation suggests a positive linear relationship in the sample: Higher self-esteem scores (suggesting greater self-esteem) tended to be associated with higher GPAs, lower self-esteem scores with lower GPAs. The t test is used to evaluate whether we have evidence that a positive relationship also exists in the population as a whole. The nondirectional null hypothesis suggests there is no population relationship between the two variables:

$$H_0: \rho_{XY} = 0,$$

where ρ_{XY} represents the correlation coefficient for the entire population. The alternative hypothesis suggests a relationship exists:

$$H_1: \rho_{XY} \neq 0.$$

17.3 TESTING THE NULL HYPOTHESIS

The formula for the t test for a correlation coefficient is

$$t_r = \frac{r_{XY}\sqrt{N-2}}{\sqrt{1-r_{XY}^2}}$$

The symbol t_r indicates this is a t test for a correlation coefficient. The computation of t_r for our study is demonstrated in Procedure Box 17.1.

17.4 MAKING A DECISION ABOUT THE NULL HYPOTHESIS

Critical values of the t test may be found in Table D–1 of Appendix D. The degrees of freedom for the t test for a correlation coefficient equal $N - 2$. In our study the two-tailed critical value for testing the non-directional null hypothesis is $t_{\alpha=.05, df=3} = \pm 3.182$; we can reject the null hypothesis if

$$|t_r| \geq 3.182.$$

The computed t_r value of $+.41$ indicates we are not close to significance.

There are only two variables in the formula for the t test for a correlation coefficient: the degrees of freedom and r_{XY}. This means it is possible to make a decision about the null hypothesis without computing t. Table D–3 provides the minimum r_{XY} value you would need for a certain degrees of freedom before you could reject the null hypothesis with a desired probability of a Type I error. For example, in our study with $df = 3$, the absolute value of r_{XY} would have to equal .878 or greater before we would be able to reject the null hypothesis at $\alpha = .05$. Our $r_{XY} = +.2281$, which does not allow rejection of the null hypothesis.

Interpreting the Results. Our data do not provide sufficient evidence to conclude that a relationship exists between self-esteem and GPA in the population from which our sample was randomly drawn. This may be because there is no relationship or, as you will see, because of insufficient power. If t_r had been significant, a positive t value would suggest

The *t* Test for a Correlation Coefficient

Goal   Compute t_r where $r_{XY} = +.2281$ and $N = 5$.

$$t_r = \frac{r_{XY}\sqrt{N-2}}{\sqrt{1-r_{XY}^2}}$$

Step 1   *Square r_{XY}, subtract from 1, and find the square root.*

$$\sqrt{1-r_{XY}^2} = \sqrt{1-.2281^2} = .9736$$

Step 2   *Find the square root of $N - 2$.*

$$\sqrt{5-2} = \sqrt{3} = 1.73205$$

Step 3   *Multiply r_{XY} by the result of Step 2, and divide by the result of Step 1.*

$$t_r = \frac{(.2281)(1.7321)}{.9736} = +.41$$

a positive linear relationship in the population between X and Y, while a negative t value would suggest a negative linear relationship.

Note that a significant result indicates only that the evidence suggests the population correlation coefficient does not equal zero. A significant t test does not say anything about how large ρ_{XY} is, or how strong the relationship between X and Y is, only that a relationship exists in the population.

17.5 CONDITIONS FOR USING THE TEST

Conditions. The t test for a correlation coefficient can be used when (1) members of the sample produce an X variable which can be any type of variable except a nominal variable with more than two values, (2) members of the sample also produce a quantitative Y variable, and (3) the null hypothesis has to do with whether $\rho_{XY} = 0$.

I mentioned at the beginning of the chapter that the correlation coefficient can be computed as a descriptive statistic for any two variables so long as neither is a nominal variable with more than two values. The conditions for using the t test for a correlation coefficient are slightly more restrictive, requiring at least one quantitative variable. For example, the phi coefficient is used to represent the strength of the relationship between two dichotomous variables. The t test should not be used to evaluate whether a population phi coefficient equals zero, since neither variable is quantitative. The same is true for the Spearman correlation, which is used with discrete ordinal variables.

The Point-Biserial Correlation. Although not appropriate for phi or Spearman coefficients, the t test can be used to evaluate whether a population point-biserial correlation equals zero. The point-biserial correlation is used to represent the strength of the relationship between a dichotomous variable and a quantitative variable. If the t test for a correlation coefficient is used to evaluate whether a population point-biserial correlation equals zero, it is equivalent to using the independent groups t test to evaluate whether a relationship exists between a dichotomous variable and a quantitative variable.

To demonstrate this point, I will use the data on college professors and anxiety introduced for the independent groups t test. Groups of liberal arts and behavioral science professors produced the following scores on the MMPI Psychasthenia scale:

Liberal Arts	Behavioral Sciences
45	58
63	59
62	63
51	68
54	74
63	68
52	52
54	66
64	69
49	57

Psychasthenia scores will be considered variable Y. Suppose we use variable X to refer to the group, and we assign every liberal arts professor a value of 1 on X and every behavioral science professor a 2. The data can now be listed in the following form:

X	Y	X	Y
1	45	2	58
1	63	2	59
1	62	2	63
1	51	2	68
1	54	2	74
1	63	2	68
1	52	2	52
1	54	2	66
1	64	2	69
1	49	2	57

Using these data we can compute the point-biserial correlation between X and Y:

$$r_{XY} = \frac{\displaystyle\sum_{i=1}^{N} X_i Y_i - \frac{\left(\displaystyle\sum_{i=1}^{N} X_i\right)\left(\displaystyle\sum_{i=1}^{N} Y_i\right)}{N}}{\sqrt{\left[\displaystyle\sum_{i=1}^{N} X_i^2 - \frac{\left(\displaystyle\sum_{i=1}^{N} X_i\right)^2}{N}\right]\left[\displaystyle\sum_{i=1}^{N} Y_i^2 - \frac{\left(\displaystyle\sum_{i=1}^{N} Y_i\right)^2}{N}\right]}}$$

$$= \frac{1825 - \frac{30(1191)}{20}}{\sqrt{\left[50 - \frac{30^2}{20}\right]\left[2382 - \frac{1191^2}{20}\right]}}$$

$$= +.513.$$

Complete instructions for computing the correlation coefficient may be found in Procedure Box 7.1. The *t* value for this correlation equals

$$t_r = \frac{.513\sqrt{20 - 2}}{\sqrt{1 - .513^2}} = +2.54.$$

This *t* value equals the *t* value computed for the independent groups *t* test in Chapter 16. Notice the sign has changed: in Chapter 16 $t_{\overline{Y}_1 - \overline{Y}_2} = -2.54$; now $t_r = +2.54$. This simply reflects the arbitrary decision concerning which group to consider Group 1 and which to consider Group 2. Had we assigned 1s to behavioral science professors and 2s to liberal arts professors, t_r would have been negative. The degrees of freedom are also the same, $N - 2 = 18$.

Assumptions. The *t* test for a correlation coefficient requires the following statistical assumptions (Binder, 1959):

1. random and independent sampling
2. the normality assumption: for each value of *X* in the population, the corresponding *Y* scores in the population are normally distributed
3. the homogeneity of variance assumption: for each value of *X* in the population, the corresponding *Y* scores have equal variances

For example, if you took every member of the population with an *X* score of 12, the second assumption suggests that the distribution of *Y* scores for these members would be normal. The third assumption suggests that the variance of these *Y* scores would equal the variance of *Y* scores associated with any other *X* value. It is because of these assumptions that the *t* test is not recommended for phi coefficients. If *Y* only has two values, the *Y* values associated with any *X* score clearly cannot be normally distributed. Notice that if *X* is a dichotomous variable, these assumptions are equivalent to the assumptions required for the independent groups *t* test.

TABLE 17.1   Selected Aspects of the t Test for a Correlation Coefficient

Symbol Used	Degrees of Freedom	Type of Statistical Hypotheses	General Form of Statistical Hypotheses	Type of Test	Symbol for Alpha	Critical Region in
t_r	$N-2$	nondirectional	$H_0: \rho_{XY} = 0$ $H_1: \rho_{XY} \neq 0$	two-tailed	α	both tails (both positive and negative critical values)
		directional	$H_0: \rho_{XY} \leq 0$ $H_1: \rho_{XY} > 0$	one-tailed	$\alpha(\mathrm{D})$	upper tail (critical value is positive)
		directional	$H_0: \rho_{XY} \geq 0$ $H_1: \rho_{XY} < 0$	one-tailed	$\alpha(\mathrm{D})$	lower tail (critical value is negative)

17.6 DIRECTIONAL VERSUS NONDIRECTIONAL HYPOTHESES

If we wanted to use a directional hypothesis suggesting a positive linear relationship exists between two population variables, the null and alternative hypotheses would be

$$H_0: \rho_{XY} \leq 0$$
$$H_1: \rho_{XY} > 0,$$

and the critical value would be positive. If we wanted to test the hypothesis that a negative linear relationship exists between two variables, the null and alternative hypotheses would be

$$H_0: \rho_{XY} \geq 0$$
$$H_1: \rho_{XY} < 0,$$

and the critical value would be negative. This and other aspects of the t test for a correlation coefficient are summarized in Table 17.1. The critical values for one-tailed tests may be found in Table D–1; the minimum sample r_{XY} value necessary to achieve significance may be found in Table D–3.

For the one-tailed test of the directional hypothesis that self-esteem and GPA are positively related in the population, $t_{\alpha(\mathrm{D})=.05, df=3} = +2.353$; r_{XY} would have to equal or exceed .805 to reject the null hypothesis. Similarly, to test the directional hypothesis that self-esteem and GPA are negatively related in the population, $t_{\alpha(\mathrm{D})=.05, df=3} = -2.353$ and the critical r_{XY} value would be $-.805$.

17.7 POWER AND SAMPLE SIZE ISSUES

The power of the t test for a correlation coefficient is determined by the alpha level, sample size, and effect size. The effect size is determined by the size of the correlation between X and Y in the population; the larger ρ_{XY} is, the larger the effect size. Table C–5 in Appendix C provides recommended sample sizes for achieving power of .80 ($\beta = .20$) and .90 ($\beta = .10$). For example, for $\alpha(\mathrm{D}) = .01$, $\beta = .10$, and a large effect size the appropriate sample size is 45. Even if the effect size were large, the sample size of 5 in the study of GPA and self-esteem is not sufficient to insure an adequate level of power. The failure to find a relationship between self-esteem and GPA in our population may have occurred because of a very high probability of a Type II error.

KEY TERMS

directional hypothesis
homogeneity of variance assumption
linear relationship
negative linear relationship
nominal variable
nondirectional hypothesis
normality assumption
one-tailed test
Pearson product-moment correlation
    coefficient

phi coefficient
point-biserial correlation coefficient
positive linear relationship
power
quantitative variable
sample size
t distribution
two-tailed test
Type II error

EXERCISES

Answers to all exercises may be found in Appendix B.

1. A researcher is interested in whether students who spend more time on homework tend to be liked less by other students. For one semester, eighth grade students record the amount of time spent on homework each day. They are also asked to rate their liking of all other students in their class on a scale from 1 (Dislike Very Much) to 5 (Like Very Much). The mean number of hours of homework completed per weekday in a semester is then compared to the liking score averaged across all classmates.

    a. Is this a *true experiment, quasi-experiment,* or *observational study?*

    b. State the null and alternative directional hypotheses for this study.

    c. Assuming a large effect size is considered the smallest important effect, and the researcher would like to use $\alpha(D) = .01$, $\beta = .10$, what is the appropriate sample size for this study?

    d. Compute r_{XY} and the *t* test for a correlation coefficient using the following data:

Hours	Liking
1.5	4.1
2.0	1.2
1.7	3.6
.9	1.2
1.3	4.7
1.9	3.2

    e. What is the critical value for $\alpha(D) = .01$? What is the minimum r_{XY} value that can result in significance in the present case? Can the researcher reject the null hypothesis?

    f. How might these results be interpreted?

2. In the exercises for the last chapter, a true experiment was described in which five-day-old rat pups were injected with either fenfluramine and amphetamine to evaluate the impact of injection on subsequent percent weight gain. Suppose we reorganize the data from that study in the following way:

X	Y	X	Y
1	2	2	8
1	3	2	10
1	3	2	4
1	4	2	7
1	4	2	9
1	5	2	3
1	6	2	7
1	6	2	12
1	6	2	6
1	7	2	8

The variable X represents group ($1 =$ fenfluramine, $2 =$ amphetamine), the variable Y percent weight gain.

    a. State the nondirectional statistical hypotheses for this study.

b. Compute r_{XY}. Is this a *point-biserial correlation*, a *phi coefficient*, or a *Spearman correlation coefficient*?

c. Compute the t test for a correlation coefficient.

d. What is the critical value for $\alpha = .05$? Can the researcher reject the null hypothesis?

3. Challenge question: Suppose the study in the previous question consisted of three groups: rat pups who received fenfluramine, pups who received amphetamine, and pups who received plain salt water. On the X variable there would then be 3 values, to represent groups 1, 2, and 3. It would no longer be appropriate to use the t test for a correlation coefficient. Why? *Hint:* Think about the meaning of linear relationships.

4. For each of the following, indicate the minimum correlation coefficient necessary to achieve significance. Indicate whether the correlation coefficient would need to be positive, negative, or either to reject the null hypothesis:

a. A researcher believes that the longer a Senator has been in office, the more money that politician is able to raise for reelection campaigns. Data are collected for 30 Senators on length in office and amount of money raised the last time they ran for office. The hypothesis test will be conducted with $\alpha = .05$.

b. A researcher believes that the longer a Senator has been in office, the less time that Senator spends in the home state. Data are collected for 62 Senators on length in office and the number of days spent in the home state during the last year. The hypothesis test will be conducted with $\alpha(D) = .05$.

c. A researcher believes that the longer the time since a rat's last feeding, the greater the rat's activity level. Data are collected for 62 rats on number of minutes since last feeding and amount of movement (measured by a device attached to the floor of the cage). The hypothesis test will be conducted with $\alpha(D) = .01$.

5. For each of the following studies, indicate how you would interpret the finding:

a. A researcher hypothesizes that more attractive females tend to be perceived as less intelligent by males. The correlation was $+.625$, which was significant at $\alpha = .05$.

b. A researcher hypothesizes that more attractive females tend to be perceived as less intelligent by males. The correlation was $+.923$, which was not significant at $\alpha(D) = .05$.

c. A researcher hypothesizes that more attractive females tend to be perceived as less intelligent by males. The correlation was $-.325$, which was significant at $\alpha = .01$.

The One-Way Independent
Groups Analysis of Variance

18.1 INTRODUCTION

Family-Wise Error Rate. Research studies often involve more than two groups. Suppose we are interested in whether Catholics, Protestants, or Jews have the highest average yearly income. The study has to do with the relationship between the variables religious preference, a nominal variable with three values, and annual income, a discrete ratio variable. We could compute separate independent groups t tests for each pair of groups. This would require a t test comparing Jews and Catholics, a second comparing Catholics and Protestants, and a third comparing Jews and Protestants. The problem with this analysis is that it results in a rapid increase in the probability of a Type I error.

To understand why this happens, let's compare it to flipping a coin. There are two possible outcomes to a coin flip, a head (H) or a tail (T). The probability of a head is .50. Flipping a coin two times results in one of four possible outcomes: HH, HT, TH, and TT. The probability of *at least* one head has increased to .75. The probability of at least one head increases to .875 when a coin is flipped three times. The more times a coin is flipped, the greater the probability of at least one head.

For a single independent groups t test evaluated at $\alpha = .05$, the probability of a Type I error is .05. For two t tests, each evaluated at $\alpha = .05$, the probability of *at least* one Type I error increases to as much as .0975 depending on circumstances surrounding the analysis. Computing three t tests at $\alpha = .05$ increases the probability of at least one Type I error to as much as .1426. The more inferential statistics are computed, the greater the probability of at least one Type I error. If we define the **family-wise error rate** as *the probability of at least one Type I error across a set, or family, of analyses*, we would say that using multiple t tests to analyze differences among more than two group means does not control family-wise error rate.

The Analysis of Variance. The statistician R. A. Fisher introduced the analysis of variance, or ANOVA, as a procedure for controlling the Type I error rate when comparing two or more groups in experimental studies. The analysis of variance is not actually an inferential statistic. The term applies to various procedures for computing variances from a set of data. These variances are then used in the computation of inferential statistics.

Hypothesis tests associated with the analysis of variance use an inferential statistic called the F test in Fisher's honor. Before discussing the analysis of variance in detail it will help to know a little about the F test.

18.1.1 The *F* Test

Comparing Variance Estimates. The *F* test may be used whenever the statistical hypotheses have to do with whether two population variances are equal. Suppose we hypothesize that males tend to be more variable in their level of intelligence than females, that males produce more very high scores and very low scores on intelligence tests. The null and alternative hypotheses for this study could be stated as

$$H_0: \sigma_1^2 = \sigma_2^2$$
$$H_1: \sigma_1^2 \neq \sigma_2^2.$$

The null hypothesis suggests that the two population variances are equal, the alternative hypothesis that they are unequal.

This null hypothesis could be tested using the *F* test, which uses the following formula:

$$F = \frac{s_1^2}{s_2^2},$$

where s_1^2 is always the larger of the two population variance estimates, s_2^2 the smaller.

The *F* Distribution. Suppose we were able to create an *F* **distribution**, a *sampling distribution of F values for all random samples of a given size from some population*. The shape of the sampling distribution is determined by the degrees of freedom for the numerator of $F(df_1)$ and the degrees of freedom for the denominator (df_2), where:

$$df_1 = n_1 - 1$$
$$df_2 = n_2 - 1.$$

If the null hypothesis is true and $\sigma_1^2 = \sigma_2^2$, then the expected sample *F* value would be 1.0. Since the numerator and denominator are both squared values, *F* must be a positive number. There is no limit to how large an *F* value can be, but *F* values can be no less than 0. This tends to produce a positively skewed sampling distribution of *F* values, as illustrated in Figure 18.1(a). However, with greater degrees of freedom the positive tail contracts, as in Figure 18.1(b), reducing the amount of skew.

Table D–4 in Appendix D provides critical *F* values for various degrees of freedom. For example, the critical value for $df_1 = 10$ and $df_2 = 15$ is

$$F_{\alpha=.05, df_1=10, df_2=15} = 2.55.$$

If the computed *F* value equals or exceeds 2.55, it suggests that σ_1^2 is larger than σ_2^2.

The *F* test is not used very often to examine whether two sample variances represent equal population variances. This is because the *F* test, when used for this purpose, requires the assumption that both variance estimates came from populations that are normally distributed, and it is never robust against violation of this assumption. As we have seen, a normally distributed population is very unlikely (Micceri, 1989), so the results of the test are usually questionable. In practice, the *F* test is used almost exclusively for the analysis of variance.

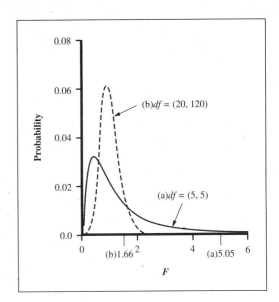

FIGURE 18.1   The F distributions for $df = (5, 5)$ and $df = (20, 120)$ when the null hypothesis is assumed to be true.

18.1.2 The One-Way Independent Groups ANOVA

The one-way independent groups ANOVA is also called the one-way between-subjects ANOVA. The conditions required for using the one-way independent groups ANOVA are similar to those required for the independent groups t test: (1) members of the sample fall into two or more groups based on a discrete variable, (2) the groups are independent, (3) members of the sample produce a quantitative variable, and (4) the null hypothesis has to do with whether the quantitative variable μ is different for the populations represented by the groups.

Unlike the t test, the ANOVA is not limited to the comparison of two groups. Technically, the one-way ANOVA can handle an infinite number of groups, although in practice the number rarely surpasses four or five.

The analysis of variance was originally developed specifically for the analysis of true experiments. In that context the discrete variable was the independent variable, and the quantitative variable was the dependent variable. The term *one-way* implies the presence of one independent variable, although the ANOVA is referred to as one-way even when the study is observational. Other ANOVA procedures are available to handle cases where there is more than one independent variable; an example is provided in Chapter 21.

18.2 DEFINING THE NULL AND ALTERNATIVE HYPOTHESES

Describing the Study. Fenfluramine is a drug that increases the amount of a chemical called serotonin in the brain, while amphetamine enhances the activity of the chemical norepinephrine. Both serotonin and norepinephrine are believed to play a role in the suppression of appetite. Suppose we would like to compare the appetite suppression effects of injecting equal amounts of fenfluramine and amphetamine into 15-day-old

Long-Evans hooded rats. This study would require two groups of rats, each of which is injected with one of the two drugs. The results could be analyzed using an independent groups *t* test.

Now suppose we wanted to add a third group to be injected with plain saltwater. The rats who receive saltwater injections represent a control group to examine the impact of injection alone on food intake.

Twelve rats were each randomly assigned to one of the groups, producing three groups of four rats. The group of rats that is assigned to receive fenfluramine injection may be considered representative of a population of rats randomly assigned to receive fenfluramine. The group of rats that is assigned to receive amphetamine injection may be considered representative of a population of rats randomly assigned to receive amphetamine. The group of rats that is assigned to receive saltwater injection may be considered representative of a population of rats randomly assigned to receive saltwater.

For rats receiving fenfluramine and amphetamine injections, 0.5 milligrams of the appropriate drug for each kilogram of body weight was mixed with saltwater. After injection they were allowed to feed with milk for 2 hours. Weight gain was then evaluated as a percentage of starting weight. The study is evaluating whether a relationship exists between the variables type of drug (a nominal variable with three values: amphetamine, fenfluramine, and saltwater) and percent weight gain (a continuous ratio variable).

The Statistical Hypotheses. The null and alternative hypotheses in this study may be stated as

$$H_0: \mu_1 = \mu_2 = \mu_3$$

$$H_1: \mu_1 \neq \mu_2 \text{ and/or } \mu_1 \neq \mu_3 \text{ and/or } \mu_2 \neq \mu_3.$$

Since the one-way independent groups ANOVA is not limited to three groups, the statistical hypotheses could be stated more generally as

$$H_0: \text{all } \mu\text{s are equal}$$

$$H_1: \text{not all } \mu\text{s are equal.}$$

That is, the one-way independent groups ANOVA *F* test evaluates whether the entire set of μs is equal.

An Alternate Form. These statistical hypotheses can also be stated in terms of the variance of the three μs. Suppose we took the μs from our three populations and computed a variance. If the μs are all equal, as the null hypothesis suggests, then the variance of the μs (σ_μ^2) will equal zero; if the alternative hypothesis is true and there is some variability among the μs, then the variance of the μs (σ_μ^2) is some value greater than 0. The null and alternative hypotheses may therefore be written

$$H_0: \sigma_\mu^2 = 0$$

$$H_1: \sigma_\mu^2 \neq 0.$$

It is important to understand the difference between σ_Y^2 and σ_μ^2. σ_μ^2 represents the variance *among* the μs of several populations. For example, if we knew the μs for the percent weight gain in the population of rats receiving fenfluramine, amphetamine, and saltwater, σ_μ^2 would be the variance of these three μs. σ_Y^2 represents the variance *within* a single population. It is computed by finding deviation scores for each member of a population from the population μ.

Notice that we have moved from talking about *differences between* μs as we did with the *t* test, to talking about *variances among* μs. This is one of the implications of the term *analysis of variance*.

18.3 TESTING THE NULL HYPOTHESIS

Section 18.1.1 indicated that the F test may be used to evaluate whether two population variances are equal. *Population variance estimates computed for the analysis of variance* are referred to as **mean squares**, and the two variance estimates computed for the one-way independent groups ANOVA are called the mean square between groups and the mean square within groups. The next two sections briefly describe the computation of the two variance estimates. This is followed by a demonstration of the computation of F, and a discussion of the implications of this F value for the null hypothesis

$$H_0\colon \sigma_\mu^2 = 0.$$

18.3.1 The Mean Square Between Groups

The **mean square between groups** (MS_{BG}) is *a population variance estimate based on the variability among group means. The numerator of the mean square between groups* is called the **sum of squares between groups** (SS_{BG}). *The denominator of the mean square between groups* (df_{BG}) is called the **degrees of freedom between groups**.

If the group sizes are equal, the definitional formula for the sum of squares between groups may be stated as

$$SS_{\text{BG}} = n \sum_{j=1}^{k} (\overline{Y}_j - \overline{Y}_s)^2,$$

where $\overline{Y}_j$ refers to the means for the groups, $\overline{Y}_s$ to the mean for the entire sample of N subjects. In our study, k (the number of groups) $= 3$. I will use $j = 1$ to refer to the fenfluramine group, $j = 2$ to the amphetamine group, and $j = 3$ to the saltwater group. If our study includes 12 rats, $\overline{Y}_1$ refers to the mean percent weight gain for the 4 rats who receive fenfluramine, $\overline{Y}_2$ to the mean percent weight gain for the 4 rats who receive amphetamine, and $\overline{Y}_3$ to the mean percent weight gain for the 4 rats who receive saltwater. $\overline{Y}_S$ would refer to the mean percent weight gain for all 12 rats.

The following computational formula may be used instead:

$$SS_{\text{BG}} = \left[\frac{\left(\sum \text{first group}\right)^2}{n} + \cdots \frac{\left(\sum \text{last group}\right)^2}{n} \right] - \frac{\left(\sum \text{scores}\right)^2}{N}.$$

First, the scores for each group are summed, squared, and divided by n. The resulting values are then added together. Second, all the scores are summed, squared, and divided by N. The second quantity is then subtracted from the first.

The formula for the degrees of freedom between groups is

$$df_{BG} = k - 1.$$

Computation of all formulas will be demonstrated in Procedure Box 18.1 later in the chapter.

18.3.2 The Mean Square Within Groups

The **mean square within groups** (MS_{WG}) is a *population variance estimate based on the variability within the groups*. The definitional formula for MS_{WG} is

$$MS_{WG} = \frac{\sum_{j=1}^{k} SS_j}{N - k}.$$

SS_j refers to the sum of squares for each of the k groups. These are summed and divided by the sample size minus the number of groups. This formula indicates that the variability within each of the groups is pooled to produce a single population variance estimate. Like the independent groups t test in Chapter 16, the one-way independent groups ANOVA uses a pooled variance formula, so the homogeneity of variance assumption is required.

The numerator of the mean square within groups is called the **sum of squares within groups** (SS_{WG}). *The denominator of the mean square within groups* is called the **degrees of freedom within groups** (df_{WG}). The computational formula for SS_{WG} is

$$SS_{WG} = \left(\sum \text{squared scores} \right) - \left[\frac{(\sum \text{first group})^2}{n} + \cdots \frac{(\sum \text{last group})^2}{n} \right].$$

The scores for each group are summed, squared, and divided by n. The resulting values are then added together. This quantity is then subtracted from the sum of the squared values. The formula for the degrees of freedom within groups is

$$df_{WG} = N - k.$$

18.3.3 The *F* Test

The formula for F is

$$F = \frac{MS_{BG}}{MS_{WG}}.$$

Procedure Box 18.1 demonstrates the computation of the F test for the appetite suppression study.

The One-Way Independent Groups ANOVA *F* Test

Goal   Twelve rats were randomly assigned to receive one of three drugs. Subsequent percent weight gains were:

Fenfluramine	Amphetamine	Saltwater
1	3	10
2	6	8
4	9	12
6	5	10

Compute the *F* value.

$$SS_{BG} = \left[\frac{(\sum \text{first group})^2}{n} + \cdots \frac{(\sum \text{last group})^2}{n}\right] - \frac{(\sum \text{scores})^2}{N}$$

$$SS_{WG} = \left(\sum \text{squared scores}\right) - \left[\frac{(\sum \text{first group})^2}{n} + \cdots \frac{(\sum \text{last group})^2}{n}\right].$$

$$df_{BG} = k - 1 \qquad df_{wg} = N - k$$

$$MS_{BG} = \frac{SS_{BG}}{df_{BG}} \quad MS_{WG} = \frac{SS_{WG}}{df_{WG}} \quad F = \frac{MS_{BG}}{MS_{WG}}$$

Step 1   *Compute the sum of Y and Y^2 for each group.*

Y	Y^2	Y	Y^2	Y	Y^2
1	1	3	9	10	100
2	4	6	36	8	64
4	16	9	81	12	144
6	36	5	25	10	100
Sums: 13	57	23	151	40	408

Step 2   *Square the sum of the scores for each group, divide by n, and sum the resulting values.*

$$\left[\frac{(\sum \text{first group})^2}{n} + \cdots \frac{(\sum \text{last group})^2}{n}\right] = \frac{13^2}{4} + \frac{23^2}{4} + \frac{40^2}{4} = 574.5$$

Continued

The one-way independent groups ANOVA F test continued

Step 3   *Square the sum of all the scores and divide by N.*

$$\frac{(\sum \text{scores})^2}{N} = \frac{(13 + 23 + 40)^2}{12} = 481.3333$$

Step 4   *Sum the squared scores.*

$$\left(\sum \text{squared scores}\right) = 57 + 151 + 408 = 616$$

Step 5   *Subtract the result of Step 3 from the result of Step 2.*

$$SS_{BG} = 574.5 - 481.3333 = 93.1667 \longleftarrow \textit{This number must be positive}$$

Step 6   *Subtract the result of Step 2 from the result of Step 4.*

$$SS_{WG} = 616 - 574.5 = 41.5 \longleftarrow \textit{This number must be positive}$$

Step 7   *Divide the result of Step 5 by $k - 1$.*

$$MS_{BG} = \frac{93.1667}{3 - 1} = 46.5834$$

Step 8   *Divide the result of Step 6 by $N - k$.*

$$MS_{WG} = \frac{41.5}{12 - 3} = 4.6111$$

Step 9   *Divide the result of Step 7 by the result of Step 8.*

$$F = \frac{46.5834}{4.6111} = 10.10$$

The results may be used to create an ANOVA summary table (see Section 18.4):

Source	df	SS	MS	F
Between Groups	2	93.17	46.58	10.10
Within Groups	9	41.50	4.61	

18.3.4 Understanding the ANOVA *F* Test

The Analysis of Variance. Some additional information about the analysis of variance itself is appropriate. Suppose I ignored the groups and computed a population variance estimate using every subject in the sample:

$$\frac{\sum_{i=1}^{N}(Y_i - \overline{Y}_s)^2}{N - 1}$$

(remember that $\overline{Y}_s$ is the mean for the entire sample). *The numerator of the variance estimate based on the entire sample* is called the **sum of squares total** (SS_T), and *the denominator of the variance estimate based on the entire sample* is the **degrees of freedom total** (df_T).

One characteristic of the one-way independent groups ANOVA is that the sum of squares total equals the sum of squares between groups plus the sum of squares within groups, and the degrees of freedom total equals the degrees of freedom between groups plus the degrees of freedom within groups:

$$SS_{BG} + SS_{WG} = SS_T$$

$$n\sum_{j=1}^{k}(\overline{Y}_j - \overline{Y}_s)^2 + \frac{\sum_{j=1}^{k} SS_j}{N - k} = \sum_{i=1}^{N}(Y_i - \overline{Y}_s)^2$$

$$df_{BG} + df_{WG} = df_T$$

$$(k - 1) + (N - k) = N - 1.$$

This demonstrates the formal meaning of the term **analysis of variance**: *a set of statistical procedures for which the common element is the division of the variability in a set of scores into meaningful subcomponents.* In the case of the one-way independent groups ANOVA, the variability of the scores is divided into variability between the groups and variability within the groups. Other ANOVA procedures will involve dividing variability in other ways.

The *F* Test. You know already that the *F* test is used to evaluate whether two population variances are equal. If the *F* test is significant, it suggests that the population parameter estimated by MS_{BG} is larger than the parameter estimated by MS_{WG}. So what parameters are estimated by MS_{BG} and MS_{WG}?

Remember that σ_Y^2 represents the variance of all the Y scores within a population. The variances for the three populations in our study—the population of 15-day-old rats injected with fenfluramine, the population of 15-day-old rats injected with amphetamine, and the population of 15-day-old rats injected with saltwater—were assumed to be equal in order to use a pooled variance formula for MS_{WG}. It can be demonstrated that MS_{WG} estimates σ_Y^2, the variance for any of the three populations. In other words, if a large number of random samples from these populations were collected, and MS_{WG} was computed for each sample, it would be possible to generate a sampling distribution of MS_{WG}. The mean of this sampling distribution would equal σ_Y^2.

MS_{BG} estimates the value

$$\sigma_Y^2 + c(\sigma_\mu^2).$$

The c refers to a constant that varies depending on certain conditions which need not trouble us here. What is important to understand is the relationship between MS_{BG} and the null hypothesis.

If the null hypothesis is true, $\sigma_\mu^2 = 0$ and MS_{BG} estimates

$$\sigma_Y^2 + c(0) = \sigma_Y^2.$$

MS_{WG} also estimates σ_Y^2. The two mean squares are estimating the same population value, so the F test should not be significant.

If the null hypothesis is false it means the variance of the μs is greater than 0. Therefore, MS_{BG} is estimating a larger value than MS_{WG}. The F test should be significant, assuming adequate power. This in turn indicates that at least some of the population μs are not equal.

18.4 MAKING A DECISION ABOUT THE NULL HYPOTHESIS

Critical values for F may be found in Table D–4 of Appendix D. The degrees of freedom for the numerator are the degrees of freedom between groups; the degrees of freedom for the denominator are the degrees of freedom within groups. In our appetite suppression study,

$$df_1 = k - 1 = 3 - 1 = 2$$

$$df_2 = N - k = 12 - 3 = 9$$

$$F_{\alpha=.05, df_1=2, df_2=9} = 4.26.$$

We can reject the null hypothesis if

$$F \geq 4.26.$$

The computed F value 10.10 from Procedure Box 18.1 allows us to reject the null hypothesis. There is evidence that the three population μs are not equal.

The results of the ANOVA are often presented in the following format, sometimes referred to as an ANOVA summary table:

Source	df	SS	MS	F
Between Groups	2	93.17	46.58	10.10*
Within Groups	9	41.50	4.61	

*$p < .05$

The "$p < .05$" at the bottom of the table indicates that the asterisked F value surpasses the critical value when $\alpha = .05$, so rejecting the null hypothesis is associated with a Type I error probability of less than .05.

Interpreting the Results. Rejecting the null hypothesis suggests that a relationship exists between the type of drug and percent weight gain. The study was conducted as a true experiment, with rats randomly assigned to a type of drug. Assuming the random assignment has been successful, and assuming there are no unmentioned situational confounds, we have strong evidence that the type of drug has a direct effect on percent weight gain. Of course, given the small groups sizes it may be unreasonable to assume random assignment was successful (see Section 3.2.1.3, "Explaining the Findings," for a discussion of the relationship between group size and random assignment in true experiments).

If $k = 2$ (a dichotomous variable) we could stop right now; the direction of the difference would be evident from a comparison of the group means. When $k > 2$, additional analyses are necessary to determine what differences between means suggest differences between μs.

We have rejected the null hypothesis that $\mu_1 = \mu_2 = \mu_3$, but we do not yet know if the difference is between μ_1 and μ_2, μ_1 and μ_3, μ_2 and μ_3, or some combination of these possibilities. So far, we have only determined that a difference exists. This was accomplished by conducting an **omnibus test**, *an analysis of variance test that includes all the μs of interest, to determine whether there is evidence of differences in a set of μs.* Determining where these differences lie is accomplished by conducting additional tests which are discussed in the next chapter.

To summarize, the analysis of variance is a sequential process. The first step involves conducting an omnibus test to determine whether there is evidence of a difference among μs. If there is evidence of differences, the next step involves conducting additional analyses to see where the differences lie. If the omnibus test fails to suggest there are differences, then the analysis is concluded.

18.5 CONDITIONS FOR USING THE TEST

Conditions. As I stated previously, the conditions required for using the one-way independent groups ANOVA are similar to those required for the independent groups t test: (1) members of the sample fall into two or more groups based on a discrete variable, (2) the groups are independent, (3) members of the sample produce a quantitative variable, and (4) the null hypothesis has to do with whether the quantitative variable μ is different for the populations represented by the groups. Such a difference would suggest the existence of a population relationship between the two variables.

The similarity to the independent groups t test does not stop there. If the discrete variable has only two values you could compute either the independent groups t test or the one-way independent groups ANOVA. In this case the computed F value would be the square of the computed t value. Furthermore, the critical F value would be the square of the critical t value. When the discrete variable is dichotomous, the t and F tests are equivalent: using either test will result in the same decision concerning the null hypothesis.

The appetite suppression study represents a true experiment. The one-way independent groups ANOVA can also be used to analyze quasi-experimental studies in which there is nonrandom assignment to independent treatment groups, or observational studies where there are independent groups. The example that began this chapter, comparing

TABLE 18.1   Selected Aspects of the One-Way Independent Groups ANOVA

Symbol Used	Degrees of Freedom	Type of Statistical Hypotheses	General Form of Statistical Hypotheses	Type of Test	Symbol for Alpha	Critical Region in
F	$k - 1$ $N - k$	nondirectional	H_0: all μs are equal H_1: not all μs are equal	one-tailed	α	upper tail

members of three religions on annual income, is an example of an observational study in which use of the one-way independent groups ANOVA would be appropriate.

Assumptions.   The test requires the following statistical assumptions:

1. Random and independent sampling.
2. The normality assumption: the populations represented by each group are all normally distributed. The one-way independent groups ANOVA is generally considered robust against violation of this assumption if $n \geq 30$ for all groups.
3. The homogeneity of variance assumption: the variances of the populations are all equal. This assumption was necessary to develop the pooled variance formula. The one-way independent groups ANOVA is generally considered robust against violation of this assumption if all group sizes are equal.

18.6 DIRECTIONAL VERSUS NONDIRECTIONAL HYPOTHESES

Like the χ^2 test, the ANOVA F test is always one-tailed. The larger the differences in the group means, the larger the computed F value will be. The ANOVA F test has an advantage over the t test in that the equality of many μs can be evaluated simultaneously. The disadvantage is that the F test can only indicate that the μs are not all equal; it does not indicate which μs are unequal. The only exception to this rule occurs when the discrete variable is dichotomous. Then the one-way independent groups ANOVA is essentially equivalent to the independent groups t test, and the larger group mean suggests which population μ is larger. Like the χ^2 goodness of fit test, the ANOVA F test is always one-tailed, yet only nondirectional hypotheses can be tested. This and other aspects of the one-way independent groups ANOVA are summarized in Table 18.1.

18.7 POWER AND SAMPLE SIZE ISSUES

The power of the ANOVA F test depends upon the alpha level, the sample size, the degrees of freedom for the numerator, and the effect size. The effect size of the ANOVA F test is determined by the variance of the μs, σ_μ^2, and the variance within each population (which are assumed to be equal), σ_Y^2. The larger the variance of the μs, the larger the effect size. The smaller the variance within the populations, the larger the effect size.

Table C–6 in Appendix C provides the group size table for the ANOVA F test. Note that these values represent n, not N. The desired sample size is the number in the table multiplied by k, the number of groups.

A medium effect size is reasonable as the smallest meaningful effect in the present study. A difference so small as to be unobservable to the eye does not provide strong evidence of a difference in the impact of norepinephrine and serotonin on appetite. On the other hand, the effect need not be grossly obvious before it suggests a meaningful difference. With $\alpha = .05$, $\beta = .20$, $df_1 = 2$, and a medium effect size, the desired group size is 52. Since there are three groups, the desired sample size is $3(52) = 156$. If there is a medium-sized effect in the population, a sample size of 156 would be required to assure rejection of the null hypothesis 80% of the time at $\alpha = .05$.

KEY TERMS

analysis of variance

degrees of freedom between groups

degrees of freedom total

degrees of freedom within groups

dichotomous variable

directional hypothesis

discrete variable

F distribution

family-wise error rate

homogeneity of variance assumption

mean square

mean square between groups

mean square within groups

nondirectional hypothesis

normality assumption

omnibus test

one-tailed test

power

quantitative variable

sample size

sampling distribution

sum of squares between groups

sum of squares total

sum of squares within groups

Type I error

EXERCISES

Answers to all exercises may be found in Appendix B.

1. Chapter 16 introduced the independent groups t test. One of the assumptions of that test is that the two population variances are equal. This assumption was necessary to develop a best estimate of the standard error that pooled data from the two groups. To evaluate whether this is a reasonable hypothesis, some statistical computer programs compute the F test comparing the variance of the first group to the variance of the second group. If the F test is significant, it may be taken as evidence that the two population variances are not equal, suggesting that an unpooled formula should be used for the t test. What is the problem with this strategy; that is, why are the results of the F test in this case questionable?

2. For which of the following studies would the one-way independent groups ANOVA be an appropriate analysis?

   a. Subjects are randomly assigned to one of five different treatments for anxiety. Anxiety is measured using a rating scale.

   b. Rats are placed at the center of a maze which allows them to run either left or right. Food is placed in the right tunnel, and the rats are placed at the center of the maze until they choose the right tunnel 20 times in a row. They are then randomly assigned to one of three conditions. In one, food is placed at the end of the left tunnel and none in the right. In the second, food is still placed in the right tunnel, but so is a device that administers a mild shock. In the third condition neither food nor shock is administered in either tunnel. The rats are returned to the center of the maze six more times. The first five are meant to allow the rats to learn the new situations. The number in each group that turn right on the sixth trial is recorded as the dependent variable.

c. The study described in part b is repeated. This time, the rats are returned to the maze 15 more times once the conditions are introduced. The number of times each rat turns right during trials 6–15 is recorded.

3. A researcher is interested in comparing the average annual income of families that describe themselves as Jewish, Protestant, or Catholic. Subjects are recruited through local religious organizations.
   a. Is this a *true experiment, quasi-experiment,* or *observational study*?
   b. State the statistical hypotheses for this study.
   c. Assuming a small effect size is considered the smallest important effect, and the researcher would like to use $\alpha = .05$, $\beta = .20$, what is the appropriate sample size for this study?
   d. Compute the one-way independent groups ANOVA using the following data (in units of $10,000, rounded to the nearest whole number). After completing your work construct an ANOVA summary table:

Jewish	Protestant	Catholic
12	7	8
4	9	10
3	5	2
5	3	6
2	8	5
3	4	9
5	8	7
4	9	10
8	2	1
5	3	2

   e. What is the critical value for $\alpha = .05$? Can the researcher reject the null hypothesis?
   f. How might these results be interpreted?

4. A statistics professor is curious whether students learn more about the analysis of variance from a certain textbook called *Understanding Statistics: A Research Perspective* (which we will call *US*) than they do from other texts. Students are randomly assigned to read either the chapter from *US* that

introduces the analysis of variance, or the corresponding chapter from one of three other texts. A test of their understanding and ability to compute the analysis of variance is then administered. Results are as follows:

US	Alternate A	Alternate B	Alternate C
15	15	13	10
14	19	10	11
17	18	9	6
21	12	14	17
16	14	13	12

(I feel a disclaimer is appropriate here: these are not true data; I made them up for the purposes of this exercise.)
   a. Is this a *true experiment, quasi-experiment,* or *observational study*?
   b. What types of variables are textbook and understanding of ANOVA: *nominal, ordinal, interval,* or *ratio*; *continuous* or *discrete*?
   c. Compute the one-way independent groups ANOVA for these data, and construct the ANOVA summary table.
   d. What is the critical value for $\alpha = .05$? What decision should be made about the null hypothesis?
   e. How would you interpret these findings?

5. Patients hospitalized for depression are divided into three groups according to severity: severe, moderate, and mild. All receive a two-week course of electroconvulsive therapy (ECT), a treatment which involves passing an electric current through the brain. The researcher is interested in whether there is a difference in the amount of improvement in response to ECT.
   a. What type of study is this: a *true experiment, quasi-experiment,* or *observational study*?
   b. What type of variable is severity: *nominal, ordinal, interval,* or *ratio*; *continuous* or *discrete*?
   c. Each patient's improvement is computed by subtracting his or her score on a depression rating scale after treatment from the score before treatment. What type of variable is this: *nominal, ordinal, interval,* or *ratio*; *continuous* or *discrete*?
   d. State the nondirectional statistical hypotheses.
   e. What would be the desired sample size in the following circumstances?
      (1) $\alpha = .01$, $1 - \beta = .80$, large effect
      (2) $\alpha = .10$, $\beta = .10$, small effect
      (3) $\alpha = .05$, $\beta = .20$, medium effect

f. Using the following data for amount of improvement, compute the one-way independent groups ANOVA. Construct an ANOVA summary table when you are done:

Severe	Moderate	Mild
26	12	4
18	14	6
24	13	12
16	11	9
22	19	3
20	4	7

g. What is the critical value for $\alpha = .01$; can you reject the null hypothesis?

h. How would you interpret these results?

6. a. If the null hypothesis is true, what is MS_{BG} estimating? What is MS_{WG} estimating? What value would you expect for F?

b. If the null hypothesis is false, what is MS_{BG} estimating? What is MS_{WG} estimating? What does this information imply about the value you would expect for F?

7. The statistical hypotheses for the independent groups t test may be stated in terms of the difference between two μs. The statistical hypothesis for the one-way independent groups ANOVA, which has to do with differences among two or more μs, is instead stated in terms of the variance of μs. Explain why.

8. Examine the following incomplete ANOVA summary table:

Source	df	SS	MS	F
Between Groups				
Within Groups	16	64.00		
Total	19	85.00		

The total degrees of freedom equal 19, and the total sums of squares equals 85.00. Answer the following questions:

a. How many groups are there?

b. What is SS_{BG}?

c. What is MS_{BG}?

d. What is MS_{WG}?

e. What is F?

f. How many subjects are there per group?

9. If there were only one subject in each group, which mean square in the one-way independent groups ANOVA would have to equal 0?

CHAPTER 19

Multiple Comparison Tests

19.1 INTRODUCTION

In the last chapter I suggested that a significant omnibus F test indicates evidence of a difference among population μs. In the case where the number of groups is $k = 2$, inspection of the means will indicate which μ is believed to be larger. When k is greater than 2 it is still unclear where the difference lies. In a study where $k = 5$, a significant omnibus test may occur because all five μs are unequal, or because only four of the five are equal, or because of any other possibility in between.

A study was described in the last chapter in which rats were injected with either fenfluramine, amphetamine, or saltwater. The omnibus F test demonstrated that the three groups subsequently differed significantly on percent weight gain. If the omnibus test is significant, additional analyses are used to determine the location of potential differences among μs when $k > 2$. These analyses are referred to as **multiple comparison tests**, *hypothesis tests designed to control family-wise error rate across a set of comparisons.* Each comparison involves a subset of the k means, usually two of the means at a time.[1]

Multiple comparison tests fall into two groups. A **planned comparison** is *a comparison of means planned on the basis of the central scientific hypothesis.* For example, if we consider the central scientific hypothesis of the appetite suppression study to be that fenfluramine and amphetamine will differ in their effect on appetite suppression, then the comparison of these two groups represents a planned comparison. The researcher should be able to determine what comparisons may be considered planned even before the collection of data begins.

An **unplanned comparison** is *a comparison of means which does not follow from the central scientific hypothesis.* In the appetite suppression study, the saltwater group was added to serve as a comparison for the other two groups; it does not play a role in the central scientific hypothesis. A comparison of the fenfluramine or amphetamine group to the saltwater group may be considered an unplanned comparison.

The next two sections discuss the computation of planned and unplanned comparisons. The chapter will conclude with a discussion of general issues surrounding comparisons among means.

---

[1]Statistics textbooks are very inconsistent in the guidelines they offer for using multiple comparisons. This reflects continuing debate among statisticians on the topic. I have chosen selectively from several sources and modified some definitions to offer what I believe are practical recommendations on this topic.

19.2 PLANNED COMPARISONS

Planned comparisons of group means may be conducted using a variation of the independent groups t test. The t test for planned comparisons is used to compare two of the means from the omnibus test at a time.

The formula for the t test for planned comparisons is

$$t_P = \frac{\overline{Y}_i - \overline{Y}_j}{\sqrt{MS_{WG}\left(\dfrac{1}{n_i} + \dfrac{1}{n_j}\right)}}.$$

The symbol t_P will be used to indicate this is a t test of a planned comparison.

The subscripts i and j require explanation. If the omnibus test included five means, you could conceivably conduct 3 or 4 planned comparisons. One planned comparison might include Groups 1 and 2, another Groups 2 and 4, and so forth. The subscripts i and j in the formula refer simply to the two groups included in each comparison.

Compare this formula to that for the independent groups t test:

$$t_{\overline{Y}_1 - \overline{Y}_2} = \frac{\overline{Y}_1 - \overline{Y}_2}{\sqrt{\dfrac{SS_1 + SS_2}{N - 2}\left(\dfrac{1}{n_1} + \dfrac{1}{n_2}\right)}}.$$

If the variances of the two populations are equal, the value $(SS_1 + SS_2)/(N - 2)$ is the best sample estimate of σ_Y^2, the variance of scores within either population (which are assumed to be equal). In the one-way independent groups ANOVA, the within-groups variance estimate MS_{WG} is the best single estimate of σ_Y^2 if the population variances are all equal, since it includes variability from all the groups (as discussed in Section 18.3.4). So, the t test for planned comparisons is essentially the same statistic as the independent groups t test, except that it uses the more accurate MS_{WG} instead of $(SS_1 + SS_2)/(N - 2)$ as the best estimate of σ_Y^2.

When group sizes are equal, the formula can also be stated

$$t_P = \frac{\overline{Y}_i - \overline{Y}_j}{\sqrt{\dfrac{2MS_{WG}}{n}}},$$

where n is the group size for any group.

I have already suggested that the comparison of the fenfluramine and amphetamine groups represents a planned comparison in our study. The null and alternative hypotheses for this t test are

$$H_0: \mu_F = \mu_A$$

$$H_1: \mu_F \neq \mu_A.$$

Procedure Box 19.1 demonstrates the computation of t_P for this comparison.

PROCEDURE BOX 19.1

The *t* Test for Planned Comparisons

Goal   Compute the *t* test for planned comparisons comparing percent weight gain after injection with fenfluramine and amphetamine. The data are (as originally provided in Procedure Box 18.1 in Chapter 18):

Fenfluramine	Amphetamine	Saltwater
1	3	10
2	6	8
4	9	12
6	5	10

$$t_P = \frac{\overline{Y}_i - \overline{Y}_j}{\sqrt{\dfrac{2MS_{WG}}{n}}}$$

Step 1   *Compute the means for each group and find the difference.*

	Fenfluramine	Amphetamine
	1	3
	2	6
	4	9
	6	5
Means:	3.25	5.75

$$\overline{Y}_i - \overline{Y}_j = 3.25 - 5.75 = -2.5$$

Step 2   *Multiply MS_{WG} from the omnibus test by 2/n and find the square root.*

$$\sqrt{\frac{2(4.6111)}{4}} = 1.5184$$

Step 3   *Divide the result of Step 1 by the result of Step 2.*

$$t_P = \frac{-2.5}{1.5184} = -1.65$$

Critical values for t tests may be found in Table D–1 of Appendix D. The degrees of freedom equal df_{WG}:

$$N - k = 12 - 3 = 9.$$

The two-tailed critical value for the nondirectional null hypothesis is $t_{\alpha=.05,\,df=9} = \pm 2.262$; we can reject the null hypothesis for the planned comparison if

$$|t_p| \geq 2.262.$$

We are unable to reject the null hypothesis since $t_p = -1.65$; we do not have evidence of a difference in the effect of fenfluramine and amphetamine on appetite, at least at the dosage used.

At the beginning of the last chapter I suggested that the analysis of variance was developed as an alternative to multiple t tests when $k > 2$ to control family-wise error rate. Now I seem to be suggesting the use of multiple t tests as a method for analyzing group differences. Is this a contradiction? In fact, the two procedures differ in two important ways. First, according to the method of analysis described here, planned comparisons are not permitted unless the omnibus test first proves to be significant. Second, in any study only a few comparisons may be treated as planned comparisons. These conditions for the use of planned comparisons are meant to offer some control over the family-wise error rate.

19.3 UNPLANNED COMPARISONS

A number of procedures have been developed for conducting unplanned comparisons.[2] I will limit the discussion here to the most popular and generally applicable procedure, called the Tukey Honestly Significant Difference test, or the Tukey test or HSD test for short. The formula is

$$Q = \frac{\overline{Y}_i - \overline{Y}_j}{\sqrt{\dfrac{MS_{WG}}{n}}}$$

where $\overline{Y}_i$ is the larger of the two means being compared and $\overline{Y}_j$ is the smaller. This means that Q will always be a positive number, and that the Tukey test represents a one-tailed test of a nondirectional null hypothesis. The Tukey test requires equal group sizes, although a variant called the Tukey-Kramer test is available when group sizes are unequal.

Suppose we decide to conduct the unplanned comparison of the fenfluramine and saltwater groups based on the sample means. The null and alternative hypotheses for this Q test are

$$H_0 : \mu_F = \mu_S$$

$$H_1 : \mu_F \neq \mu_S.$$

Procedure Box 19.2 demonstrates the computation of Q for this comparison.

---

[2]A review of the various techniques for conducting unplanned comparisons is beyond the scope of the present text. The interested reader is referred to Zwick (1993).

PROCEDURE BOX 19.2

The Q Test for Unplanned Comparisons

Goal   Compute the Q value comparing percent weight gain after injection with fenfluramine and saltwater (complete data for this study may be found in Procedure Box 19.1).

$$Q = \frac{\overline{Y}_1 - \overline{Y}_2}{\sqrt{\dfrac{MS_{WG}}{n}}}$$

Step 1   *Compute the means for both groups, and subtract the smaller from the larger.*

	Fenfluramine	Saltwater
	1	10
	2	8
	4	12
	6	10
Means:	3.25	10.0

$$\overline{Y}_i - \overline{Y}_j = 10 - 3.25 = 6.75$$

Step 2   *Divide MS_{WG} from the omnibus test by n and square root.*

$$\sqrt{\frac{4.6111}{4}} = 1.0737$$

Step 3   *Divide the result of Step 1 by the result of Step 2.*

$$Q = \frac{6.75}{1.0737} = 6.29$$

The critical values for Q may be found in Table D–5 of Appendix D. The critical value depends upon the desired alpha level, the number of groups included in the omnibus test (k), and df_{WG}. Our critical value is $Q_{\alpha = .05,\, k = 3,\, df = 9} = 3.95$. We can reject the null hypothesis since $Q = 6.29$. Examination of the means indicates the percent weight gain is lower after fenfluramine injection than saltwater injection, suggesting

TABLE 19.1   Selected Aspects of the t_P and Tukey (Q) Tests

Symbol Used	Degrees of Freedom	Type of Statistical Hypotheses	General Form of Statistical Hypotheses	Type of Test	Symbol for Alpha	Critical Region in
t_P	$N - k$	nondirectional	$H_0: \mu_1 - \mu_2 = 0$ $H_0: \mu_1 - \mu_2 \neq 0$	two-tailed	α	both tails (both positive and negative critical values)
Q	$N - k$	nondirectional	$H_0: \mu_1 - \mu_2 = 0$ $H_0: \mu_1 - \mu_2 \neq 0$	one-tailed	α	upper tail (subtract smaller mean from larger mean)

fenfluramine suppresses appetite more than does saltwater. A general summary of the t_P and Tukey tests is provided in Table 19.1.

19.4 GENERAL ISSUES IN TESTING MULTIPLE COMPARISONS

The correct method of conducting multiple comparisons is perhaps the most controversial aspect of the analysis of variance. The controversy exists because methods of conducting multiple comparisons that offer the best control over family-wise error rate (the probability of at least one Type I error) also tend to demonstrate the poorest power. For example, the Tukey test is less powerful than the t test for a planned comparison, but offers greater control of the Type I error rate. Even if you compare every pair of group means in the sample, the family-wise error rate associated with the Tukey test remains at .05.

I recommend the following guidelines for multiple comparisons testing based on both statistical literature and research practice:

1. When conducting multiple comparisons based on a single omnibus test, treat no more than 2–3 of the tests as planned comparisons.
2. If you will be conducting both planned and unplanned comparisons you have two options. You can analyze the planned comparisons with t tests and the unplanned comparisons with another test such as the Tukey. Some researchers instead treat all the comparisons as if they were unplanned, and will consistently use one test such as the Tukey. This has the advantage of simplicity and efficiency, although tests of the planned comparisons will be less powerful than they would have been if evaluated using t tests.
3. An omnibus test is technically unnecessary before a test such as the Tukey which controls the family-wise error rate by itself. However, many researchers choose to conduct an omnibus test first anyway.

Unlike other hypothesis testing procedures described so far, standard procedures for multiple comparison testing in the analysis of variance remains an area in development. New methods of comparison continue to be suggested, and I expect it will be some time before there is a standard procedure accepted for controlling family-wise error rate.

KEY TERMS

family-wise error rate
group size
mean square within groups
multiple comparison tests

omnibus test
planned comparison
Type I error
unplanned comparison

EXERCISES

Answers to all exercises may be found in Appendix B.

1. Which of the following represent *planned comparisons?* Which represent *unplanned comparisons?*
   a. A researcher is interested in whether Asians demonstrate higher scores on the Wechsler Adult Intelligence Scale (WAIS; Wechsler, 1981) than blacks and whites.
      (1) The Asian-white comparison
      (2) The Asian-black comparison
      (3) The black-white comparison
   b. A researcher believes that exposing phobics to feared situations is a more effective treatment than teaching them relaxation techniques, but that either will be superior to placebo. Individuals suffering from social phobia (a fear of social situations) are randomly assigned to an exposure treatment, a relaxation treatment, a placebo treatment in which they discuss their phobia in a group and encourage each other to overcome it, or a "wait list" group in which they receive no treatment.
      (1) The exposure-relaxation comparison.
      (2) The exposure-wait list comparison.
      (3) The relaxation-wait list comparison.
      (4) The placebo-wait list comparison.
      (5) The exposure-placebo comparison.
      (6) The relaxation-placebo comparison.
   c. Are crack addicts on average able to function more effectively in society than heroin addicts? A researcher collects groups of subjects addicted to crack, to heroin, and to both, and measures their annual income.
      (1) The crack-heroin comparison.
      (2) The crack-both comparison.
      (3) The heroin-both comparison.

2. It has been demonstrated that 5 milligrams (mg) of diazepam reduces self-reported feelings of anxiety. A researcher believes that 2-mg increases in the dosage results in significant increases in effectiveness, but 1 mg increases should be insufficient. Subjects are randomly assigned to receive either 5, 6, 7, or 8 mg of diazepam.
   a. Indicate which comparisons could be considered planned, which unplanned.
   b. How many planned comparisons are there? Is this consistent with the guidelines offered in the chapter? If not, how could you deal with this inconsistency?

3. Conduct the unplanned comparison of the amphetamine and saltwater conditions for the appetite suppression example from the chapter. The data are as follows:

Fenfluramine	Amphetamine	Saltwater
1	3	10
2	6	8
4	9	12
6	5	10

   a. Compute Q.
   b. What is the critical value, assuming $\alpha = .05$? Can the researcher reject the null hypothesis?
   c. How might these results be interpreted?

4. Using the data provided in the appetite suppression example, conduct the comparison of the amphetamine and saltwater conditions as if this were a planned comparison.
   a. Compute t_P.
   b. What is the critical value, assuming $\alpha = .05$? Can the researcher reject the null hypothesis?
   c. How might these results be interpreted?

5. In the exercises for the last chapter, a study was described in which students were randomly assigned to read the ANOVA chapter from one of four textbooks: *Understanding Statistics: A Research Perspective* (called *US*), or one of three alternative texts. The question of interest was whether students

who read *US* did better on a test of their understanding of ANOVA. Test results were as follows:

US	Alternate A	Alternate B	Alternate C
15	15	13	10
14	19	10	11
17	18	9	6
21	12	14	17
16	14	13	12

(These data were made up for the present example.) The omnibus test proved to be significant, so multiple comparisons are now necessary.

a. Which analyses may be considered planned, which unplanned?

b. Conduct the six possible comparisons. Hint: this isn't as time-consuming as it sounds. Remember that all the planned comparisons share the same denominator, as do the unplanned comparisons.

c. What are the critical values for the planned and unplanned comparisons, assuming $\alpha = .05$?

d. In which cases can you reject the null hypothesis? What conclusions can you draw?

6. If a researcher has a choice between conducting a planned and unplanned comparison, why might a planned comparison be preferred? Why might an unplanned comparison be preferred?

CHAPTER 20

The One-Way Dependent
Groups ANOVA

It was indicated in Chapter 18 that the one-way independent groups ANOVA may be used when (1) members of the sample fall into two or more groups based on a discrete variable, (2) the groups are independent, (3) members of the sample produce a quantitative variable, and (4) the null hypothesis has to do with whether the quantitative variable μ is different for the populations represented by the groups. There are a number of other ANOVA models besides the one-way independent groups ANOVA. Each divides the total variability of the quantitative variable scores differently, depending on the type of data collected.

The present chapter introduces the one-way dependent groups ANOVA. The next chapter will focus on the two-way independent groups ANOVA. The discussion in these two chapters offers little more than an introduction to these analyses; the student who wishes to learn more about these procedures should turn to more advanced sources (Keppel, 1991; Kirk, 1995; Myers & Well, 1991).

20.1 INTRODUCTION

In Chapter 15, which introduced the dependent groups t test, I described a study in which college students reported the frequency of behaviors that increase the risk of HIV infection before and after an AIDS awareness presentation. Using the data provided we found evidence of a reduction in the self-reported frequency of risk behaviors after the presentation. Suppose we would like to evaluate whether the improvement lasts for six months. Six months after participating in the workshop, the 10 college students again complete the rating scale concerning the frequency of risk behaviors over the last two weeks. The study represents a repeated measures study examining the relationship between a nominal independent variable with three levels (time of measurement) and a continuous ordinal dependent variable (self-reported frequency of risk behaviors).

The one-way dependent groups ANOVA may be used whenever you are interested in the relationship between two variables, one of which is a quantitative variable, and the other is a discrete variable that produces at least two dependent groups. As defined in Chapter 15, groups are dependent when each score in one group is associated with a score in the other group. In the case of the dependent groups ANOVA all groups are dependent: each score in one group is associated with a score in every other group. This may be because the same subjects served in every group (as in the present example) or because subjects have been matched (as in a matched groups study).

20.2 DEFINING THE NULL AND ALTERNATIVE HYPOTHESES

The null and alternative hypotheses for the omnibus test of the one-way dependent groups ANOVA are the same as those for the independent groups ANOVA:

$$H_0: \text{all } \mu\text{s are equal}$$

$$H_1: \text{not all } \mu\text{s are equal,}$$

or

$$H_0: \sigma_\mu^2 = 0$$

$$H_1: \sigma_\mu^2 \neq 0.$$

As with all ANOVA procedures, the one-way dependent groups ANOVA can only be used to evaluate nondirectional hypotheses.

20.3 TESTING THE NULL HYPOTHESIS

The mean square between groups for the one-way dependent groups ANOVA is computed using the same formulas used for the independent groups ANOVA:

$$SS_{\text{BG}} = \left[\frac{(\sum \text{first group})^2}{n} + \cdots \frac{(\sum \text{last groups})^2}{n} \right] - \frac{(\sum \text{scores})^2}{N},$$

$$df_{\text{BG}} = k - 1,$$

and

$$MS_{\text{BG}} = \frac{SS_{\text{BG}}}{df_{\text{BG}}}.$$

The denominator variance estimate is somewhat different. Called the **mean square residual** (MS_R), it is computed by dividing the **sum of squares residual** (SS_R) by the **degrees of freedom residual** (df_R). The computational formula for the sum of squares residual is

$$SS_R = \left(\sum \text{squared scores} \right) + \frac{(\sum \text{scores})^2}{N} - \left[\frac{(\sum \text{first group})^2}{n} + \cdots \frac{(\sum \text{last group})^2}{n} \right]$$
$$- \left[\frac{(\sum \text{first block})^2}{k} + \cdots \frac{(\sum \text{last block})^2}{k} \right].$$

The first three components in this formula were also used to compute SS_{BG} and SS_{WG} in Sections 18.3.1 and 18.3.2. The last component is new.

The concept of a block was introduced in Chapter 15. A block refers to the set of associated scores across all the groups. In the present case each block consists of the three scores produced by a single subject. To compute the fourth component, all the scores in the first block are summed, squared, and divided by k, the number of scores in each block (which equals the number of groups). This is repeated for each block, and the resulting values are added together.

The degrees of freedom residual equal

$$df_R = (n - 1)(k - 1),$$

and

$$MS_R = \frac{SS_R}{df_R}.$$

F is computed from the formula

$$F = \frac{MS_{BG}}{MS_R}.$$

Computation of the dependent groups ANOVA omnibus F test is demonstrated in Procedure Box 20.1.

20.4 MAKING A DECISION ABOUT THE NULL HYPOTHESIS

The degrees of freedom for the numerator equal df_{BG}; the degrees of freedom for the denominator equal df_R. In the AIDS presentation study:

$$df_1 = k - 1 = 3 - 1 - = 2$$
$$df_2 = (n - 1)(k - 1) = (10 - 1)(3 - 1) = 18$$
$$F_{\alpha=.05, df_1=2, df_2=18} = 3.55 \quad \text{(from Table D–4 in Appendix D)}$$

The computed F value 3.43 does not equal or exceed this value, so we cannot reject the null hypothesis. The ANOVA summary table may be found at the end of Procedure Box 20.1.

Interpreting the Results. Even if the omnibus test were significant, since $k > 2$ we would not know where the differences suggested by this finding lie until we conducted multiple comparison tests for dependent groups ANOVAs. This is a particularly interesting example, in that we already know there was a significant difference between scores before treatment and two weeks after treatment. The improvements found immediately after the presentation are washed out when the data from six months later are added.

20.5 CONDITIONS FOR USING THE TEST

Conditions. The conditions for using the one-way dependent groups ANOVA are similar to those required for the dependent groups t test: (1) members of the sample fall into two or more groups based on a discrete variable, (2) the groups are dependent, (3) members of

The One-Way Dependent Groups ANOVA *F* Test

Goal   Ten students completed a rating scale concerning the frequency of risk behaviors before, 2 weeks after, and 6 months after an AIDS awareness presentation:

	Before	2 weeks	6 months
Student 1	15	9	17
Student 2	22	16	18
Student 3	18	15	12
Student 4	16	3	13
Student 5	9	10	15
Student 6	8	6	3
Student 7	17	9	20
Student 8	11	5	6
Student 9	4	6	8
Student 10	10	10	4

Compute the *F* value using these data.

$$SS_{BG} = \left[\frac{\left(\sum \text{first group}\right)^2}{n} + \cdots \frac{\left(\sum \text{last group}\right)^2}{n} \right] - \frac{\left(\sum \text{scores}\right)^2}{N}$$

$$SS_R = \left(\sum \text{squared scores} \right) + \frac{\left(\sum \text{scores}\right)^2}{N} - \left[\frac{\left(\sum \text{first group}\right)^2}{n} \right.$$

$$+ \cdots \left. \frac{\left(\sum \text{last group}\right)^2}{n} \right] - \left[\frac{\left(\sum \text{first block}\right)^2}{k} + \cdots \frac{\left(\sum \text{last block}\right)^2}{k} \right]$$

$$df_{BG} = k - 1 \qquad df_R = (n - 1)(k - 1)$$

$$MS_{BG} = \frac{SS_{BG}}{df_{BG}} \qquad MS_R = \frac{SS_R}{df_R} \qquad F = \frac{MS_{BG}}{MS_R}$$

Continued

The one-way dependent groups ANOVA F test continued

Step 1   *Sum the Y and Y^2 scores for each group.*

Y	Y^2	Y	Y^2	Y	Y^2
15	225	9	81	17	289
22	484	16	256	18	324
18	324	15	225	12	144
16	256	3	9	13	169
9	81	10	100	15	225
8	64	6	36	3	9
17	289	9	81	20	400
11	121	5	25	6	36
4	16	6	36	8	64
10	100	10	100	4	16
Sums: 130	1960	89	949	116	1676

Step 2   *Sum the Y scores for each block (row of scores).*

$$15 + 9 + 17 = 41$$

$$22 + 16 + 18 = 56$$

$$18 + 15 + 12 = 45$$

$$16 + 3 + 13 = 32$$

$$9 + 10 + 15 = 34$$

$$8 + 6 + 3 = 17$$

$$17 + 9 + 20 = 46$$

$$11 + 5 + 6 = 22$$

$$4 + 6 + 8 = 18$$

$$10 + 10 + 4 = 24$$

Step 3   *Square the sum of the scores for each group, divide by n, and sum the resulting values.*

$$\left[\frac{(\sum \text{first group})^2}{n} + \cdots \frac{(\sum \text{last group})^2}{n}\right] = \frac{130^2}{10} + \frac{89^2}{10} + \frac{116^2}{10} = 3827.7$$

Step 4   *Square the sum of all scores and divide by N.*

$$\frac{(\sum \text{scores})^2}{N} = \frac{(130 + 89 + 116)^2}{30} = 3740.8333$$

Step 5   *Sum the squared scores.*

$$\left(\sum \text{squared scores}\right) = 1960 + 949 + 1676 = 4585$$

Continued

The one-way dependent groups ANOVA F test continued

Step 6   Square the sum of the scores for each block, divide by k, and sum the resulting values.

$$\left[\frac{(\sum \text{first block})^2}{k} + \cdots \frac{(\sum \text{last block})^2}{k} \right] = \frac{41^2}{3} + \frac{56^2}{3} + \frac{45^2}{3} + \frac{32^2}{3} + \frac{34^2}{3}$$

$$+ \frac{17^2}{3} + \frac{46^2}{3} + \frac{22^2}{3} + \frac{18^2}{3} + \frac{24^2}{3}$$

$$= 4270.3333$$

Step 7   Subtract the result of Step 4 from the result of Step 3.

$$SS_{\text{BG}} = 3827.7 - 3740.8333 = 86.8667 \longleftarrow \text{This number must be positive}$$

Step 8   Sum the results of Step 4 and 5, and subtract the results of Steps 3 and 6.

$$SS_{\text{R}} = 3740.8333 + 4585 - 3827.7 - 4270.3333$$
$$= 277.8 \longleftarrow \text{This number must be positive}$$

Step 9   Divide the result of Step 7 by k − 1.

$$MS_{\text{BG}} = \frac{86.8667}{3 - 1} = 43.4334$$

Step 10   Divide the result of Step 8 by (n − 1)(k − 1).

$$MS_{\text{R}} = \frac{227.8}{(10 - 1)(3 - 1)} = 12.6556$$

Step 11   Divide the result of Step 9 by the result of Step 10.

$$F = \frac{43.4334}{12.6556} = 3.432$$

The results may be used to create an ANOVA summary table:

Source	df	SS	MS	F
Between Groups	2	86.87	43.43	3.43
Residual	18	227.80	12.66	

the sample produce a quantitative variable, and (4) the null hypothesis has to do with whether the μ of the quantitative variable is equal for the populations represented by the groups. Such a difference would suggest the existence of a relationship between the two variables in the population.

Examples of other studies for which the one-way dependent groups ANOVA may be used include:

TABLE 20.1   Selected Aspects of the One-Way Dependent Groups ANOVA

Symbol Used	Degrees of Freedom	Type of Statistical Hypotheses	General Form of Statistical Hypotheses	Type of Test	Symbol for Alpha	Critical Region in
F	$k - 1$	nondirectional	H_0: all μs are equal	one-tailed	α	upper tail
	$N - k$		H_1: not all μs are equal			

1. A true experiment in which subjects are matched on level of depression before they are randomly assigned to one of four treatments for depression.
2. An observational study in which self-esteem scores for mothers, fathers, and their oldest child are compared.

   Like the independent groups t test, the independent groups ANOVA may be more appropriate than the dependent groups ANOVA even in some cases where groups are dependent. Specifically, in cases where associated scores are likely to correlate highly — as in repeated measures studies or matched groups studies with a well-chosen matching variable — the dependent groups ANOVA is appropriate. In cases where the matching variable is not strongly correlated with the dependent variable, the independent groups ANOVA may be more appropriate. The supplement contains more information on the power of the two tests.

   Assumptions. The assumptions of the dependent groups ANOVA are complicated and will not be discussed here. The interested reader is again referred to the more detailed texts on analysis of variance methods mentioned earlier in the chapter.

20.6 DIRECTIONAL VERSUS NONDIRECTIONAL HYPOTHESES

Like the one-way independent groups ANOVA, the dependent groups ANOVA F test is always one-tailed. The larger the differences in the group means, the larger the computed F value will be. Rejection of the null hypothesis indicates that a difference seems to exist among the μs, but does not indicate which μs seem to be different. The only exception to this rule occurs when the discrete variable is dichotomous. Then the one-way dependent groups ANOVA is essentially equivalent to the dependent groups t test, and the larger group mean indicates the population μ that seems to be larger. The ANOVA F test is always one-tailed, yet only nondirectional hypotheses can be tested. This and other aspects of the one-way dependent groups ANOVA are summarized in Table 20.1.

KEY TERMS

block
computational formula
degrees of freedom between groups
degrees of freedom residual
dependent groups
discrete variable
matched groups study

mean square between groups
mean square residual
quantitative variable
repeated measures study
sum of squares between groups
sum of squares residual

EXERCISES

Answers to all exercises may be found in Appendix B.

1. For which of the following studies is the one-way dependent groups ANOVA an appropriate analysis?
   a. Assembly line workers responsible for driving rivets into car bodies are randomly assigned to one of three programs to enhance job performance. The number of rivets they insert per hour serves as the outcome measure.
   b. Subjects are asked to rate which of three cheeses they like best. The number preferring each cheese is tallied.
   c. Blocks of subjects defined on the basis of performance on a memory task are randomly assigned to memorize either meaningless or meaningful three-letter words. The number of words they remember three hours later is the dependent variable. *Challenge:* what other inferential statistic you have learned about could be used to analyze the data from this study?

2. The study described in the chapter involved self-reported frequency of HIV risk behaviors before and after a workshop on avoiding HIV infection. Now consider another study with a similar design. One of the effects of HIV is a drastic reduction in the number of T4 cells in the blood stream. T4 cells are an important component of the immune system, so AIDS sufferers are extremely susceptible to infection. A medical researcher measures the number of T4 cells in the blood stream before initiating treatment with AZT (a drug used to fight AIDS), and again after three months of treatment.
   a. The study in the chapter was considered a fairly weak study (see the section titled "Interpreting the Results"). Why should the study described above be any better?
   b. An alternative to the study described above would be a true experiment in which AIDS sufferers are randomly assigned to receive either AZT or a placebo alternative. Explain why the study described above is ethically more acceptable than this true experiment.

3. High school students are divided into blocks of three on the basis of grade point average, then randomly assigned within blocks to three groups. One group participates in a peer-led self-esteem training program. The second group participates in a self-esteem training program led by a professional counselor. The third group is assigned to read material on how to enhance self-esteem. The dependent variable is the difference in self-esteem score from before treatment to after treatment. Is it possible that the dependent groups ANOVA may not be the most appropriate analysis for this study? Explain your answer.

4. A researcher wanted to study the effectiveness of two weight loss programs, versus just having people weigh themselves and record their weight each morning. Subjects were matched on the basis of percent overweight, and assigned to one of the three treatments based on their availability at the times the treatment groups were to meet.
   a. Is this a *true experiment, quasi-experiment,* or *observational study*?
   b. The following data represent percent weight lost during treatment. Compute the one-way dependent groups ANOVA, and construct an ANOVA table:

Treatment 1	Treatment 2	Control
12	7	8
4	9	10
3	5	2
5	3	6
2	8	5
3	4	9
5	8	7
4	9	10
8	2	1
5	3	2

   c. What is the critical value using $\alpha = .01$? Can the researcher reject the null hypothesis?
   d. How might these results be interpreted?

5. Individuals suffering from depression are divided into blocks of four depending on initial depression score on a rating scale. They are then randomly assigned within blocks to receive either an antidepressant drug, psychotherapy, a placebo drug, or an unled discussion group.
   a. Is this a *true experiment, quasi-experiment,* or *observational study*?
   b. Upon completing treatment the following depression scores are observed, where lower scores suggest less depression:

Anti-depressant	Psycho-therapy	Placebo	Discussion
18	17	27	26
16	26	18	24
19	32	21	35
21	19	26	32
14	25	32	29

Compute the one-way dependent groups ANOVA, and construct the ANOVA table

c. What is the critical value for $\alpha = .05$? Can you reject the null hypothesis?

d. Compute the means for the four groups. Based on inspection of the means, what would you expect multiple comparisons will indicate?

6. An exercise was provided in Chapter 15 concerning statistical regression. *Statistical regression* refers to the tendency for individuals with extreme scores on some scale to move towards the mean over time. For example, people with the highest scores on a rating scale should tend to show a decline in scores over time, and those with the lowest score should tend to show an increase. To demonstrate this phenomenon, a researcher administered a measure of self-esteem to 300 college students. One month later she administered the scale again to those 10 students who had the lowest scores on the first administration.

a. Compute the one-way dependent groups ANOVA using the following data:

Time 1	Time 2
2	8
3	10
3	4
4	7
4	9
5	3
6	7
6	12
6	6
7	8

b. What is the critical value for $\alpha = .01$? Can the researcher reject the null hypothesis?

c. How might these results be interpreted? Note that there are only two levels to the discrete variable time; multiple comparisons are not necessary to make a full interpretation of the results.

7. A researcher is interested in whether there are racial differences in scores on the Wechsler Adult Intelligence Scale (WAIS; Wechsler, 1981). To insure the groups are comparable, subjects are selected so that the groups as a whole are equal in terms of socioeconomic status (based on level of education and job status). For example, at first the Asian group was of higher status on average than the other groups, so more Asians of relatively low status were solicited. Should the dependent groups ANOVA be used to analyze these data?

S20.1 POWER FOR THE DEPENDENT AND INDEPENDENT GROUPS ANOVAS

The larger the F value, the more likely you will be able to reject the null hypothesis, and therefore the more powerful the test is. Since the numerator of both the dependent and independent groups ANOVA F tests is MS_{BG}, the relative size of the two F values depends on the denominators of the two formulas. Ignoring for now differences in the critical value, if MS_R is smaller than MS_{WG}, then the dependent groups ANOVA is more powerful than the independent groups ANOVA; if MS_R is larger than MS_{WG}, then the dependent groups ANOVA is less powerful than the independent groups ANOVA

The formula for SS_R is

$$SS_R = \left(\sum \text{squared scores} \right) + \frac{(\sum \text{scores})^2}{N} - \left[\frac{(\sum \text{first group})^2}{n} + \ldots \frac{(\sum \text{last group})^2}{n} \right]$$
$$- \left[\frac{(\sum \text{first block})^2}{k} + \ldots \frac{(\sum \text{last block})^2}{k} \right].$$

If you compare this formula to that of the SS_{WG} from the independent groups ANOVA (from Section 18.3.1),

$$SS_{WG} = \left(\sum \text{squared scores} \right) - \left[\frac{(\sum \text{first group})^2}{n} + \ldots \frac{(\sum \text{last group})^2}{n} \right],$$

you will see they are very similar. SS_R is equal to the SS_{WG} with the quantity $(\sum \text{scores})^2/N$ added, and the quantity $[(\sum \text{first block})^2/k + \ldots (\sum \text{last block})^2/k]$ subtracted. It can be demonstrated that $(\sum \text{scores})^2/k$ will always be less than or equal to $[(\sum \text{first block})^2/k + \ldots (\sum \text{last block})^2/k]$, which means that SS_R must be less than or equal to SS_{WG}.

On the other hand, df_R equals $(n-1)(k-1)$, as opposed to $df_{WG} = k(n-1)$. df_R will therefore always be less than df_{WG}. The dependent groups ANOVA will only be more powerful than the independent groups ANOVA if the quantity subtracted from SS_{WG},

$$\left[\frac{(\sum \text{first block})^2}{k} + \ldots \frac{(\sum \text{last block})^2}{k} \right] + \frac{(\sum \text{scores})^2}{N},$$

is large enough to offset the smaller degrees of freedom. The quantity $[(\sum \text{first block})^2/k + \ldots (\sum \text{last block})^2/k]$ represents variability attributable to the blocks. The larger the correlation between the associated scores, the greater the proportion of the total variance that can be attributed to the blocks (you may note that the wording here is similar to that used to describe the index of association in Chapter 7), and therefore the larger $[(\sum \text{first block})^2/k + \ldots (\sum \text{last block})^2/k]$ will be. When associated scores correlate well the dependent groups ANOVA is more powerful; when associated scores correlate poorly the independent groups ANOVA is more powerful.

CHAPTER 21

The Two-Way Independent Groups ANOVA

2.1 INTRODUCTION

In Chapter 18 the one-way independent groups ANOVA was illustrated with a study comparing the appetite suppressing effects of fenfluramine, amphetamine, and saltwater injections in 15-day old hooded rats. We were able to reject the null hypothesis for the omnibus test, indicating that a relationship exists in the population between the variables type of drug (a nominal variable with three values: fenfluramine, amphetamine, and saltwater) and percent weight gain (a continuous ratio variable). Because the study represented a true experiment, this was considered evidence that type of drug has a direct effect on percent weight gain. We then used multiple comparison tests to learn more about the relationship. We found evidence that fenfluramine results in greater appetite suppression than saltwater in the population, but no evidence of a population difference was found between fenfluramine and amphetamine.

Suppose we believe that the relationship between type of drug and appetite suppression varies depending on whether rats are 5 or 15-days-old. This suggests the existence of a **moderator effect:** *a relationship involving three variables in which the relationship between two of the variables differs depending upon the third variable.* This is the first (and only) example in this text of a relationship that involves three variables. A moderator effect exists when the relationship between two variables changes for different values of a third variable. For example, if the relationship between drug and percent weight gain varies depending on the age of the rats, then age *moderates* the relationship between type of drug and weight gain.

The two-way independent groups ANOVA may be used when a discrete variable moderates a relationship between a second discrete variable and an interval or ratio variable. In experimental studies the two discrete variables are the independent variables, and the interval or ratio variable are the dependent variable. The term *two-way* refers to the presence of two discrete variables. *An ANOVA with more than one discrete variable* is called a **factorial ANOVA,** and *discrete variables in a factorial ANOVA are called* **factors.**

21.2 DEFINING THE NULL AND ALTERNATIVE HYPOTHESES

The null and alternative hypotheses for the two-way independent groups ANOVA are more complicated than those we have seen so far. This is because there is an omnibus test for each factor, and an omnibus test for the moderator effect. In two-way ANOVA, *the omnibus test of a single factor ignoring any other factors* is called a **main effect**. *The omnibus test of a moderator effect* is called an **interaction.**

The Age Main Effect Hypotheses. Let's start with the null and alternative hypotheses for the two main effects, since these will seem more familiar to you. For the age factor the omnibus test evaluates whether the percent weight gain is different for 5-day-old rats than for 15-day-old rats:

$$H_0: \mu_5 = \mu_{15}$$

$$H_1: \mu_5 \neq \mu_{15}.$$

Except for the subscripts, which are used to identify them as the statistical hypotheses for the age main effect, these look like most of the other null and alternative hypotheses you have seen. However, there is an important difference in terms of the populations represented. These μs do not refer to general populations of 5- and 15-day-old hooded rats. Since every rat in the study receives some type of injection, μ_5 refers to percent weight gain in a population of 5-day-old rats who have received injections of either fenfluramine, amphetamine, or saltwater.

The Drug Main Effect Hypotheses. For the drug main effect the omnibus test evaluates whether there are differences in percent weight gain depending on whether the rat is injected with fenfluramine, amphetamine, or saltwater in a population of 5- and 15-day-old rats:

$$H_0: \mu_F = \mu_A = \mu_S$$

$$H_1: \text{not all } \mu \text{s are equal.}$$

The Age-Drug Interaction Hypotheses. Now we must translate the moderator effect into statistical hypotheses. If the proposed moderator effect exists, then the relationship between type of drug and percent weight gain should be different depending on age, and the relationship between age and percent weight gain should be different depending on the type of drug. This suggests the following statistical hypotheses:

$$H_0: (\mu_{5F} - \mu_{15F}) = (\mu_{5A} - \mu_{15A}) = (\mu_{5S} - \mu_{15S})$$

$$H_1: \text{differences between } \mu \text{s at different ages}$$
$$\text{vary depending on the type of drug.}$$

The null hypothesis suggests that the relationship between age and percent weight gain is consistent for all three drugs. The alternative hypothesis suggests the relatio\nship is not consistent for all three drugs. For example, if the difference between the μs for 5- and 15-day old rats receiving fenfluramine is different than the difference between the μs for 5- and 15-day old rats receiving amphetamine, then the null hypothesis is false.

Graphing Population μs. Figure 21.1 provides some possible patterns of the μs to help understand the nature of main effects and interactions in factorial ANOVA. The X axes represent the drug variable. The Y axes represent the mean percent weight gain for each population. The age variable is represented by the two lines, one for each age. The points on the lines represent the individual populations. For example, the left-most point on the 5-day-old line indicates the mean percent weight gain for 5-day-old rats who received fenfluramine.

No Effects. Figure 21.1(a) illustrates the case in which there are no main effects or interaction. The μ for 5-day-olds equals the μ for 15-day-olds, the μ for fenfluramine equals the μ for amphetamine and the μ for saltwater, and the differences between age groups for each drug group are the same. Graphically, the two age lines fall on top of each other and the lines are flat. If any of the omnibus tests in a sample are significant it represents a Type I error.

When a Drug Main Effect Exists. Figures 21.1(b), (d), (f), and (h) illustrate cases in which the drug main effect should be significant. For example, the following data are found in Figure 21.1(b):

		Type of Drug			
		Fen	Amph	Salt	
	5 Days	13	11	13	12.33
Age	15 Days	13	11	13	12.33
		13	11	13	12.33

Remember that this is a table of μs.

A drug main effect exists if there is a difference between the three μs at the bottom of the columns labeled Fen (fenfluramine), Amph (amphetamine), and Salt (saltwater). Looking at the bottom row of the table, it is evident that the μs for all rats receiving amphetamine and saltwater (13) are greater than the μ for all rats receiving fenfluramine (11). This indicates that a drug main effect exists. In this case, failure to reject the null hypothesis for the drug main effect would represent a Type II error.

Compare this with the data from Figure 21.1(c):

		Type of Drug			
		Fen	Amph	Salt	
	5 Days	13	13	13	13
Age	15 Days	11	11	11	11
		12	12	12	12

In this case, the μ for all rats receiving fenfluramine (12) equals the μ for all rats receiving amphetamine (12), which equals the μ for all rats receiving saltwater alone (12). There is no drug main effect in this case.

When an Age Main Effect Exists. Figures 21.1(c), (d), (g), and (h) illustrate cases in which the age main effect should be significant. In each case there is a difference in the μs for all 5- and 15-day-old rats. Examine the data tables above for Figures 21.1(b) and 21.1(c).

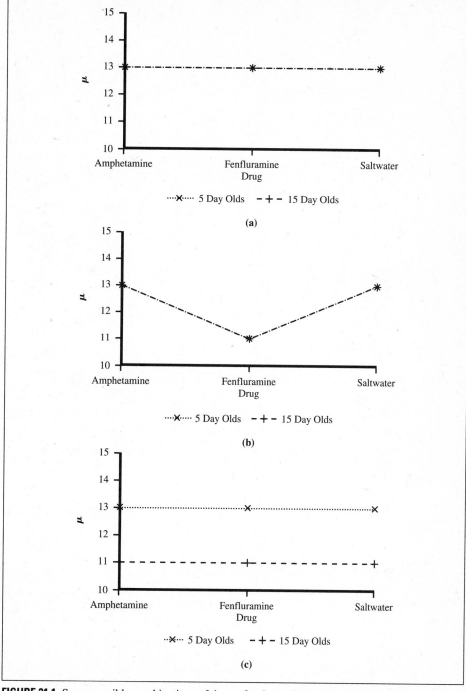

FIGURE 21.1 Some possible combinations of the μs for the study on age and type of drug. (a) No significant main effects or interactions expected. (b) A significant main effect is expected for type of drug; a significant interaction or main effect for age is not expected. (c) A significant main effect is expected for age; a significant interaction or main effect for type of drug is not expected (*continued on next page*).

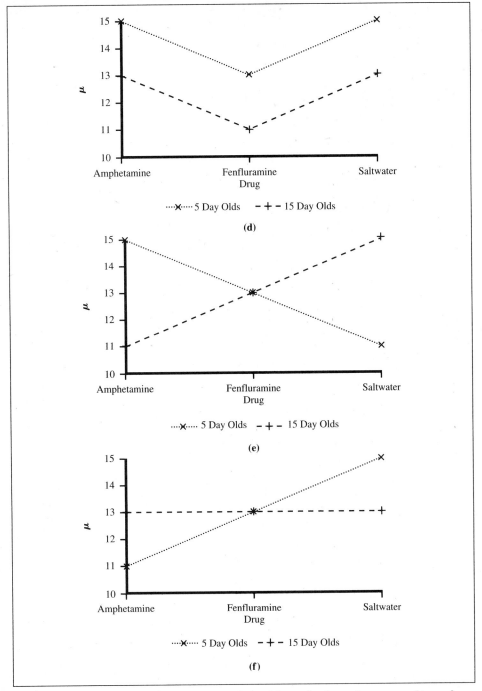

FIGURE 21.1 (*continued*) Some possible combinations of the μs for the study on age and type of drug. (d) Significant main effects for age and type of drug are expected; a significant interaction is not expected. (e) A significant interaction is expected; significant main effects are not expected. (f) A significant interaction and main effect for type of drug is expected; a significant main effect for age is not expected (*continued on next page*).

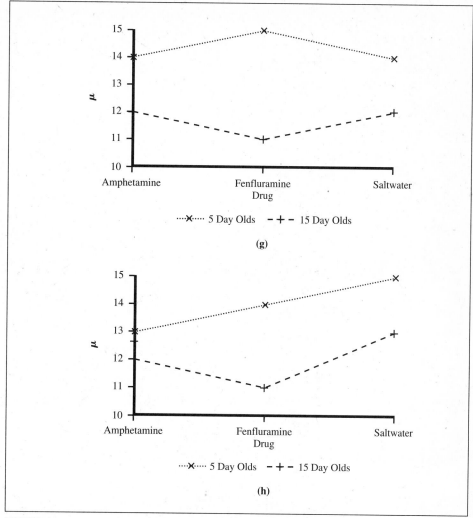

FIGURE 21.1 (*continued*) Some possible combinations of the μs for the study on age and type of drug. (g) A significant interaction and main effect for age is expected; a significant main effect for type of drug is not expected. (h) Both main effects and the interaction are expected to be significant.

In Figure 21.1(c), the μ for all 5-day-old rats (13) is greater than the μ for all 15-day-old rats (11). In this case failure to reject the null hypothesis for the age main effect would represent a Type II error. In Figure 21.1(b), the μ for all 5-day-old rats (12.33) equals the μ for all 15-day-old rats (12.33); there is no age main effect.

When an Age-Drug Interaction Exists. Figures 21.1(e), (f), (g), and (h) represent cases in which the interaction should be significant. Notice that in each case the two age lines are not parallel. In these cases failure to reject the null hypothesis for the interaction of drug and age would represent a Type II error. Compare this to Figure 21.1(d) where the two lines are parallel, indicating the absence of an interaction between age and drugs.

The following table was generated using data from Figure 21.1(e):

		Type of Drug		
		Amph	Fen	Salt
Age	5 Days	15	13	11
	15 Days	11	13	15
	$\mu_{15} - \mu_5$	-4	0	4

The fact that the differences between μ_{15} and μ_5 changes for different drugs suggests the presence of a moderator effect: one variable moderates the relationship with the other variable and percent weight gain.

Graphing Group Means. Figure 21.1 represents a graph of population μs. You do not typically know the population μs, but you do have access to the group means from your study. Graphing these group means in the manner that the μs are graphed in Figure 21.1 can be an effective method of communicating information about main effects and interactions in the analysis of variance. With some experience, you will be able to examine graphs of means and detect where you would expect significant effects to occur. Just as the frequency distribution can help you interpret measures of central tendency and measures of variability, and the scatterplot can help you interpret correlation coefficients, the graph of means can help you interpret main effects and interactions.

21.3 TESTING THE NULL HYPOTHESIS

The Denominator Mean Square. A separate F test is required for each main effect and the interaction. In each case the denominator will be the mean square within groups,

$$SS_{WG} = \left(\sum \text{squared scores} \right) - \left[\frac{(\sum \text{first group})^2}{n} + \cdots \frac{(\sum \text{last group})^2}{n} \right],$$

$$df_{WG} = N - k(q),$$

and

$$MS_{WG} = \frac{SS_{WG}}{df_{WG}}$$

where k is the number of groups defined by the first factor and q is the number of groups defined by the second factor.

Numerator Sums of Squares. The numerator will differ for the three F tests. If we consider age as Factor A and type of drug as Factor B, then the numerator for the F test of the age main effect will be called *mean square A* (MS_A), the numerator for the F test of the drug main effect will be called *mean square B* (MS_B), and the numerator for the F test of the age-drug interaction will be called *mean square A $\times$ B* ($MS_{A \times B}$).

The data for our study may be laid out in the following manner:

		Type of Drug (B)		
		Amph	Fen	Salt
Age (A)	5 days	5A	5F	5S
	15 days	15A	15F	15S

This layout can be used as the basis for the following computational formulas:

$$SS_A = \left[\frac{(\sum \text{first row})^2}{n_{row}} + \cdots \frac{(\sum \text{last row})^2}{n_{row}} \right] - \frac{(\sum \text{scores})^2}{N}$$

$$SS_B = \left[\frac{(\sum \text{first column})^2}{n_{column}} + \cdots \frac{(\sum \text{last column})^2}{n_{column}} \right] - \frac{(\sum \text{scores})^2}{N}$$

$$SS_{A \times B} = \left[\frac{(\sum \text{first group})^2}{n} + \cdots \frac{(\sum \text{last group})^2}{n} \right] + \frac{(\sum \text{scores})^2}{N}$$

$$- \left[\frac{(\sum \text{first row})^2}{n_{row}} + \cdots \frac{(\sum \text{last row})^2}{n_{row}} \right] - \left[\frac{(\sum \text{first column})^2}{n_{column}} + \cdots \frac{(\sum \text{last column})^2}{n_{column}} \right].$$

n_{row} refers to the number of subjects per row of the table. In our example, n_{row} is the number of rats in each age group. n_{column} is the number of subjects per column in the table, the number of rats receiving each drug. n without a subscript is the number of rats in each of the six groups (assuming the group sizes are equal).

Numerator Degrees of Freedom. The degrees of freedom for each numerator mean square equal

$$df_A = k-1$$
$$df_B = q-1$$
$$df_{A \times B} = (k-1)(q-1)$$

Computation of the omnibus F tests is demonstrated in Procedure Box 21.1.

21.4 MAKING A DECISION ABOUT THE NULL HYPOTHESIS

For each F test the df_1 is defined by the degrees of freedom for the numerator mean square. This means the critical value for the omnibus tests can differ. The critical values and decisions for each hypothesis test are as follows (critical F values come from Table D–4 in Appendix D).

21.4.1 A × B Interaction

$$F_{A \times B} = 9.43$$
$$F_{\alpha=.05, df_1=2, df_2=6} = 5.14$$
decision: reject H_0.

The Two-Way Independent Groups ANOVA *F* Test

Goal   Six 5-day-old and six 15-day-old rats were injected with one of three drugs: fenfluramine, amphetamine, or saltwater. Subsequent percent weight gains were:

		Type of Drug (B)		
		Fen	Amph	Salt
Age (A)	5 days	1 2	3 6	10 8
	15 days	4 6	15 14	12 10

Compute the two-way independent groups *F* value using these data.

$$SS_A = \left[\frac{(\sum \text{first row})^2}{n_{\text{row}}} + \cdots \frac{(\sum \text{last row})^2}{n_{\text{row}}} \right] - \frac{(\sum \text{scores})^2}{N}$$

$$SS_B = \left[\frac{(\sum \text{first column})^2}{n_{\text{column}}} + \cdots \frac{(\sum \text{last column})^2}{n_{\text{column}}} \right] - \frac{(\sum \text{scores})^2}{N}$$

$$SS_{A \times B} = \left[\frac{(\sum \text{first group})^2}{n} + \cdots \frac{(\sum \text{last group})^2}{n} \right] + \frac{(\sum \text{scores})^2}{N}$$
$$- \left[\frac{(\sum \text{first row})^2}{n_{\text{row}}} + \cdots \frac{(\sum \text{last row})^2}{n_{\text{row}}} \right]$$
$$- \left[\frac{(\sum \text{first column})^2}{n_{\text{column}}} + \cdots \frac{(\sum \text{last column})^2}{n_{\text{column}}} \right]$$

$$SS_{\text{WG}} = \left(\sum \text{squared scores} \right) - \left[\frac{(\sum \text{first group})^2}{n} + \cdots \frac{(\sum \text{last group})^2}{n} \right]$$

$$df_A = k - 1 \qquad df_B = q - 1 \qquad df_{A \times B} = (k-1)(q-1) \qquad df_{\text{WG}} = N - k(q)$$

$$MS_A = \frac{SS_A}{df_A} \qquad MS_B = \frac{SS_B}{df_B} \qquad MS_{A \times B} = \frac{SS_{A \times B}}{df_{A \times B}} \qquad MS_{\text{WG}} = \frac{SS_{\text{WG}}}{df_{\text{WG}}}$$

Continued

The two-way independent groups ANOVA F test continued

$$F_A = \frac{MS_A}{MS_{WG}} \qquad F_B = \frac{MS_B}{MS_{WG}} \qquad F_{A \times B} = \frac{MS_{A \times B}}{MS_{WG}}$$

Step 1 Compute the sum of Y and Y^2 for each group, the sum of Y for each row and column, and the sum of Y for all subjects.

	Fen	Amph	Salt	
5	$\sum Y = 3$ $\sum Y^2 = 5$	$\sum Y = 9$ $\sum Y^2 = 45$	$\sum Y = 18$ $\sum Y^2 = 164$	$3 + 9 + 18 = 30$
15	$\sum Y = 10$ $\sum Y^2 = 52$	$\sum Y = 29$ $\sum Y^2 = 421$	$\sum Y = 22$ $\sum Y^2 = 244$	$10 + 29 + 22 = 61$
	$3 + 10 = 13$	$9 + 29 = 38$	$18 + 22 = 40$	$30 + 61 = 13 +$ $38 + 40 = 91$

Step 2 Square the sum of the scores for each group, divide each by n, and sum the resulting values.

$$\left[\frac{(\sum \text{first group})^2}{n} + \cdots \frac{(\sum \text{last group})^2}{n} \right] = \frac{3^2}{2} + \frac{9^2}{2} + \frac{18^2}{2} + \frac{10^2}{2} + \frac{29^2}{2} + \frac{22^2}{2} = 919.5$$

Step 3 Square the sum of all scores and divide by N.

$$\frac{(\sum \text{scores})^2}{N} = \frac{91^2}{12} = 690.0833$$

Step 4 Sum the squared scores.

$$\left(\sum \text{squared scores} \right) = 5 + 45 + 164 + 52 + 421 + 244 = 931$$

Step 5 Square the sum of the scores for each row, divide by n_{row}, and sum the resulting values.

$$\left[\frac{(\sum \text{first row})^2}{n_{\text{row}}} + \cdots \frac{(\sum \text{last row})^2}{n_{\text{row}}} \right] = \frac{30^2}{6} + \frac{61^2}{6} = 770.1667$$

Step 6 Square the sum of the scores for each column, divide by n_{column}, and sum the resulting values.

$$\left[\frac{(\sum \text{first column})^2}{n_{\text{column}}} + \cdots \frac{(\sum \text{last column})^2}{n_{\text{column}}} \right] = \frac{13^2}{4} + \frac{38^2}{4} + \frac{40^2}{4} = 803.25$$

Continued

The two-way independent groups ANOVA F test continued

Step 7 Compute the sums of squares.

SS_{WG} = Step 4 − Step 2 = 931 − 919.5 = 11.5 ⟵——————————— *These*

SS_A = Step 5 − Step 3 = 770.1667 − 690.0833 = 80.0833 ⟵——————— *numbers*

SS_B = Step 6 − Step 3 = 803.25 − 690.0833 = 113.1667 ⟵——————— *must be*

$SS_{A \times B}$ = Step 2 + Step 3 − Step 5 − Step 6

= 919.5 + 690.0833 − 770.1667 − 803.25

= 36.1667 ⟵————————————————————————— *positive*

Step 8 *Divide each sum of squares by the corresponding degrees of freedom.*

$$MS_{WG} = \frac{SS_{WG}}{N - k(q)} = \frac{11.5}{12 - 3(2)} = 1.9167$$

$$MS_A = \frac{SS_A}{k - 1} = \frac{80.0833}{2 - 1} = 80.0833$$

$$MS_B = \frac{SS_B}{q - 1} = \frac{113.1667}{3 - 1} = 56.5834$$

$$MS_{A \times B} = \frac{SS_{A \times B}}{(k - 1)(q - 1)} = \frac{36.1667}{(2 - 1)(3 - 1)} = 18.0834$$

Step 9 *Divide MS_A, MS_B, and $MS_{A \times B}$ by MS_{WG}.*

$$F_A = \frac{MS_A}{MS_{WG}} = \frac{80.0833}{1.9167} = 41.78$$

$$F_B = \frac{MS_B}{MS_{WG}} = \frac{56.5834}{1.9167} = 29.52$$

$$F_{A \times B} = \frac{MS_{A \times B}}{MS_{WG}} = \frac{18.0834}{1.9167} = 9.43$$

The results may be used to create an ANOVA summary table:

Source	df	SS	MS	F
Age (A)	1	80.08	80.08	41.78*
Drug (B)	2	113.17	56.58	29.52*
Interaction	2	36.17	18.08	9.43*
Within Groups	6	11.50	1.92	

$*p < .05$

Interpretation of the Results. The results suggest that the effect of type of injection on appetite suppression differs depending on age. The decision to reject the null hypothesis is followed by multiple comparison tests designed for the analysis of interactions. If you examine the original data table in Procedure Box 21.1, you may suspect that multiple comparison tests will demonstrate that the relationship between age and percent weight is very different for amphetamine than it is for fenfluramine or saltwater. Specifically, 15-day-olds gained more weight after receiving amphetamine than did 5-day-olds. The differences were much smaller for the other two drugs. However, this conclusion must be considered tentative in the absence of multiple comparisons.

21.4.2 A Main Effect

$$F_A = 6.7368$$
$$F_{\alpha=.05, df_1=1, df_2=6} = 5.99$$
$$\text{decision: reject } H_0$$

Interpretation of the Results. The results suggest that appetite suppression differed depending on age. Since $k = 2$, examination of the means indicates the expected difference between the population μs. The mean percent weight gain for 5-day-olds was 5.0%, compared to 10.2% for 15-day-olds. The direction of the means suggests 15-day-old rats demonstrate greater weight gain after injection than 5-day-olds regardless of which drug they received.

21.4.3 B Main Effect

$$F_B = 14.7105$$
$$F_{\alpha=.05, df_1=2, df_2=6} = 5.14$$
$$\text{decision: reject } H_0$$

Interpretation of the Results. The results suggest that appetite suppression at both ages differs depending on the type of injection. Since $q = 3$, multiple comparison tests are necessary to explore which population μs seem to be different, although the data suggest greater weight gain after injection with amphetamine or saltwater than after fenfluramine.

Interactions and Main Effects. Although I have provided an interpretation of the results for the two main effects as well as the interaction, in practice it is not appropriate to interpret significant main effects if the interaction is significant. This is because the interaction suggests a straightforward interpretation of the main effects is not appropriate. For example, a significant drug main effect might suggest fenfluramine results in less weight gain than saltwater. This would be a misleading finding in the present circumstances, since the significant interaction suggests that the differences in weight gain for different drugs varies depending on the age of the rat.

21.5 CONDITIONS FOR USING THE TEST

Conditions. The conditions required for using the two-way independent groups ANOVA are: (1) members of the sample fall into two or more groups based on two discrete variables, (2) the groups are independent, (3) members of the sample produce an interval or ratio variable, and (4) you are interested in whether one discrete variable moderates the relationship between the second discrete variable and the interval or ratio variable. Rejection of the null hypothesis would suggest the existence of a moderator effect in the population.

Unlike the one-way ANOVA, use of the two-way ANOVA with continuous ordinal variables is not recommended. Tests of interactions with ordinal variables can produce inaccurate results (Davison & Sharma, 1990).

Examples of other studies for which the two-way independent groups ANOVA may be used include:

1. An observational study in which black males, black females, white males, and white females are compared on body temperature. The two factors would be ethnicity and gender.
2. A true experiment in which the effect of size and color of print on the number of words read per minute is evaluated. This is a case in which the experimenter is manipulating two independent variables.

Assumptions. The test requires the following statistical assumptions:

1. Random and independent sampling.
2. Normality: the populations represented by the groups are all normally distributed. The two-way independent groups ANOVA is generally considered robust against violation of this assumption if $n \geq 30$ for all groups.
3. Homogeneity of variance: the variances of the populations are all equal. The two-way independent groups ANOVA is generally considered robust against violation of this assumption if all group sizes are equal.

21.6 DIRECTIONAL VERSUS NONDIRECTIONAL HYPOTHESES

Like the other ANOVA models discussed, the two-way independent groups ANOVA F test is always one-tailed. The larger the computed F value, the larger the size of the main effect or interaction. Rejection of the null hypothesis for a main effect indicates that a difference seems to exist among the μs, but does not indicate which μs seem to be different. The only exception to this rule occurs when the discrete variable is dichotomous. Rejection of the null hypothesis for an interaction indicates that the size of differences among μs for one variable differ depending on the value of the other variable, but not where the differences occur. The ANOVA F test is always one-tailed, yet only nondirectional hypotheses can be tested. This and other aspects of the two-way independent groups ANOVA are summarized in Table 21.1.

TABLE 21.1   Selected Aspects of the Two-Way Independent Groups ANOVA

Symbol Used	Degrees of Freedom	Type of Statistical Hypotheses	General Form of Statistical Hypotheses	Type of Test	Symbol for Alpha	Critical Region in
F	$k-1$ $q-1$ $(k-1)(q-1)$ $N-k(q)$	nondirectional	*main effects:* H_0: all row (or column) μs are equal H_1: not all row (or column) μs are equal *interaction:* H_0: differences between μs for variable 1 are equal at every level of variable 2 H_1: not all differences between μs for variable 1 are equal at every level of variable 2	one-tailed	α	upper tail

KEY TERMS

degrees of freedom within groups
dependent groups
discrete variable
factor
factorial ANOVA
homogeneity of variance assumption
interaction
interval variable

main effect
mean square within groups
moderator effect
normality assumption
quantitative variable
ratio variable
robust
sum of squares within groups

EXERCISES

Answers to all exercises may be found in Appendix B.

1. In which of the following studies would the two-way independent groups ANOVA be an appropriate analysis?
   a. Subjects are randomly assigned to two smoking cessation programs. The number of cigarettes smoked per day before versus after treatment is measured.
   b. A researcher examines the frequency of common illnesses among black and white children from low- versus high-income families.
   c. Average family income is compared in families with black and white children who frequently experience common illnesses.

2. A study is conducted in which first- and sixth-grade teachers identify students they believe demonstrate poor social skills. The students are randomly assigned

either to two hours per week of formal social skills training with an adult, or two hours per week of unstructured activity with a same-age student that teachers identified as socially skilled.
   a. Is this a *true experiment, quasi-experiment,* or *observational study*?
   b. Subjects are observed through a two-way mirror as they interact with peers. Trained raters evaluate the adequacy of the children's social skills. The following data represent the differences between their scores after three months of treatment, and their scores prior to treatment. Positive scores suggest improved social skills, negative scores a decline. Compute the two-way independent groups ANOVA, and construct an ANOVA table (assume $\alpha = .05$):

		Grade	
		First	Sixth
Program	Adult	8	−1
		6	1
		12	3
	Peer	7	8
		9	6
		13	9

c. What is the critical value for each analysis using $\alpha = .05$? Can the researcher reject the null hypotheses?

d. What is the mean for each group? What is the mean for first and sixth graders, and for students in the formal and peer social skills programs? On the basis of these means, how might the results be interpreted?

3. Examine the following graphs of μs that could potentially occur in the populations used for the social skills study described in question 2. In each case, indicate which effects should be significant (assuming sufficient power):

a.

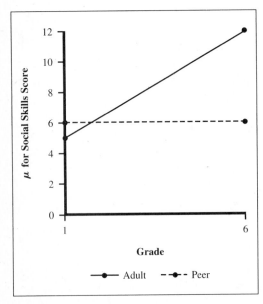

b.

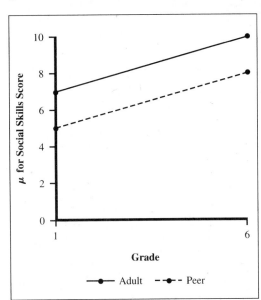

c.

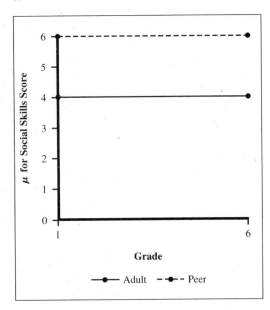

4. Examine the following tables of μs that could potentially occur in the populations used for the social skills study described in question 2. In each case, indicate which effects should be significant (assuming sufficient power):

a.

		Grade	
		First	Sixth
Program	Adult	11	8
	Peer	6	3

b.

		Grade	
		First	Sixth
Program	Adult	6	8
	Peer	8	6

c.

		Grade	
		First	Sixth
Program	Adult	8	8
	Peer	8	8

5. A researcher believes that overall, college students feel more comfortable speaking to instructors of the same gender than they do speaking to instructors of the opposite gender. Male and female students are randomly assigned to speak either to a male or female instructor. The mean number of words the student speaks per minute in a 10-minute conversation about the student's progress in college is taken as evidence of comfort level.

a. Is this a *true experiment, quasi-experiment,* or *observational study*?

b. What type of variable is number of words spoken: *nominal, ordinal, interval,* or *ratio; continuous* or *discrete*?

c. State the null and alternative hypotheses for the two-way independent groups ANOVA.

d. Using the following data, construct the ANOVA table:

		Student	
		Male	Female
Instructor	Male	32	12
		25	16
	Female	26	14
		23	18

e. What are the critical values for $\alpha = .05$? Which null hypotheses can be rejected? What conclusions can you draw?

CHAPTER 22

The Chi-Square Test
of Independence

The next four chapters focus on *nonparametric* alternatives to some of the tests discussed previously. The concept of the nonparametric test was introduced in Chapter 12, and defined as an inferential statistic which requires no assumptions about the shape of the population distribution. The parametric tests discussed in the last several chapters — the *t* and *F* tests —require making certain assumptions about the population distributions from which samples are drawn, most commonly that these distributions are normally distributed. It is usually not difficult to meet the robustness conditions for the use of these tests, such as setting $N \geq 30$.

However, there are some circumstances where these tests are not appropriate. They may produce inaccurate results when a discrete ordinal variable is used instead of a continuous one. Even under conditions where the test is usually robust the critical value may not be correct if the population distribution is extremely nonnormal. You may also find circumstances where achieving robustness is not practical, for example where group sizes are very different. In such cases a nonparametric alternative may be suggested. This chapter will focus on the most commonly used nonparametric hypothesis test, the chi-square test of independence.

22.1 INTRODUCTION

The chi-square goodness of fit test, a test used to evaluate null hypotheses concerning the probability associated with each value of a variable, was introduced in Chapter 14. The chi-square test of independence can be used to examine whether two or more variables are related based on information about probabilities. Only the two-variable case will be discussed here.

To demonstrate the chi-square goodness of fit test I used an example evaluating the pattern of political views in the general adult population. Suppose in the same survey we gathered information about the gender of our subjects. The chi-square test of independence could be used to evaluate whether a relationship exists between political view and gender.

22.2 DEFINING THE NULL AND ALTERNATIVE HYPOTHESES

Gender is a dichotomous variable. Political view was measured in Chapter 14 as an ordinal variable with three values: conservative, moderate, and liberal. The combination of the two variables creates six possible categories: conservative males, conservative females, moderate males, moderate females, liberal males, and liberal females.

If these two variables are unrelated, then the probability that a female is conservative will equal the probability that a male is conservative, the probability that a female is moderate will equal the probability that a male is moderate, and the probability that a female is liberal will equal the probability that a male is liberal. In other words, knowing a person's gender offers no information about the person's political view, and vice versa. The null hypothesis might be stated as

$$H_0: p(\text{conservative} \mid \text{female}) = p(\text{conservative} \mid \text{male}), \quad \text{and}$$

$$p(\text{moderate} \mid \text{female}) = p(\text{moderate} \mid \text{male}), \quad \text{and}$$

$$p(\text{liberal} \mid \text{female}) = p(\text{liberal} \mid \text{male}).$$

where the symbol $p(\text{conservative} \mid \text{female})$ represents the *conditional probability* of a conservative among female subjects. The conditional probability was introduced in Section 9.1.2: $p(\text{conservative} \mid \text{female})$ indicates the probability that a member of the population is conservative *given* that the subject is female. The corresponding alternative hypothesis is

$$H_1: p(\text{conservative} \mid \text{female}) \neq p(\text{conservative} \mid \text{male}), \quad \text{and/or}$$

$$p(\text{moderate} \mid \text{female}) \neq p(\text{moderate} \mid \text{male}), \quad \text{and/or}$$

$$p(\text{liberal} \mid \text{female}) \neq p(\text{liberal} \mid \text{male}).$$

The statistical hypotheses could be stated more generally as

H_0: The probability of each value for one variable is consistent across all values of the other variable (values of one variable are independent of values of the other).

H_1: The probability of at least one value for one variable is not consistent across all values of the other variable (at least some values of one variable are dependent on values of the other).

In our example, the variable gender has two possible values while the variable political view has three possible values. For the null hypothesis to be true, in every case the probability of a certain political view must be the same for males and females. The alternative hypothesis is true if in at least one case the probability of a certain political view is not the same for males and females. I could also have stated the statistical hypotheses the other way, in terms of the probability that a conservative is male versus female for example.

22.3 TESTING THE NULL HYPOTHESIS

The chi-square test of independence requires determining the expected frequencies for each possible combination of the two variables, assuming the null hypothesis is true. In Chapter 14 the sample frequencies associated with the three political views in a sample of 1000 adults were

liberal: 246

conservative: 349

moderate: 40.

Suppose we find the number of males and females in our sample to be

male: 447

female: 553.

The data for our study may be laid out in the following manner:

Political View

		Liberal	Conservative	Moderate	
	Male	Male Liberal	Male Conservative	Male Moderate	447
Gender					
	Female	Female Liberal	Female Conservative	Female Moderate	553
		246	349	40	1000

If the null hypothesis is true, then the probability of a male should be the same regardless of political view. Based on our sample, our best guess of the probability of a male in the population is $447/1000 = .447$, and our best guess of the probability of a female is $553/1000 = .553$. If the null hypothesis is true, then 44.7% of liberals should be male, 44.7% of conservatives should be male, and 44.7% of moderates should be male. This information can be used to determine the expected frequencies: if the null hypothesis is true, then

$$\frac{447}{1000}(246) = 109.96$$

subjects in a sample of 1000 should be male liberals, while

$$\frac{553}{1000}(246) = 136.04$$

subjects should be female liberals. Repeating this process for each of the six combinations suggests the following expected frequencies:

EXPECTED FREQUENCIES

		Political View			
		Liberal	Conservative	Moderate	
Gender	Male	109.96	156.00	181.04	447
	Female	136.04	193.00	223.96	553
		246	349	405	1000

Notice that $109.96/246 = 156.00/349 = 181.04/405 = 447/1000 = .447$. This is consistent with the null hypothesis; the expected proportion of liberals who are male equals the expected proportion of conservatives who are male equals the expected proportion of moderates who are male. Furthermore, each equals the proportion of the entire sample that is male.

The procedure for computing the expected frequency for a cell can be stated generally as

$$f_{E_{\text{row } i \text{ column } j}} = \frac{n_{\text{row } i}(n_{\text{column } j})}{N}.$$

That is, the expected frequency for the cell in row i, column j is defined by multiplying the n for row i by the n for row j, and dividing by the N.

Suppose the sample frequencies prove to be as follows:

OBSERVED FREQUENCIES

		Political View			
		Liberal	Conservative	Moderate	
Gender	Male	73	161	213	447
	Female	173	188	192	553
		246	349	405	1000

Do the differences between the expected and observed frequencies reflect chance sample variation, or does a relationship exist between gender and political view in the population?

The chi-square test of independence is computed using the same formula used for the chi-square goodness of fit test:

$$\chi^2 = \sum_{j=1}^{k} \frac{(f_{0_j} - f_{E_j})^2}{f_{E_j}}.$$

For the test of independence the subscript j refers to the various combinations of the two variables, so j ranges in this example from 1 to 6. Computation of the chi-square value for our study is demonstrated in Procedure Box 22.1.

The Chi-Square Test of Independence

Goal   Compute the chi-square value for the sample data provided.

$$\chi^2 = \sum_{j=1}^{k} \frac{(f_{0_j} - f_{E_j})^2}{f_{E_j}}$$

Step 1   *Subtract the expected from observed frequencies, square the differences, and divide by the expected frequency.*

	Observed	Expected	Difference	Squared	Divided	
liberal males	73	109.96	−36.96	1366.04	12.42 ←	*These*
liberal females	173	136.04	36.96	1366.04	10.04 ←	*numbers*
conservative males	161	156.00	5.00	25.00	0.16 ←	*must*
conservative females	188	193.00	−5.00	25.00	0.13 ←	*be*
moderate males	213	181.04	31.96	1021.44	5.64 ←	*positive*
moderate females	192	223.96	−31.96	1021.44	4.56	

Step 2   *Sum the values in the last column of Step 1.*

$$\chi^2 = 12.42 + 10.04 + .16 + .13 + 5.64 + 4.56 = 32.95$$

22.4 MAKING A DECISION ABOUT THE NULL HYPOTHESIS

While the goodness of fit test and the test of independence use the same formula, they differ in terms of the appropriate degrees of freedom. For the chi-square test of independence,

$$df = (k - 1)(q - 1),$$

where k is the number of values for the first discrete variable, and q is the number of values for the second. Since gender has two values and political view has three values, the degrees of freedom are

$$df = (2 - 1)(3 - 1) = 2.$$

Critical values for χ^2 may be found in Table D–2 of Appendix D: $\chi^2_{\alpha=.05, df=2} = 5.991$. We can reject the nondirectional null hypothesis if

$$\chi^2 \geq 5.991.$$

Since the computed chi-square value of 32.95 exceeds 5.991 we can reject the null hypothesis. The results suggest a relationship exists between gender and political view.

Interpreting the Results. If $k = 2$ and $q = 2$ we could stop right now. The direction of the differences between observed and expected frequencies would indicate the nature of the relationship between the two variables. When either k or q is greater than 2, additional analyses are necessary to determine where the population differences seem to lie (see Marascuilo & McSweeney, 1977).

Looking at the contribution for each combination of the two variables (see the last column of Step 1 in Procedure Box 22.1), the gender composition for liberals is particularly discrepant from the expected frequencies. The data suggest that females are more likely to describe themselves as liberals, and males less likely to describe themselves as liberals, than would be expected if the variables were unrelated. In addition, the proportion of moderate males is somewhat higher, and the proportion of moderate females somewhat lower, than would be expected if the two variables were unrelated. The proportion of male and female conservatives are consistent with the expected frequencies. However, as with the χ^2 goodness of fit test (and ANOVA F tests) these conclusions must be considered tentative until additional analyses are conducted.

22.5 CONDITIONS FOR USING THE TEST

Other Examples. The chi-square test of independence can be used when the scientific hypothesis has to do with whether two variables demonstrate dependent outcomes (are related). Other examples of studies that could use the chi-square test of independence include the following:

1. A researcher is interested in whether students with above average academic performance are more likely to be left-handed than students with average or below average academic performance.
2. A researcher is interested in whether honor students and special education students differ in their pattern of responding to the statement "I feel good about myself" on a scale from 1 (Strongly Disagree) to 5 (Strongly Agree).
3. Rats are randomly assigned to receive either a low or high dose of electric shock. The dependent variable is the proportion of rats that freeze versus the proportion that flee within three seconds after administration of the shock.

Either of the first two examples could also have been analyzed using the two-group independent t test. In the first example, GPA (a continuous ordinal variable) could have been related to handedness using the independent groups t test. Instead, GPA is reduced to three values: above average, average, or below average GPA. In the second case the self-esteem variable (a continuous ordinal variable) has a relatively small number of measured values.

When you have the option of choosing between the chi-square test of independence and the two-group independent t test, the t test is generally preferred. For one thing, the t test usually requires a smaller N than the χ^2 test to achieve a desired level of power. In addition, transforming a continuous variable into a variable with a small number of values can be tricky. What is the best GPA to use as the dividing line between "below average" and "average," or between "average" and "above average"? This decision is often arbitrary, and can reduce the power of the test.

Statistical Conditions. The chi-square test of independence requires the same conditions as the goodness of fit test:

1. random and independent sampling
2. a certain minimum number of subjects, although if all expected frequencies are 5 or greater the sample size is more than sufficient
3. the set of combinations for the two variables are mutually exclusive and exhaustive

None of these conditions requires a parametric assumption, making the chi-square test of independence a nonparametric test.

22.6 DIRECTIONAL VERSUS NONDIRECTIONAL HYPOTHESES

Like the goodness of fit test, the test of independence is always one-tailed, because differences between the observed and expected frequencies are always squared. The greater the difference from the expected proportion in either direction, the larger the χ^2 value will be. The only critical value lies in the upper tail of the χ^2 distribution. The χ^2 test of independence can only evaluate nondirectional hypotheses. This and other aspects of the chi-square test of independence are summarized in Table 22.1.

22.7 POWER AND SAMPLE SIZE ISSUES

The power of the chi-square test of independence is equivalent to the power of the chi-square goodness of fit test, so the same sample size table may be used. Table C–3 in Appendix C provides sample sizes necessary for .80 and .90 power for small, medium, and large effect sizes. If we assume a small effect size is the smallest meaningful effect as we did in Chapter 14, for $\alpha = .05$, $\beta = .20$, and $df = 2$ the required sample size is 964. Even if the population effect size is small, our sample size of 1000 is sufficient for the present study.

TABLE 22.1 Selected Aspects of the Chi-Square Test of Independence

Symbol Used	Degrees of Freedom	Type of Statistical Hypotheses	General Form of Statistical Hypotheses	Type of Test	Symbol for Alpha	Critical Region in
χ^2	$(k-1)(q-1)$	nondirectional	H_0: two variables are independent H_1: two variables are not independent	one-tailed	α	upper tail

KEY TERMS

χ^2 distribution
conditional probability
dependent values
dichotomous variable
directional hypothesis
discrete variable
frequency

independent values
nondirectional hypothesis
nonparametric test
one-tailed test
power
probability
sample size

EXERCISES

Answers to all exercises may be found in Appendix B.

1. For which of the following studies is the chi-square test of independence an appropriate statistic:
   a. A study is conducted to investigate whether there is a difference in the the rate of learning disability among right- versus left-handed students.
   b. A researcher finds that the frequency of church attendance is greater in low income subjects than high income subjects.
   c. A researcher is interested in whether the rate of child abuse is higher in families where the father is alcoholic.

2. A market researcher is interested in whether males and females demonstrate a difference in their preference for two colas. Subjects consist of shoppers at a mall. Subjects taste cola 1, then cola 2, and indicate which they prefer.
   a. Is this a *true experiment*, *quasi-experiment*, or *observational study*?
   b. State the null and alternative hypotheses for this study.
   c. Assuming a large effect size is considered the smallest important effect, and the researcher would like to use $\alpha = .05$, $\beta = .20$, what is the appropriate sample size for this study?
   d. The researcher is able to gather a sample of 46 shoppers to taste the colas. She finds that of the 18 males, 12 prefer cola 1 and 6 prefer cola 2. Of the 28 females, 10 prefer cola 1, 18 prefer cola 2. Generate the expected frequencies for these data.
   e. Compute the χ^2 test of independence.
   f. What is the critical value for $\alpha = .05$? Can the researcher reject the null hypothesis?
   g. How might these results be interpreted?

   h. It is said that the χ^2 test can only address nondirectional hypotheses, yet it was possible in step g to directly interpret the results without additional analyses. Why was this possible?

3. A researcher randomly assigns cardiac patients to receive a new heart medication or a previously approved heart medication. Over the next three years, the researcher records the number in each group who suffer at least one more heart attack.
   a. Is this a *true experiment*, *quasi-experiment*, or *observational study*?
   b. State the null and alternative hypotheses for this study.
   c. The following data are collected:

		Heart Attack		
		0	≥ 1	
Medication	New	364	86	450
	Old	388	62	450
		752	148	900

   Generate the expected frequencies for these data.
   d. Compute the chi-square test of independence.
   e. What is the critical value for $\alpha = .01$? Can the researcher reject the null hypothesis?
   f. How might these results be interpreted? In particular, would you recommend that cardiac patients use this medication?

4. The chi-square test of independence is still a goodness of fit test. Can you explain what this statement means?

5. Five different ethnic groups are compared on political position:

Ethnicity

		White	Black	Latino	Asian	Native American	
	Conservative	72	42	34	65	26	239
Political Position	Moderate	102	91	107	113	82	495
	Liberal	26	67	59	22	92	266
		200	200	200	200	200	1000

a. Is this a *true experiment*, *quasi-experiment*, or *observational study*?

b. What type of variables are ethnicity and political position: *nominal*, *ordinal*, *interval*, or *ratio*; *continuous* or *discrete*?

c. Compute the expected frequencies for this table.

d. Compute the chi-square test of independence.

e. What is the critical value at $\alpha = .05$? Can the researcher reject the null hypothesis?

f. What conclusions can you draw on the basis of these findings? If the results are significant, what would you expect additional analyses to reveal?

6. Explain in words why the expected frequency in each cell is computed from the formula

$$f_{E_{\text{row } i \text{ column } j}} = \frac{n_{\text{row } i}(n_{\text{column } j})}{N}.$$

CHAPTER 23

The Wilcoxon *T* Test

23.1 INTRODUCTION

The Wilcoxon *T* test may be used to evaluate whether a relationship exists between a dichotomous variable with dependent groups and a non-nominal variable. The Wilcoxon *T* test is recommended as an alternative to the dependent groups *t* test when the sample size is too small to insure robustness against violation of the normality assumption (when N_D is less than 30 and/or the population distribution is believed to be severely nonnormal), or when the study involves a discrete ordinal variable, since the *t* test is not recommended for this class of variables. However, under certain circumstances the Wilcoxon *T* test will not detect the presence of a relationship that the dependent groups *t* test can detect.

23.2 DEFINING THE NULL AND ALTERNATIVE HYPOTHESES

A study comparing the frequency of self-reported risk behaviors before and after an AIDS awareness presentation was used to illustrate the dependent groups *t* test. The two groups (which include the same subjects) are representative of a population of college students before an AIDS awareness presentation, and the same population of students after the presentation. Each member of the first population is also a single member of the second population.

Suppose we had access to the entire population of students from which our sample was randomly drawn, and performed the following steps:

1. computed the difference score for each pair of associated scores
2. rank ordered the absolute values of these difference scores from lowest to highest (Table 23.1 reviews the steps involved in rank ordering; see Procedure Box 6.2 in Chapter 6 for a more thorough description)
3. summed the ranks associated with positive difference scores ($\sum R_+$), and the ranks associated with negative difference scores ($\sum R_-$)

If the presentation has no impact on the self-reported frequency of risk behaviors, then the sum of the positive difference score ranks should equal the sum of the negative difference score ranks:

$$H_0: \sum R_+ = \sum R_-,$$

TABLE 23.1	Review of the Transformation to Ranks
Step 1	Order the values from lowest to highest.
Step 2	Replace unique values (values with a frequency of 1) with their position in the list. The lowest score is replaced with a rank of 1, and so on.
Step 3	Replace tied scores with the mean of their positions in the list.

or

$$\sum R_+ - \sum R_- = 0.$$

The alternative hypothesis may be stated as

$$H_1 : \sum R_+ \neq \sum R_-,$$

or

$$\sum R_+ - \sum R_- \neq 0.$$

For example, suppose our population consisted of only four students:

Before	After	Difference	Absolute Difference	Rank	R_+	R_-
1	3	−2	2	1		1
5	22	−17	17	4		4
19	16	3	3	2	2	
15	11	4	4	3	3	
Sums:					5	5

The null hypothesis for the Wilcoxon *T* test is true here; the sum of the two sets of ranks are equal. Note, however, that the null hypothesis for the dependent groups *t* test is not true;

$$\mu_D = \frac{(-2) + (-17) + 3 + 4}{4} = -3,$$

not 0. Although the Wilcoxon *T* test is considered an alternative to the dependent groups *t* test, it may not be able to detect a relationship that is detectable by the *t* test because of the transformation of scores to ranks.

23.3 TESTING THE NULL HYPOTHESIS

The computational procedure begins with the steps described previously:

1. Compute the difference score for each associated pair of values.
2. Rank order the absolute value of these difference scores from lowest to highest.
3. Sum the ranks associated with positive difference scores ($\sum_{i=1}^{n_+} R_i$)then sum the ranks associated with negative difference scores ($\sum_{i=1}^{n_-} R_i$). The computed *T* value is the smaller sum.

Procedure Box 23.1 provides an example of the computation of the T value for the AIDS awareness study. In practice, you usually do not need to compute both $\sum_{i=1}^{n_+} R_i$ and $\sum_{i=1}^{n_-} R_i$; you can determine which will be the smaller sum by sight. However, you do need to compute both if you want to use the computation check described in the Procedure Box.

23.4 MAKING A DECISION ABOUT THE NULL HYPOTHESIS

The critical values for the T test may be found in Table D–6 of Appendix D. For any given alpha level, the critical value is determined, not by degrees of freedom, but by N_D, the number of difference scores. In a sample of 10 difference scores the critical value is $T_{\alpha=.05, N_D=10} = 8$. If the computed T value is *less than* the critical value, you may reject the null hypothesis. This means you always compare the computed T value to the lower tail of the T distribution. Even so, the test may be considered two-tailed since the smaller of the two computed T values is always compared to the critical value. The T value computed in Procedure Box 23.1 (5.5) allows us to reject the null hypothesis.

Interpreting the Results. Since the smaller sum was associated with the negative difference scores, this suggests that the self-reported frequency of risk behaviors was lower after attending the presentation than before. Problems with the interpretation of this study were noted in Section 15.4.

23.5 CONDITIONS FOR USING THE WILCOXON T TEST

The conditions for using the Wilcoxon T test are similar to those required for the dependent groups t test: (1) members of the sample fall into two groups based on a dichotomous variable, (2) the two groups are dependent, (3) members of the sample produce a non-nominal variable, and (4) you are interested in whether the sum of the ranks for the positive differences in the population equals the sum of the ranks for the negative differences. If they are unequal it suggests the existence of a population relationship between the two variables.

TABLE 23.2   A Critical Tie in the AIDS Presentation Study

The following data are repeated from Step 2 in Procedure Box 23.1:

D	$|D|$	R	
6	6	7	
6	6	7	
3	3	5	
13	13	10	
−1	1	2	
2	2	3.5	⟵
8	8	9	
6	6	7	
−2	2	3.5	⟵
0	0	1	

The two $|D|$ values indicated are tied at 2. In the first case $D = 2$, a positive difference score. In the second case $D = -2$, a negative difference score. This represents a critical tie.

PROCEDURE BOX 23.1

The Wilcoxon *T* test

Goal   Ten students completed a rating scale concerning the frequency of risk behaviors before and after an AIDS awareness presentation:

	Before	After
Student 1	15	9
Student 2	22	16
Student 3	18	15
Student 4	16	3
Student 5	9	10
Student 6	8	6
Student 7	17	9
Student 8	11	5
Student 9	4	6
Student 10	10	10

Compute the Wilcoxon *T* test using these data.

Step 1   *For each pair of scores subtract the second from the first.*

Before	After	Difference
15	9	6
22	16	6
18	15	3
16	3	13
9	10	−1
8	6	2
7	9	8
11	5	6
4	6	−2
10	10	0

Continued

There are no statistical assumptions required for the use of the Wilcoxon *T* test other than the random and independent sampling assumption, making it a nonparametric test. However, the results of the Wilcoxon *T* test may be inaccurate if there are *critical ties*. A critical tie occurs in the Wilcoxon test when a positive difference score is tied with a negative difference score. Table 23.2 demonstrates the presence of a critical tie in the data from the AIDS presentation study. If there are one or more critical ties the results of the analysis should be considered suspect, particularly if the computed *T* value is near the critical value. When critical ties are present the results of the test should be adjusted (see Leach, 1979).

The Wilcoxon T test continued

Step 2 *Transform the absolute values of the difference scores to ranks from lowest to highest.*

D	$|D|$	R
6	6	7
6	6	7
3	3	5
13	13	10
-1	1	2
2	2	3.5
8	8	9
6	6	7
-2	2	3.5
0	0	1

Step 3 *Sum the ranks associated with positive difference scores, and the ranks associated with negative difference scores.*

$$\sum_{i=1}^{n_+} R_i = 7 + 7 + 5 + 10 + 3.5 + 9 + 7 + 1 = 49.5$$

$$\sum_{i=1}^{n_-} R_i = 2 + 3.5 = 5.5$$

Step 4 *T is the smaller sum.*

$$T = 5.5$$

Computation Check

The sum of the ranks must equal $N_D(N_D + 1)/2$.

$$\frac{N_D(N_D + 1)}{2} = \sum_{i=1}^{n_+} R_i + \sum_{i=1}^{n_-} R_i$$

$$\frac{10(11)}{2} = 49.5 + 5.5$$

$$55 = 55$$

The Wilcoxon *T* test may be used in any study where the dependent groups *t* test would also be appropriate, and may be preferred when you cannot meet the robustness requirements for the normality assumption and/or fear a seriously nonnormal population distribution. In addition, its use can be recommended for studies involving discrete ordinal variables. However, there is a tradeoff in that some relationships cannot be detected by the Wilcoxon test that can be detected using the *t* test.

23.6 DIRECTIONAL VERSUS NONDIRECTIONAL HYPOTHESES

When testing a nondirectional hypothesis with the Wilcoxon test, T equals the smaller of $\sum_{i=1}^{n_+} R_i$ and $\sum_{i=1}^{n_-} R_i$. To test a directional hypothesis, T is the sum of the ranks the alternative hypothesis suggests should be smaller (see Table 23.3). For example, suppose we wanted to evaluate whether attending an AIDS awareness presentation reduces self-reported risk behavior as a one-tailed test. The difference scores were computed by subtracting scores after the presentation from scores before the presentation. If participation results in lower scores, then $\sum_{i=1}^{n_-} R_i$ should be smaller than $\sum_{i=1}^{n_+} R_i$. This suggests the following null and alternative hypotheses:

$$H_0: \sum R_+ \leq \sum R_-$$
$$H_1: \sum R_+ > \sum R_-.$$

In this case you need only compute $\sum_{i=1}^{n_-} R_i$. If upon inspecting the data you find $\sum_{i=1}^{n_-} R_i$ is going to be larger than $\sum_{i=1}^{n_+} R_i$, you know already you will not be able to reject the null hypothesis.

If $\sum_{i=1}^{n_-} R_i$ is the smaller sum, you can use the values for a one-tailed test provided in Table D–6. In the AIDS awareness study

$$T_{\alpha(D)=.05,\,N_D=10} = 10.$$

Notice that the one-tailed critical value is greater than the two-tailed critical value. Since the computed T value is smaller than 10 we can reject the null hypothesis.

TABLE 23.3   Selected Aspects of the Wilcoxon *T* Test

Symbol Used	Type of Statistical Hypotheses	General Form of Statistical Hypotheses	Type of Test	Symbol for Alpha	Critical Region in
T	nondirectional	$H_0: \sum R_+ - \sum R_- = 0$ $H_1: \sum R_+ - \sum R_- \neq 0$	one-tailed	α	lower tail (compared to the smaller of $\sum_{i=1}^{n_+} R_i$ and $\sum_{i=1}^{n_-} R_i$)
	directional	$H_0: \sum R_+ - \sum R_- \leq 0$ $H_1: \sum R_+ - \sum R_- > 0$	one-tailed	$\alpha(D)$	lower tail (compared to $\sum_{i=1}^{n_-} R_i$)
	directional	$H_0: \sum R_+ - \sum R_- \geq 0$ $H_1: \sum R_+ - \sum R_- < 0$	one-tailed	$\alpha(D)$	lower tail (compared to $\sum_{i=1}^{n_+} R_i$)

Suppose we instead wanted to evaluate whether the presentation increases the frequency of risk behaviors as a one-tailed test. Since difference scores are being computed by subtracting scores after the presentation from scores before the presentation, $\sum_{i=1}^{n_+} R_i$ should be the smaller of the two sums. This suggests the following null and alternative hypotheses:

$$H_0: \sum R_+ \geq \sum R_-$$
$$H_1: \sum R_+ < \sum R_-.$$

The critical value would still be 10. However, if you look back at the data it is clear that the sum of the positive ranks is larger than the sum of the negative ranks. You know that you would not be able to reject this null hypothesis, so no further computations are necessary.

23.7 POWER AND SAMPLE SIZE ISSUES

As was demonstrated above, under certain conditions the Wilcoxon test is unable to detect a relationship that the t test can detect. However, the Wilcoxon test can be more powerful than the dependent groups t test if the assumptions of the t test are grossly violated. If you believe the population of difference scores from which your sample was drawn is severely nonnormal, then the Wilcoxon test may be more powerful even if you meet the condition under which the t test is generally considered robust ($N_D \geq 30$).

KEY TERMS

alternative hypothesis
critical value
dependent groups
dichotomous variable
directional hypothesis
nominal variable
nondirectional hypothesis

normality assumption
null hypothesis
one-tailed test
power
robust
two-tailed test

EXERCISES

Answers to all exercises may be found in Appendix B.

1. For which of the following studies could the Wilcoxon T test be an appropriate analysis? (Remember: the test is still potentially applicable even if no variable is rank ordered, so long as a variable can be converted into rank orders.)
   a. Subjects are randomly assigned to two different programs aimed at eliminating cigarette smoking.
   b. Subjects are divided into blocks of two on the basis of number of cigarettes smoked per day, and randomly assigned within blocks to two programs to stop cigarette smoking.
   c. For a sample of 100 dogs, number of drops of saliva in the mouth are counted before and after hearing a bell that has previously been associated with receiving food.
   d. Rats are placed at the center of a maze which allows the rat to run in one of three directions. The number of rats out of 100 who choose to turn

left instead of right or going straight is recorded before and after placing food in the alley to the left of the rat.

2. In Chapter 15 an example was used involving the concept of *statistical regression*, the tendency for individuals with extreme scores on some scale to move towards the mean over time. A researcher administered a measure of self-esteem to 300 college students. One month later she administered the scale again to those 10 students who had the lowest scores on the first administration.

a. If the researcher chooses to use the Wilcoxon *T* test to analyze these data, state the directional statistical hypotheses. Assume scores at the second measurement will be subtracted from scores at the first measurement.

b. Compute the Wilcoxon *T* test using the following data:

Time 1	Time 2
2	8
3	10
3	4
4	7
4	9
5	3
6	7
6	12
6	6
7	8

c. What is the critical value using $\alpha(D) = .01$? Can the researcher reject the null hypothesis?

d. How might these results be interpreted?

e. Are there any critical ties in these data? If so, what are the implications for the data analysis?

3. The number of words correctly defined in a vocabulary test by high school students is measured before and after participation in a 3-hour language skills workshop, to see whether the workshop enhances performance on the test.

a. Is this a *true experiment*, *quasi-experiment*, or *observational study*?

b. State the nondirectional null and alternative hypotheses for the Wilcoxon *T* test.

c. Use the following data to compute the Wilcoxon *T* test:

Before	After
12	14
14	16
16	20
10	14
9	10
7	5

d. What is the critical value for $\alpha = .05$? Can the researcher reject the null hypothesis?

e. How might these results be interpreted?

f. Are there critical ties in these data? If so, what are the implications for the data analysis?

CHAPTER 24

The Mann-Whitney *U* Test

24.1 INTRODUCTION

The Mann-Whitney U test may be used to evaluate whether a relationship exists between a dichotomous variable with independent groups and a non-nominal variable. The Mann-Whitney U test is recommended as an alternative to the independent groups t test when the group sizes are too small or unequal to insure robustness against violation of the parametric assumptions required by the t test, or when the study involves a discrete ordinal variable. However, under certain circumstances the Mann-Whitney test will not detect the presence of a relationship that the independent groups t test can detect.

24.2 DEFINING THE NULL AND ALTERNATIVE HYPOTHESES

Let's return to the example used to introduce the independent groups t test. We are interested in whether there is a difference between liberal arts professors and behavioral science professors in level of anxiety as measured by the MMPI Psychasthenia scale.

Suppose we could combine the two populations represented by our groups and rank order every member from lowest anxiety score to highest. If there is no relationship between type of professor and level of anxiety, then the sum of the ranks for the liberal arts professors should equal the sum of the ranks for the behavioral science professors:

$$H_0: \sum R_1 = \sum R_2,$$

or

$$\sum R_1 - \sum R_2 = 0.$$

The alternative hypothesis may be stated as

$$H_1: \sum R_1 \neq \sum R_2,$$

or

$$\sum R_1 - \sum R_2 \neq 0.$$

However, like the Wilcoxon test, this test may not be able to detect a relationship that is detectable using the independent groups *t* test because of the transformation of scores to ranks; in some cases the sum of the ranks for the two populations will be equal but the μs will not.

24.3 TESTING THE NULL HYPOTHESIS

The computational procedure requires the following steps:

1. Combine the data from the two groups.
2. Rank order the data from lowest to highest (rank ordering was reviewed in Table 23.1 in Chapter 23).
3. Compute the *U* value for each group, where

$$U_1 = n_1 n_2 + \frac{n_2(n_2 + 1)}{2} - \sum_{i=1}^{n_2} R_i,$$

$$U_2 = n_1 n_2 + \frac{n_1(n_1 + 1)}{2} - \sum_{i=1}^{n_1} R_i.$$

An explanation of these *U* values is offered in the supplement. Notice that the *U* value for the first group uses the *n* and the sum of the ranks for the second group, and vice versa. The Mann-Whitney *U* value is the smaller of U_1 and U_2.

Procedure Box 24.1 illustrates the computation of the *U* value for the college professor study. When $n_1 = n_2$ the smaller *U* is associated with the group with the larger sum of the ranks, so you do not need to compute the *U* for the other group. However, you do need to compute both if you want to use the computation checks described in the Procedure Box.

24.4 MAKING A DECISION ABOUT THE NULL HYPOTHESIS

The critical values for the *U* test may be found in Table D−7 of Appendix D. For any given alpha level, the critical value is determined by n_1 and n_2, the two group sizes. In the college professors study the critical value is

$$U_{\alpha=.05, n_1=10, n_2=10} = 23.$$

If the computed *U* value is less than the critical value, you may reject the null hypothesis. Like the Wilcoxon test, since the smaller of U_1 and U_2 is compared to the critical value this may be considered a one-tailed test of a nondirectional hypothesis. The computed *U* value is 20.5, so we can reject the null hypothesis.

Interpreting the Results. The smaller *U* was associated with the first group, liberal arts professors. This suggests that liberal arts professors demonstrate less anxiety on the MMPI Psychasthenia scale than behavioral science professors.

PROCEDURE BOX 24.1

The Mann-Whitney *U* Test

Goal Compute the Mann-Whitney *U* value for the study on anxiety in college professors (data may be found in Procedure Box 16.1 in Chapter 16 as well as below).

$$U_1 = n_1 n_2 + \frac{n_2(n_2 + 1)}{2} - \sum_{i=1}^{n_2} R_i,$$

$$U_2 = n_1 n_2 + \frac{n_1(n_1 + 1)}{2} - \sum_{i=1}^{n_1} R_i$$

Step 1 *Rank order all scores from lowest to highest and sum the ranks for each group.*

Group	Y	Rank	Group 1	Group 2
Liberal arts	45	1	1	
Liberal arts	49	2	2	
Liberal arts	51	3	3	
Liberal arts	52	4.5	4.5	
Behavioral science	52	4.5		4.5
Liberal arts	54	6.5	6.5	
Liberal arts	54	6.5	6.5	
Behavioral science	57	8		8
Behavioral science	58	9		9
Behavioral science	59	10		10
Liberal arts	62	11	11	
Liberal arts	63	13	13	
Liberal arts	63	13	13	
Behavioral science	63	13		13
Liberal arts	64	15	15	
Behavioral science	66	16		16
Behavioral science	68	17.5		17.5
Behavioral science	68	17.5		17.5
Behavioral science	69	19		19
Behavioral science	74	20		20
Sums:			75.5	134.5

Step 2 *Compute U_1 and U_2.*

$$U_1 = 10(10) + \frac{10(11)}{2} - 134.5 = 20.5 \longleftarrow This\ number\ must\ be\ positive$$

$$U_2 = 10(10) + \frac{10(11)}{2} - 75.5 = 79.5 \longleftarrow This\ number\ must\ be\ positive$$

Continued

The Mann-Whitney U Test continued

Step 3   *U is the smaller of U_1 and U_2.*

$$U = 20.5$$

Computation Checks

1. The sum of the ranks for the two groups must equal $N(N+1)/2$.

$$\frac{N(N+1)}{2} = \sum_{i=1}^{n_1} R_i + \sum_{i=1}^{n_2} R_i$$

$$\frac{20(21)}{2} = 75.5 + 134.5$$

$$210 = 210$$

2. The sum of U_1 and U_2 must equal $n_1 n_2$.

$$U_1 + U_2 = n_1(n_2)$$

$$20.5 + 79.5 = 10(10)$$

$$100 = 100$$

24.5 CONDITIONS FOR USING THE TEST

The conditions for using the Mann-Whitney U test are similar to those required for the independent groups t test: (1) members of the sample fall into two groups based on a dichotomous variable, (2) the two groups are independent, (3) members of the sample produce a non-nominal variable, and (4) you are interested in whether the sums of the ranks for the non-nominal variable for the two populations are equal. If they are unequal it suggests the existence of a population relationship between the two variables.

There are no assumptions required for the use of the Mann-Whitney U test other than the random and independent sampling assumption, making it a nonparametric test. However, like the Wilcoxon T test the results of the Mann-Whitney U test may be inaccurate if there are critical ties. In the case of the U test a critical tie occurs when a score in the first group is tied with a score in the second group. The results of the test can be adjusted for critical ties (Leach, 1979).

The Mann-Whitney U test may be used in any study where the independent groups t test would also be appropriate, and may be preferred when you cannot meet the robustness requirements for the parametric assumptions of the t tests and/or there is concern that the assumptions are grossly violated. In addition, its use can be recommended for studies involving discrete ordinal variables. However, there is a tradeoff in that some relationships cannot be detected by the Mann-Whitney test that can be detected using the t test.

24.6 DIRECTIONAL VERSUS NONDIRECTIONAL HYPOTHESES

When the Mann-Whitney test is used to evaluate a nondirectional hypothesis, U equals the smaller of U_1 and U_2. To test a directional hypothesis, U is the U for the group the alternative hypothesis suggests should be smaller (see Table 24.1).

Suppose we wanted to use directional hypotheses based on the scientific hypothesis that liberal arts professors are more anxious than behavioral science professors. This would indicate that the ranks associated with the population of behavioral science professors should be smaller than the ranks associated with the population of liberal arts professors. The appropriate null and alternative hypotheses would be

$$H_0: \sum R_1 \le \sum R_2$$
$$H_1: \sum R_1 > \sum R_2.$$

Since U_2 should be the smaller of the two Us if the alternative hypothesis is true, you need only compute this value. If upon inspecting the data you find U_2 is going to be larger than U_1, you know already you will not be able to reject the null hypothesis. This is true in the present case.

Suppose we instead wanted to evaluate whether liberal arts professors are less anxious than behavioral science professors using a directional hypothesis. This would suggest that the ranks associated with the population of liberal arts professors should be smaller

TABLE 24.1   Selected Aspects of the Mann-Whitney Test

Symbol Used	Type of Statistical Hypotheses	General Form of Statistical Hypotheses	Type of Test	Symbol for Alpha	Critical Region in
U	nondirectional	$H_0: \sum R_1 - \sum R_2 = 0$ $H_1: \sum R_1 - \sum R_2 \ne 0$	one-tailed	α	lower tail (compared to the smaller of U_1 and U_2
	directional	$H_0: \sum R_1 - \sum R_2 \le 0$ $H_1: \sum R_1 - \sum R_2 > 0$	one-tailed	$\alpha(D)$	lower tail (compared to U_2)
	directional	$H_0: \sum R_1 - \sum R_2 \ge 0$ $H_1: \sum R_1 - \sum R_2 < 0$	one-tailed	$\alpha(D)$	lower tail (compared to U_1)

than the ranks associated with the population of behavioral science professors. The appropriate null and alternative hypotheses would be

$$H_0: \sum R_1 \geq \sum R_2$$
$$H_1: \sum R_1 < \sum R_2.$$

If U_1 is the smaller sum, we can use the values for a one-tailed test provided in Table D–7. In the college professors study

$$U_{\alpha(D)=.05, n_1=10, n_2=10} = 27.$$

U is smaller than 27 so we can reject the null hypothesis.

24.7 POWER AND SAMPLE SIZE ISSUES

As was stated above, under certain conditions the Mann-Whitney test is unable to detect a relationship that the *t* test can detect. However, the Mann-Whitney test can be more powerful than the independent groups *t* test if the assumptions of the *t* test are grossly violated. If you believe that at least one of the populations involved from which your sample was drawn is severely nonnormal, or that the population variances are very different, then the Mann-Whitney test may be more powerful even if you meet the conditions under which the *t* test is generally considered robust (n_1 and $n_2 \geq 30$, and $n_1 = n_2$).

KEY TERMS

alternative hypothesis
critical value
dichotomous variable
directional hypothesis
independent groups
nominal variable

nondirectional hypothesis
null hypothesis
one-tailed test
power
two-tailed test

EXERCISES

Answers to all exercises may be found in Appendix B.

1. For which of the following studies is the Mann-Whitney *U* test a potentially appropriate analysis? (Remember: none of the variables need to be rank ordered for the test to be appropriate; however, one variable must be capable of being transformed to ranks.)

   a. A researcher randomly assigns subjects to receive either medication or placebo for the treatment of a rash. The dependent variable is change in severity of the rash.

   b. A researcher blocks subjects on the severity of rash, and randomly assigns them within blocks to receive either medication or placebo.

   c. Catholics and Muslims are compared on the frequency with which they attend religious services.

   d. Subjects are randomly assigned to one of three weight loss programs. Percent over desired body weight is measured before and after treatment. The difference between percent overweight before and after treatment serves as the dependent variable. The researcher would like to compute three U tests, one for each of the possible pairs of groups.

e. For each of the 50 states, the number of speeding tickets distributed in 1995 is divided by the state population, to compute the average number of tickets written per resident. The number of tickets per resident is compared for states that forbid the use of radar detectors to those that allow their use.

2. A researcher is interested in comparing the appetite suppression effects of two drugs, fenfluramine and amphetamine, in rat pups. Five-day old pups are randomly assigned to be injected with one of the two drugs. After two hours of free feeding, percent weight gain is measured.

a. State the nondirectional statistical hypotheses for the Mann-Whitney U test.

b. Compute the Mann-Whitney U test using the following data:

Fenfluramine	Amphetamine
2	8
3	10
3	4
4	7
4	9
5	3
6	7
6	12
6	6
7	8

c. What is the critical value using $\alpha = .01$? Can the researcher reject the null hypothesis?

d. How might these results be interpreted?

e. Are there any critical ties in these data? If so, what are the implications for the data analysis?

3. A researcher is interested in whether political liberals or conservatives tend to be more publicly informed. A 75-item multiple choice test is composed using questions drawn from recent national and international news stories to test political knowledge.

a. Is this study a *true experiment, quasi-experiment,* or *observational study*?

b. The following data are gathered from 30 college students. Higher scores suggest better performance on the test. Assume the researcher has decided to evaluate the directional null hypothesis based on the scientific hypothesis that liberals are more politically knowledgeable than conservatives. Compute the Mann-Whitney U Test test:

Liberal	Conservative
26	18
32	25
18	32
42	53
15	27
16	26
23	19
45	35
53	42
47	51
32	26
23	63
51	42
62	40
19	36

c. What is the critical value for $\alpha(D) = .01$? Can you reject the null hypothesis?

d. Again, assuming the researcher has decided to evaluate the directional null hypothesis based on the scientific hypothesis that liberals are more politically knowledgeable than conservatives, how would you interpret these results? Is the direction of the results consistent with the direction suggested by the scientific hypothesis?

e. Are there any critical ties in these data? If so, what are the implications for the data analysis?

S24.1 THE MEANING OF *U*

Suppose that for the college professor study we only collected 3 liberal arts professors and 3 behavioral science professors, and their scores on the Psychasthenia scale were as follows:

Group	Y	Rank	Group 1	Group 2
Liberal arts	53	1	1	
Behavioral science	57	2		2
Liberal arts	58	3	3	
Liberal arts	61	4	4	
Behavioral science	62	5		5
Behavioral science	66	6		6
Sums:			8	13

U_1 and U_2 equal:

$$U_1 = 3(3) + 3(4)/2 - 13 = 2$$

$$U_2 = 3(3) + 3(4)/2 - \ 8 = 7.$$

The purpose of this section is to provide an understanding of what these values mean.

The null hypothesis for the Mann-Whitney U test suggests that if the populations represented by the two groups were combined and transformed to rank scores, the sum of the ranks for the first population would equal the sum of the ranks for the second population:

$$\sum R_1 = \sum R_2.$$

For this to occur, the scores from the two populations would need to be distributed equally in the set of combined scores. If we place the six scores in rank order we get the following:

L_1	B_1	L_2	L_3	B_2	B_3
53	57	58	61	62	66

where L refers to a liberal arts professor's score, B to a behavioral science professor's score. Now suppose for each score we determine the number of scores from the other group which are lower than that score:

$$B \text{ scores} < L_1 = 0 \qquad L \text{ scores} < B_1 = 1$$
$$B \text{ scores} < L_2 = 1 \qquad L \text{ scores} < B_2 = 3$$
$$B \text{ scores} < L_3 = 1 \qquad L \text{ scores} < B_3 = 3$$

Sums: 2   7

These are the values we computed for U_1 and U_2 above. U_1 equals the number of scores from the second group that are lower than scores from the first group; U_2 equals the number of scores from the second group that are lower than scores from the first group. If the null hypothesis is true, these numbers should tend to be approximately equal, and larger than the critical value. A value lower than the critical value suggests the two populations are not equally distributed within the combined set.

CHAPTER 25

The Kruskal-Wallis *H* Test

25.1 INTRODUCTION

The Kruskal-Wallis *H* test may be used to evaluate whether a relationship exists between a discrete variable with independent groups and a non-nominal variable. The *H* test is recommended as a nonparametric alternative to the one-way independent groups ANOVA when the group sizes are too small or unequal to insure robustness against violation of the parametric assumptions required by the *F* test, when populations are believed to be severely nonnormal, or when the study involves a discrete ordinal variable. However, like the *T* and *U* tests, the Kruskal-Wallis test will sometimes fail to detect the presence of a relationship that the one-way independent groups ANOVA can detect.

25.2 DEFINING THE NULL AND ALTERNATIVE HYPOTHESES

To illustrate the *H* test I will use the fenfluramine, amphetamine, and saltwater study used to introduce the one-way independent groups ANOVA. Twelve rats were randomly assigned to receive injections of one of the three drugs. Suppose we could combine the three populations represented by the three groups and rank order every member from lowest percent weight gain to highest. If there is no relationship between type of drug and percent weight gain, then the sum of the ranks for the three populations should be equal:

$$H_0: \sum R_1 = \sum R_2 = \sum R_3.$$

The alternative hypothesis may be stated as

$$H_1: \text{not all sums of ranks are equal.}$$

Testing this null hypothesis does not require parametric assumptions like the independent groups ANOVA. However, this test is not equivalent to testing whether $\sigma_\mu^2 = 0$. In some cases the sum of the population ranks can be equal even though the μs are unequal.

25.3 TESTING THE NULL HYPOTHESIS

The computational procedure requires the following steps:

1. combine the data from the groups
2. rank order the data (rank ordering is reviewed in Table 23.1 of Chapter 23)
3. compute the *H* value for the sample:

$$H = \frac{12}{N(N+1)} \left[\frac{(\sum \text{first group ranks})^2}{n} + \cdots \frac{(\sum \text{last group ranks})^2}{n} \right] - 3(N+1)$$

Unlike the Wilcoxon *T* test and the Mann-Whitney *U* test, the Kruskal-Wallis test only requires the computation of one *H* value. Procedure Box 25.1 illustrates the computation of *H* for the appetite suppression study.

25.4 MAKING A DECISION ABOUT THE NULL HYPOTHESIS

If the *n* for each group is at least 6, and if *k* (the number of groups) is greater than 2, the distribution of *H* looks much like the χ^2 distribution, and critical values can be taken from the table of χ^2 critical values (Table D–2 in Appendix D). According to the table, the critical value for the appetite suppression study is $\chi^2_{\alpha=.05,\, df=2} = 5.99$; we may reject the null hypothesis if

$$H \geq 5.99.$$

Since the computed *H* value surpasses the critical value, we can reject the null hypothesis. In this regard the *H* test is more like the χ^2 test than the *T* and *U* tests in that rejection of the null hypothesis depends on equaling or surpassing the critical value.

   Interpreting the Results. A significant *H* value when $k > 2$ indicates only that a difference exists across populations, not the location of that difference. Determining the location requires additional comparisons, similar to the multiple described for the one-way independent groups ANOVA. One option is to conduct multiple Mann-Whitney *U* tests, although it is then recommended that you reduce the α level for each test to control the family-wise error rate. For example, if you wanted to conduct four *U* tests but keep the family-wise error rate at .05, you should set the α for each *U* test to .05/4 = .0125.

25.5 CONDITIONS FOR USING THE TEST

The conditions for using the Kruskal-Wallis *H* test are similar to those required for the one-way independent groups ANOVA: (1) members of the sample fall into two or more groups based on a discrete variable, (2) the groups are independent, (3) members of the sample produce a non-nominal variable, and (4) you are interested in whether the sums of the non-nominal variable ranks are equal for each population. A difference would suggest the existence of a population relationship between the two variables.

PROCEDURE BOX 25.1

The Kruskal-Wallis *H* test

Goal   Compute the *H* value for the following data:

Fenfluramine	Amphetamine	Saltwater
1	3	10
2	6	8
4	9	12
6	5	10

$$H = \frac{12}{N(N+1)} \left[\frac{(\sum \text{first group ranks})^2}{n} + \cdots \frac{(\sum \text{last group ranks})^2}{n} \right] - 3(N+1)$$

Step 1   *Rank order all scores from lowest to highest and sum the ranks for each group.*

Group	Y	Rank	Group 1	Group 2	Group 3
Fenfluramine	1	1.0	1.0		
Fenfluramine	2	2.0	2.0		
Amphetamine	3	3.0		3.0	
Fenfluramine	4	4.0	4.0		
Amphetamine	5	5.0		5.0	
Fenfluramine	6	6.5	6.5		
Amphetamine	6	6.5		6.5	
Saltwater	8	8.0			8.0
Amphetamine	9	9.0		9.0	
Saltwater	10	10.5			10.5
Saltwater	10	10.5			10.5
Saltwater	12	12.0			12.0
Sums:			13.5	23.5	41.0

Step 2   *Square each group sum, divide by the group size, and sum the resulting values.*

$$\left[\frac{(\sum \text{first group ranks})^2}{n} + \cdots \frac{(\sum \text{last group ranks})^2}{n} \right]$$

$$= \frac{13.5^2}{4} + \frac{23.5^2}{4} + \frac{41^2}{4} = 603.875$$

Step 3   *Multiply the result of Step 2 by* $12/N(N+1)$.

$$\frac{12(603.875)}{12(12+1)} = 46.4519$$

Continued

The Kruskal-Wallis H test continued

Step 4 *Subtract* $3(N + 1)$ *from the result of Step 3.*

$$H = 46.4519 - 3(12 + 1) = 7.45 \quad \longleftarrow \quad \textit{This number must be positive}$$

Computation Check

The sum of the ranks for all groups must equal $N(N + 1)/2$.

$$\frac{N(N + 1)}{2} = \left(\sum \text{first group ranks} \right) + \cdots \left(\sum \text{last group ranks} \right)$$

$$\frac{12(13)}{2} = 13.5 + 23.5 + 41$$

$$78 = 78$$

There are no statistical assumptions required for the use of the Kruskal-Wallis H test other than the random and independent sampling assumption, making it a nonparametric test. However, like the Wilcoxon T and Mann-Whitney U tests, the results may be inaccurate if there are critical ties. In the case of the H test a critical tie occurs when a score in one group is tied with a score in another group. The results of the test can be adjusted for critical ties (Leach, 1979). In addition, the n for any group should be no smaller than 6, and k should be greater than 2. If the last two conditions are not met, the χ^2 critical values may not be accurate for the H test.

The Kruskal-Wallis H test can be used in any study where the one-way independent groups ANOVA would be appropriate, and may be preferred when you cannot meet the robustness requirements for the ANOVA or there is concern that the assumptions are grossly violated. In addition, its use can be recommended for studies involving discrete ordinal variables. However, there is a tradeoff in that some relationships cannot be detected by the Kruskal-Wallis test that can be detected using the F test.

25.6 DIRECTIONAL VERSUS NONDIRECTIONAL HYPOTHESES

Issues surrounding the testing of directional hypotheses with the H test are similar to those discussed earlier for the χ^2 tests and the independent groups ANOVA. The Kruskal-Wallis test is always one-tailed (see Table 25.1). Since the H test as described here should only be used when $k > 2$, identifying which groups' sums of ranks are significantly different always requires additional comparisons. If $k = 2$ the Mann-Whitney test should be used instead.

TABLE 25.1   Selected Aspects of the Kruskal-Wallis *H* Test

Symbol Used	Degrees of Freedom	Type of Statistical Hypotheses	General Form of Statistical Hypotheses	Type of Test	Symbol for Alpha	Critical Region in
H	$k - 1$	nondirectional	H_0: all sums of ranks are equal H_1: not all sums of ranks are equal	one-tailed	α	upper tail

25.7 POWER AND SAMPLE SIZE ISSUES

Although under certain conditions the Kruskal-Wallis test is unable to detect a relationship that the ANOVA can detect, it can be more powerful than the one-way independent groups ANOVA test if the assumptions of the *F* test are grossly violated. If you believe that at least one of the populations involved from which your sample was drawn is severely non-normal, or that the population variances are very different, then the Kruskal-Wallis test may be more powerful even if you meet the conditions under which the independent groups ANOVA *F* test is usually considered robust (all *ns* $\geq$ 30, and all *ns* equal).

KEY TERMS

alternative hypothesis
critical value
directional hypothesis
discrete variable
independent groups

nominal variable
nondirectional hypothesis
null hypothesis
one-tailed test
power

EXERCISES

Answers to all exercises may be found in Appendix B.

1. For which of the following studies could the Kruskal-Wallis *H* test be an appropriate analysis? (Remember: none of the variables need to be rank ordered for the test to be appropriate; however, one variable must be capable of being transformed to ranks.)
   a. Subjects are randomly assigned to one of five different treatments for anxiety. Anxiety is measured using a rating scale.
   b. Rats are placed at the center of a maze which allows them to run either left or right. Food is placed in the right tunnel, and the rats are placed at the center of the maze until they choose the right tunnel 20 times in a row. They are then randomly assigned to one of three conditions. In one food is placed at the end of the left tunnel and none in the right. In the second, food is still placed in the right tunnel, but so is a device that administers a mild shock. In the third condition neither food nor shock is administered in either tunnel. The rats are returned to the center of the maze six more times. The first five are meant to allow the rats to learn the new situation. The number in each group that turn right on the sixth trial is recorded.
   c. The study described in part b is repeated. This time, the rats are returned to the maze 15 more times once the conditions are introduced. The

number of times each rat turns right during trials 6–15 is recorded.

d. Runners in a marathon are divided into three groups on the basis of how long they trained for the event (minimal, moderate, or extensive). Their final position (first, second, third, etc.) is recorded. The researcher is interested in whether extensive training is any more valuable than moderate training.

2. A researcher is interested in comparing the average annual income of families that describe themselves as Jewish, Protestant, or Catholic. Subjects are recruited through local religious organizations.
   a. State the statistical hypotheses for the Kruskal-Wallis *H* test.
   b. Compute the Kruskal-Wallis *H* test using the following data (in units of $10,000, rounded to the nearest whole number):

Jewish	Protestant	Catholic
12	7	8
4	9	10
3	5	2
5	3	6
2	8	5
3	4	9
5	8	7
4	9	10
8	2	1
5	3	2

c. What is the critical value using $\alpha = .01$? Can the researcher reject the null hypothesis?
d. How might these results be interpreted?
e. Are there any critical ties in these data? If so, what are the implications for the analysis?

3. Patients hospitalized for depression are divided into three groups according to severity: severe, moderate, and mild. All receive a two-week course of electroconvulsive therapy (ECT), a treatment which involves passing an electric current through the brain. The researcher is interested in whether there is a difference in the amount of improvement in response to ECT.
   a. What type of study is this: a *true experiment, quasi-experiment,* or *observational study*?
   b. Using the following data for amount of improvement, compute the Kruskal-Wallis *H* test:

Severe	Moderate	Mild
26	12	2
18	14	6
24	13	9
16	11	9
22	19	3
20	4	7

c. What is the critical value for $\alpha = .05$; can you reject the null hypothesis?
d. How would you interpret these results?
e. Are there any critical ties in these data? If so, what are the implications for the analysis?

CHAPTER 26

Choosing the Right Statistics

One of the most difficult tasks faced by students is deciding which statistic to use in which situations. The purpose of this chapter is to attempt to make this task easier, by summarizing the types of variables and situations for which each statistic discussed so far is appropriate. Models will be provided for choosing the right descriptive and inferential statistics, followed by examples.

26.1 CHOOSING DESCRIPTIVE STATISTICS

Which descriptive statistics will be most useful for your research project depends primarily on the answers to two questions:

1. What types of variables are used?
2. What type of information do you want?

The answers to these questions requires information introduced in the very first chapters of this text. Chapter 1 introduced the 7 types of variables: discrete nominal variables, discrete and continuous ordinal variables, discrete and continuous interval variables, and discrete and continuous ratio variables. You may want to review Table 1.1 in Chapter 1 to refresh your memory about the 7 types of variables.

The type of information you want depends upon the nature of the scientific hypothesis. As discussed in Chapter 3, a scientific hypothesis may have to do with the pattern of data for a single variable, or the relationship between two (or more) variables. The right statistics will depend on the type of pattern or relationship you are studying.

26.1.1 Finding the Acceptable Statistics

Table 26.1 indicates the descriptive statistics appropriate for various combinations of variables. The following rules may be used to read this table.

1. The acceptable descriptive statistics are identified on the basis of the types of variables you are measuring. For example, if the first variable is a discrete ordinal variable, and there is no second variable (in other words, you are interested in the pattern of

TABLE 26.1 Types of Variables and Descriptive Statistics

Second Variable	First Variable: None	Discrete — Dichotomous	Nominal	Ordinal	Interval	Ratio	Continuous — Ordinal	Interval	Ratio
None		ungrouped frequency, proportion, percent; mode	ungrouped frequency, proportion, percent; mode	grouped or ungrouped frequency, proportion, percent; mode, mean, median; range, standard deviation, variance	grouped or ungrouped frequency, proportion, percent; mode, mean, median; range, standard deviation, variance	grouped or ungrouped frequency, proportion, percent; mode, mean, median; range, standard deviation, variance	grouped frequency, proportion, percent; mode, mean, median; range, standard deviation, variance	grouped frequency, proportion, percent; mode, mean, median; range, standard deviation, variance	grouped frequency, proportion, percent; mode, mean, median; range, standard deviation, variance
Discrete — Dichotomous		phi coefficient	phi coefficient		point-biserial correlation coefficient	point-biserial correlation coefficient		point-biserial correlation coefficient	point-biserial correlation coefficient
Nominal		phi coefficient	phi coefficient						
Ordinal				Spearman rank-order correlation coefficient, Pearson product-moment correlation coefficient; simple regression	Spearman rank-order correlation coefficient, Pearson product-moment correlation coefficient; simple regression	Spearman rank-order correlation coefficient, Pearson product-moment correlation coefficient; simple regression			
Interval		point-biserial correlation coefficient			Pearson product-moment correlation coefficient; simple regression	Pearson product-moment correlation coefficient; simple regression	Pearson product-moment correlation coefficient; simple regression	Pearson product-moment correlation coefficient; simple regression	Pearson product-moment correlation coefficient; simple regression
Ratio		point-biserial correlation coefficient			Pearson product-moment correlation coefficient; simple regression	Pearson product-moment correlation coefficient; simple regression	Pearson product-moment correlation coefficient; simple regression	Pearson product-moment correlation coefficient; simple regression	Pearson product-moment correlation coefficient; simple regression
Continuous — Ordinal									
Interval									
Ratio									

Note: "Nominal" here refers to nominal variables with three or more values. Nominal variables with two values are treated under Dichotomous.

data for the first variable), then the following statistics are acceptable: the frequency, proportion, and percent; the mode, mean, and median; and the range, standard deviation, and variance. If the first variable you are studying is a discrete interval variable, and the second variable is a continuous ordinal variable (in other words, you are interested in the relationship between two variables), then the Pearson product-moment correlation coefficient and simple regression are acceptable.

2. None of the descriptive statistics described in this text are appropriate for the combinations that are darkened in. These represent relatively unusual combinations of variables.

3. Since many statistics are specifically designed for use with dichotomous variables, the dichotomous variable has been treated as if it were another category of variable. Dichotomous variables are usually either discrete nominal or ordinal variables.

4. The row labeled "None" for the second variable indicates statistics used to identify patterns in a single variable. The rest of the table (below the dotted line) deals with descriptive statistics for relationships. The table below the dotted line is symmetrical: when looking at the relationship between variables, according to the table the same statistics apply regardless of which variable you think of as the "first" variable and which you think of as the "second."

26.1.2 Choosing the Appropriate Statistics

Once you have identified the acceptable descriptive statistics, the next step requires determining which statistic provides the type of information you want. Table 26.2 summarizes the type of information provided by each descriptive statistic discussed in this text. The number in parentheses indicates the chapter in which the statistic was described.

26.1.3 An Example: Gender and Income

Suppose you are interested in conducting a study on the relationship between gender and income. After gathering income and gender data from a random sample of 500 American adults, the next step is to determine which descriptive statistics to compute. What are the right descriptive statistics?

First, what descriptive statistics might be of interest for your gender variable? This is a dichotomous variable, so the available statistics are the frequency, proportion, percent, or mode. In the present case, you may want to find the frequency of males and females in the sample.

What descriptive statistics might be of interest for your income variable? This is a discrete ratio variable, so the available statistics are the frequency, proportion, or percent; the mode, mean, or median; and the range, standard deviation, or variance. Since the variable income is likely to have a large number of values, the frequency, proportion, percent, or mode would only be useful in grouped form. The mean may be useful, since it provides an indicator of central tendency that reflects the exact position of each score in the sample. The median may also be useful, since income is likely to be very positively skewed. The range is not likely to be helpful here because of the amount of skew in income data, but

---

TABLE 26.2 Types of Information Provided by Descriptive Statistics

---

Measures of Frequency

frequency (4): the frequency of occurrence for each variable value
proportion, percent (4): the relative frequency of occurrence for each variable value

Measures of Central Tendency

mode (5): the most commonly occurring value
mean (5): an indicator of central tendency sensitive to the exact position of each score in the
    distribution
median (5): the middle score in a distribution

Measures of Variability

range (6): the difference between the lowest and highest scores
variance (6): the average squared deviation from the mean
standard deviation (6): an indicator of average deviation from mean in the same units of
    measure as the original scores

Measures of Linear Relationship

Pearson product-moment correlation coefficient (7): the strength and direction of the relation-
    ship between two variables
phi coefficient (7): a variant of the Pearson statistic for two dichotomous variables
point-biserial correlation coefficient (7): a variant of the Pearson statistic where one variable is
    dichotomous
Spearman rank-order correlation coefficient (7): a variant of the Pearson statistic for two
    rank-ordered variables
Simple regression (8): indicates the best estimate of one variable from the values of another

---

the standard deviation or variance may be recommended as an indicator of variability within the sample. Remember that of the two the standard deviation is generally preferred for descriptive purposes because it measures variability in the same units as the original variable (in the present case, dollars). Of the available options, the mean, median, and standard deviation seem the most useful.

Finally, what descriptive statistics might be used to indicate the relationship between gender and income? Since gender is dichotomous and income is a discrete ratio variable, the correct statistic is the point-biserial correlation coefficient.

Two points should be drawn from this example. First, even though the purpose of the study was to examine a relationship between two variables, it is usually still worthwhile to compute some descriptive statistics that reflect the pattern of data for each of your variables individually. It is important to know the number of males and females in your sample, for example. For the income variable, the mean, median, and standard deviation would all provide useful information concerning the pattern of income data in your sample. You might even want to compute the mean and standard deviation for males and females separately.

Second, notice the title to this section is "Choosing the Right Statistics," plural. It may be that several different statistics will be needed to provide the descriptive information you want. In any good study, means and standard deviations, at the very least, are provided in addition to other statistics more relevant to the hypothesis of the study.

26.2 CHOOSING INFERENTIAL STATISTICS

26.2.1 Finding the Acceptable Statistics

We start with the same two questions:

1. What types of variables are used?
2. What type of information do you want?

Table 26.3 indicates the hypothesis testing statistics appropriate for various combinations of variables. The rules provided for Table 26.1 apply here as well. For example, the t test of a correlation coefficient is the appropriate statistic to evaluate whether a relationship exists in the population between a discrete ratio variable and a continuous interval variable. An additional column for two discrete variables is provided to include the case of the two-way independent groups ANOVA, in which the combination of two discrete variables is related to a third variable.

26.2.2 Choosing the Appropriate Statistics

Once you have identified the acceptable inferential statistics, the next step involves determining which statistic provides the type of information you want. Table 26.4 summarizes the type of information provided by each hypothesis testing statistic discussed in this text. The number in parentheses after each indicates the chapter in which the statistic was discussed.

Although not specifically mentioned in the table, it should be noted that in certain circumstances the corresponding confidence intervals provide more useful information than the hypothesis test listed. Hypothesis tests evaluate whether some condition is true of a parameter; confidence intervals estimate the value of the parameter. If you are more interested in the actual value of the parameter than whether you can rule out some possible value for that parameter, the confidence interval is the appropriate statistic.

Table 26.5 summarizes much of the statistical information about the various hypothesis testing statistics discussed in the text. All of this information has been provided in previous tables, but you may find this table useful as a quick source for information about the nature of each test.

26.2.3 An Example: Religion and Attitudes towards Abortion

It is your hypothesis that members of the most popular religions in the United States—Protestantism, Catholicism, and Judaism—tend to differ in terms of their attitudes towards abortion. A sample of 500 American adults who report belonging to one of the three religions listed are asked to indicate their support for the statement "Abortion is an acceptable choice for women," on a scale from 1 (Strongly Agree) to 5 (Strongly Disagree). What is the appropriate inferential statistic in this case?

Religion represents a nominal variable with three possible values in this study. Response to the abortion question is a continuous ordinal variable. The acceptable options are therefore the Kruskal-Wallis H test, the one-way independent groups ANOVA, and the one-way dependent groups ANOVA. Since this is an observational study without group assignment, matching has not occurred. The dependent groups ANOVA can be ruled out as an option.

TABLE 26.3 Types of Variables and Hypothesis Testing Statistics

Second Variable \ First Variable	Dichotomous	Nominal	Two Discrete	Ordinal	Interval	Ratio	Ordinal (Continuous)	Interval (Continuous)	Ratio (Continuous)
None	binomial test; χ² goodness of fit test	χ² goodness of fit test		χ² goodness of fit test	χ² goodness of fit test; one-group z and t tests	χ² goodness of fit test; one-group z and t tests	one-group z and t tests	one-group z and t tests	one-group z and t tests
Dichotomous	χ² test of independence								
Nominal	χ² test of independence	χ² test of independence							
Ordinal	Wilcoxon T, Mann-Whitney U, Kruskal-Wallis H tests	Kruskal-Wallis H test		t test for a correlation coefficient					
Interval	Wilcoxon T, Mann-Whitney U, Kruskal-Wallis H tests; t test for a point-biserial correlation coefficient; dependent and independent groups t tests; one-way dependent and independent groups ANOVA	Kruskal-Wallis H test; one-way independent and dependent-groups ANOVA	two-way independent groups ANOVA	t test for a correlation coefficient	t test for a correlation coefficient				
Ratio	Wilcoxon T, Mann-Whitney U, Kruskal-Wallis H tests; t test for a point-biserial correlation coefficient; dependent and independent groups t tests; one-way dependent and independent groups ANOVA	Kruskal-Wallis H test; one-way independent and dependent-groups ANOVA	two-way independent groups ANOVA	t test for a correlation coefficient	t test for a correlation coefficient	t test for a correlation coefficient			
Ordinal (Continuous)	Wilcoxon T, Mann-Whitney U, Kruskal-Wallis H tests	Kruskal-Wallis H test		t test for a correlation coefficient	t test for a correlation coefficient	t test for a correlation coefficient	t test for a correlation coefficient		
Interval (Continuous)	Wilcoxon T, Mann-Whitney U, Kruskal-Wallis H tests; t test for a point-biserial correlation coefficient; dependent and independent groups t tests; one-way dependent and independent groups ANOVA	Kruskal-Wallis H test; one-way independent and dependent groups ANOVA	two-way independent groups ANOVA	t test for a correlation coefficient	t test for a correlation coefficient	t test for a correlation coefficient	t test for a correlation coefficient	t test for a correlation coefficient	
Ratio (Continuous)	Wilcoxon T, Mann-Whitney U, Kruskal-Wallis H tests; t test for a point-biserial correlation coefficient; dependent and independent groups t tests; one-way dependent and independent groups ANOVA	Kruskal-Wallis H test; one-way independent and dependent groups ANOVA	two-way independent groups ANOVA	t test for a correlation coefficient	t test for a correlation coefficient	t test for a correlation coefficient	t test for a correlation coefficient	t test for a correlation coefficient	t test for a correlation coefficient

Note: "Nominal" here refers to nominal variables with three or more values. Nominal variables with two values are treated under Dichotomous.

TABLE 26.4 Types of Information Provided by Hypothesis Testing Statistics

Parametric Tests of Pattern Hypotheses

one-group z test (12): whether a population μ differs from some predefined value where σ is known

one-group t test (13): whether a population μ differs from some predefined value; knowing σ is unnecessary

Nonparametric Tests of Pattern Hypotheses

binomial test (10): whether a population probability for a dichotomous variable differs from some predefined value

χ^2 goodness of fit test (14): whether a set of population probabilities differ from a set of predefined values

Parametric Tests of Relationship Hypotheses

dependent groups t test (15): whether a dichotomous variable is related to a quantitative variable in the population when groups defined by the dichotomous variable are dependent

independent groups t test (16): whether a dichotomous variable is related to a quantitative variable in the population when groups defined by the dichotomous variable are independent

t test for a correlation coefficient (17): whether the population ρ_{XY} between two variables differs from 0

one-way independent groups ANOVA (18): whether a discrete variable is related to a quantitative variable in the population when groups defined by the discrete variable are independent

one-way dependent groups ANOVA (20): whether a discrete variable is related to a quantitative variable in the population when groups defined by the discrete variable are dependent

two-way independent groups ANOVA (21): whether the combination of two discrete variables is related to an interval or ratio variable in the population when groups defined by the discrete variables are independent

Nonparametric Tests of Relationship Hypotheses

χ^2 test of independence (22): whether two variables demonstrate dependent outcomes in the population

Wilcoxon T test (23): whether a dichotomous variable is related to an ordinal, interval, or ratio variable in the population when groups defined by the dichotomous variable are dependent

Mann-Whitney U test (24): whether a dichotomous variable is related to an ordinal, interval, or ratio variable in the population when groups defined by the dichotomous variable are independent

Kruskal-Wallis H test (25): whether a discrete variable is related to an ordinal, interval, or ratio variable in the population when groups defined by the discrete variable are independent

If we were concerned that the population distribution of responses to the abortion question were severely nonnormal for any of the three religions, or if the group sizes are extremely different, the Kruskal-Wallis might be the preferred statistic. Barring these potential problems, the one-way independent groups ANOVA would be the statistic of choice.

26.3 STATISTICS AND RESEARCH DESIGN

It seems appropriate to end this text by reinforcing an important concept raised very early in the discussion. Although this book focuses almost exclusively on statistics, statistical analysis in fact plays only a small (though absolutely essential) part in the entire research

TABLE 26.5 Summary of Statistical Aspects for Hypothesis Tests

Test	Symbol Used	Degrees of Freedom	Type of Statistical Hypotheses	General Form of Statistical Hypotheses	Type of Test	Symbol for Alpha	Critical Region in
binomial test	None		nondirectional	$H_0: p(V) = ?$ $H_1: p(V) \neq ?$	two-tailed	α	both tails
			directional	$H_0: p(V) \leq ?$ $H_1: p(V) > ?$	one-tailed	$\alpha(D)$	upper tail
			directional	$H_0: p(V) \geq ?$ $H_1: p(V) < ?$	one-tailed	$\alpha(D)$	lower tail
one-group z test	$z_{\overline{Y}}$		nondirectional	$H_0: \mu = ?$ $H_1: \mu \neq ?$	two-tailed	α	both tails (both positive and negative critical values)
			directional	$H_0: \mu \leq ?$ $H_1: \mu > ?$	one-tailed	$\alpha(D)$	upper tail (critical value is positive)
			directional	$H_0: \mu \geq ?$ $H_1: \mu < ?$	one-tailed	$\alpha(D)$	lower tail (critical value is negative)
one-group t test	$t_{\overline{Y}}$	$N - 1$	nondirectional	$H_0: \mu = ?$ $H_1: \mu \neq ?$	two-tailed	α	both tails (both positive and negative critical values)
			directional	$H_0: \mu \leq ?$ $H_1: \mu > ?$	one-tailed	$\alpha(D)$	upper tail (critical value is positive)
			directional	$H_0: \mu \geq ?$ $H_1: \mu < ?$	one-tailed	$\alpha(D)$	lower tail (critical value is negative)
χ^2 goodness of fit test	χ^2	$k - 1$	nondirectional	$H_0:$ all probabilities equal expected values $H_1:$ all probabilities do not equal expected values	one-tailed	α	upper tail
dependent groups t test	$t_{\overline{D}}$	$N_D - 1$	nondirectional	$H_0: \mu_1 - \mu_2 = 0$ $H_1: \mu_1 - \mu_2 \neq 0$	two-tailed	α	both tails (both positive and negative critical values)
			directional	$H_0: \mu_1 - \mu_2 \leq 0$ $H_1: \mu_1 - \mu_2 > 0$	one-tailed	$\alpha(D)$	upper tail (critical value is positive)
			directional	$H_0: \mu_1 - \mu_2 \geq 0$ $H_1: \mu_1 - \mu_2 < 0$	one-tailed	$\alpha(D)$	lower tail (critical value is negative)
independent groups t test	$t_{\overline{Y}_1 - \overline{Y}_2}$	$N - 2$	nondirectional	$H_0: \mu_1 - \mu_2 = 0$ $H_1: \mu_1 - \mu_2 \neq 0$	two-tailed	α	both tails (both positive and negative critical values)
			directional	$H_0: \mu_1 - \mu_2 \leq 0$ $H_1: \mu_1 - \mu_2 > 0$	one-tailed	$\alpha(D)$	upper tail (critical value is positive)

(continued on next page)

TABLE 26.5 (*continued*) Summary of Statistical Aspects for Hypothesis Tests

Test	Symbol Used	Degrees of Freedom	Type of Statistical Hypotheses	General Form of Statistical Hypotheses	Type of Test	Symbol for Alpha	Critical Region in
independent groups *t* test (cont. from p. 338)			directional	$H_0: \mu_1 - \mu_2 \geq 0$ $H_1: \mu_1 - \mu_2 < 0$	one-tailed	$\alpha(D)$	lower tail (critical value is negative)
t test for a correlation coefficient	t_r	$N-2$	nondirectional	$H_0: \rho_{XY} = 0$ $H_1: \rho_{XY} \neq 0$	two-tailed	α	both tails (both positive and negative critical values)
			directional	$H_0: \rho_{XY} \leq 0$ $H_1: \rho_{XY} > 0$	one-tailed	$\alpha(D)$	upper tail (critical value is positive)
			directional	$H_0: \rho_{XY} \geq 0$ $H_1: \rho_{XY} < 0$	one-tailed	$\alpha(D)$	lower tail (critical value is negative)
one-way independent groups ANOVA	F	$k-1$ $N-k$	nondirectional	H_0: all μs are equal H_1: not all μs are equal	one-tailed	α	upper tail
t test for a planned comparison	t_p	$N-k$	nondirectional	$H_0: \mu_1 - \mu_2 = 0$ $H_1: \mu_1 - \mu_2 \neq 0$	two-tailed	α	both tails (both positive and negative critical values)
Tukey test	Q	$N-k$	nondirectional	$H_0: \mu_1 - \mu_2 = 0$ $H_1: \mu_1 - \mu_2 \neq 0$	one-tailed	α	upper tail (subtract smaller mean from larger mean)
one-way dependent groups ANOVA	F	$k-1$ $N-k$	nondirectional	H_0: all μs are equal H_1: not all μs are equal	one-tailed	α	upper tail
two-way independent groups ANOVA	F	$k-1$ $q-1$ $(k-1)(q-1)$ $N-k(q)$	nondirectional	*main effects:* H_0: all row (or column) μs are equal H_1: not all row (or column) μs are equal *interaction:* H_0: differences between μs for variable 1 are equal at every level of variable 2 H_1: not all differences between μs for variable 1 are equal at every level of variable 2	one-tailed	α	upper tail

(continued on next page)

TABLE 26.5 *(continued)* Summary of Statistical Aspects for Hypothesis Tests

Test	Symbol Used	Degrees of Freedom	Type of Statistical Hypotheses	General Form of Statistical Hypotheses	Type of Test	Symbol for Alpha	Critical Region in
χ^2 test of independence	χ^2	$(k-1)(q-1)$	nondirectional	H_0: two variables are independent H_1: two variables are not independent	one-tailed	α	upper tail
Wilcoxon T test	T		nondirectional	H_0: $\sum R_+ - \sum R_- = 0$ H_0: $\sum R_+ - \sum R_- \neq 0$	one-tailed	α	lower tail (compared to the smaller of $\sum\limits_{i=1}^{n+} R_i$ and $\sum\limits_{i=1}^{n-} R_i$)
			directional	H_0: $\sum R_+ - \sum R_- \geq 0$ H_1: $\sum R_+ - \sum R_- < 0$	one-tailed	$\alpha(\mathrm{D})$	lower tail (compared to $\sum\limits_{i=1}^{n+} R_i$)
			directional	H_0: $\sum R_+ - \sum R_- \leq 0$ H_1: $\sum R_+ - \sum R_- > 0$	one-tailed	$\alpha(\mathrm{D})$	lower tail (compared to $\sum\limits_{i=1}^{n-} R_i$)
Mann-Whitney U Test	U		nondirectional	H_0: $\sum R_1 - \sum R_2 = 0$ H_1: $\sum R_1 - \sum R_2 \neq 0$	one-tailed	α	lower tail (compared to the smaller of U_1 and U_2)
			directional	H_0: $\sum R_1 - \sum R_2 \leq 0$ H_1: $\sum R_1 - \sum R_2 > 0$	one-tailed	$\alpha(\mathrm{D})$	lower tail (compared to U_2)
			directional	H_0: $\sum R_1 - \sum R_2 \geq 0$ H_1: $\sum R_1 - \sum R_2 < 0$	one-tailed	$\alpha(\mathrm{D})$	lower tail (compared to U_1)
Kruskal-Wallis H Test	H	$k-1$	nondirectional	H_0: all sums of ranks are equal H_1: not all sums of ranks are equal	one-tailed	α	upper tail

Note: ? in a statistical hypothesis refers to some value chosen by the researcher.

process. Statistics can only provide evidence about the existence and sometimes the strength of a pattern or relationship. It is the quality of the research design that allows the researcher to explain those findings with confidence. Knowledge of statistical methods provides only one of the skills necessary to become a competent researcher in the behavioral sciences. In order to conduct research projects of a high quality, that knowledge must be combined with an understanding of the principles of research design. To enhance your understanding of research issues, the supplement to this chapter offers an example of a research study followed from start to finish.

KEY TERMS

continuous variable
descriptive statistic
dichotomous variable
discrete variable
hypothesis testing statistics
inferential statistic

interval estimation statistics
interval variable
nominal variable
ordinal variable
ratio variable

EXERCISES

Answers to all exercises may be found in Appendix B.

1. Rats are randomly divided into two groups. One group is trained so that turning left in a maze consistently leads to food. The other group is trained so that turning right consistently leads to food. Now they are placed in a new maze in which turning in the previously trained direction results in a mild electrical shock. The researcher is interested in whether they will turn in the direction that formerly led to food the next time they are placed in the maze after they have been shocked once. In answering the following questions, list all *acceptable* statistics:
   a. Is this a *true experiment, quasi-experiment*, or *observational study*?
   b. What types of variables are group and turning choice: *nominal, ordinal, interval*, or *ratio*; *continuous* or *discrete*?
   c. What descriptive statistics could be used to describe the frequency of turning left or right for the sample as a whole, or within each group?
   d. What descriptive statistics could be used to describe the relationship between group and turning choice?
   e. What inferential statistic could be used to evaluate whether a relationship exists in the population between group and the direction in which they choose to turn after they have been shocked once?

2. A random sample of American adults are asked to rate their financial security on a scale from 1 (Very Insecure) to 5 (Very Secure). In answering the following questions, list only the *appropriate* statistics:
   a. Is this a *true experiment, quasi-experiment*, or *observational study*?
   b. The researcher would like to describe characteristics of the sample so that others can examine whether it really seems to be a representative sample of American adults. What descriptive statistics would be the best choice for the following variables: gender, number of years of education, state of residence, ethnic status, and age?
   c. The researcher believes that the modal response for American adults would be 2 (Somewhat Insecure). What inferential statistic could be used to test this hypothesis?
   d. The researcher believes that the mean response for American adults would be 2 (Somewhat Insecure). What inferential statistic could be used to test this hypothesis?

3. Members of a sample of 1000 hypertensives (people with high blood pressure) are randomly assigned to receive one of 20 different dosages of a new blood pressure medication. The hypothesis is that diastolic

blood pressure will tend to decrease as dosage is increased.

   a. Is this a *true experiment*, *quasi-experiment*, or *observational study*?

   b. What types of variables are dosage and diastolic blood pressure reading: *nominal*, *ordinal*, *interval*, or *ratio*; *continuous* or *discrete*? Hint: diastolic blood pressure is measured in millimeters of mercury.

   c. For each of the 20 groups, what descriptive statistic could be computed that would best describe the group pattern?

   d. What descriptive statistic best describes the relationship between dosage and diastolic blood pressure? What inferential statistic would best be used to evaluate whether a relationship exists between these two variables in the population?

4. A researcher would like to demonstrate that birth weight can be used to successfully predict intelligence test score at age 21.

   a. Is this a *true experiment*, *quasi-experiment*, or *observational study*?

   b. What types of variables are birth weight and intelligence test score: *nominal*, *ordinal*, *interval*, or *ratio*; *continuous* or *discrete*?

   c. What inferential statistic would best be used to determine whether a relationship exists between birth weight and intelligence test score?

   d. What descriptive statistic could be used to predict intelligence test score at age 21 from birth weight?

5. A researcher believes that successful police officers must be particularly empathic. A sample of police officers nominated by colleagues for being exceptional officers are administered an empathy self-rating scale for which the mean and standard deviation of the general adult population are known.

   a. Is this a *true experiment*, *quasi-experiment*, or *observational study*?

   b. What type of variable is score on an empathy rating scale: *nominal*, *ordinal*, *interval*, or *ratio*; *continuous* or *discrete*?

   c. What would be the most appropriate descriptive statistics to generate in this example?

   d. Given that the standard deviation for the general population is known, what inferential statistic might one use in this situation?

   e. If the researcher suspects the standard deviation for the population of successful police officers may be different than that for the general population, what inferential statistic might she use instead?

6. Quantity of the chemical serotonin is measured in blood serum before and after a meal rich in carbohydrates.

   a. Is this a *true experiment*, *quasi-experiment*, or *observational study*?

   b. What types of variable are time of measurement (before versus after the meal) and quantity of the chemical serotonin: *nominal*, *ordinal*, *interval*, or *ratio*; *continuous* or *discrete*?

   c. What two descriptive statistics might best be computed before and after the meal to describe the pattern of serotonin data at each point?

   d. What inferential statistics could be used to examine the scientific hypothesis that a high-carbohydrate meal will increase serotonin level? Of those, which would you most likely use?

7. A researcher is interested in whether popularity is related to academic performance. In a grade school class, students list their friends in the class, and are ranked from most to least popular. Class rank is also recorded.

   a. Is this a *true experiment*, *quasi-experiment*, or *observational study*?

   b. What types of variable are rank orders: *nominal*, *ordinal*, *interval*, or *ratio*; *continuous* or *discrete*?

   c. What descriptive statistic would best be used to describe the relationship between these two variables? Discuss what related statistical formula might also be used in this analysis.

   d. Is there an inferential statistic discussed in this textbook which would be appropriate for analyzing these data?

8. A researcher believes males are better at ignoring annoying stimuli than females. Subjects are instructed to read pages of random digits and cross out every 3 they find. Half are randomly assigned to listen to a soft hiss over headphones while completing the task, half to loud jarring noises. The number of 3s correctly crossed out in 10 minutes, minus the number of non–3s crossed out, is recorded.

   a. Is this a *true experiment*, *quasi-experiment*, or *observational study*?

   b. What types of variable are gender, type of noise, and score on the task: *nominal*, *ordinal*, *interval*, or *ratio*; *continuous* or *discrete*?

c. What descriptive statistic would you compute for each group to examine whether there are differences among the groups?

d. What inferential statistic would be most useful for evaluating this scientific hypothesis?

9. For each of the following studies, indicate whether a hypothesis testing statistic or confidence interval would be the more appropriate analysis. Remember that confidence intervals can indirectly provide information about the results of the corresponding hypothesis test, so that the answer confidence interval is technically always correct. For this exercise, assume that "confidence intervals" can only provide parameter estimates, and do not provide information about the accuracy of hypotheses:

a. A researcher is interested in the average number of hours school children spend per day watching TV.

b. A researcher believes that older school children tend to watch more TV per day than younger children.

c. A researcher is interested in whether participation in a motivational workshop increases workers' level of job motivation.

d. A researcher is interested in how large a change in workers' level of job motivation occurs after they participate in a motivational workshop.

This supplement will be devoted to following the conduct of a research study from beginning to end. Although the study described is relatively simple, it illustrates many of the concepts essential to designing and conducting a study.

Before you begin this section you may want to review the supplement to Chapter 3, particularly Figure S3.1, which provides a general summary of the research process. You may also want to refresh your memory from the Terms to Remember at the end of previous chapters, as many of these terms will be used here.

S26.1 SELECT A RESEARCH IDEA

The original research idea can emerge from several sources: personal interests, personal observations, previous research, or scientific theories. This example will be based on a personal interest. Grace is a college student who decided to conduct a research project for her senior thesis. Grace takes a nutritional supplement daily, and has often wondered if the supplement could be having any effect on her intellectual abilities. Grace decided to explore this as her research idea: do nutritional supplements affect intellectual functioning among normal adults?

S26.2 REVIEW THE LITERATURE

The first step in refining her research idea required reviewing the literature on nutritional or vitamin supplements and intellectual functioning. To begin, Grace accessed *Psychological Abstracts* from a computer at her university library. As of August 1993, Grace found 154 article entries which included some reference to both nutritional supplements and intellectual ability. Because of the flexibility of the computer version of *Psychological Abstracts*, several methods can be used to reduce this to a more reasonable number. For example, the search can be limited to articles written in English, articles about adults, or articles in which nutrition and intellectual functioning are considered major topics. Grace requested full copies of those entries she believed were relevant to her research idea. By reading the abstract of the article included with each entry she identified the articles important enough to read in full.

From her review of the literature Grace discovered several useful pieces of information. First, she found there has been no previous research concerning the effects of nutritional supplements on intellectual functioning in normal adults. There are a number of studies examining the use of nutritional supplements to enhance intellectual performance in the elderly

(Deijen, van der Beek, Orlebeke, & van den Berg, 1992), and in mentally retarded children and adults (Davis, 1987; Ellis & Tomporowski, 1983). There are also several studies using normal children, most of which supported the hypothesis that nutritional supplements improve intellectual performance on nonverbal tasks (Benton, 1992). However, none used normal adults. Second, by reviewing the methods used in previous studies Grace found measures of the variables in which she was interested that are generally accepted as construct valid.

S26.3 STATE THE SCIENTIFIC HYPOTHESIS

Her review of the literature led Grace to the following central scientific hypothesis: *adults provided a nutritional supplement treatment will on average demonstrate better intellectual functioning than adults who do not receive a nutritional supplement.* In addition, she is curious whether the strength of the nutritional supplement treatment is related to its effect on intellectual functioning.

S26.4 THE TYPE OF STUDY

This scientific hypothesis could be examined using either a true experiment, a quasi-experiment, or an observational study. If Grace compared intellectual functioning among adults who already use a nutritional supplement and adults who do not, the study would be observational. However, an observational study would not allow her to control the many potential subject confounds effectively. The most serious of these potential confounds is the possibility that adults who take nutritional supplements were brighter to begin with. Grace recognized that an experimental study would be preferable. Since Grace finds there are no obstacles to random assignment, she decides to conduct a true experiment in which subjects will be randomly assigned to receive either a basic nutritional supplement treatment, a high-intensity nutritional supplement treatment, or a placebo alternative.

S26.5 EXTERNAL VALIDITY

Grace decided to recruit subjects by placing an advertisement in local newspapers asking for people over the age of 18 willing to participate in a study in return for free nutritional supplements. Although similar methods are common in behavioral research, it is a method that creates some problems for the external validity of the study. Those who respond to the ad are members of a single community who read the newspaper, and are likely to be more interested in nutritional supplements than the typical person. It is unreasonable to assume this is a valid sample of the American adult population; however, it is not unreasonable to assume this is a valid sample of the adults from similar communities who read the newspaper and would respond to such an ad.

The method used to solicit subjects defines the appropriate population for which the sample may be considered representative. Anyone reading the results of this study would need to keep this in mind when deciding whether or not to generalize the results to other populations of adults.

S26.6 CONSTRUCT VALIDITY

The Nutritional Supplement Variable. Grace based her nutritional supplement treatment on one which has previously been used safely with mentally retarded children (Harrell, Capp, Davis, Peerless, & Ravitz, 1981) and adults (Chanowitz, Ellman, Silverstein, Zingarelli, & Ganger, 1985). Consistent with the studies mentioned, Grace set the length of treatment at four months, during which subjects would be instructed to take the nutritional supplement treatment once daily.

The basic nutritional supplement consisted of the recommended daily allowance (RDA) as defined by the federal government for each ingredient in the supplement. The supplement consisted of 5000 International Units (a unit of measure used for certain drugs), or IUs, of Vitamin A; 1.5 milligrams (mg) of Vitamin B_1; 400 IUs of Vitamin D; 30 IUs of vitamin E; 18 mg of iron; and 400 mg of magnesium. The high-intensity treatment consisted of 10,000 IUs vitamin A; 300 mg vitamin B_1; 1000 IUs of vitamin D; 12,000 IUs of vitamin E; 18 mg iron; and 1200 mg magnesium. Grace consulted with a registered pharmacist to insure the amounts given were appropriate as basic and high-intensity nutritional supplements.

Both supplements came in the form of a powder which subjects were instructed to mix with 8 ounces of orange juice. A placebo powder was also available which had no active ingredient.

A four-month supply of supplements, a daily journal, and four postage-paid envelopes were given to each subject before beginning treatment. Subjects were instructed to take one dose of the nutritional supplement each morning, and to record the time of taking the supplement in the journal. In addition, subjects were instructed not to take any other nutritional supplements during this period. Journals were returned monthly in the postage-paid envelope to Grace. Subjects who failed to return their journal, or who reported failing to take the nutritional supplement for three days in a row, were not included in the analysis of the results.

Intellectual Functioning. The Wechsler Adult Intelligence Scale, or WAIS (1981), is the most commonly used measure of adult intellectual ability, and Grace decided to use it to represent intellectual functioning. The WAIS consists of a series of verbal and nonverbal intellectual tasks supervised by a trained test administrator. The administrator scores the subject on each task and computes a total score. Based on a national sample of adults, total scores on the WAIS are transformed so that the mean score in the adult population is 100 with a standard deviation of 15.

The WAIS demonstrates a high level of test reliability, and WAIS scores correlate well with variables which should be related to intellectual functioning such as academic performance and occupational status (Matarazzo, 1972). Accordingly, it is believed the WAIS demonstrates adequate construct validity. Grace hired doctoral students who had received course training in the administration of the WAIS to administer the tests.

S26.7 INTERNAL VALIDITY

Insuring adequate internal validity requires identifying the potential confounds in a study and implementing research strategies to reduce or eliminate their potential impact. If Grace found her groups differed in level of intellectual functioning at the end of four months, what else besides the nutritional supplements might explain this pattern? Here are some possibilities, and what Grace did to try to control each:

Potential confound 1: Subjects who ended up in the nutritional supplement conditions differ in some important way from those in the control condition (for example, were brighter, or were more motivated). These represent potential subject confounds. Grace tried to control for this confound through random assignment.

We know that the probability of random assignment proving effective is relatively high once the *n* for each group is 40 or more (Hsu, 1989). If she still found that groups were different on an important subject confound, she might use a more sophisticated statistical analysis to achieve statistical equalization. Alternatively, she could have modified the random assignment procedure to achieve equalization.

Potential confound 2: Subjects in the nutritional supplement conditions would behave differently than control subjects because they know they are in the active treatment group. For example, they might try harder when administered the WAIS, or might decide to take evening classes because participating in the treatment has made them feel more optimistic. This represents a potential situational confound. Grace tried to control this confound through equalization, by equalizing the treatments as much as possible. Subjects in the placebo condition were also told they were receiving nutritional supplements, and were given a placebo supplement under the same instructions as those who received the vitamins and minerals.

This strategy creates certain ethical and validity difficulties. First, failure to inform subjects they may be placed in a placebo group has been seen by some as a violation of the principle of informed consent. However, this information may lead subjects to try to guess their group, and these guesses may influence their performance on the test. Second, if the results suggest nutritional supplements have an effect on intellectual functioning, the researcher has an ethical responsibility to offer the supplement to the control subjects at the end of the study.

Potential confound 3: Knowing the goals of the study, the WAIS administrators may tend to score subjects receiving nutritional supplements too leniently. This represents a potential situational confound. Grace tried to control this confound through equalization, by keeping the WAIS administrators blind to the goals of the study and subjects' group membership until the study was completed.

Potential confound 4: The WAIS administrators for the nutritional supplement groups may happen to be more generous graders than the WAIS administrators for the placebo group. This represents a potential situational confound. Grace tried to control this confound through equalization, making sure that each administrator tested an equal number of subjects from each group.

As you can see, Grace was able to control the potential confounds fairly effectively through a combination of random assignment and equalization techniques.

S26.8 ETHICAL TREATMENT OF SUBJECTS

The ethical treatment of subjects requires that each subject sign an informed consent form prior to participating in the study. A sample consent form for this study is provided in Table S26.1, containing the following elements:

TABLE S26.1   Informed Consent Form

Informed Consent Form

Description of the Study:
You have been asked to participate in a study on the psychological effects of nutritional supplements on healthy adults.

Your Activities:
The study will last for a period of 4 months, during which you will be provided with one of several different nutritional supplement treatments free of charge. You will be expected to:
1.   take one dose of the supplement daily.
2.   record the time at which you took the supplement each day in the journal provided you.
3.   return the journal monthly to the researcher.
4.   complete some psychological tests at the end of the treatment period. If you foresee any significant life changes during the next four months, you should discuss them with the researcher. If significant life changes occur during the course of the study, please contact the researcher at _____.

Potential Risks:
The supplement is unlikely to cause any harm or side effects. If you do experience any physical problems you suspect may be associated with taking the supplement, please contact the researcher immediately at _____.

Potential Benefits:
You may experience any of the benefits of using a nutritional supplement regularly. In addition, the study may enhance our understanding of the psychological effects of using nutritional supplements. Once the study is completed you will be provided with complete information about the purposes of the study, the findings, and your test results. Finally, if another treatment proves to have more positive effects that the treatment you received, you will be offered the opportunity to receive the better treatment free of charge for a period of four months.

Confidentiality:
Any materials you complete as a participant in this study will be kept completely confidential.

Voluntary Participation:
Your participation in this study is completely voluntary. You may decide to terminate your participation at any time without prejudice.

I have read and agreed to the above conditions of my participation in the study:

_____   _____
Date   Signature

                                                                  _____
                                                                  Name (please print)

                                                                  _____
                                                                  Witness

1. A brief description of the purpose of the study. Notice that the purpose of the study is described in vague terms, so subjects are not aware of the true purpose of the study.
2. What the subjects are expected to do, including how much time is required.
3. Any potential risks, and what to do if the subject is harmed.
4. Possible benefits of the study to the subject and to science.
5. A statement that all information is confidential.
6. A statement that participation is voluntary.

Once the study is completed, all participants should be debriefed. This usually includes a detailed discussion of the purposes of the study, the findings, and, when appropriate, feedback on the subject's personal test results. Also, if one of the supplements proves superior to the other treatments, it is considered desirable to offer that treatment to the subjects who did not receive it.

Grace must also be sure to minimize any potential risks to the subjects. Before initiating the treatment the registered pharmacist with whom she consulted assured her that the dosages she was providing were completely safe.

S26.9 COLLECT THE DATA

To summarize Grace's research design briefly, adult volunteers were randomly assigned to three groups. One group received a basic nutritional supplement treatment, the second a high intensity treatment, and the third a placebo alternative. After four months of treatment subjects were administered the WAIS.

It is very helpful to state the entire research design in written form before beginning the study. In doing so, every question concerning how the study is to be conducted should be addressed. For Grace's study, this would include the following:

- how do potential participants contact the researcher?
- where and when do meetings with potential subjects take place to discuss the study and sign the consent form?
- where will the vitamin supplements and placebo come from?
- how are vitamins and placebo delivered?
- how often should the researcher check in with subjects?
- how and when are journals returned to the researcher?
- how are appointments for completing the WAIS scheduled?
- where will the WAIS test materials come from?
- when and where will debriefing sessions take place?

I think you will see that once you start considering every aspect of the study all sorts of practical questions can arise. In reading the example so far, you probably had not even considered most of these problems. I find that students usually underestimate the complexity involved in conducting a study until the problems are upon them. Plan every detail ahead, and do not be surprised if during the course of the study it becomes necessary to redesign portions of the study because of unexpected problems.

The next step is the determination of the appropriate sample size required to achieve a desirable level of power for hypothesis testing. To find the best sample size, Grace must select the hypothesis test she will use, and decide on an expected effect size.

The appropriate hypothesis test depends on the types of variables Grace is collecting. The independent variable, type of treatment, is a discrete variable with three values. The dependent variable, WAIS score, is a continuous ordinal (quantitative) variable. The study therefore meets the conditions necessary for the one-way independent groups ANOVA.

Nutritional supplementation is a low-risk and low-cost treatment. However, the long-term impact of taking nutritional supplements is not completely known. Furthermore, very small changes in WAIS scores are unlikely to be of practical value. For these reasons, Grace decided to consider a medium effect to be the smallest meaningful effect size. Since there are three groups, df_1 for the one-way independent groups ANOVA equal

$$k - 1 = 2.$$

For $\alpha = .05$, $\beta = .20$ (power $= .80$), $df_1 = 2$, and a medium effect size, the desired minimum group size is

$$n = 52$$

(see Table C–6 in Appendix C). With three groups, this suggests a sample size of

$$N = 3(52) = 156.$$

Notice that this number is also greater than the number needed for reasons of robustness ($n = 30$) and random assignment ($n = 40$).

S26.10 ANALYZE AND INTERPRET THE FINDINGS

Data Analysis. Four months later, 108 subjects (36 in each group) had completed the study. The rest either dropped out or missed too many days. This is a common problem in studies which extend over long periods of time, and Grace might have been better off recruiting more subjects than she needed at first.

Grace collected WAIS scores for each subject who completed treatment, and was ready to analyze the data. Grace followed the three steps required for hypothesis testing:

1. *develop the null and alternative hypotheses.* For her study these were

H_0: $\mu_1 = \mu_2 = \mu_3$ (all μs are equal)
H_1: $\mu_1 \neq \mu_2$ and/or $\mu_2 \neq \mu_3$ and/or $\mu_1 \neq \mu_3$ (not all μs are equal).

2. *test the null hypothesis.* Suppose Grace found the following group statistics:
   Basic Treatment: $\overline{Y}_1 = 108.30$, $SS_1 = 468.48$
   High Intensity Treatment: $\overline{Y}_2 = 110.63$, $SS_2 = 529.76$
   Placebo Treatment: $\overline{Y}_3 = 105.62$, $SS_3 = 535.68$
   Sample Mean: $\overline{Y}_s = 108.1833$.

The one-way independent groups ANOVA may be computed as follows:

$$SS_{BG} = n \sum_{j=1}^{k} (\overline{Y}_j - \overline{Y}_s)^2$$

$$= 36[(108.30 - 108.1833)^2 + (110.63 - 108.1833)^2$$

$$+ (105.62 - 108.1833)^2]$$

$$= 452.5372$$

$$df_{BG} = k - 1$$

$$= 3 - 1$$

$$= 2$$

$$MS_{BG} = \frac{452.5372}{2}$$

$$= 226.2686$$

$$MS_{WG} = \frac{\sum_{j=1}^{k} SS_j}{N - k}$$

$$= \frac{468.48 + 529.76 + 535.68}{108 - 3}$$

$$= 14.6088$$

$$F = \frac{226.2686}{14.6088} = 15.4885.$$

3. *make a decision about the null hypothesis.* The degrees of freedom are 2 and 105. Although $df_2 = 105$ is not tabled, according to the steps for determining the significance for untabled degrees of freedom described in Table 13.2 from Chapter 13, $F = 15.4885$ is significant at $\alpha = .05$. The interpolation formula suggests the true critical value is

$$F_{\alpha=.05, df_1=2, df_2=105} = F_S + \frac{df_L - df_D}{df_L - df_S}(F_L - F_S)$$

$$= 3.07 + \frac{125 - 105}{125 - 100}(3.09 - 3.07)$$

$$= 3.086.$$

The omnibus test indicated the presence of a difference among μs. Post hoc testing was then necessary to decide where the differences seem to lie. The original scientific hypothesis, that a nutritional supplement enhances intellectual functioning, suggests the comparison between the basic and placebo treatments may be considered a planned comparison. The t test for this planned comparison is

$$t_P = \frac{\overline{Y}_i - \overline{Y}_j}{\sqrt{\dfrac{2MS_{WG}}{n}}}$$

$$= \frac{108.30 - 105.62}{\sqrt{\dfrac{2(14.6088)}{36}}}$$

$$= 2.9748.$$

The critical value is $t_{\alpha=.05,df=105} = 1.985$ (again determined using the interpolation formula), so Grace rejected the null hypothesis. The basic treatment was found superior to placebo.

Comparisons of the high-intensity treatment to the basic and placebo treatments were analyzed as unplanned comparisons. The Q statistic for high-intensity versus basic treatment proved to be

$$Q = \frac{\overline{Y}_i - \overline{Y}_j}{\sqrt{\dfrac{MS_{WG}}{n}}}$$

$$= \frac{110.63 - 108.30}{\sqrt{\dfrac{14.6008}{36}}}$$

$$= 3.6576.$$

The critical value (by interpolation) is $Q_{\alpha=.05,k=3,df=105} = 3.37$, so Grace rejected the null hypothesis; the high-intensity treatment was superior to the basic treatment. Not surprisingly, she also found the high-intensity treatment superior to the placebo, $Q = 7.86$ compared to the same critical value.

Interpreting Findings. The analysis suggested that the μ for WAIS scores in the population receiving the high-intensity treatment is higher than the μ for the basic treatment, and both are higher than the μ in the population that receives the placebo. Grace would like to interpret this as evidence in support of her scientific hypothesis, that nutritional supplement treatment enhances intellectual functioning in adults. However, the results of the study must be interpreted in light of the external validity, construct validity, and internal validity of the study.

As mentioned previously, people who respond to an advertisement for a vitamin supplement study are not likely to represent the general adult population. It is important to recognize that the results are only applicable to the types of people who would have responded to such an ad. Grace would have to be cautious about drawing conclusions concerning adults in general.

When evaluating the external validity of the study, it is often helpful to examine the descriptive statistics for the sample. Does the mean age suggest this is a representative sample of the general adult population? Does the proportion of males and females suggest it is a representative sample? If the sample's descriptive statistics are not consistent with those for the population of interest, it can be an indicator that the external validity of the study is questionable.

The construct validity of the study is relatively good. Grace used commonly accepted variables representing intellectual performance and nutritional supplement treatment. However, while the construct validity of the WAIS is considered sound, she did not directly evaluate how accurate her WAIS administrators were. Inconsistency (technically referred to as *unreliability*) in the scoring of the test could have been a potential explanation if Grace had failed to find a difference between the groups.

One might also question the construct validity of the nutritional supplement treatment in several ways. If the results had not been significant, one might question whether the treatment was long enough, frequent enough, or intense enough. Given that Grace's results were significant, one must wonder which components of the treatment are necessary to achieve the results; perhaps only the mineral supplements affect intellectual functioning, or vitamin B_1.

Through a combination of random assignment and equalization Grace did a good job of insuring adequate internal validity. The possibility always exists that the random assignment failed. However, her efforts meet generally accepted standards.

In summary, the study demonstrated a decent level of construct and internal validity. It is reasonable to conclude that the rejection of the null hypothesis was directly due to a difference between the nutritional supplements and the placebo. The external validity is somewhat weaker, and in preparing a description of her findings, Grace should make clear the nature of the sample used.

This example again demonstrates the complementary roles of statistics and research design. Inferential statistics can provide evidence for the presence or absence of some pattern or relationship in a population. The interpretation of why such a pattern or relationship exists or does not exist depends upon the external validity, construct validity, and internal validity of the study. The greater the validity of the study, the more confidence the researcher can place in the desired explanation for the findings.

Appendices

A. REFERENCES

B. ANSWERS TO EXERCISES

C. SAMPLE AND GROUP SIZE TABLES

D. CRITICAL VALUE TABLES

E. OTHER TABLES

APPENDIX A

References

Abelson, R. P. (1985). A variance explanation paradox: When a little is a lot. *Psychological Bulletin, 97,* 129–133.

Allen, M. J., & Yen, W. M. (1979). *Introduction to measurement theory.* Monterey, CA: Brooks/Cole.

Benton, D. (1992). Vitamin/mineral supplementation and the intelligence of children: A review. *Journal of Orthomolecular Medicine, 7,* 31–38.

Binder, A. M. (1959). Considerations of the place of assumptions in correlational analysis. *American Psychologist, 14,* 504–510.

Butcher, J. N., Dahlstrom, W. G., Graham, J. R., Tellegen, A. M., & Kaemmer, B. (1989). *MMPI–2: Manual for administration and scoring.* Minneapolis, MN: University of Minnesota Press.

Campbell, D. T., & Stanley, J. C. (1966). *Experimental and quasi-experimental designs for research.* Skokie, IL: Rand McNally.

Chanowitz, J., Ellman, G., Silverstein, C. I., Zingarelli, G., & Ganger, E. (1985). Thyroid and vitamin-mineral supplement fail to improve IQ of mentally retarded adults. *American Journal of Mental Deficiencies, 90,* 217–219.

Cohen, J. (1988). *Statistical power analysis for the behavioral sciences* (2nd ed.). Hillsdale, NJ: Lawrence Erlbaum.

Cohen, J. (1992). A power primer. *Psychological Bulletin, 112,* 155–159.

Cohen, J., & Cohen, P. (1983). *Applied multiple regression/correlation analysis for the behavioral sciences* (2nd ed.). Hillsdale, NJ: Lawrence Erlbaum.

Cook, T. D., & Campbell, D. T. (1979). *Quasi-experimentation: Design and analysis issues for field settings.* Chicago: Rand McNally.

Crocker, L., & Algina, J. (1986). *Introduction to classical and modern test theory.* New York: Holt, Rinehart & Winston.

Davis, D. R. (1987). The Harrell study and seven follow-up studies: A brief review. *Journal of Orthomolecular Medicine, 2,* 111–114.

Davison, M. L., & Sharma, A. R. (1988). Parametric statistics and levels of measurement. *Psychological Bulletin, 104,* 137–144.

Davison, M. L., & Sharma, A. R. (1990). Parametric statistics and levels of measurement: Factorial designs and multiple regression. *Psychological Bulletin, 107,* 394–400.

Deijen, J. B., van der Beek, E. J., Orlebeke, J. F., & van den Berg, H. (1992). Vitamin B–6 supplementation in elderly men: Effects on mood, memory, performance and mental effort. *Psychopharmacology, 109,* 489–496.

Delucchi, K. L. (1993). On the use and misuse of chi-square. In G. Keren & C. Lewis (Eds.), *A handbook for data analysis in the behavioral sciences: Statistical issues.* Hillsdale, NJ: Lawrence Erlbaum, pp. 295–320.

Dewan, M. J., & Koss, M. (1989). The clinical impact of the side effects of psychotropic drugs. In S. Fisher & R. P. Greenberg (Eds.), *The limits of biological treatments for psychological distress: Comparisons with psychotherapy and placebo*, pp. 189–234. Hillsdale, NJ: Lawrence Erlbaum.

Edwards, A. L. (1979). *Multiple regression and the analysis of variance and covariance.* San Francisco: W. H. Freeman.

Ellis, N. R., & Tomporowski, P. D. (1983). Vitamin/mineral supplements and intelligence of institutionalized mentally retarded adults. *American Journal of Mental Deficiency, 88,* 211–214.

Harrell, R. F., Capp, R. H., Davis, D. R., Peerless, J., & Ravitz, L. R. (1981). Can nutritional supplements help mentally retarded children? An exploratory study. *Proceedings of the National Academy of Science, 78,* 574–578.

Hsu, L. (1989). Random sampling, randomization, and equivalence of contrasted groups in psychotherapy outcome research. *Journal of Consulting and Clinical Psychology, 57,* 131–137.

Huitema, B. E. (1980). *The analysis of covariance and alternatives.* New York: Wiley.

Keppel, G. (1991). *Design and analysis: A researcher's handbook (3rd ed.).* Englewood Cliffs, NJ: Prentice-Hall.

Kirk, R. E. (1995). *Experimental design: Procedures for the behavioral sciences* (3rd ed.). Belmont, CA: Brooks/Cole.

Kraemer, H. C., & Thiemann, S. (1987). *How many subjects? Statistical power analysis in research.* Newbury Park, CA: Sage Publications.

Leach, C. (1979). *Introduction to statistics: A nonparametric approach for the social sciences.* Chichester, England: Wiley.

Lem, S. (1983). *His master's voice* (M. Kandel, Trans.). San Diego, CA: Harcourt Brace Jovanovich. (Original work published 1968)

Lipsey, M. W., & Wilson, D. B. (1993). The efficacy of psychological, educational, and behavioral treatment: Confirmation from meta-analysis. *American Psychologist, 48,* 1181–1209.

Marascuilo, L. A., & McSweeney, M. (1977). *Nonparametric and distribution-free methods for the social sciences.* Monterey, CA: Brooks/Cole.

Matarazzo, J. D. (1972). *Wechsler's measurement and appraisal of adult intelligence.* New York: Oxford University Press.

Micceri, T. (1989). The unicorn, the normal curve, and other improbable creatures. *Psychological Bulletin, 105,* 156–166.

Michael, R. T., Gagnon, J. H., Laumann, E. O., & Kolata, G. (1994). *Sex in America: A definitive survey.* New York: Little, Brown.

Moses, L. E., & Oakford, R. V. (1963). *Tables of random permutations.* Stanford, CA: Stanford University Press.

Murphy, E. A. (1964). One cause? Many causes? The argument from the bimodal distribution. *Journal of Chronic Disease, 17,* 301–324.

Myers, J. L., & Well, A. D. (1991). *Research design and statistical analysis.* New York: HarperCollins.

National Center for Health Statistics, Najjar, M. F., & Rowland, M. (1987). *Anthropometric reference data and prevalence of overweight, United States, 1976–1980.* DHHS Pub. No. (PHS) 87–1688. Washington, DC: U. S. Government Printing Office.

The RAND Corporation. (1955). *A million random digits with 100,000 normal deviates.* New York: The Free Press.

Range, L. M., Turzo, A. P., & Ellis, J. B. (1990). On the difficulties of recruiting men as undergraduate subjects. *College Student Journal, 23,* 340–342.

Rosenthal, R., & Rubin, D. B. (1982). A simple, general purpose display of magnitude of experimental effect. *Journal of Educational Psychology, 74,* 166–169.

Spence, J. T., Cotton, J. W., Underwood, B. J., & Duncan, C. P. (1990). *Elementary statistics* (5th ed.). Englewood Cliffs, NJ: Prentice-Hall.

Stevens, S. S. (1946). On the theory of scales of measurement. *Science, 103,* 677–680.

Stevens, S. S. (1951). Mathematics, measurement, and psychophysics. In S. S. Stevens (Ed.), *Handbook of experimental psychology* (pp. 1–49). New York: Wiley.

Terman, J. S., Terman, M., Schlager, D., Rafferty, B. Rosofsky, M., Link, M. J., Gallin, P.F., & Quitkin, F. M. (1990). Efficacy of brief, intense light exposure for treatment of winter depression. *Psychopharmacology Bulletin, 26,* 3–11.

Tobias, A. (1982). *The invisible bankers: Everything the insurance industry never wanted you to know.* New York: Linden.

Tukey, J. W. (1977). *Exploratory data analysis.* Reading, MA: Addison-Wesley.

Wechsler, D. (1981). *WAIS-R: Wechsler Adult Intelligence Scale -Revised manual.* San Antonio, TX: Psychological Corporation.

Wechsler, D. (1991). *WISC-III: Wechsler Intelligence Scale for Children — Third Edition manual.* San Antonio, TX: Psychological Corporation.

Willard, J. E., Lange, R. A., & Hillis, L. D. (1992). The use of aspirin in ischemic heart disease. *New England Journal of Medicine, 327,* 175–181.

Zwick, R. (1993). Pairwise comparison procedures for one-way analysis of variance designs. In G. Keren & C. Lewis (Eds.), *A handbook for data analysis in the behavioral sciences: Statistical issues.* Hillsdale, NJ: Lawrence Erlbaum, pp. 43–71.

Answers to Exercises

CHAPTER 1   Basic Statistical Concepts

1. a. The purpose of Part 1 is to introduce basic statistical concepts and the research process.

2. Interviewing alcoholics is an example of scientific research, because the student is directly observing events. Reading about alcoholism is not in and of itself an example of scientific research, although the books may include summaries of scientific research studies.

3. a. This is a constant.
   b. This is a variable, since different routes will involve different lengths.
   c. This is a constant in the given context.
   d. This is a variable, since age in months can vary between 24 and 35 in two-year-olds.
   e. This is a constant.

4. a. A discrete ratio variable, since it involves counting.
   b. A discrete ordinal variable, since it involves rank ordering.
   c. A discrete nominal variable.
   d. A discrete ratio variable, since it involves counting.
   e. A discrete nominal variable.
   f. A continuous ratio variable.
   g. A discrete ratio variable: since currency values are limited to two decimal places, exact measurement is possible.
   h. A continuous ratio variable.
   i. A discrete ratio variable, since it involves counting the number of words.
   j. A continuous interval variable.
   k. A continuous ordinal variable.
   l. A continuous ratio variable.
   m. A discrete ordinal variable, since it involves rank ordering.
   n. A discrete nominal variable: the values gold, silver, and bronze are arbitrary values.

5. a. lower real limit: 67.5″
       upper real limit: 68.5″
       midpoint: 68″
   b. lower real limit: 71.25″
       upper real limit: 71.75″
       midpoint: 71.5″
   c. lower real limit: 68.75″
       upper real limit: 69.25″
       midpoint: 69″

    d. lower real limit: 101.25°
       upper real limit: 101.35°
       midpoint: 101.3°

CHAPTER 2   Sampling

1. a. A sample; the population is all shoppers at that mall.
  b. A population.
  c. A sample; the population is all voters in the election.
  d. A sample; the population is all Long-Evans rat pups.
  e. A population.
  f. A sample (unless all students attended on Thursday); the population is all students in the class.
  g. A sample; the population is all sips from the container.
  h. A population of closets.
  i. A sample; the population is all possible coin flips with that coin.

2. a. Random sampling.
  b. Stratified random sampling, because the proportion of males and females in the sample is consistent with that in the population.
  c. Random sampling.
  d. Convenience sampling.
  e. Convenience sampling: although the form was assigned on a random basis, the sample was chosen on the basis of convenience to the teacher.
  f. Convenience sampling.
  g. Random sampling.
  h. Stratified random sampling.

3. This is an example of convenience sampling. The problem is that voters who call their congressional officials may not be very representative of the entire population of voters.

4. 712, 698, 228, 456, 203, 896, 837, 204, 133, 476

5. 1, 12, 16, 11, 13, 3, 15, 5

6. a. An inferential statistic.
  b. A descriptive statistic.
  c. A descriptive statistic.
  d. An inferential statistic.
  e. An inferential statistic.

CHAPTER 3   Basic Concepts in Research Design

1. a. A scientific hypothesis, because it is *possible* to design a study to test the hypothesis.
  b. Not a scientific hypothesis.
  c. A scientific hypothesis.

d. A scientific hypothesis, tested by asking John whether he is thinking of the color blue right now.

2. a. Pattern: the presence or absence of life.
   b. Pattern: the percentage of heads (or tails) differs from 50%.
   c. Relationship between gender and height.
   d. Pattern: the percentage of adults who are Democrats is greater than the percentage who are Republicans.

3. a. Observational study.
   b. Observational study.
   c. Quasi-experiment.
   d. True experiment.
   e. Quasi-experiment.

4. a. Observational: there is no manipulation of the variables under investigation, only of the conditions for measurement.
   b. Blood pressure is higher in white adults than in black adults; blood pressure is lower in white adults than in black adults; or there is no difference in blood pressure between white adults and black adults.

5. a. Quasi-experiment.
   b. Quasi-experiment.
   c. True experiment.
   d. Observational study.

6.
Group 1	Group2	Group 3
42	30	28
59	4	76
44	87	58
13	97	27
23	47	98

7.
Group 1	Group 2	Group 3	Group 4
80	74	69	10
8	51	17	91
59	41	82	65

8. The following are examples of alternative potential interpretations; you may think of others.
   a. Police may tend to pull red cars over more than cars of other colors.
   b. Social factors may lead females to manifest emotional problems through depression more than men.
   c. The number of people taking baths at any time is much larger than the number of people who are driving.
   d. Larger towns have both more churches and more bars.
   e. Those who took the treatment expected improvement.
   f. Given the sample size, random assignment had a high likelihood of failing. For example, those who used the computer may have been brighter on average than those who used paper.

CHAPTER 4   Frequency Distributions

1. a. This is a discrete ratio variable.

b.

V	f	cum f	p	cum p
10	4	4	.0667	.0667
11	4	8	.0667	.1333
12	7	15	.1167	.2500
13	2	17	.0333	.2833
14	9	26	.1500	.4333
15	3	29	.0500	.4833
16	8	37	.1333	.6167
17	5	42	.0833	.7000
18	3	45	.0500	.7500
19	8	53	.1333	.8833
20	6	59	.1000	.9833
21	1	60	.0167	1.0000
N	60			

2. a. This is a continuous ratio variable.

b. $V_{Max} = 21.8$ (the largest value), $V_{Min} = 10.2$ (the smallest value), so

$$w = \frac{21.8 - 10.2}{10} = 1.16,$$

which is rounded to 1.2. The smallest value in the sample (10.2) is not a multiple of 1.2. The first multiple of 1.2 below 10.2 is 9.6.

V	f
9.6–10.7	2
10.8–11.9	6
12.0–13.1	8
13.2–14.3	4
14.4–15.5	8
15.6–16.7	8
16.8–17.9	6
18.0–19.1	5
19.2–20.3	9
20.4–21.5	3
21.6–22.7	1
N	60

3. a. This is a discrete nominal variable.

b. Brown Hair: $360° \left(\dfrac{11}{28}\right) = 141.43°$

Red Hair: $\qquad$ $360° \left(\dfrac{2}{28} \right) = 25.71°$

Blonde Hair: $\qquad$ $360° \left(\dfrac{7}{28} \right) = 90.00°$

Black Hair: $\qquad$ $360° \left(\dfrac{8}{28} \right) = 102.86°$

c.

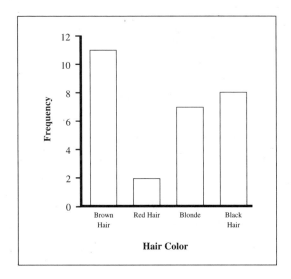

4. For each of the figures below, the first X axis uses the interval limits, the second the midpoint.

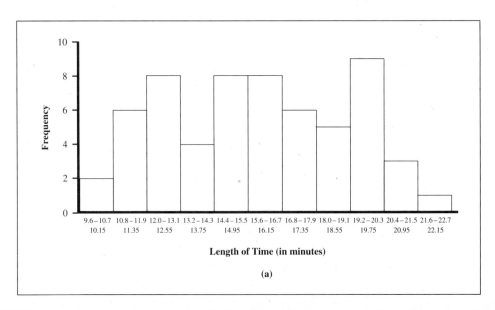

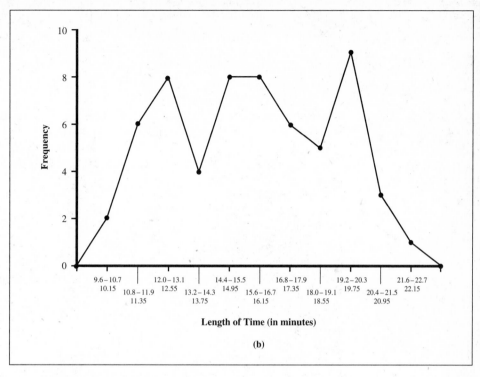

Length of Time (in minutes)

(b)

5. a. This is a convenience sample.
   b. This is a true experiment.
   c. The independent variable is the type of group (led versus unled), a discrete nomi-
      nal variable. The dependent variable is the level of anxiety reported. It is a contin-
      uous ordinal variable because subjects are classified according to level of anxiety.

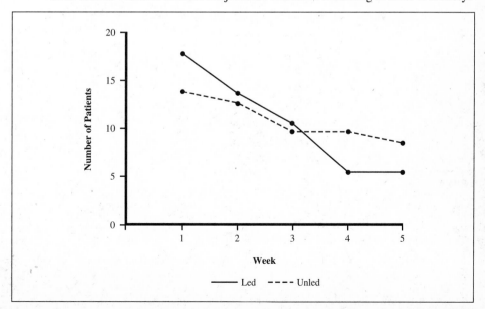

Week

——— Led   ---- Unled

Notice that the endpoints of the lines are not connected to the X axis, because this is an example of using the frequency distribution with a discrete variable.

   f. While more patients in the led group reported severe anxiety at first, over time the number of cases was lower than in the unled group.

6. a. Negatively skewed: most scores should be very high, with a few that are lower.
   b. This will probably be symmetrical: some people will finish quickly, some will take their time, and most will finish in the middle.
   c. Positively skewed: most people have never seen a UFO, but a few will report they have seen many.
   d. Symmetrical: the number of days with very high and very low temperatures should be about the same.
   e. Symmetrical: the number of very tall and very short subjects should be about the same.
   f. Positively skewed: almost all will be 14–15 years old, but a few could be as old as 17–18 because they did not pass earlier grades.
   g. Negatively skewed: most should require the entire hour, but a few students will finish more quickly.

7. a. When the goal is to grab the viewer's attention.
   b. When the goal is to provide specific information, or when producing the figure by hand.
   c. When the variable is continuous.
   d. When the variable is discrete, when the variable is cumulative, when producing the figure by hand, or when smoothing is desired.

CHAPTER 5   Summation and Measure of Central Tendency

1. a. $10 + 6 + 14 + 8 = 38$
   b. $10 + 6 = 16$
   c. $6 + 14 = 20$
   d. $10^2 + 6^2 + 14^2 + 8^2 = 100 + 36 + 196 + 64 = 396$
   e. $(10 + 6 + 14 + 8)^2 = 1444$

2. a. There are two modes, 16 and 19, both with a frequency of 8.
   b. The sample may include representatives of two populations which should be separated for further analysis.

3. a. Median: Not pulled by extreme scores.
   b. Mode: This is a nominal variable.
   c. Mean: Demonstrates less variability across samples than the median or mode.

4. a. Can be used with nominal variables; easy to compute; can indicate the mixture of two populations.
   b. Best sample estimate of μ; sensitive to the position of every score.
   c. Not affected by extreme scores.

5. a. $\overline{Y} = 14.9, Md = 15, Mo = 20$

b. Negatively skewed

6. a. True experiment

b. The independent variable is type of pill, a discrete nominal (dichotomous) variable. The dependent variable is time to completion, a continuous ratio variable.

c. $\overline{Y}_{\text{Supplement}} = 8.80$ seconds, $\overline{Y}_{\text{Placebo}} = 9.67$ seconds

d. Subjects who used the nutritional supplement completed the maze more quickly. However, given the small sample size, random assignment may not have been effective.

7. a. These are μs, the means for populations.

b. The average SAT score for male students at College A is higher than the average SAT score for female students. On average, the males at College A tended to do better on the SATs than females who attend College A.

8. a. Negatively skewed; $\overline{Y}$ should be less than 3.

b. Positively skewed; Md should fall between 6 and 8.

c. Symmetrical; Mo should be 8.9.

CHAPTER 6   Measure of Variability and Transformations

1. $Rn = 20.5 - 5.5 = 15$

$s_Y^2 = 18.62$

$S_Y = 4.32$

2. When the goal is to compute a measure of variability very quickly.

3. a. $s_{\text{Supplement}} = 2.026$, $s_{\text{Placebo}} = 2.137$

b. The placebo group appears more variable.

4. a. 34.134%

b. 47.725%

c. 81.859%

5–7.	Ordered Scores	5. Ranks	6. Percentiles	7. z scores
	6	1	0	−2.06
	8	2	5	−1.60
	10	3.5	10	−1.14
	10	3.5	10	−1.14
	11	5	20	−0.90
	12	6	25	−0.67
	14	8	30	−0.21
	14	8	30	−0.21
	14	8	30	−0.21
	15	10.5	45	0.02
	15	10.5	45	0.02

16	12	55	0.25
17	13	60	0.49
18	14	65	0.72
19	15.5	70	0.95
19	15.5	70	0.95
20	18.5	80	1.18
20	18.5	80	1.18
20	18.5	80	1.18
20	18.5	80	1.18

8. a. 91.149
   b. 26.763
   c. 50.000
9. When you must present results to people with little or no background in statistics.

CHAPTER 7   Scatterplots and the Correlation Coefficient

1. a. Observational study
   b. Rating scale scores are generally continuous ordinal variables.
   c.

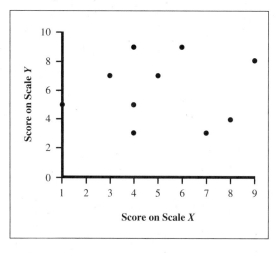

   d. $r_{XY} = +.04$
   e. No, the level of agreement between the two scales is very poor. If the two scales are measuring the same variable, you would expect a very high positive correlation between the two sets of scores.
2. a. There will be a strong but not perfect tendency for low X values to be associated with high Y values, and high X values to be associated with low Y values.
   b. There will be a slight tendency for low X values to be associated with low Y values, and high X values to be associated with high Y values.
   c. Either the left half of the scatterplot will be a mirror image of the right half, or the top half will be a mirror image of the bottom half.

3. a. Quasi-experiment
   b. Program is a discrete nominal (dichotomous) variable; improvement in number of words read per minute is a continuous ratio variable.
   c. Point-biserial (although the Pearson formula can be used to compute r).
   d.

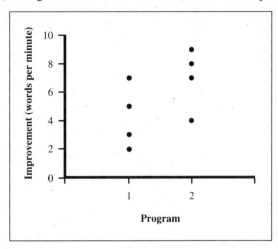

   e. $r_{pb} = +.402$
   f. Subjects who participated in program 2 showed greater improvements in reading speed than subjects receiving program 1.

4. a. True experiment
   b. Treatment is a discrete nominal (dichotomous) variable; improvement is a discrete ordinal (dichotomous) variable.
   c. Phi coefficient (although the Pearson formula can be used to compute r).
   d. $r_\phi = +.816$
   e. Subjects receiving ibuprofen were much more likely to report improvement than subjects receiving aspirin.

5. The results suggest that performance on the advanced placement test accounts for only 12% of the variance in college history course grades. However, given that students come from honors history courses, the possibility exists of a restricted range on both variables. Also, one should consider the possibility of a nonlinear relationship.

6. a. Observational study
   b. The estimates represent a discrete ratio variable. The actual measurements represent a continuous ratio variable.
   c. $r_{XY} = +.812$.
   d. There is a strong tendency for students who estimate they will take a longer time to take a longer time; students who estimate they will take less time tend to take less time.

e.

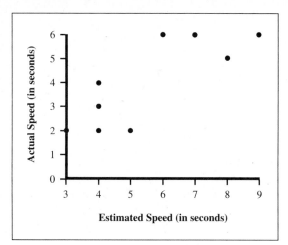

The scatterplot indicates a curve in the line; no matter what the estimate, students completed the maze within 6 seconds.

7. a. Observational study
   b. These are both continuous ratio variables.
   c. lower real limit: 3.75
      upper real limit: 4.25
      midpoint: 4.0
   d. $r_{XY} = +.715$. This is a Pearson correlation coefficient.
   e.

X	Y
2.0	5.0
1.0	1.0
6.0	8.0
3.0	3.0
7.0	2.0
4.0	4.0
5.0	7.0
10.0	10.0
9.0	6.0
8.0	9.0

   These are now discrete ordinal variables.
   f. $r_{XY} = .685$. This is a Spearman rank-order correlation coefficient.
   g. When there are tied scores, only the Pearson formula produces the correct value.

CHAPTER 8   Simple Regression

1. a. Simple regression would be appropriate: both variables are continuous ratio variables.
   b. Simple regression would be appropriate: one variable is dichotomous, the other a continuous ratio variable.
   c. Simple regression would not be appropriate: the study involves two predictor variables. Multiple regression could be used instead.

d. Simple regression would not be appropriate: one variable is a nominal variable with more than two values.

e. Simple regression would not be appropriate: the strength of a relationship is estimated using measures of linear relationship.

2. The formulas for the slope and y-intercept are different, and regression lines can be computed for less than perfectly linear data.

3. a. The best estimate of variable Y for subject i.

   b. The regression coefficient (or slope) for the regression line when variable Y is regressed onto variable X (when Y is the criterion and X is the predictor).

   c. The regression coefficient (or slope) for the regression line when variable X is regressed onto variable Y.

   d. The regression constant (or y-intercept) for the regression line when variable Y is regressed onto variable X.

   e. The error of estimate for subject i when variable Y is regressed onto variable X.

   f. The standard error of estimate for the regression line when variable Y is regressed onto variable X; also the amount of error to be expected for the estimated Y values.

   g. The standard error of estimate for the regression line when variable X is regressed onto variable Y; also the amount of error to be expected for the estimated X values.

4. a. $b_{Y \cdot X} = .038$, $a_{Y \cdot X} = 5.807$

   b.

$\hat{Y}$	Error
5.845	−0.845
5.921	1.079
6.034	2.966
5.958	−2.958
5.958	−0.958
5.996	1.004
5.958	3.042
6.147	1.853
6.110	−2.110
6.072	−3.072

   c. $s_{Y \cdot X} = 2.45$. On average, estimates differ from the actual Y values by over 2 points. Given the small range of actual Y values, these are relatively poor estimates.

5. a. $b_{X \cdot Y} = .042$, $a_{X \cdot Y} = 4.850$

$\hat{X}$	Error	$\hat{X}$	Error
5.058	−4.058	5.142	−0.142
5.142	−2.142	5.225	−1.225
5.225	0.775	5.183	3.817
4.975	−0.975	5.017	2.983
5.058	−1.058	4.975	2.025

$s_{X \cdot Y} = 2.47$, Estimates on average are off by $2\frac{1}{2}$ points, again a fairly large margin of error for these data.

6. a. The slope is 1.8 and the constant is 32.

b. The slope is $10/18 = .556$, and the constant is

$$\frac{10}{18}(-32) = -17.778.$$

7. a. Every $\hat{Y}$ will exactly equal the corresponding Y value.

b. $b_{Y \cdot X} = 2$, $b_{X \cdot Y} = \frac{1}{2}$

c. $a_{Y \cdot X} = 5 - 2(10) = -15$

$a_{X \cdot Y} = 10 - \frac{1}{2}(5) = 7.5$

d. Both standard errors of estimate must equal 0.

CHAPTER 9   Concepts Underlying Inferential Statistics

1. a. No, this refers to a level of confidence about our planet.
   b. Yes.
   c. No, this refers to a level of confidence about the value of μ.
   d. Yes.
   e. No, this refers to a level of confidence about this candidate in this election.
   f. Yes.
   g. Yes.

2. a. Mutually exclusive.
   b. Mutually exclusive and exhaustive.
   c. Neither.
   d. Mutually exclusive.
   e. Mutually exclusive and exhaustive.
   f. Mutually exclusive.
   g. Mutually exclusive and exhaustive.

3. a. Independent outcomes.
   b. Dependent outcomes.
   c. Independent outcomes.
   d. Dependent outcomes.
   e. Independent outcomes.
   f. Dependent outcomes.

4. a. This is the probability of being infected both times (infection the first time and infection the second time). Since infection either time will mean she is infected, the true probability must be larger than this.
   b. This is only correct if getting infected the first time and getting infected the second time are mutually exclusive; as we have seen in the answer to part a, this is not true.

c. One way is to correct the answer given in part b by the probability of infection at both times:

$$p(\text{Time 1 or Time 2}) = p(\text{Time 1}) + p(\text{Time 2}) - p(\text{Time 1 and Time 2})$$

$$= .002 + .002 - .000004 = .003996.$$

The second method is more difficult to figure out. To avoid infection, this woman must not be infected both at Time 1 and at Time 2. The probability of noninfection at both times is:

$$p(\text{Time 1 and Time 2}) = .998(.998) = .996004.$$

The probability of infection is therefore

$$1 - .996004 = .003996.$$

5. When he suggests that the probability of an accident involving the ladder is .08, this is a conditional probability: given that a household accident has occurred, the probability is .08 that the accident involved a ladder:

$$p(L \mid A) = .08.$$

To compute the probability that this boy will have a accident at home when he climbs the ladder, the multiplication rule is

$$p(L \text{ and } A) = p(A)p(L \mid A).$$

If the probability of a household accident at any time is .00001 (1 in a hundred thousand), for example, so that at any time 1 in every hundred thousand Americans are involved in a household accident, the true probability of getting into an accident when he climbs the ladder is

$$p(L \text{ and } A) = .00001(.08) = .0000008.$$

The second problem is that household accidents involving ladders and household accidents involving a tree overlap. The correct addition rule is therefore

$$p(T \text{ or } L) = p(T) + p(L) - p(T \text{ and } L).$$

6. a. $p(AT \text{ or } CC) = p(AT) + p(CC) = \dfrac{260}{500} + \dfrac{42}{500} = .604.$

b. $p(AT \text{ or } UB) = p(AT) + p(UB) - p(AT \text{ and } UB)$

$$= .52 + .92 - .44 = 1.00$$

c. $p(AT \text{ and } UB) = p(AT)p(UB \mid AT) = .52\left(\dfrac{220}{260}\right) = .44.$

7. a. True.
   b. False: this will only be true for some samples.
   c. False.
   d. False.
   e. True.
   f. True.

CHAPTER 10   The Logic of Hypothesis Testing

1. The statistical hypothesis is translated into a pair of statistical hypotheses. The null hypothesis suggests the absence of the pattern or relationship discussed in the scientific hypothesis, the alternative hypothesis suggests its presence. The absence of a pattern or relationship always implies some equality, so the null hypothesis always includes an equal sign.

2. a. Directional: Nondirectional:

   $H_0: \sigma_E \leq \sigma_w$ $H_0: \sigma_E = \sigma_w$

   $H_1: \sigma_E > \sigma_w$ $H_1: \sigma_E \neq \sigma_w$

   Note that in this example the variance could have been used instead of the standard deviation.

   b. Directional: Nondirectional:

   $H_0: \rho_{PA} \leq 0$ $H_0: \rho_{PA} = 0$

   $H_1: \rho_{PA} > 0$ $H_1: \rho_{PA} \neq 0$

   The scientific hypothesis suggests that as pitching speed increases, so will distance from the target.

   c. Directional: Nondirectional:

   $H_0: \mu_A \leq \mu_N$ $H_0: \mu_A = \mu_N$

   $H_1: \mu_A > \mu_N$ $H_1: \mu_A \neq \mu_N$

   d. Directional:

   $H_0: p(> .300)_A \geq p(> .300)_N$

   $H_1: p(> .300)_A < p(> .300)_N$

   Nondirectional:

   $H_0: p(> .300)_A = p(> .300)_N$

   $H_1: p(> .300)_A \neq p(> .300)_N$.

3. a. Not acceptable: the null hypothesis should indicate the absence of a pattern, not the alternative hypothesis.
   b. Not acceptable: these are not mutually exhaustive.
   c. Acceptable.
   d. Not acceptable: these are not mutually exclusive; also, the null hypothesis should indicate the absence of a pattern, not the alternative hypothesis.

4. a. $H_1: \rho_{XY} < .10$

   $H_0: \rho_{XY} \geq .10$.

   b. $H_0: \mu \leq 10$

   $H_1: \mu > 10$.

   c. $H_1: \rho_{XY} \neq .10$

   $H_0: \rho_{XY} = .10$.

d. H_0: $\sigma = 3.5$

H_1: $\sigma \neq 3.5$.

5. a. False: A Type I error can only occur if the null hypothesis is true.

   b. True.

   c. True.

   d. False: If the alternative hypothesis is true, then the only possible outcomes for a study are correct rejection or incorrect non-rejection.

   e. True.

   f. False: $1 - \alpha$ is used to symbolize the probability of a correct non-rejection if the null hypothesis is true.

   g. False: If the jury convicts, but the defendant is actually innocent, the jury has committed a case of incorrect rejection, or a Type I error.

   h. False: If the null hypothesis is true, and a study is repeated many times with α set at .01, then the null hypothesis should be rejected in 1% of the studies.

6. An alpha level of .01 is more conservative. It would require a more extreme sample value to reject the null hypothesis.

7. If the alternative hypothesis is true, the probability of a Type II error becomes 1.0.

CHAPTER 11 Type II Error and Power

1. If the null hypothesis is true, the probability of a Type I error becomes 1.0.

2. b and d.

3. Increasing the alpha level will improve the power of the study if the alternative hypothesis is true. However, if the null hypothesis is instead true, increasing the alpha level increases the probability of a Type I error.

4. The following are reasonable decisions about effect size; you may make others as long as they are justified:

   a. At the minimum a medium effect size may be assumed, and a large effect size may be preferable.

   b. Since this phenomenon is supposed to occur in all males, a large effect may be assumed.

   c. Since this is one element in a series for which effects will probably sum together, a small effect size is appropriate.

   d. This difference should be "grossly perceptible," suggesting a large effect size.

   e. In the general population even a small effect size would mean large differences in absolute numbers.

   f. This is a case where a medium effect might be appropriate. Minor dissatisfaction with the course may be considered unimportant, but it need not be grossly obvious before it can be considered important.

   g. This is similar to e, and so one could argue for a small effect size. However, it was noted in the chapter that .15 represents a medium effect, and since

$$|.35 - .50| = |.65 - .50| = .15,$$

   one could also argue for a medium effect. Either answer may be considered acceptable.

5. a. $N = 853$.
   b. $N = 19$.
   c. $N = 85$.
6. a. 2, 3, 5, and 6 are consistent with the null hypothesis, since these values fall within the range of values associated with the null hypothesis.
   b. 3 would result in the most powerful test of the null hypothesis, because it is the value furthest from the range of values associated with the alternative hypothesis.
   c. 6 would result in the least powerful test of the null hypothesis, because it is the value closest to the range of values associated with the alternative hypothesis.
   d. Assuming $\rho_{XY} = .45$ provides the least powerful test of the null hypothesis if the alternative hypothesis is true.

CHAPTER 12   The One-Group z Test and Interval Estimation

1. a. No: this is a study about a variable relationship.
   b. No: if the questionnaire has not been used before, the population standard deviation is not known.
   c. Yes: if the population variance is known, so is the population standard deviation.

2. a. $H_0: \mu = 112.73$

   $H_1: \mu \neq 112.73$
   b. Observational study.

   c. $N = 25$.

   d. $z_{\bar{Y}} = 1.149$

   e. $z_{\alpha=.01} = \pm 2.575$; do not reject

   f. There may be no difference between the average IQ of medical school applicants and the general college graduate population, or the study had insufficient power to uncover the difference.

3. a. False: this is only true if the population distribution is normally distributed, or if N is sufficiently large.
   b. False: the variability decreases with larger sample sizes.
   c. True.
   d. True.
   e. True.

4. a. 1.2 hours.
   b. .04 hours.
   c. .02275.

5. a. $LL_{.99} = 107.84$

   $UL_{.99} = 125.49$

   b. The results are consistent, in that the null hypothesis value for μ (112.73) falls within the confidence interval, so the possibility that $\mu = 112.73$ cannot be ruled out.
6. If the 95% confidence interval (for example) includes the null hypothesis value, then one cannot be 95% confident in the decision to reject the null hypothesis.

CHAPTER 13   The One-Group t Test

1. a. No
   b. Yes
   c. Yes: although the population variance (and standard deviation) is known, there is no reason you could not use the one-group t test.

2. a. $H_0: \mu \leq 112.73$

   $H_1: \mu > 112.73$

   b. $N = 26$.

   c. $t_{\bar{Y}} = +2.139$

   d. $t_{\alpha_{(D)}=.05,\, df=14} = +1.761$; reject

   e. There is evidence of a difference between the average IQ of medical school applicants and the general college graduate population, assuming a Type I error has not occurred. The sign of the t value suggests medical school applicants are on average brighter than the average college graduate.

3. a. This is a case where a population difference in either direction from the neutral point would be important to know about.
   b. Since a μ of 4 would suggest no preference in the population,

   $$H_0: \mu = 4$$
   $$H_1: \mu \neq 4.$$

   c. Since there is no manipulation of the variable, this is an observational study.
   d. $N = 198$.
   e. $t_{\bar{Y}} = .742$
   f. $t_{\alpha=.05, df=19} = \pm 2.093$; do not reject the null hypothesis
   g. Since the null hypothesis was not rejected, the results do not offer evidence that the population μ differs from the neutral point of 4. The results do not provide evidence that members of this population have a preference one way or the other on this issue. However, the power of the study may have been inadequate.

4. a. It would be as important to know that nutritional supplements reduce intelligence as it would be to know they increase intelligence.
   b. Since a mean value of 100 on the WAIS after completion of the treatment would mean the nutritional supplements had no effect,

   $$H_0: \mu = 100$$
   $$H_1: \mu \neq 100.$$

   c. There is a manipulation, but no random assignment; all subjects receive the treatment. This is a quasi-experiment.
   d. In this case, the treatment should have at least a medium effect on WAIS scores before it would be appropriate to recommend the nutritional supplement as an intelligence booster.
   e. $N = 22$.

f. $t_{\bar{Y}} = 3.198$

g. $t_{\alpha=.05, df=11} = \pm 2.201$; reject the null hypothesis

h. Since the computed t value is a positive number, it suggests the average intelligence test score in the population represented by this sample is above the null hypothesis value of 100. However, there are several problems with attributing this finding to the treatment. First, there is the situational confound of expectations: the expectation of improvement may lead them to try harder on the WAIS. Also, people willing to participate in such a treatment may be smarter than the average person to begin with.

5. a. $LL_{.95} = 112.72$

   $UL_{.95} = 120.61$

   It is not appropriate to use the critical value used above, since the computation of the confidence interval should be based on the two-tailed critical value

   $t_{\alpha=.05, df=14} = \pm 2.145.$

b. They are not consistent with the results of the hypothesis test, since the confidence interval includes the null hypothesis value from the hypothesis test. This occurred because the hypothesis test was conducted as a one-tailed test, which is more powerful than a two-tailed test when results are in the expected direction.

6. a. $LL_{.99} = 3.456$

   $UL_{.99} = 5.144$

   It is appropriate to use the critical t value from Question 2f, since this is a two-tailed critical value for the appropriate alpha level.

b. The results of the confidence interval are consistent with those for the hypothesis test, in that the null hypothesis value for μ (4) is contained in the confidence interval.

7. a. $LL_{.99} = 100.22$

   $UL_{.99} = 115.11$

   It is not appropriate to use the critical value for Question 3g; although it is a two-tailed critical value, it is the critical value for the wrong α level.

b. The results of the confidence interval are consistent with the results of the hypothesis test, in that the null hypothesis value for μ (100) does not appear within the confidence interval. This suggests we could have rejected the null hypothesis even if we had set $\alpha = .01$.

8. a. 0; 0.

b. The sampling distribution of z will always be normal; the sampling distribution of t will be normal when the degrees of freedom $(N - 1)$ are very large.

c. The t distribution; when $df > 120$.

CHAPTER 14   The Chi-Square Goodness of Fit Test

1. a. No: this is a study about a variable relationship.
    b. No: The scientific hypothesis has to do with the mean, not the probabilities of occurrence for variable values.
    c. Yes: The scientific hypothesis has to do with the probabilities of occurrence for variable values.
    d. Yes
    e. Yes

2. a. Quasi-experiment: there is a manipulation without random assignment.
    b. Arm choice is a discrete nominal variable.
    c. H_0: $p(E) = .25$ and $p(N, W, S) = .75$

    H_ϕ: $p(E) \neq .25$ and $p(N, W, S) \neq .75$

    d. A small effect size would probably be a trivial finding, so one should assume at least a medium effect size.
    e. $N = 130$.
    f. $\chi^2 = 77.01$
    g. $\chi^2_{\alpha=.05, df=1} = 3.841$; reject the null hypothesis
    h. The results suggest that rats are able to maintain learning over periods of at least six months.

3. a. Quasi-experiment.
    b.
    H_0: $p(\text{Cola 1}) = .333$, and
    $p(\text{Cola 2}) = .333$, and
    $p(\text{Cola 3}) = .333$.
    H_1: $p(\text{Cola 1}) \neq .333$, and/or
    $p(\text{Cola 2}) \neq .333$, and/or
    $p(\text{Cola 3}) \neq .333$.

    or, H_0: all probabilities are equal
    H_1: some probabilities are not equal.

    c. $N = 86$.
    d. $\chi^2 = 3.6$.

    $\chi^2_{\alpha=.10, df=2} = 4.605$; do not reject.

    e. The results do not support the existence of a difference in preference. This may be due to insufficient power.

4. a. Quasi-experiment: there is a manipulation without random assignment.
    b. Outcome is a discrete ordinal variable.

c. H_0: $p(I) = p(U) = p(D) = .333$

   H_1: One or more of the null hypothesis probabilities is incorrect

d. Based on these considerations, a large effect size seems clearly appropriate as the smallest meaningful effect size.

e. (1) $N = 1743$

   (2) $N = 39$

   (3) $N = 141$

f. $\chi^2 = .14$

g. $\chi^2_{\alpha=.10,\, df=2} = 4.605$; do not reject the null hypothesis

h. There is no evidence that this surgery results in improvement any more frequently than it leads to deterioration or no change.

5. a. H_0: $p(I) = .11$ and $p(U) = .14$ and $p(D) = .75$

   H_1: One or more of the null hypothesis probabilities is incorrect

b. $\chi^2 = 287.19$

c. The critical value is still 4.605; reject the null hypothesis.

d. The findings suggest the surgery does result in a significantly greater number of positive outcomes than no surgery.

6. a. If the null hypothesis is true, the expected value for the z and t distributions equals 0; the expected value for the χ^2 distribution increases as the degrees of freedom increase.

b. The t and z distributions are symmetrical; the χ^2 is skewed unless the degrees of freedom are large.

c. The χ^2 distribution does not allow two-tailed tests; the z and t distributions do.

d. The χ^2 distribution cannot be used to evaluate directional hypotheses unless $k = 2$; the z and t distributions always can.

CHAPTER 15   The Dependent Groups t Test

1. a. No: these are not dependent groups.

b. Yes

c. Yes

d. No: Both time of measurement (before versus after) and choice of alley are nominal variables.

2. a. Observational study.

b. H_0: $\mu_1 \geq \mu_2$

   H_1: $\mu_1 < \mu_2$,

   or H_0: $\mu_D \geq 0$

   H_1: $\mu_D < 0$, assuming μ_2 was subtracted from μ_1

   c. $N = 252$.

   d. $t_{\overline{D}} = -2.905$.

   e. $t_{\alpha(D)=.01, df=9} = -2.821$; reject

   f. Among students who report very low self-esteem, there is a tendency for scores to increase over a period of a month (assuming a Type I error has not occurred).

3. a. Quasi-experiment
   b. Time of measurement is a discrete nominal variable; vocabulary skill is a continuous ordinal variable.

   c. $H_0: \mu_B = \mu_A$

      $H_1: \mu_B \neq \mu_A,$

  or $H_0: \mu_D = 0$

      $H_1: \mu_D \neq 0$

   d. A medium effect size is probably appropriate.
   e. (1) $N = 20$

      (2) $N = 166$

      (3) $N = 26$

   f. $t_{\overline{D}} = -2.015$

   g. $t_{\alpha=.05, df=5} = \pm 2.571$; do not reject the null hypothesis
   h. The results do not provide evidence of a difference due to the treatment. In this case the failure to find significance could have been due to relatively low power.

4. a. $LL_{.99} = -5.93$

      $UL_{.99} = .33$

    No, because the confidence interval should be computed using the two-tailed critical value.
   b. They are not consistent, because the null hypothesis value 0 falls within the confidence interval. This occurred because the more powerful one-tailed hypothesis test was conducted.

5. a. $LL_{.95} = -.729$

      $UL_{.95} = 4.395$

    Yes, because both are based on the two-tailed critical value $\alpha = .05$.
   b. They are consistent; failure to reject the null hypothesis is consistent with finding the null hypothesis value for μ_D (0) lies within the confidence interval.

6. Since two subjects are needed to generate each difference score, the sample size is actually twice the value provided in the table.

CHAPTER 16   The Independent Groups *t* Test

1. a. Yes
   b. No: these are dependent groups.
   c. Yes
   d. Yes
   e. Yes

2. a. True experiment.

   b. $H_0: \mu_1 = \mu_2$
      $H_1: \mu_1 \neq \mu_2$

   c. $n = 26; N = 2(26) = 52.$

   d. $t_{\bar{Y}_1 - \bar{Y}_2} = -2.82.$

   e. $t_{\alpha=.05, df=18} = \pm 2.878$; do not reject.

   f. No difference was found in the impact of fenfluramine and amphetamine on subsequent weight gain. However, this may have been due to insufficient power.

3. a. Observational study
   b. Political position is a discrete nominal (dichotomous) variable; political knowledge is a continuous ordinal variable.

   c. (1) $H_0: \mu_L \leq \mu_C$
          $H_1: \mu_L > \mu_C$

      (2) $H_0: \mu_L \geq \mu_C$
          $H_1: \mu_L < \mu_C$

      (3) $H_0: \mu_L = \mu_C$
          $H_1: \mu_L \neq \mu_C$

      (4) The nondirectional statistical hypotheses seem the most appropriate, since findings in either direction would be meaningful.

   d. This is a case where even small differences would represent meaningful differences at the level of the entire American population.

   e. (1) $n = 27, N = 2(27) = 54$

      (2) $n = 82, N = 2(82) = 164$

      (3) $n = 226, N = 2(226) = 452$

   f. $t_{\bar{Y}_1 - \bar{Y}_2} = -.399$

   g. $t_{\alpha(D)=.01, df=28} = 2.467$; do not reject

   h. The results do not support the contention that liberals are more knowledgeable than conservatives. In fact, the mean for conservatives (35.667) was actually higher than the mean for liberals (33.600).

4. a. $LL_{.80} = -4.1211$

      $UL_{.80} = -1.4789$

No, because the critical value for $\alpha = .05$ is not appropriate for the 80% confidence interval.

b. No; the hypothesis test did not allow rejection of the null hypothesis, but the null hypothesis value of 0 was not contained in the confidence interval. This is because the more liberal standard of 80% confidence was used for the confidence interval. Had the alpha level of the hypothesis test been set at $\alpha = .20$, the null hypothesis could have been rejected.

5. a. $LL_{.95} = -4.1211$

$UL_{.95} = -1.4789$

No, because the critical value for question 3g was one-tailed; the confidence interval requires the two-tailed critical value.

b. Yes: the failure to reject the null hypothesis in question 3 is consistent with finding the value 0 contained within the 95% confidence interval.

6. The test is robust against neither violation of the normality assumption (since $n_1 < 30$) nor the homogeneity of variance assumption (since $n_1 \neq n_2$).

CHAPTER 17 The *t* Test for a Correlation Coefficient

1. a. Observational study.

b. H_0: $\rho_{XY} \geq 0$

H_1: $\rho_{XY} < 0$

c. $N = 45$.

d. $r_{XY} = +.0132$, $t_r = +.026$.

e. $t_{\alpha(D)=.01,df=4} = -3.747$; critical $r_{XY} = -.882$; do not reject.

f. There is no evidence that spending more time on homework is associated with being disliked; in fact, students who did more homework received higher liking ratings in this sample.

2. a. H_0: $\rho_{XY} = 0$

H_1: $\rho_{XY} \neq 0$

b. $r_{XY} = +.553$; this is a point-biserial correlation coefficient.

c. $\dfrac{.553\sqrt{18}}{\sqrt{1 - .553^2}} = +2.82$

d. $t_{\alpha=.05,df=18} = \pm 2.878$; do not reject.

3. The correlation coefficient measures the strength of linear relationships. There is no reason to expect that the amount of weight gain is linearly related to group; for example, weight gain could be greatest for Group 2, and less for Groups 1 and 3. The study therefore needs to examine nonlinear relationships as well.

4. a. $\pm .361$

b. $-.211$

c. $+.295$

5. a. The findings suggest that more attractive females are actually seen as more intelligent by males in this population.
    b. The failure to find significance probably stems from the use of a one-tailed test, since the results were opposite in direction to what was expected by the research; had a two-tailed test been used instead the results probably would have been significant, assuming a reasonable sample size.
    c. The scientific hypothesis was supported.

CHAPTER 18   The One-Way Independent Groups Analysis of Variance

1. When the F test is used to evaluate whether two population variances are equal, the test is not robust against violation of the normality assumption. Since this assumption rarely applies, it means the results of an F test used for this purpose must be considered suspect.

2. a. Yes
    b. No: the dependent variable is whether the rat chooses to turn left or right, a discrete nominal variable.
    c. Yes: the dependent variable is now the number of right turns, which is a discrete ratio variable.

3. a. Observational study.

    b. $H_0 : \mu_J = \mu_P = \mu_c$(all μs are equal)
            $H_1 :$ not all μs are equal,

        or $H_0 : \sigma_\mu^2 = 0$
            $H_1 : \sigma_\mu^2 \neq 0$

    c. $n = 322; N = 3(322) = 966.$

    d.
Source	df	SS	MS	F
Between Groups	2	4.467	2.233	.245
Within Groups	27	246.500	9.130	

    e. $F_{\alpha=.05,df_1=2,df_2=27} = 3.35$; do not reject.

    f. No relationship was found between religious affiliation and annual income. This may have been due to insufficient power.

4. a. True experiment
    b. Textbook is a discrete nominal variable; understanding of ANOVA is a continuous ordinal variable.

c.

Source	df	SS	MS	F
Between Groups	3	109.20	36.40	6.04
Within Groups	16	144.00	9.00	

d. $F_{\alpha=.05, df_1=3, df_2=16} = 3.24$; reject the null hypothesis.

e. There is a difference between texts in terms of the level of understanding demonstrated on the test.

5. a. This is a quasi-experimental study: there is a manipulation, but not random assignment

b. Severity as defined here is a continuous ordinal variable.

c. Amount of improvement is a continuous ordinal variable.

d. $H_0 : \mu_{Sev} = \mu_{Mod} = \mu_{Mild}$ (all μs are equal)

$H_1 :$ not all μs are equal,

or $H_0 : \sigma_\mu^2 = 0$

$H_1 : \sigma_\mu^2 \neq 0$

e. (1) $n = 30, N = 3(30) = 90$

(2) $n = 349, N = 3(349) = 1047$

(3) $n = 52, N = 3(52) = 156$

f.

Source	df	SS	MS	F
Between Groups	2	614.333	307.167	18.909*
Within Groups	15	203.667	16.244	

$*p < .05$

g. $F_{\alpha=.01, df_1=2, df_2=15} = 6.36$; reject the null hypothesis.

h. There is a difference in amount of improvement after ECT for severely, moderately, or mildly depressed individuals.

6. a. If the null hypothesis is true, MS_{BG} is estimating the variance within any of the populations (which are assumed to be equal), σ_Y^2. So is MS_{WG}, so F is expected to equal 1.0.

b. If the null hypothesis is false, MS_{WG} is still estimating σ_Y^2. MS_{BG} is instead estimating

$$\sigma_Y^2 + c(\sigma_\mu^2),$$

a larger value. F therefore should be some value larger than 1.0.

7. Because it is the variance of the μs that is directly examined by the one-way independent groups ANOVA. If there is evidence that the variance of the μs is greater than 0, it indicates the μs are not all equal.

8. a. The df_{BG} must equal 3, so there are 4 groups.

b. $SS_{BG} = 21.0$

    c. $MS_{BG} = 21/3 = 7.0$

    d. $MS_{WG} = 4.0$

    e. $F = 1.75$

    f. $n = 5$

9. MS_{WG} would have to equal zero, since there would be no variability within the groups.

CHAPTER 19   Multiple Comparison Tests

1. a. (1) Planned comparison
    (2) Planned comparison
    (3) Unplanned comparison

  b. (1) Planned comparison
    (2) Unplanned comparison
    (3) Unplanned comparison
    (4) Unplanned comparison
    (5) Planned comparison
    (6) Planned comparison

  c. (1) Planned comparison
    (2) Unplanned comparison
    (3) Unplanned comparison

2. a. Planned: 5 vs. 6, 6 vs. 7, 7 vs. 8, 5 vs. 7, 6 vs. 8
    Unplanned: 5 vs. 8
  b. The chapter recommends limiting the number of planned comparisons to at most 2–3; there are 5 here. It would probably be better to conduct all 6 comparisons using the Tukey test.

3. a. $Q = 3.96$.
  b. $Q_{\alpha=.05,k=3,df=9} = 3.95$; reject.
  c. Amphetamine was found superior to placebo as an appetite suppressant.

4. a. $t = -2.80$.
  b. $t_{\alpha=.05,df=9} = \pm2.262$; reject.
  c. Amphetamine was found superior to placebo as an appetite suppressant.

5. a. Planned comparisons would include the comparison of US to the other three texts. Unplanned comparisons would include the comparisons between the alternate texts.
  b. Planned Comparisons:
    US vs. A: $t_p = .527$
    US vs. B: $t_p = 2.530$
    US vs. C: $t_p = 2.846$

Unplanned Comparisons:

$$\text{A vs. B: } Q = 2.832$$
$$\text{A vs. C: } Q = 3.280$$
$$\text{B vs. C: } Q = .447$$

c. $t_{\alpha=.05,df=16} = \pm 2.120$

$Q_{\alpha=.05,k=4,df=16} = 4.05$

d. The comparison of US to alternate texts B and C are significant; no other analyses were significant. Students did seem to learn more from US than from texts B and C, but there was no difference evident between US and text A.

6. The planned comparison is likely to be more powerful than the unplanned comparison. However, the unplanned comparison might be preferred for the sake of simplicity if unplanned comparisons will have to be conducted anyway.

CHAPTER 20   The One-Way Dependent Groups ANOVA

1. a. No: these are independent groups.
   b. No: this is a study of the probabilities associated with variable values, for which the chi-square goodness of fit would be the most appropriate statistic.
   c. Yes; the dependent groups t test could also be used for this analysis.

2. a. Since the dependent variable is an objective physiological measure (number of T4 cells) rather than a self-report, this study is not susceptible to the problems noted for the study described in the chapter.
   b. If AZT is a more effective treatment for AIDS than placebo, using an experimental study would mean that members of the placebo group could die unnecessarily by withholding effective treatment.

3. It is questionable whether grade point average is that strongly related to response to a self-esteem enhancement program. This is a case in which the one-way independent groups ANOVA could be more appropriate even though the groups were matched.

4. a. Quasi-experiment (since assignment was nonrandom).
   b.

Source	df	SS	MS	F
Between Groups	2	4.467	2.233	.294
Residual	18	136.867	7.604	

c. $F_{\alpha=.01,df_1=2,df_2=18} = 6.01$; do not reject.

d. There is no evidence that either treatment is any more effective than having people observe and record their weight each morning.

5. a. True experiment
   b.

Source	df	SS	MS	F
Between Groups	3	376.950	125.650	7.22*
Residual	8	208.800	17.400	

$*p < .05$

c. $F_{\alpha=.05,df_1=3,df_2=12} = 3.49$; reject the null hypothesis.

d. $\overline{Y}_{\text{Antidepressant}} = 17.6$

$\overline{Y}_{\text{Psychotherapy}} = 23.8$

$\overline{Y}_{\text{Placebo}} = 26.8$

$\overline{Y}_{\text{Discussion}} = 29.2$

Antidepressant drugs were the most effective treatment (since level of depression was lowest), the unled discussion group the least effective.

6. a.

Source	df	SS	MS	F
Between Groups	1	39.200	39.200	8.44
Residual	9	41.800	4.644	

b. $F_{\alpha=.01,df_1=1,df_2=9} = 10.6$; do not reject the null hypothesis

c. The results do not suggest that self-esteem scores increased over time.

7. The dependent groups ANOVA is not appropriate, because the subjects were not individually matched in blocks.

CHAPTER 21   The Two-Way Independent Groups ANOVA

1. a. No: the second discrete variable (before versus after treatment) involves dependent groups.

b. Yes: the two nominal variables are race and household income, and the third variable is a ratio variable.

c. No: since frequency of illness is a constant here, only two variables are being investigated.

2. a. True experiment.

b.

Source	df	SS	MS	F
Program	1	44.083	44.233	7.05*
Grade	1	70.083	70.083	11.21*
Interaction	1	24.083	24.083	3.85
Within Groups	8	50.000	6.250	

$*p < .05$

c. In each case $F_{\alpha=.05,df_1=1,df_2=8} = 5.32$. The two main effects are significant, the interaction is not.

d.

		Grade		
		First	Sixth	
Program	Formal	8.667	1.000	4.833
	Peer	9.667	7.667	8.667
		9.167	4.333	

The results suggest that first-graders performed better than sixth-graders regardless of program, and students in the peer program performed better than students in the formal program regardless of grade.

3. a. All three tests should be significant.
   b. The main effects for grade and program should be significant, but not the interaction.
   c. The main effect for program should be the only significant effect.

4. a. The two main effects should be significant, but not the interaction.
   b. The interaction should be significant, but not the main effects.
   c. None of the effects should be significant.

5. a. True experiment
   b. Number of words spoken per minute is a discrete ratio variable.
   c. main effects:

   $$\text{Student Gender:} \quad H_0: \mu_F = \mu_M$$
   $$H_1: \mu_F \neq \mu_M$$
   $$\text{Instructor Gender:} \quad H_0: \mu_F = \mu_M$$
   $$H_1: \mu_F \neq \mu_M$$

   interaction: H_0: differences between μs for the Student Gender variable are equal at every level of the Instructor Gender variables
   H_1: differences between μs for the Student Gender variable are not equal at every level of the Instructor Gender variable.

   d.

Source	df	SS	MS	F
Instructor	1	2.000	2.000	0.178
Student	1	264.500	264.500	23.511*
Interaction	1	18.000	18.000	1.600
Within Groups	4	45.000	11.250	

   $*p < .05$

   e. In each case $F_{\alpha=.05, df_1=1, df_2=4} = 7.71$. Only the null hypothesis for the student main effect could be rejected, suggesting that male students in this population tend to talk more than female students, regardless of the instructor's gender.

CHAPTER 22 The Chi-Square Test of Independence

1. a. Yes
   b. No: this is a study about the mean frequency of church attendance, which suggests the use of the independent groups t test or one-way independent groups ANOVA.
   c. Yes

2. a. Quasi-experiment.
   b. H_0: $p(\text{cola 1} \mid \text{female}) = p(\text{cola 1} \mid \text{male})$, and
      $p(\text{cola 2} \mid \text{female}) = p(\text{cola 2} \mid \text{male})$,
   H_1: $p(\text{cola 1} \mid \text{female}) \neq p(\text{cola 1} \mid \text{male})$, and/or
      $p(\text{cola 2} \mid \text{female}) \neq p(\text{cola 2} \mid \text{male})$,

These could also be stated the opposite way, for example, p (female | cola 1). An acceptable alternative answer would be

H_0:   values of one variable are independent of the other

H_1:   at least some values of one variable are dependent on values of the other

c. $N = 31$.

d.

		Cola		
		1	2	
Gender	Male	8.6087	9.3913	18
	Female	13.3913	14.6087	28
		22	24	42

e. $\chi^2 = 4.21$.

f. $\chi^2_{\alpha=.05, df=1} = 3.841$; reject.

g. Females show a preference for cola 2 over cola 1, while males tend to prefer cola 1.

h. Direct interpretation of results is possible when both variables are dichotomous, even if the statistical hypotheses are nondirectional.

3. a. True experiment

   b. H_0: values of one variable are independent of the other

             H_1: at least some values of one variable are dependent on values of the other

      or

             H_0: $p(HA \mid$ new drug$) = P(HA \mid$ old drug$)$, and

                   $p($no HA $\mid$ new drug$) = P($no HA $\mid$ old drug$)$

             H_1: $p(HA \mid$ new drug$) \neq P(HA \mid$ old drug$)$, and

                   $p($no HA $\mid$ new drug$) \neq P($no HA $\mid$ old drug$)$

   c. Expected frequencies are:

		Heart Attack	
		0	≥ 1
Medication	New	376	74
	Old	376	74

   d. $\chi^2 = 4.66$.

   e. $\chi^2_{\alpha=.01, df=1} = 6.635$; do not reject.

   f. Given that no difference was found when compared to an established treatment, one could recommend use of this medication, assuming it has no more serious side effects or costs than the old medication.

4. The purpose of the goodness of fit test is to determine whether some preconceived idea about the probabilities is consistent with, or fit, the true probabilities. In the case of the test of independence, the preconceived idea is that the variables are independent.

5. a. Observational study.
   b. Ethnic group is a discrete nominal variable. Political position is a continuous ordinal variable.
   c. The expected frequencies are:

Ethnicity

		White	Black	Latino	Asian	Native American
	Conservative	47.8	47.8	47.8	47.8	47.8
Political Position	Moderate	99	99	99	99	99
	Liberal	53.2	53.2	53.2	53.2	53.2

   d. $\chi^2 = 104.068$
   e. $\chi^2_{\alpha=.05, df=8} = 15.507$; reject the null hypothesis
   f. The results suggest that within this population there seems to be a relationship between ethnicity and political position. Specifically, examining the group contributions to the chi square, Native Americans are more likely to be liberal than expected, Asians and whites to be more conservative than expected. However, these results must be considered tentative until additional tests are conducted.

6. Suppose we study two variables X and Y, each of which have two values, 1 and 2. If these variables are independent, then among subjects whose Y value equals 1, the proportion of subjects with an X value of 1 should equal the overall proportion of an X value of 1. The overall proportion of subjects with an X value of 1 is provided by the formula

$$p(X = 1) = \frac{n_{\text{row } 1}}{N},$$

assuming X refers to the rows in the table. Therefore, multiplying the number of subjects with a Y value of 1 ($n_{\text{column } 1}$) by this proportion will provide the number of subjects who should have both variables X and Y equal to 1 if the variables are independent. This logic can be repeated for each of the four groups in the study.

CHAPTER 23   The Wilcoxon *T* Test

1. a. No: these are not dependent groups.
   b. Yes
   c. Yes
   d. No: Both time of measurement (before versus after) and choice of alley are nominal variables.

2. a. H_0: $\sum R_- \leq \sum R_+$
      H_1: $\sum R_- > \sum R_+$

   b. $T = 7.5$.
   c. $T_{\alpha(D)} = .01$, $N_D = 10 = 5$; do not reject.
   d. The results do not provide evidence of statistical regression.
   e. No.

3. a. Quasi-experiment

   b. H_0: $\sum R_+ - \sum R_- = 0$
      H_1: $\sum R_+ - \sum R_- \neq 0$

   c. $T = 3$

   d. $T_{\alpha=.05, N_D=6} = 0$; do not reject

   e. The results do not provide evidence for an improvement in vocabulary performance as a function of participation in this workshop.

   f. Yes: there is one positive difference of 2 points, and two negative differences of 2 points. This brings into question the accuracy of the findings.

CHAPTER 24   The Mann–Whitney *U* Test

1. a. Yes
   b. No: these are dependent groups.
   c. Yes
   d. Yes
   e. Yes

2. a. H_0: $\sum R_1 = \sum R_2$
      H_1: $\sum R_1 \neq \sum R_2$

   b. $U = 16.5$.

   c. $U_{\alpha(D)=.01, n_1=10, n_2=10} = 16$; do not reject.

   d. The results do not provide evidence of a difference in the appetite suppressing effects of fenfluramine and amphetamine.

   e. Yes: one pup in each group demonstrated 4% weight gain, while one pup who received fenfluramine and two who received amphetamine demonstrated 7% weight gain. This brings into question the accuracy of the findings.

3. a. Observational study

   b. $U = 98$

   b. $U_{\alpha(D)=.01, n_1=15, N_2=15} = 56$; do not reject

   d. The results do not suggest a difference in how politically knowledgeable people are based on political position. The direction of the outcome is actually inconsistent with the initial scientific hypothesis.

   e. There are a number of critical ties across groups. This places the accuracy of the findings in doubt.

CHAPTER 25   The Kruskal-Wallis *H* Test

1. a. Yes
   b. No: the dependent variable is whether the rat chooses to turn left or right, a discrete nominal variable.
   c. Yes
   d. Yes

2. a. H_0: all sums of ranks are equal

   H_1: not all sums of ranks are equal

   b. $H = 3.69$.

   c. $\chi^2_{\alpha=.01,df=2} = 9.210$; do not reject.

   d. The results do not support the position that a relationship exists between religious affiliation and annual income.
   e. Yes: there are multiple cases where subjects in different groups are tied. This brings into question the accuracy of the findings.

3. a. Quasi-experiment: there is a manipulation without random assignment.

   b. $H = 12.772$

   c. $\chi^2_{\alpha=.05,df=2} = 5.991$; reject the null hypothesis
   d. The results suggest a difference in improvement rates for ECT depending on initial severity.
   e. No

CHAPTER 26   Choosing the Right Statistics

1. a. True experiment.
   b. Nominal; nominal (both are also dichotomous).
   c. Ungrouped frequency, proportion, percent; mode.
   d. Phi coefficient.
   e. χ^2 test of independence.
2. a. Observational study.
   b. Gender: frequency, proportion, percent
      Years of education: mean, median, standard deviation
      State of residence: frequency, proportion, percent
      Ethnic status: frequency, proportion, percent
      Age: mean, median, standard deviation
   c. χ^2 test of independence.
   d. One-group *t* test.
3. a. True experiment
   b. Both are continuous ratio variables.
   c. The mean

    d. The correlation coefficient would be the most useful descriptive statistic for describing the relationship between the two variables; the t test for a correlation coefficient could be used to evaluate whether a relationship exists in the population.

4. a. Observational study
   b. Birth weight is a continuous ratio variable; intelligence test score is a continuous ordinal variable
   c. The t test for a correlation coefficient could be used in this situation.
   d. Simple regression

5. a. Observational study
   b. Rating scale score is a continuous ordinal variable
   c. The mean and standard deviation would be most appropriate here
   d. The one-group z test
   e. The one-group t test

6. a. Quasi-experiment
   b. Time of measurement is a discrete nominal (dichotomous) variable; quantity of serotonin is a continuous ratio variable.
   c. The mean and standard deviation
   d. Since the groups are dependent and one variable is dichotomous, the possibilities include the Wilcoxon T test, the dependent groups t test, and the one-way dependent groups ANOVA. The most likely choice would be one of the last two.

7. a. Observational study
   b. Rank orders are discrete ordinal variables
   c. The Spearman rank order correlation coefficient, although the Pearson formula could technically be used to compute the correlation, and would be more appropriate if there are tied ranks.
   d. No

8. a. True experiment
   b. Gender and type of noise are discrete nominal (dichotomous) variables; number of correct cross-outs is a discrete ratio variable
   c. The mean
   d. The two-way independent groups ANOVA

9. a. Confidence interval
   b. Hypothesis test
   c. Hypothesis test
   d. Confidence interval

APPENDIX C

Sample and Group Size Tables

TABLE C-1   SAMPLE SIZE TABLE FOR TESTING H_0: $p(V) = .50$

How To Use This Table: Choose the desired alpha level and estimated effect size; this will indicate the appropriate column. Choose the desired level of power; this will indicate the appropriate row. The number located where the appropriate column and row meet is the recommended sample size.

	Alpha Level														
	two-tailed														
	.01			.02			.05			.10			.20		
	one-tailed														
	.005			.01			.025			.05			.10		
	Estimated Effect Size														
Power	Small	Medium	Large	Small	Medium	Large	Small	Medium	Large	Small	Medium	Large	Small	Medium	Large
.80	1165	127	44	1001	109	37	783	85	30	616	67	23	449	48	19
.90	1483	160	54	1297	140	50	1047	113	40	853	91	33	654	70	26

TABLE C-2 SAMPLE SIZE TABLE FOR THE ONE-GROUP z AND t TESTS AND THE DEPENDENT GROUPS t TEST

How To Use This Table: Choose the desired alpha level and estimated effect size; this will indicate the appropriate column. Choose the desired level of power; this will indicate the appropriate row. The number located where the appropriate column and row meet is the recommended sample size. In the case of the dependent groups t test, the number provided indicates the desirable number of difference scores. In a repeated measures study, this will equal the number of subjects. In a matched groups study, this number is half the necessary sample size.

	\<two-tailed\>														
	.01			.02			.05			.10			.20		
	\<one-tailed\>														
	.005			.01			.025			.05			.10		
	Estimated Effect Size														
Power	Small	Medium	Large	Small	Medium	Large	Small	Medium	Large	Small	Medium	Large	Small	Medium	Large
.80	293	48	20	252	42	17	198	33	15	156	26	12	114	20	9
.90	373	61	25	327	54	22	264	44	18	215	36	16	166	28	12

Alpha Level

TABLE C-3 SAMPLE SIZE TABLE FOR THE CHI-SQUARE TEST

How To Use This Table: Choose the desired alpha level and estimated effect size; this will indicate the appropriate column. Choose the desired level of power and the degrees of freedom; this will indicate the appropriate row. The number located where the appropriate column and row meet is the recommended sample size.

					Alpha Level					
		.01			.05			.10		
					Estimated Effect Size					
Power	df	Small	Medium	Large	Small	Medium	Large	Small	Medium	Large
.80	1	1168	130	47	785	87	31	618	69	25
	2	1388	154	56	964	107	39	771	86	31
	3	1546	172	62	1090	121	44	880	98	35
	4	1648	183	66	1194	133	48	1288	143	52
	5	1787	199	71	1283	143	51	1382	154	55
	6	1887	210	75	1362	151	54	1465	163	59
.90	1	1488	165	60	1051	117	42	856	95	34
	2	1743	194	70	1265	141	51	1046	116	42
	3	1925	214	77	1417	157	57	1180	131	47
	4	2074	230	83	1540	171	62	1288	143	52
	5	2203	245	88	1647	183	66	1382	154	55
	6	2318	258	93	1742	194	70	1465	163	59

TABLE C-4   GROUP SIZE TABLE FOR THE INDEPENDENT GROUPS *t* TEST

How To Use This Table: Choose the desired alpha level and estimated effect size; this will indicate the appropriate column. Choose the desired level of power; this will indicate the appropriate row. The number located where the appropriate column and row meet is the recommended group size. The recommended sample size is twice the number in the table.

												Alpha Level												
								two-tailed						
	.01			.02			.05			.10			.20		
							one-tailed						
	.005			.01			.025			.05			.10		
							Estimated Effect Size						
Power	Small	Medium	Large	Small	Medium	Large	Small	Medium	Large	Small	Medium	Large	Small	Medium	Large
.80	586	95	38	503	82	33	393	64	26	310	50	20	226	36	14
.90	746	120	48	652	105	42	526	85	34	429	69	27	329	53	21

TABLE C-5 SAMPLE SIZE TABLE FOR THE *t* TEST OF A CORRELATION COEFFICIENT

How To Use This Table: Choose the desired alpha level and estimated effect size; this will indicate the appropriate column. Choose the desired level of power; this will indicate the appropriate row. The number located where the appropriate column and row meet is the recommended sample size.

	Alpha Level														
	two-tailed .01			two-tailed .02			two-tailed .05			two-tailed .10			two-tailed .20		
	one-tailed .005			one-tailed .01			one-tailed .025			one-tailed .05			one-tailed .10		
	Estimated Effect Size														
Power	Small	Medium	Large	Small	Medium	Large	Small	Medium	Large	Small	Medium	Large	Small	Medium	Large
.80	1163	125	41	1000	108	36	783	85	28	617	68	22	451	49	17
.90	1481	158	51	1296	139	45	1047	113	37	854	92	31	656	72	24

TABLE C-6 GROUP SIZE TABLE FOR THE ONE-WAY INDEPENDENT GROUPS ANOVA

How To Use This Table: Choose the desired alpha level and estimated effect size; this will indicate the appropriate column. Choose the desired level of power and the numerator degrees of freedom; this will indicate the appropriate row. The number located where the appropriate column and row meet is the recommended group size. The recommended sample size is the number in the table multiplied by the number of groups.

Power	df_1	.01 Small	.01 Medium	.01 Large	.05 Small	.05 Medium	.05 Large	.10 Small	.10 Medium	.10 Large
.80	1	586	95	38	393	64	26	310	50	20
	2	464	76	30	322	52	21	258	41	17
	3	388	63	25	274	45	18	221	36	15
	4	336	55	22	240	39	16	193	32	13
	5	299	49	20	215	35	14	174	28	12
	6	271	44	18	195	32	13	159	26	11
.90	1	746	120	48	526	85	34	429	69	27
	2	582	95	38	421	68	27	349	57	23
	3	483	78	31	354	58	23	296	48	19
	4	416	68	27	309	50	20	258	42	17
	5	368	60	24	275	45	18	231	37	15
	6	332	54	22	250	41	16	210	34	14

Alpha Level

Estimated Effect Size

Critical Value Tables

TABLE D-1   CRITICAL VALUES FOR THE *t* TEST

How To Use This Table: Choose the desired alpha level; this will indicate the appropriate column. Choose the degrees of freedom for your study; this will indicate the appropriate row. The number located where the appropriate column and row meet is the critical value.

	Alpha Level two-tailed				
	.20	.10	.05	.02	.01
	one-tailed				
df	.10	.05	.025	.01	.005
1	3.078	6.314	12.706	31.821	63.657
2	1.886	2.920	4.303	6.965	9.925
3	1.638	2.353	3.182	4.541	5.841
4	1.533	2.132	2.776	3.747	4.604
5	1.476	2.015	2.571	3.365	4.032
6	1.440	1.943	2.447	3.143	3.707
7	1.415	1.895	2.365	2.998	3.499
8	1.397	1.860	2.306	2.896	3.355
9	1.383	1.833	2.262	2.821	3.250
10	1.372	1.812	2.228	2.764	3.169
11	1.363	1.796	2.201	2.718	3.106
12	1.356	1.782	2.179	2.681	3.055
13	1.350	1.771	2.160	2.650	3.012
14	1.345	1.761	2.145	2.624	2.977
15	1.341	1.753	2.131	2.602	2.947
16	1.337	1.746	2.120	2.583	2.921
17	1.333	1.740	2.110	2.567	2.898
18	1.330	1.734	2.101	2.552	2.878
19	1.328	1.729	2.093	2.539	2.861
20	1.325	1.725	2.086	2.528	2.845
21	1.323	1.721	2.080	2.518	2.831
22	1.321	1.717	2.074	2.508	2.819
23	1.319	1.714	2.069	2.500	2.807
24	1.318	1.711	2.064	2.492	2.797
25	1.316	1.708	2.060	2.485	2.787
26	1.315	1.706	2.056	2.479	2.779
27	1.314	1.703	2.052	2.473	2.771
28	1.313	1.701	2.048	2.467	2.763
29	1.311	1.699	2.045	2.462	2.756
30	1.310	1.697	2.042	2.457	2.750
40	1.303	1.684	2.021	2.423	2.704
60	1.296	1.671	2.000	2.390	2.660
120	1.289	1.658	1.980	2.358	2.617
∞	1.282	1.645	1.960	2.326	2.576

Source: Adapted from Tables II, III, IV, and VII of Fisher & Yates; STATISTICAL TABLES FOR BIOLOGICAL, AGRICULTURAL AND MEDICAL RESEARCH. Published by Longman Group UK Ltd., 1974. I am grateful to the Longman Group UK Ltd., on behalf of the Literary Executor of the late Sir Ronald A. Fisher, F. R. S. and Dr. Frank Yates, F. R. S. for permission to adapt Tables II, III, IV, and VII from *Statistical Tables for Biological, Agricultural and Medical Research 6/E* (1974).

TABLE D-2   CRITICAL VALUES FOR THE CHI-SQUARE TEST

How To Use This Table: Choose the desired alpha level; this will indicate the appropriate column. Choose the degrees of freedom for your study; this will indicate the appropriate row. The number located where the appropriate column and row meet is the critical value.

df	Alpha Level .20	.10	.05	.02	.01
1	1.642	2.706	3.841	5.412	6.635
2	3.219	4.605	5.991	7.824	9.210
3	4.642	6.251	7.815	9.837	11.345
4	5.989	7.779	9.488	11.668	13.277
5	7.289	9.236	11.070	13.388	15.086
6	8.558	10.645	12.592	15.033	16.812
7	9.803	12.017	14.067	16.622	18.475
8	11.030	13.362	15.507	18.168	20.090
9	12.242	14.684	16.919	19.679	21.666
10	13.442	15.987	18.307	21.161	23.209
11	14.631	17.275	19.675	22.618	24.725
12	15.812	18.549	21.026	24.054	26.217
13	16.985	19.812	22.362	25.472	27.688
14	18.151	21.064	23.685	26.873	29.141
15	19.311	22.307	24.996	28.259	30.578
16	20.465	23.542	26.296	29.633	32.000
17	21.615	24.769	27.587	30.995	33.409
18	22.760	25.989	28.869	32.346	34.805
19	23.900	27.204	30.144	33.687	36.191
20	25.038	28.412	31.410	35.020	37.566
21	26.171	29.615	32.671	36.343	38.932
22	27.301	30.813	33.924	37.659	40.289
23	28.429	32.007	35.172	38.968	41.638
24	29.553	33.196	36.415	40.270	42.980
25	30.675	34.382	37.652	41.566	44.314
26	31.795	35.563	38.885	42.856	45.642
27	32.912	36.741	40.113	44.140	46.963
28	34.027	37.916	41.337	45.419	48.278
29	35.139	39.087	42.557	46.693	49.588
30	36.250	40.256	43.773	47.962	50.892

Source: Adapted from Tables II, III, IV, and VII of Fisher & Yates; STATISTICAL TABLES FOR BIOLOGICAL, AGRICULTURAL AND MEDICAL RESEARCH. Published by Longman Group UK Ltd., 1974. I am grateful to the Longman Group UK Ltd., on behalf of the Literary Executor of the late Sir Ronald A. Fisher, F. R. S. and dr. Frank Yates, F. R. S. for permission to adapt Tables II, III, IV, and VII from *Statistical Tables for Biological, Agricultural and Medical Research 6/E* (1974).

TABLE D-3   CRITICAL r_{XY} VALUES

How To Use This Table: Choose the desired alpha level; this will indicate the appropriate column. Choose the degrees of freedom for your study; this will indicate the appropriate row. The number located where the appropriate column and row meet is the correlation needed to reject the null hypothesis.

	Alpha Level two-tailed					Alpha Level two-tailed			
	.10	.05	.02	.01		.10	.05	.02	.01
	one-tailed					one-tailed			
df	.05	.025	.01	.005	df	.05	.025	.01	.005
1	.988	.997	.9995	.9999	23	.337	.396	.462	.505
2	.900	.950	.980	.990	24	.330	.388	.453	.496
3	.805	.878	.934	.959	25	.323	.381	.445	.487
4	.729	.811	.882	.917	26	.317	.374	.437	.479
5	.669	.754	.833	.874	27	.311	.367	.430	.471
6	.622	.707	.789	.834	28	.306	.361	.423	.463
7	.582	.666	.750	.798	29	.301	.355	.416	.456
8	.549	.632	.716	.765	30	.296	.349	.409	.449
9	.521	.602	.685	.735	35	.275	.325	.381	.418
10	.497	.576	.658	.708	40	.257	.304	.358	.393
11	.476	.553	.634	.684	45	.243	.288	.338	.372
12	.458	.532	.612	.661	50	.231	.273	.322	.354
13	.441	.514	.592	.641	60	.211	.250	.295	.325
14	.426	.497	.574	.623	70	.195	.232	.274	.302
15	.412	.482	.558	.606	80	.183	.217	.256	.283
16	.400	.468	.542	.590	90	.173	.205	.242	.267
17	.389	.456	.528	.575	100	.164	.195	.230	.254
18	.378	.444	.516	.561	120	.150	.178	.210	.232
19	.369	.433	.503	.549	150	.134	.159	.189	.208
20	.360	.423	.492	.537	200	.116	.138	.164	.181
21	.352	.413	.482	.526	300	.095	.113	.134	.148
22	.344	.404	.472	.515	400	.082	.098	.116	.128
					500	.073	.088	.104	.115

Source: Adapted from Tables II, III, IV, and VII of Fisher & Yates; Statistical Tables For Biological, Agricultural and Medical Research. Published by Longman Group UK Ltd., 1974. I am grateful to the Longman Group UK Ltd., on behalf of the Literary Executor of the late Sir Ronald Fisher, F. R. S. and Dr. Frank Yates, F. R. S. for permission to adapt Tables II, III, IV, and VII from *Statistical Tables for Biological, Agricultural and Medical Research 6/E (1974).*

TABLE D-4   CRITICAL F VALUES

How To Use This Table: Choose the degrees of freedom for the numerator (df_1); this will indicate the appropriate column. Choose the degrees of freedom for the denominator (df_2) and the desired alpha level; this will indicate the appropriate row. The number located where the appropriate column and row meet is the critical value.

df_2	α	df_1 1	2	3	4	5	6	7	8	9	10	11	12
1	.25	5.83	7.50	8.20	8.58	8.82	8.98	9.10	9.19	9.26	9.32	9.36	9.41
	.10	39.90	49.50	53.60	55.80	57.20	58.20	58.90	59.40	59.90	60.20	60.50	60.70
	.05	161.00	200.00	216.00	225.00	230.00	234.00	237.00	239.00	241.00	242.00	243.00	244.00
2	.25	2.57	3.00	3.15	3.23	3.28	3.31	3.34	3.35	3.37	3.38	3.39	3.39
	.10	8.53	9.00	9.16	9.24	9.29	9.33	9.35	9.37	9.38	9.39	9.40	9.41
	.05	18.50	19.00	19.20	19.20	19.30	19.30	19.40	19.40	19.40	19.40	19.40	19.40
	.01	98.50	99.00	99.20	99.20	99.30	99.30	99.40	99.40	99.40	99.40	99.40	99.40
3	.25	2.02	2.28	2.36	2.39	2.41	2.42	2.43	2.44	2.44	2.44	2.45	2.45
	.10	5.54	5.46	5.39	5.34	5.31	5.28	5.27	5.25	5.24	5.23	5.22	5.22
	.05	10.10	9.55	9.28	9.12	9.01	8.94	8.89	8.85	8.81	8.79	8.76	8.74
	.01	34.10	30.80	29.50	28.70	28.20	27.90	27.70	27.50	27.30	27.20	27.10	27.10
4	.25	1.81	2.00	2.05	2.06	2.07	2.08	2.08	2.08	2.08	2.08	2.08	2.08
	.10	4.54	4.32	4.19	4.11	4.05	4.01	3.98	3.95	3.94	3.92	3.91	3.90
	.05	7.71	6.94	6.59	6.39	6.26	6.16	6.09	6.04	6.00	5.96	5.94	5.91
	.01	21.20	18.00	16.70	16.00	15.50	15.20	15.00	14.80	14.70	14.50	14.40	14.40
5	.25	1.69	1.85	1.88	1.89	1.89	1.89	1.89	1.89	1.89	1.89	1.89	1.89
	.10	4.06	3.78	3.62	3.52	3.45	3.40	3.37	3.34	3.32	3.30	3.28	3.27
	.05	6.61	5.79	5.41	5.19	5.05	4.95	4.88	4.82	4.77	4.74	4.71	4.68
	.01	16.30	13.30	12.10	11.40	11.00	10.70	10.50	10.30	10.20	10.10	9.96	9.89
6	.25	1.62	1.76	1.78	1.79	1.79	1.78	1.78	1.78	1.77	1.77	1.77	1.77
	.10	3.78	3.46	3.29	3.18	3.11	3.05	3.01	2.98	2.96	2.94	2.92	2.90
	.05	5.99	5.14	4.76	4.53	4.39	4.28	4.21	4.15	4.10	4.06	4.03	4.00
	.01	13.70	10.90	9.78	9.15	8.75	8.47	8.26	8.10	7.98	7.87	7.79	7.72
7	.25	1.57	1.70	1.72	1.72	1.71	1.71	1.70	1.70	1.69	1.69	1.69	1.68
	.10	3.59	3.26	3.07	2.96	2.88	2.83	2.78	2.75	2.72	2.70	2.68	2.67
	.05	5.59	4.74	4.35	4.12	3.97	3.87	3.79	3.73	3.68	3.64	3.60	3.57
	.01	12.20	9.55	8.45	7.85	7.46	7.19	6.99	6.84	6.72	6.62	6.54	6.47
8	.25	1.54	1.66	1.67	1.66	1.66	1.65	1.64	1.64	1.63	1.63	1.63	1.62
	.10	3.46	3.11	2.92	2.81	2.73	2.67	2.62	2.59	2.56	2.54	2.52	2.50
	.05	5.32	4.46	4.07	3.84	3.69	3.58	3.50	3.44	3.39	3.35	3.31	3.28
	.01	11.30	8.65	7.59	7.01	6.63	6.37	6.18	6.03	5.91	5.81	5.73	5.67
9	.25	1.51	1.62	1.63	1.63	1.62	1.61	1.60	1.60	1.59	1.59	1.58	1.58
	.10	3.36	3.01	2.81	2.69	2.61	2.55	2.51	2.47	2.44	2.42	2.40	2.38
	.05	5.12	4.26	3.86	3.63	3.48	3.37	3.29	3.23	3.18	3.14	3.10	3.07
	.01	10.60	8.02	6.99	6.42	6.06	5.80	5.61	5.47	5.35	5.26	5.18	5.11
10	.25	1.49	1.60	1.60	1.59	1.59	1.58	1.57	1.56	1.56	1.55	1.55	1.54
	.10	3.29	2.92	2.73	2.61	2.52	2.46	2.41	2.38	2.35	2.32	2.30	2.28
	.05	4.96	4.10	3.71	3.48	3.33	3.22	3.14	3.07	3.02	2.98	2.94	2.91
	.01	10.00	7.56	6.55	5.99	5.64	5.39	5.20	5.06	4.94	4.85	4.77	4.71
11	.25	1.47	1.58	1.58	1.57	1.56	1.55	1.54	1.53	1.53	1.52	1.52	1.51
	.10	3.23	2.86	2.66	2.54	2.45	2.39	2.34	2.30	2.27	2.25	2.23	2.21
	.05	4.84	3.98	3.59	3.36	3.20	3.09	3.01	2.95	2.90	2.85	2.82	2.79
	.01	9.65	7.21	6.22	5.67	5.32	5.07	4.89	4.74	4.63	4.54	4.46	4.40

df_2	α	df_1 15	20	24	30	40	50	60	100	120	200	500	∞
1	.25	9.49	9.58	9.63	9.67	9.71	9.74	9.76	9.78	9.80	9.82	9.84	9.85
	.10	61.20	61.70	62.00	62.30	62.50	62.70	62.80	63.00	63.10	63.20	63.30	63.30
	.05	246.00	248.00	249.00	250.00	251.00	252.00	252.00	253.00	253.00	254.00	254.00	254.00
2	.25	3.41	3.43	3.43	3.44	3.45	3.45	3.46	3.47	3.47	3.48	3.48	3.40
	.10	9.42	9.44	9.45	9.46	9.47	9.47	9.47	9.48	9.48	9.49	9.49	9.40
	.05	19.40	19.40	19.50	19.50	19.50	19.50	19.50	19.50	19.50	19.50	19.50	19.50
	.01	99.40	99.40	99.50	99.50	99.50	99.50	99.50	99.50	99.50	99.50	99.50	99.50
3	.25	2.46	2.46	2.46	2.47	2.47	2.47	2.47	2.47	2.47	2.47	2.47	2.47
	.10	5.20	5.18	5.18	5.17	5.16	5.15	5.15	5.14	5.14	5.14	5.14	5.13
	.05	8.70	8.66	8.64	8.62	8.59	8.58	8.57	8.55	8.55	8.54	8.53	8.50
	.01	26.90	26.70	26.60	26.50	26.40	26.40	26.30	26.20	26.20	26.20	26.10	26.10
4	.25	2.08	2.08	2.08	2.08	2.08	2.08	2.08	2.08	2.08	2.08	2.08	2.08
	.10	3.87	3.84	3.83	3.82	3.80	3.80	3.79	3.78	3.78	3.77	3.76	3.76
	.05	5.86	5.80	5.77	5.75	5.72	5.70	5.69	5.66	5.66	5.65	5.64	5.63
	.01	14.20	14.00	13.90	13.80	13.70	13.70	13.70	13.60	13.60	13.50	13.50	13.50
5	.25	1.89	1.88	1.88	1.88	1.88	1.88	1.87	1.87	1.87	1.87	1.87	1.87
	.10	3.24	3.21	3.19	3.17	3.16	3.15	3.14	3.13	3.12	3.12	3.11	3.10
	.05	4.62	4.56	4.53	4.50	4.46	4.44	4.43	4.41	4.40	4.39	4.37	4.36
	.01	9.72	9.55	9.47	9.38	9.29	9.24	9.20	9.13	9.11	9.08	9.04	9.02
6	.25	1.76	1.76	1.75	1.75	1.75	1.75	1.74	1.74	1.74	1.74	1.74	1.74
	.10	2.87	2.84	2.82	2.80	2.78	2.77	2.76	2.75	2.74	2.73	2.73	2.72
	.05	3.94	3.87	3.84	3.81	3.77	3.75	3.74	3.71	3.70	3.69	3.68	3.67
	.01	7.56	7.40	7.31	7.23	7.14	7.09	7.06	6.99	6.97	6.93	6.90	6.88
7	.25	1.68	1.67	1.67	1.66	1.66	1.66	1.65	1.65	1.65	1.65	1.65	1.65
	.10	2.63	2.59	2.58	2.56	2.54	2.52	2.51	2.50	2.49	2.48	2.48	2.47
	.05	3.51	3.44	3.41	3.38	3.34	3.32	3.30	3.27	3.27	3.25	3.24	3.23
	.01	6.31	6.16	6.07	5.99	5.91	5.86	5.82	5.75	5.74	5.70	5.67	5.65
8	.25	1.62	1.61	1.60	1.60	1.59	1.59	1.59	1.58	1.58	1.58	1.58	1.58
	.10	2.46	2.42	2.40	2.38	2.36	2.35	2.34	2.32	2.32	2.31	2.30	2.29
	.05	3.22	3.15	3.12	3.08	3.04	3.02	3.01	2.97	2.97	2.95	2.94	2.93
	.01	5.52	5.36	5.28	5.20	5.12	5.07	5.03	4.96	4.95	4.91	4.88	4.86
9	.25	1.57	1.56	1.56	1.55	1.55	1.54	1.54	1.53	1.53	1.53	1.53	1.53
	.10	2.34	2.30	2.28	2.25	2.23	2.22	2.21	2.19	2.18	2.17	2.17	2.16
	.05	3.01	2.94	2.90	2.86	2.83	2.80	2.79	2.76	2.75	2.73	2.72	2.71
	.01	4.96	4.81	4.73	4.65	4.57	4.52	4.48	4.42	4.40	4.36	4.33	4.31
10	.25	1.53	1.52	1.52	1.51	1.51	1.50	1.50	1.49	1.49	1.49	1.48	1.48
	.10	2.24	2.20	2.18	2.16	2.13	2.12	2.11	2.09	2.08	2.07	2.06	2.06
	.05	2.85	2.77	2.74	2.70	2.66	2.64	2.62	2.59	2.58	2.56	2.55	2.54
	.01	4.56	4.41	4.33	4.25	4.17	4.12	4.08	4.01	4.00	3.96	3.93	3.91
11	.25	1.50	1.49	1.49	1.48	1.47	1.47	1.47	1.46	1.46	1.46	1.45	1.45
	.10	2.17	2.12	2.10	2.08	2.05	2.04	2.03	2.00	2.00	1.99	1.98	1.97
	.05	2.72	2.65	2.61	2.57	2.53	2.51	2.49	2.46	2.45	2.43	2.42	2.40
	.01	4.25	4.10	4.02	3.94	3.86	3.81	3.78	3.71	3.69	3.66	3.62	3.60

df_2	α	df_1 1	2	3	4	5	6	7	8	9	10	11	12
12	.25	1.46	1.56	1.56	1.55	1.54	1.53	1.52	1.51	1.51	1.50	1.50	1.49
	.10	3.18	2.81	2.61	2.48	2.39	2.33	2.28	2.24	2.21	2.19	2.17	2.15
	.05	4.75	3.89	3.49	3.26	3.11	3.00	2.91	2.85	2.80	2.75	2.72	2.69
	.01	9.33	6.93	5.95	5.41	5.06	4.82	4.64	4.50	4.39	4.30	4.22	4.16
13	.25	1.45	1.55	1.55	1.53	1.52	1.51	1.50	1.49	1.49	1.48	1.47	1.47
	.10	3.14	2.76	2.56	2.43	2.35	2.28	2.23	2.20	2.16	2.14	2.12	2.10
	.05	4.67	3.81	3.41	3.18	3.03	2.92	2.83	2.77	2.71	2.67	2.63	2.60
	.01	9.07	6.70	5.74	5.21	4.86	4.62	4.44	4.30	4.19	4.10	4.02	3.96
14	.25	1.44	1.53	1.53	1.52	1.51	1.50	1.49	1.48	1.47	1.46	1.46	1.45
	.10	3.10	2.73	2.52	2.39	2.31	2.24	2.19	2.15	2.12	2.10	2.08	2.05
	.05	4.60	3.74	3.34	3.11	2.96	2.85	2.76	2.70	2.65	2.60	2.57	2.53
	.01	8.86	6.51	5.56	5.04	4.69	4.46	4.28	4.14	4.03	3.94	3.86	3.80
15	.25	1.43	1.52	1.52	1.51	1.49	1.48	1.47	1.46	1.46	1.45	1.44	1.44
	.10	3.07	2.70	2.49	2.36	2.27	2.21	2.16	2.12	2.09	2.06	2.04	2.02
	.05	4.54	3.68	3.29	3.06	2.90	2.79	2.71	2.64	2.59	2.54	2.51	2.48
	.01	8.68	6.36	5.42	4.89	4.56	4.32	4.14	4.00	3.89	3.80	3.73	3.67
16	.25	1.42	1.51	1.51	1.50	1.48	1.47	1.47	1.45	1.44	1.44	1.44	1.43
	.10	3.05	2.67	2.46	2.33	2.24	2.18	2.13	2.09	2.06	2.03	2.01	1.99
	.05	4.49	3.63	3.24	3.01	2.85	2.74	2.66	2.59	2.54	2.49	2.46	2.42
	.01	8.53	6.23	5.29	4.77	4.44	4.20	4.03	3.89	3.78	3.69	3.62	3.55
17	.25	1.42	1.51	1.50	1.49	1.47	1.46	1.45	1.44	1.43	1.43	1.42	1.41
	.10	3.03	2.64	2.44	2.31	2.22	2.15	2.10	2.06	2.03	2.00	1.98	1.96
	.05	4.45	3.59	3.20	2.96	2.81	2.70	2.61	2.55	2.49	2.45	2.41	2.38
	.01	8.40	6.11	5.18	4.67	4.34	4.10	3.93	3.79	3.68	3.59	3.52	3.46
18	.25	1.41	1.50	1.49	1.48	1.46	1.45	1.44	1.43	1.42	1.42	1.41	1.40
	.10	3.01	2.62	2.42	2.29	2.20	2.13	2.08	2.04	2.00	1.98	1.96	1.93
	.05	4.41	3.55	3.16	2.93	2.77	2.66	2.58	2.51	2.46	2.41	2.37	2.34
	.01	8.29	6.01	5.09	4.58	4.25	4.01	3.84	3.71	3.60	3.51	3.43	3.37
19	.25	1.41	1.49	1.49	1.47	1.46	1.44	1.43	1.42	1.41	1.41	1.40	1.40
	.10	2.99	2.61	2.40	2.27	2.18	2.11	2.06	2.02	1.98	1.96	1.94	1.91
	.05	4.38	3.52	3.13	2.90	2.74	2.63	2.54	2.48	2.42	2.38	2.34	2.31
	.01	8.18	5.93	5.01	4.50	4.17	3.94	3.77	3.63	3.52	3.43	3.36	3.30
20	.25	1.40	1.49	1.48	1.46	1.45	1.44	1.43	1.42	1.41	1.40	1.39	1.39
	.10	2.97	2.59	2.38	2.25	2.16	2.09	2.04	2.00	1.96	1.94	1.92	1.89
	.05	4.35	3.49	3.10	2.87	2.71	2.60	2.51	2.45	2.39	2.35	2.31	2.28
	.01	8.10	5.85	4.94	4.43	4.10	3.87	3.70	3.56	3.46	3.07	3.29	3.23
22	.25	1.40	1.48	1.47	1.45	1.44	1.42	1.41	1.40	1.39	1.39	1.38	1.37
	.10	2.95	2.56	2.35	2.22	2.13	2.06	2.01	1.97	1.93	1.90	1.88	1.86
	.05	4.30	3.34	3.05	2.82	2.66	2.55	2.46	2.40	2.34	2.30	2.26	2.23
	.01	7.95	5.72	4.82	4.31	3.99	3.76	3.59	3.45	3.35	3.26	3.18	3.12
24	.25	1.39	1.47	1.46	1.44	1.43	1.41	1.40	1.39	1.38	1.38	1.37	1.36
	.10	2.93	2.54	2.33	2.19	2.10	2.04	1.98	1.94	1.91	1.88	1.85	1.83
	.05	4.26	3.40	3.01	2.78	2.62	2.51	2.42	2.36	2.30	2.25	2.21	2.18
	.01	7.82	5.61	4.72	4.22	3.90	3.67	3.50	3.36	3.26	3.17	3.09	3.03

df_2	α	df_1 15	20	24	30	40	50	60	100	120	200	500	∞
12	.25	1.48	1.47	1.46	1.45	1.45	1.44	1.44	1.43	1.43	1.43	1.42	1.42
	.10	2.10	2.06	2.04	2.01	1.99	1.97	1.96	1.94	1.93	1.92	1.91	1.90
	.05	2.62	2.54	2.51	2.47	2.43	2.40	2.38	2.35	2.34	2.32	2.31	2.30
	.01	4.01	3.86	3.78	3.70	3.62	3.57	3.54	3.47	3.45	3.41	3.38	3.36
13	.25	1.46	1.45	1.44	1.43	1.42	1.42	1.42	1.41	1.41	1.40	1.40	1.40
	.10	2.05	2.01	1.98	1.96	1.93	1.92	1.90	1.88	1.88	1.86	1.85	1.85
	.05	2.53	2.46	2.42	2.38	2.34	2.31	2.30	2.26	2.25	2.23	2.22	2.21
	.01	3.82	3.66	3.59	3.51	3.43	3.38	3.34	3.27	3.25	3.22	3.19	3.17
14	.25	1.44	1.43	1.42	1.41	1.41	1.40	1.40	1.39	1.39	1.39	1.38	1.38
	.10	2.01	1.96	1.94	1.91	1.89	1.87	1.86	1.83	1.83	1.82	1.80	1.80
	.05	2.46	2.39	2.35	2.31	2.27	2.24	2.22	2.19	2.18	2.16	2.14	2.13
	.01	3.66	3.51	3.43	3.35	3.27	3.22	3.18	3.11	3.09	3.06	3.03	3.00
15	.25	1.43	1.41	1.41	1.40	1.39	1.39	1.38	1.38	1.37	1.37	1.36	1.36
	.10	1.97	1.92	1.90	1.87	1.85	1.83	1.82	1.79	1.79	1.77	1.76	1.76
	.05	2.40	2.33	2.29	2.25	2.20	2.18	2.16	2.12	2.11	2.10	2.08	2.07
	.01	3.52	3.37	3.29	3.21	3.13	3.08	3.05	2.98	2.96	2.92	2.89	2.87
16	.25	1.41	1.40	1.39	1.38	1.37	1.37	1.36	1.36	1.35	1.35	1.34	1.34
	.10	1.94	1.89	1.87	1.84	1.81	1.79	1.78	1.76	1.75	1.74	1.73	1.72
	.05	2.35	2.28	2.24	2.19	2.15	2.12	2.11	2.07	2.06	2.04	2.02	2.01
	.01	3.41	3.26	3.18	3.10	3.02	2.97	2.93	2.86	2.84	2.81	2.78	2.75
17	.25	1.40	1.39	1.38	1.37	1.36	1.35	1.35	1.34	1.34	1.34	1.33	1.33
	.10	1.91	1.86	1.84	1.81	1.78	1.76	1.75	1.73	1.72	1.71	1.69	1.69
	.05	2.31	2.23	2.19	2.15	2.10	2.08	2.06	2.02	2.01	1.99	1.97	1.96
	.01	3.31	3.16	3.08	3.00	2.92	2.87	2.83	2.76	2.75	2.71	2.68	2.65
18	.25	1.39	1.38	1.37	1.36	1.35	1.34	1.34	1.33	1.33	1.32	1.32	1.32
	.10	1.89	1.84	1.81	1.78	1.75	1.74	1.72	1.70	1.69	1.68	1.67	1.66
	.05	2.27	2.19	2.15	2.11	2.06	2.04	2.02	1.98	1.97	1.95	1.93	1.92
	.01	3.23	3.08	3.00	2.92	2.84	2.78	2.75	2.68	2.66	2.62	2.59	2.57
19	.25	1.38	1.37	1.36	1.35	1.34	1.33	1.33	1.32	1.32	1.31	1.31	1.30
	.10	1.86	1.81	1.79	1.76	1.73	1.71	1.70	1.67	1.67	1.65	1.64	1.63
	.05	2.23	2.16	2.11	2.07	2.03	2.00	1.98	1.94	1.93	1.91	1.89	1.88
	.01	3.15	3.00	2.92	2.84	2.76	2.71	2.67	2.60	2.58	2.55	2.51	2.49
20	.25	1.37	1.36	1.35	1.34	1.33	1.33	1.32	1.31	1.31	1.30	1.30	1.29
	.10	1.84	1.79	1.77	1.74	1.71	1.69	1.68	1.65	1.64	1.63	1.62	1.61
	.05	2.20	2.12	2.08	2.04	1.99	1.97	1.95	1.91	1.90	1.88	1.86	1.84
	.01	3.09	2.94	2.86	2.78	2.69	2.64	2.61	2.54	2.52	2.48	2.44	2.42
22	.25	1.36	1.34	1.33	1.32	1.31	1.31	1.30	1.30	1.30	1.29	1.29	1.28
	.10	1.81	1.76	1.73	1.70	1.67	1.65	1.64	1.61	1.60	1.59	1.58	1.57
	.05	2.15	2.07	2.03	1.98	1.94	1.91	1.89	1.85	1.84	1.82	1.80	1.78
	.01	2.98	2.83	2.75	2.67	2.58	2.53	2.50	2.42	2.40	2.36	2.33	2.31
24	.25	1.35	1.33	1.32	1.31	1.30	1.29	1.29	1.28	1.28	1.27	1.27	1.26
	.10	1.78	1.73	1.70	1.67	1.64	1.62	1.61	1.58	1.57	1.56	1.54	1.53
	.05	2.11	2.03	1.98	1.94	1.89	1.86	1.84	1.80	1.79	1.77	1.75	1.73
	.01	2.89	2.74	2.66	2.58	2.49	2.44	2.40	2.33	2.31	2.27	2.24	2.21

df_2	α	df_1 1	2	3	4	5	6	7	8	9	10	11	12
26	.25	1.38	1.26	1.45	1.44	1.42	1.41	1.39	1.38	1.37	1.37	1.36	1.35
	.10	2.91	2.52	2.31	2.17	2.08	2.01	1.96	1.92	1.88	1.86	1.84	1.81
	.05	4.23	3.37	2.98	2.74	2.59	2.47	2.39	2.32	2.27	2.22	2.18	2.15
	.01	7.72	5.53	4.64	4.14	3.82	3.59	3.42	3.29	3.18	3.09	3.02	2.96
28	.25	1.38	1.46	1.45	1.43	1.41	1.40	1.39	1.38	1.37	1.36	1.35	1.34
	.10	2.89	2.50	2.29	2.16	2.06	2.00	1.94	1.90	1.87	1.84	1.81	1.79
	.05	4.20	3.34	2.95	2.71	2.56	2.45	2.36	2.29	2.24	2.19	2.15	2.12
	.01	7.64	5.45	4.57	4.07	3.75	3.53	3.36	3.23	3.12	3.03	2.96	2.90
30	.25	1.38	1.45	1.44	1.42	1.41	1.39	1.38	1.37	1.36	1.35	1.35	1.34
	.10	2.88	2.49	2.28	2.14	2.05	2.98	1.93	1.88	1.85	1.82	1.79	1.77
	.05	4.17	3.32	2.92	2.69	2.53	2.42	2.33	2.27	2.21	2.16	2.13	2.09
	.01	7.56	5.39	4.51	4.02	3.70	3.47	3.30	3.17	3.07	2.98	2.91	2.84
40	.25	1.36	1.44	1.42	1.40	1.39	1.37	1.36	1.35	1.34	1.33	1.32	1.31
	.10	2.84	2.44	2.23	2.09	2.00	1.93	1.87	1.83	1.79	1.76	1.73	1.71
	.05	4.08	3.23	2.84	2.61	2.45	2.34	2.25	2.18	2.12	2.08	2.04	2.00
	.01	7.31	5.18	4.31	3.83	3.51	3.29	3.12	2.29	2.89	2.80	2.73	2.66
60	.25	1.35	1.42	1.41	1.38	1.37	1.35	1.33	1.32	1.31	1.30	1.29	1.29
	.10	2.79	2.39	2.18	2.04	1.95	1.87	1.82	1.77	1.74	1.71	1.68	1.66
	.05	4.00	3.15	2.76	2.53	2.37	2.25	2.17	2.10	2.04	1.99	1.95	1.92
	.01	7.08	4.98	4.13	3.65	3.34	3.12	2.95	2.85	2.72	2.63	2.56	2.50
120	.25	1.34	1.40	1.39	1.37	1.35	1.33	1.31	1.30	1.29	1.28	1.27	1.26
	.10	2.75	2.35	2.13	1.99	1.90	1.82	1.77	1.72	1.68	1.65	1.62	1.60
	.05	3.92	3.07	2.68	2.45	2.29	2.17	2.09	2.02	1.96	1.91	1.87	1.83
	.01	6.85	4.79	3.95	3.48	3.17	2.96	2.79	2.66	2.56	2.47	2.40	2.34
200	.25	1.33	1.39	1.38	1.36	1.34	1.32	1.31	1.29	1.28	1.27	1.26	1.25
	.10	2.73	2.33	2.11	1.97	1.88	1.80	1.75	1.70	1.66	1.63	1.60	1.57
	.05	3.89	3.04	2.65	2.42	2.26	2.14	2.06	1.98	1.93	1.88	1.84	1.80
	.01	6.76	4.71	3.88	3.41	3.11	2.89	2.73	2.60	2.50	2.41	2.34	2.27
∞	.25	1.32	1.39	1.37	1.35	1.33	1.31	1.29	1.28	1.27	1.25	1.24	1.24
	.10	2.71	2.30	2.08	1.94	1.85	1.77	1.72	1.67	1.63	1.60	1.57	1.55
	.05	3.84	3.00	2.60	2.37	2.21	2.10	2.01	1.94	1.88	1.83	1.79	1.75
	.01	6.63	4.61	3.78	3.32	3.02	2.80	2.64	2.51	2.41	2.32	2.25	2.18

df_2	α	15	20	24	30	40	50	60	100	120	200	500	∞
26	.25	1.34	1.32	1.31	1.30	1.29	1.28	1.28	1.26	1.26	1.26	1.25	1.25
	.10	1.76	1.71	1.68	1.65	1.61	1.59	1.58	1.55	1.54	1.53	1.51	1.50
	.05	2.07	1.99	1.95	1.90	1.85	1.82	1.80	1.76	1.75	1.73	1.71	1.69
	.01	2.81	2.66	2.58	2.50	2.42	2.36	2.33	2.25	2.23	2.19	2.16	2.13
28	.25	1.33	1.31	1.30	1.29	1.28	1.27	1.27	1.26	1.25	1.25	1.24	1.24
	.10	1.74	1.69	1.66	1.63	1.59	1.57	1.56	1.53	1.52	1.50	1.49	1.48
	.05	2.04	1.96	1.91	1.87	1.82	1.79	1.77	1.73	1.71	1.69	1.67	1.65
	.01	2.75	2.60	2.52	2.44	2.35	2.30	2.26	2.19	2.17	2.13	2.09	2.06
30	.25	1.32	1.30	1.29	1.28	1.27	1.26	1.26	1.25	1.24	1.24	1.23	1.23
	.10	1.72	1.67	1.64	1.61	1.57	1.55	1.54	1.51	1.50	1.48	1.47	1.46
	.05	2.01	1.93	1.89	1.84	1.79	1.76	1.74	1.70	1.68	1.66	1.64	1.62
	.01	2.70	2.55	2.47	2.39	2.30	2.25	2.21	2.13	2.11	2.07	2.03	2.01
40	.25	1.30	1.28	1.26	1.25	1.24	1.23	1.22	1.21	1.21	1.20	1.19	1.19
	.10	1.66	1.61	1.57	1.54	1.51	1.48	1.47	1.43	1.42	1.41	1.39	1.38
	.05	1.92	1.84	1.79	1.74	1.69	1.66	1.64	1.59	1.58	1.55	1.53	1.51
	.01	2.52	2.37	2.29	2.20	2.11	2.06	2.02	1.94	1.92	1.87	1.83	1.80
60	.25	1.27	1.25	1.24	1.22	1.21	1.20	1.19	1.17	1.17	1.16	1.15	1.15
	.10	1.60	1.54	1.51	1.48	1.44	1.41	1.40	1.36	1.35	1.33	1.31	1.29
	.05	1.84	1.75	1.70	1.65	1.59	1.56	1.53	1.48	1.47	1.44	1.41	1.39
	.01	2.35	2.20	2.12	2.03	1.94	1.88	1.84	1.75	1.73	1.68	1.63	1.60
120	.25	1.24	1.22	1.21	1.19	1.18	1.17	1.16	1.14	1.13	1.12	1.11	1.10
	.10	1.55	1.48	1.45	1.41	1.37	1.34	1.32	1.27	1.26	1.24	1.21	1.19
	.05	1.75	1.66	1.61	1.55	1.50	1.46	1.43	1.37	1.35	1.32	1.28	1.25
	.01	2.19	2.03	1.95	1.86	1.76	1.70	1.66	1.56	1.53	1.48	1.42	1.38
200	.25	1.23	1.21	1.20	1.18	1.16	1.14	1.12	1.11	1.10	1.09	1.08	1.06
	.10	1.52	1.46	1.42	1.38	1.34	1.31	1.28	1.24	1.22	1.20	1.17	1.14
	.05	1.72	1.62	1.57	1.52	1.46	1.41	1.39	1.32	1.29	1.26	1.22	1.19
	.01	2.13	1.97	1.89	1.79	1.69	1.63	1.58	1.48	1.44	1.39	1.33	1.28
∞	.25	1.22	1.19	1.18	1.16	1.14	1.13	1.12	1.09	1.08	1.07	1.04	1.00
	.10	1.49	1.42	1.38	1.34	1.30	1.26	1.24	1.18	1.17	1.13	1.08	1.00
	.05	1.67	1.57	1.52	1.46	1.39	1.35	1.32	1.24	1.22	1.17	1.11	1.00
	.01	2.04	1.88	1.79	1.70	1.59	1.52	1.47	1.36	1.32	1.25	1.15	1.00

Source: Adapted from Tables 18 and 29 of Pearson, E. S., and Hartley, H. O. (1966). *Biometrika tables for stastisticians*, vol. 1. (3rd ed.). New York: Cambridge University Press. I am grateful to the Biometrika Trustees for permission to adapt the table.

TABLE D-5   CRITICAL VALUES FOR Q

How To Use This Table: Choose the number of means from the omnibus test (k); this will indicate the appropriate column. Choose the degrees of freedom for the denominator of the omnibus test (df_2) and the desired alpha level; this will indicate the appropriate row. The number located where the appropriate column and row meet is the critical value.

df_2	α	k 2	3	4	5	6	7	8	9	10	11
2	.05	6.08	8.33	9.80	10.90	11.70	12.40	13.00	13.50	14.00	14.40
	.01	14.00	19.00	22.30	24.70	26.60	28.20	29.50	30.70	31.70	32.60
3	.05	4.50	5.91	6.82	7.50	8.04	8.48	8.85	9.18	9.46	9.72
	.01	8.26	10.60	12.20	13.30	14.20	15.00	15.60	16.20	16.70	17.80
4	.05	3.93	5.04	5.76	6.29	6.71	7.05	7.35	7.60	7.83	8.03
	.01	6.51	8.12	9.17	9.96	10.60	11.10	11.50	11.90	12.30	12.60
5	.05	3.64	4.60	5.22	5.67	6.03	6.33	6.58	6.80	6.99	7.17
	.01	5.70	6.98	7.80	8.42	8.91	9.32	9.67	9.97	10.24	10.48
6	.05	3.46	4.34	4.90	5.30	5.63	5.90	6.12	6.32	6.49	6.65
	.01	5.24	6.33	7.03	7.56	7.97	8.32	8.61	8.87	9.10	9.30
7	.05	3.34	4.16	4.68	5.06	5.36	5.61	5.82	6.00	6.16	6.30
	.01	4.95	5.92	6.54	7.01	7.37	7.68	7.94	8.17	8.37	8.55
8	.05	3.26	4.04	4.53	4.89	5.17	5.40	5.60	5.77	5.92	6.05
	.01	4.75	5.64	6.20	6.62	6.96	7.24	7.47	7.68	7.86	8.03
9	.05	3.20	3.95	4.41	4.76	5.02	5.24	5.43	5.59	5.74	5.87
	.01	4.60	5.43	5.96	6.35	6.66	6.91	7.13	7.33	7.49	7.65
10	.05	3.15	3.88	4.33	4.65	4.91	5.12	5.30	5.46	5.60	5.72
	.01	4.48	5.27	5.77	6.14	6.43	6.67	6.87	7.05	7.21	7.36
11	.05	3.11	3.82	4.26	4.57	4.82	5.03	5.20	5.35	5.49	5.61
	.01	4.39	5.15	5.62	5.97	6.25	6.48	6.67	6.84	6.99	7.13
12	.05	3.08	3.77	4.20	4.51	4.75	4.95	5.12	5.27	5.39	5.51
	.01	4.32	5.05	5.50	5.84	6.10	6.32	6.51	6.67	6.81	6.94
13	.05	3.06	3.73	4.15	4.45	4.69	4.88	5.05	5.19	5.32	5.43
	.01	4.26	4.96	5.40	5.73	5.98	6.19	6.37	6.53	6.67	6.79
14	.05	3.03	3.70	4.11	4.41	4.64	4.83	4.99	5.13	5.25	5.36
	.01	4.21	4.89	5.32	5.63	5.88	6.08	6.26	6.41	6.54	6.66
15	.05	3.01	3.67	4.08	4.37	4.59	4.78	4.94	5.08	5.20	5.31
	.01	4.17	4.84	5.25	5.56	5.80	5.99	6.16	6.31	6.44	6.55
16	.05	3.00	3.65	4.05	4.33	4.56	4.74	4.90	5.03	5.15	5.26
	.01	4.13	4.79	5.19	5.49	5.72	5.92	6.08	6.22	6.35	6.46
17	.05	2.98	3.63	4.02	4.30	4.52	4.70	4.86	4.99	5.11	5.21
	.01	4.10	4.74	5.14	5.43	5.66	5.85	6.01	6.15	6.27	6.38
18	.05	2.97	3.61	4.00	4.28	4.49	4.67	4.82	4.96	5.07	5.17
	.01	4.07	4.70	5.09	5.38	5.60	5.79	5.94	6.08	6.20	6.31
19	.05	2.96	3.59	3.98	4.25	4.47	4.65	4.79	4.92	5.04	5.14
	.01	4.05	4.67	5.05	5.33	5.55	5.73	5.89	6.02	6.14	6.25

df_2	α	k								
		12	13	14	15	16	17	18	19	20
2	.05	14.70	15.10	15.40	15.70	15.90	16.10	16.40	16.60	16.80
	.01	33.40	34.10	34.80	35.40	36.00	36.50	37.00	37.50	37.90
3	.05	9.72	10.20	10.30	10.50	10.70	10.80	11.00	11.10	11.20
	.01	17.50	17.90	18.20	18.50	18.80	19.10	19.30	19.50	19.80
4	.05	8.21	8.37	8.52	8.66	8.79	8.91	9.03	9.13	9.23
	.01	12.80	13.10	13.30	13.50	13.70	13.90	14.10	14.20	14.40
5	.05	7.32	7.47	7.60	7.72	7.83	7.93	8.03	8.12	8.21
	.01	10.70	10.89	11.08	11.24	11.40	11.55	11.68	11.81	11.93
6	.05	6.79	6.92	7.03	7.14	7.24	7.34	7.43	7.51	7.59
	.01	9.48	9.65	9.81	9.95	10.08	10.21	10.32	10.43	10.54
7	.05	6.43	6.55	6.66	6.76	6.85	6.94	7.02	7.10	7.17
	.01	8.71	8.86	9.00	9.12	9.24	9.35	9.46	9.55	9.65
8	.05	6.18	6.29	6.39	6.48	6.57	6.65	6.73	6.80	6.87
	.01	8.18	8.31	8.44	8.55	8.66	8.76	8.85	8.94	9.03
9	.05	5.98	6.09	6.19	6.28	6.36	6.44	6.51	6.58	6.64
	.01	7.78	7.91	8.03	8.13	8.23	8.33	8.41	8.49	8.57
10	.05	5.83	5.93	6.03	6.11	6.19	6.27	6.34	6.40	6.47
	.01	7.49	7.60	7.71	7.81	7.91	7.99	8.08	8.15	8.23
11	.05	5.71	5.81	5.90	5.98	6.06	6.13	6.20	6.27	6.33
	.01	7.25	7.36	7.46	7.56	7.65	7.73	7.81	7.88	7.95
12	.05	5.61	5.71	5.80	5.88	5.95	6.02	6.09	6.15	6.21
	.01	7.06	7.17	7.26	7.36	7.44	7.52	7.59	7.66	7.73
13	.05	5.53	5.63	5.71	5.79	5.86	5.93	5.99	6.05	6.11
	.01	6.90	7.01	7.10	7.19	7.27	7.35	7.42	7.48	7.55
14	.05	5.46	5.55	5.64	5.71	5.79	5.85	5.91	5.97	6.03
	.01	6.77	6.87	6.96	7.05	7.13	7.20	7.27	7.33	7.39
15	.05	5.40	5.49	5.57	5.65	5.72	5.78	5.85	5.90	5.96
	.01	6.66	6.76	6.84	6.93	7.00	7.07	7.14	7.20	7.26
16	.05	5.35	5.44	5.52	5.59	5.66	5.73	5.79	5.84	5.90
	.01	6.56	6.66	6.74	6.82	6.90	6.97	7.03	7.09	7.15
17	.05	5.31	5.39	5.47	5.54	5.61	5.67	5.73	5.79	5.85
	.01	6.48	6.57	6.66	6.73	6.81	6.87	6.94	7.00	7.05
18	.05	5.27	5.35	5.43	5.50	5.57	5.63	5.69	5.74	5.79
	.01	6.41	6.50	6.58	6.65	6.73	6.79	6.85	6.91	6.97
19	.05	5.23	5.31	5.39	5.46	5.53	5.59	5.65	5.70	5.75
	.01	6.34	6.43	6.51	6.58	6.65	6.72	6.78	6.84	6.89

df_2	α	k 2	3	4	5	6	7	8	9	10	11
20	.05	2.95	3.58	3.96	4.23	4.45	4.62	4.77	4.90	5.01	5.11
	.01	4.02	4.64	5.02	5.29	5.51	5.69	5.84	5.97	6.09	6.19
24	.05	2.92	3.53	3.90	4.17	4.37	4.54	4.68	4.81	4.92	5.01
	.01	3.96	4.55	4.91	5.17	5.37	5.54	5.69	5.81	5.92	6.02
30	.05	2.89	3.49	3.85	4.10	4.30	4.46	4.60	4.72	4.82	4.92
	.01	3.89	4.45	4.80	5.05	5.24	5.40	5.54	5.65	5.76	5.85
40	.05	2.86	3.44	3.79	4.04	4.23	4.39	4.52	4.63	4.73	4.82
	.01	3.82	4.37	4.70	4.93	5.11	5.26	5.39	5.50	5.60	5.69
60	.05	2.83	3.40	3.74	3.98	4.16	4.31	4.44	4.55	4.65	4.73
	.01	3.76	4.28	4.59	4.82	4.99	5.13	5.25	5.36	5.45	5.53
120	.05	2.80	3.36	3.68	3.92	4.10	4.24	4.36	4.47	4.56	4.64
	.01	3.70	4.20	4.50	4.71	4.87	5.01	5.12	5.21	5.30	5.37
∞	.05	2.77	3.31	3.63	3.86	4.03	4.17	4.29	4.39	4.47	4.55
	.01	3.64	4.12	4.40	4.60	4.76	4.88	4.99	5.08	5.16	5.23

df_2	α	k 12	13	14	15	16	17	18	19	20
20	.05	5.20	5.28	5.36	5.43	5.49	5.55	5.61	5.66	5.71
	.01	6.28	6.37	6.45	6.52	6.59	6.65	6.71	6.77	6.82
24	.05	5.10	5.18	5.25	5.32	5.38	5.44	5.49	5.55	5.59
	.01	6.11	6.19	6.26	6.33	6.39	6.45	6.51	6.56	6.61
30	.05	5.00	5.08	5.15	5.21	5.27	5.33	5.38	5.43	5.47
	.01	5.93	6.01	6.08	6.14	6.20	6.26	6.31	6.36	6.41
40	.05	4.90	4.98	5.04	5.11	5.16	5.22	5.27	5.31	5.36
	.01	5.76	5.83	5.90	5.96	6.02	6.07	6.12	6.16	6.21
60	.05	4.81	4.88	4.94	5.00	5.06	5.11	5.15	5.20	5.24
	.01	5.60	5.67	5.73	5.78	5.84	5.89	5.93	5.97	6.01
120	.05	4.71	4.78	4.84	4.90	4.95	5.00	5.04	5.09	5.13
	.01	5.44	5.50	5.56	5.61	5.66	5.71	5.75	5.79	5.83
∞	.05	4.62	4.68	4.74	4.80	4.85	4.89	4.93	4.97	5.01
	.01	5.29	5.35	5.40	5.45	5.49	5.54	5.57	5.61	5.65

Source: Adapted from Tables 18 and 29 of Pearson, E. S., and Hartley, H. O. (1966). *Biometrika tables for stastisticians, vol. 1.* (3rd ed.). New York: Cambridge University Press. I am grateful to the Biometrika Trustees for permission to adapt the table.

TABLE D-6   Critical Values for the Wilcoxon *T* Test

How To Use This Table: Choose the desired alpha level; this will indicate the appropriate column. Choose the number of difference scores (N_D) for your study; this will indicate the appropriate row. The number located where the appropriate column and row meet is the critical value. For any set of N_D difference scores, T must be less than or equal to the tabled value. Dashes indicate that no decision may be made about the null hypothesis at the indicated α level.

	Alpha Level two-tailed					Alpha Level two-tailed			
	.10	.05	.02	.01		.10	.05	.02	.01
	one-tailed					one-tailed			
N_D	.05	.025	.01	.005	N_D	.05	.025	.01	.005
5	0	-	-	-	28	130	116	101	91
6	2	0	-	-	29	140	126	110	100
7	3	2	0	-	30	151	137	120	109
8	5	3	1	0	31	163	147	130	118
9	8	5	3	1	32	175	159	140	128
10	10	8	5	3	33	187	170	151	138
11	13	10	7	5	34	200	182	162	148
12	17	13	9	7	35	213	195	173	159
13	21	17	12	9	36	227	208	185	171
14	25	21	15	12	37	241	221	198	182
15	30	25	19	15	38	256	235	211	194
16	35	29	23	19	39	271	249	224	207
17	41	34	27	23	40	286	264	238	220
18	47	40	32	27	41	302	279	252	233
19	53	46	37	32	42	319	294	266	247
20	60	52	43	37	43	336	310	281	261
21	67	58	49	42	44	353	327	296	276
22	75	65	55	48	45	371	343	312	291
23	83	73	62	54	46	389	361	328	307
24	91	81	69	61	47	407	378	345	322
25	100	89	76	68	48	426	396	362	339
26	110	98	84	75	49	446	415	379	355
27	119	107	92	83	50	466	434	397	373

Source: Adapted from Wilcoxon, F., Katte, E., & Wilcox, R. A. (1963). *Critical values and probability levels for the Wilcoxon rank sums test and the Wilcoxon signed rank test.* New York: American Cyanamid Co. Copyright © 1963, American Cyanamid Company. All Rights Reserved and Reprinted with Permission.

TABLE D-7   CRITICAL VALUES FOR THE MANN-WHITNEY U TEST

How To Use This Table: Choose the n for the first group (n_1); this will indicate the appropriate column. Choose the n for the second group (n_2) and the desired alpha level; this will indicate the appropriate row. The number located where the appropriate column and row meet is the critical value. For any group sizes n_1 and n_2, U must be less than or equal to the tabled value. Dashes indicate that it is impossible to reject the null hypothesis no matter what the value of U.

n_2	α	$\alpha(D)$	1	2	3	4	5	6	7	8	9	10	11	12	13	14	15	16	17	18	19	20
1	.10	.05	–	–	–	–	–	–	–	–	–	–	–	–	–	–	–	–	–	–	0	0
	.05	.025	–	–	–	–	–	–	–	–	–	–	–	–	–	–	–	–	–	–	–	–
	.02	.01	–	–	–	–	–	–	–	–	–	–	–	–	–	–	–	–	–	–	–	–
	.01	.005	–	–	–	–	–	–	–	–	–	–	–	–	–	–	–	–	–	–	–	–
2	.10	.05	–	–	–	–	0	0	0	1	1	1	1	2	2	2	3	3	3	4	4	4
	.05	.025	–	–	–	–	–	–	–	0	0	0	0	1	1	1	1	1	2	2	2	2
	.02	.01	–	–	–	–	–	–	–	–	–	–	–	–	0	0	0	0	0	0	1	1
	.01	.005	–	–	–	–	–	–	–	–	–	–	–	–	–	–	–	–	–	–	0	0
3	.10	.05	–	–	0	0	1	2	2	3	3	4	5	5	6	7	7	8	9	9	10	11
	.05	.025	–	–	–	–	0	1	1	2	2	3	3	4	4	5	5	6	6	7	7	8
	.02	.01	–	–	–	–	–	–	0	0	1	1	1	2	2	2	3	3	4	4	4	5
	.01	.005	–	–	–	–	–	–	–	–	0	0	0	1	1	1	2	2	2	2	3	3
4	.10	.05	–	–	0	1	2	3	4	5	6	7	8	9	10	11	12	14	15	16	17	18
	.05	.025	–	–	–	0	1	2	3	4	4	5	6	7	8	9	10	11	11	12	13	13
	.02	.01	–	–	–	–	0	1	1	2	3	3	4	5	5	6	7	7	8	9	9	10
	.01	.005	–	–	–	–	–	0	0	1	1	2	2	3	3	4	5	5	6	6	7	8
5	.10	.05	–	0	1	2	4	5	6	8	9	11	12	13	15	16	18	19	20	22	23	25
	.05	.025	–	–	0	1	2	3	5	6	7	8	9	11	12	13	14	15	17	18	19	20
	.02	.01	–	–	–	0	1	2	3	4	5	6	7	8	9	10	11	12	13	14	15	16
	.01	.005	–	–	–	–	0	1	1	2	3	4	5	6	7	7	8	9	10	11	12	13
6	.10	.05	–	0	2	3	5	7	8	10	12	14	16	17	19	21	23	25	26	28	30	32
	.05	.025	–	–	1	2	3	5	6	8	10	11	13	14	16	17	19	21	22	24	25	27
	.02	.01	–	–	–	1	2	3	4	6	7	8	9	11	12	13	15	16	18	19	20	22
	.01	.005	–	–	–	0	1	2	3	4	5	6	7	9	10	11	12	13	15	16	17	18
7	.10	.05	–	0	2	4	6	8	11	13	15	17	19	21	24	26	28	30	33	35	37	39
	.05	.025	–	–	1	3	5	6	8	10	12	14	16	18	20	22	24	26	28	30	32	34
	.02	.01	–	–	0	1	3	4	6	7	9	11	12	14	16	17	19	21	23	24	26	28
	.01	.005	–	–	–	0	1	3	4	6	7	9	10	12	13	15	16	18	19	21	22	24
8	.10	.05	–	1	3	5	8	10	13	15	18	20	23	26	28	31	33	36	39	41	44	47
	.05	.025	–	0	2	4	6	8	10	13	15	17	19	22	24	26	29	31	34	36	38	41
	.02	.01	–	–	0	2	4	6	7	9	11	13	15	17	20	22	24	26	28	30	32	34
	.01	.005	–	–	–	1	2	4	6	7	9	11	13	15	17	18	20	22	24	26	28	30
9	.10	.05	–	1	3	6	9	12	15	18	21	24	27	30	33	36	39	42	45	48	51	54
	.05	.025	–	0	2	4	7	10	12	15	17	20	23	26	28	31	34	37	39	42	45	48
	.02	.01	–	–	1	3	5	7	9	11	14	16	18	21	23	26	28	31	33	36	38	40
	.01	.005	–	–	0	1	3	5	7	9	11	13	16	18	20	22	24	27	29	31	33	36
10	.10	.05	–	1	4	7	11	14	17	20	24	27	31	34	37	41	44	48	51	55	58	62
	.05	.025	–	0	3	5	8	11	14	17	20	23	26	29	33	36	39	42	45	48	52	55
	.02	.01	–	–	1	3	6	8	11	13	16	19	22	24	27	30	33	36	38	41	44	47
	.01	.005	–	–	0	2	4	6	9	11	13	16	18	21	24	26	29	31	34	37	39	42

n_2	α	$\alpha(D)$	n_1 1	2	3	4	5	6	7	8	9	10	11	12	13	14	15	16	17	18	19	20
11	.10	.05	–	1	5	8	12	16	19	23	27	31	34	38	42	46	50	54	57	61	65	69
	.05	.025	–	0	3	6	9	13	16	19	23	26	30	33	37	40	44	47	51	55	58	62
	.02	.01	–	–	1	4	7	9	12	15	18	22	25	28	31	34	37	41	44	47	50	53
	.01	.005	–	–	0	2	5	7	10	13	16	18	21	24	27	30	33	36	39	42	45	48
12	.10	.05	–	2	5	9	13	17	21	26	30	34	38	42	47	51	55	60	64	68	72	77
	.05	.025	–	1	4	7	11	14	18	22	26	29	33	37	41	45	49	53	57	61	65	69
	.02	.01	–	–	2	5	8	11	14	17	21	24	28	31	35	38	42	46	49	53	56	60
	.01	.005	–	–	1	3	6	9	12	15	18	21	24	27	31	34	37	41	44	47	51	54
13	.10	.05	–	2	6	10	15	19	24	28	33	37	42	47	51	56	61	65	70	75	80	84
	.05	.025	–	1	4	8	12	16	20	24	28	33	37	41	45	50	54	59	63	67	72	76
	.02	.01	–	0	2	5	9	12	16	20	23	27	31	35	39	43	47	51	55	59	63	67
	.01	.005	–	–	1	3	7	10	13	17	20	24	27	31	34	38	42	45	49	53	56	60
14	.10	.05	–	2	7	11	16	21	26	31	36	41	46	51	56	61	66	71	77	82	87	92
	.05	.025	–	1	5	9	13	17	22	26	31	36	40	45	50	55	59	64	67	74	78	83
	.02	.01	–	0	2	6	10	13	17	22	26	30	34	38	43	47	51	56	60	65	69	73
	.01	.005	–	–	1	4	7	11	15	18	22	26	30	34	38	42	46	50	54	58	63	67
15	.10	.05	–	3	7	12	18	23	28	33	39	44	50	55	61	66	72	77	83	88	94	100
	.05	.025	–	1	5	10	14	19	24	29	34	39	44	49	54	59	64	70	75	80	85	90
	.02	.01	–	0	3	7	11	15	19	24	28	33	37	42	47	51	56	61	66	70	75	80
	.01	.005	–	–	2	5	8	12	16	20	24	29	33	37	42	46	51	55	60	64	69	73
16	.10	.05	–	3	8	14	19	25	30	36	42	48	54	60	65	71	77	83	89	95	101	107
	.05	.025	–	1	6	11	15	21	26	31	37	42	47	53	59	64	70	75	86	86	92	98
	.02	.01	–	0	3	7	12	16	21	26	31	36	41	46	51	56	61	66	71	76	82	87
	.01	.005	–	–	2	5	9	13	18	22	27	31	36	41	45	50	55	60	65	70	74	79
17	.10	.05	–	3	9	15	20	26	33	39	45	51	57	64	70	77	83	89	96	102	109	115
	.05	.025	–	2	6	11	17	22	28	34	39	45	51	57	63	67	75	81	87	93	99	105
	.02	.01	–	0	4	8	13	18	23	28	33	38	44	49	55	60	66	71	77	82	88	93
	.01	.005	–	–	2	6	10	15	19	24	29	34	39	44	49	54	60	65	70	75	81	86
18	.10	.05	–	4	9	16	22	28	35	41	48	55	61	68	75	82	88	95	102	109	116	123
	.05	.025	–	2	7	12	18	24	30	36	42	48	55	61	67	74	80	86	93	99	106	112
	.02	.01	–	0	4	9	14	19	24	30	36	41	47	53	59	65	70	76	82	88	94	100
	.01	.005	–	–	2	6	11	16	21	26	31	37	42	47	53	58	64	70	75	81	87	92
19	.10	.05	0	4	10	17	23	30	37	44	51	58	65	72	80	87	94	101	109	116	123	130
	.05	.025	–	2	7	13	19	25	32	38	45	52	58	65	72	78	85	92	99	106	113	119
	.02	.01	–	1	4	9	15	20	26	32	38	44	50	56	63	69	75	82	88	94	101	107
	.01	.005	–	0	3	7	12	17	22	28	33	39	45	51	56	63	69	74	81	87	93	99
20	.10	.05	0	4	11	18	25	32	39	47	54	62	69	77	84	92	100	107	115	123	130	138
	.05	.025	–	2	8	13	20	27	34	41	48	55	62	69	76	83	90	98	105	112	119	127
	.02	.01	–	1	5	10	16	22	28	34	40	47	53	60	67	73	80	87	93	100	107	114
	.01	.005	–	0	3	8	13	18	24	30	36	42	48	54	60	67	73	79	86	92	99	105

Source: Adapted from Mann, H. B., & Whitney, D. R. (1947). On a test of whether one of two random variables is stochastically larger than the other. *Annals of Mathemetical Statistics, 18*, 50–60. I am grateful to the Institute for Mathematical Statistics for permission to adapt the table.

Other Tables

TABLE E-1   RANDOM SAMPLING TABLE (RANDOM DIGITS TABLE)

How To Use This Table: This table represents a random ordering of the digits 0–9. For ease of reading the rows are broken into groups of 5 digits, and there is a break after every 5 rows. However, the numbers should be used as if they were a single unbroken row of digits. To select digits in a random order, you can drop a pencil anywhere in the table and start reading digits from that point.

93880	30067	11137	06696	77494	27526	88922	57619	02337	86662
76692	57656	99298	30095	02558	82919	25651	28120	23522	66263
04424	76978	71903	75842	31784	80399	93582	73670	02739	94643
88242	36928	66833	09970	17683	06931	09337	01020	31477	68849
21698	00855	90324	64854	64085	99148	84241	99699	85404	28371
78731	32497	56331	38406	98132	99669	25402	47197	09682	33835
82808	34677	71302	75892	49462	10275	73918	67115	20224	44925
99669	97878	35554	87900	04135	40700	02766	17443	09538	98772
08085	66902	45228	63702	97678	84155	53760	98409	65789	90750
49333	93906	43205	93404	16765	15665	32425	09293	00513	06712
19727	21123	06113	87759	71520	00040	93197	87436	09712	99234
08322	30093	19533	71269	82284	56203	89683	72041	33476	71856
06408	41290	36686	99287	18048	11168	90761	39183	93279	37994
18310	33376	12655	07615	59982	87924	93692	61118	36910	49622
97474	78227	28139	89395	60111	20995	11236	57144	90898	34917
39982	67482	78091	79694	00970	13710	64101	16277	07816	13879
28006	54888	78643	68059	67424	26880	63383	26194	97576	84261
45645	49941	04369	70130	94352	40112	43857	23164	47664	99511
13472	43394	03599	73615	49058	58048	80515	06741	56118	75052
27850	25453	21032	29743	48509	21267	03681	74642	67082	11904
59014	90744	42987	69613	20332	30392	11715	95052	58113	16536
55480	31996	85226	22210	84892	19453	80510	56212	45910	84855
24339	43283	59724	62822	15548	56141	89220	05213	36311	46352
34541	15246	09754	49137	68131	56389	64410	71732	19148	65009
49561	38668	87621	74272	67268	82594	08537	48996	83825	74170
99125	39759	25049	11813	99569	73368	50004	07974	73607	13360
04875	42765	61690	54915	31801	79108	18289	81161	97928	58360
50607	19272	53424	58923	54316	89854	71677	66815	19877	47235
30290	03075	11667	16122	32999	77755	12604	19115	97502	27969
28274	48942	27579	91896	80234	39543	95392	79920	83016	96471
16959	76737	16654	13542	20728	13928	30394	43895	21995	85942
04994	99280	94784	55171	14880	40420	15667	84423	62403	77012
25594	15045	07410	61877	55872	77197	82477	33640	06882	89657
63364	34022	88784	94445	84722	77505	64618	61370	18801	16361
08694	33467	29511	18888	57516	63467	16959	21585	35113	25620

50046	65487	22656	74729	84950	60194	80964	92915	53704	66919
28960	79829	02580	24360	40273	75814	04835	00662	29784	88808
22308	89960	58428	34381	49539	89565	73880	27768	79531	29346
98592	23403	19929	67535	74484	80083	45577	62977	13548	04909
18040	39633	74903	07420	15147	31795	84481	90974	24042	24544
04314	06864	55314	44064	68632	71109	01162	53475	24321	76906
66875	54661	48942	26027	65858	26851	72889	09511	10760	49833
29794	47770	62871	15559	49146	59030	34857	62411	60031	67962
26351	53194	42764	10192	05613	76994	67324	14248	35070	48409
45360	18780	69171	57162	59969	15610	44283	93966	03249	10961
25773	46930	91698	54007	16852	63493	16731	11774	63152	22423
34331	59199	03614	22220	64023	26306	78073	25201	02566	32066
65774	44518	93113	80244	86535	97521	27092	20736	24130	72258
40982	17521	22630	61308	90794	17845	30663	83489	35955	15812
84187	91945	63475	71413	87856	95561	88319	69211	11872	46843
22543	04824	98914	35252	94780	38482	71898	22708	90708	37177
86160	14617	93382	65976	07705	95846	85058	30360	01305	36285
37668	05644	59995	74303	18052	75216	46175	86411	38075	22125
56855	98791	55288	50820	59072	14526	39647	40210	13871	28684
27061	79252	44942	06167	39024	48704	15527	25723	85101	28363
98689	14263	23452	58231	86492	29067	81517	53630	46369	36720
24761	67296	58299	42403	18116	36978	57879	13979	74412	19322
12168	72477	65753	04397	92564	96269	50605	11449	54385	24295
85518	75304	83467	54279	42893	98840	79994	23383	70829	57754
43112	69054	58408	20068	32962	96368	05626	40435	44547	53220
34469	04112	20642	75240	53768	50416	97274	55482	65335	72559
06124	16048	71479	46340	70854	76983	71864	78202	29940	07822
07676	05094	45879	58916	76713	31828	97396	13995	28127	47905
68184	52826	85900	41488	73623	41997	61236	47352	59509	78574
54110	23945	74802	70505	39914	52606	19964	91722	57650	65738
96822	23122	06312	51650	16151	37500	18099	93210	77150	07071
79060	34403	13072	46872	71980	78778	97721	86645	67666	04008
77193	68996	63086	88657	40735	21436	39219	93172	44688	32311
78838	27993	02915	43891	00002	08535	62548	03196	72271	48395
08192	28895	48081	27465	86239	68731	37906	57188	75199	93314
33383	11480	66871	11591	58024	95560	41904	10681	32827	80995
85544	40801	22288	53780	04567	58155	32680	91181	84745	05504
21832	25724	73407	92193	16106	34170	67722	05630	31544	58393
37682	52954	50234	26513	51628	27885	92972	30168	36884	22072
56348	93463	10212	38322	34972	91894	79140	27698	53367	42779
46692	93528	58211	45684	08740	01227	93519	79555	84277	55064
83470	35241	78087	88072	72137	38349	03134	02908	95598	85118
63520	22587	59488	02138	61011	08586	45745	53366	48240	73063
29682	86193	20071	67339	36737	30521	42305	71789	37034	04311
18450	63027	09376	46280	28826	18757	86455	24431	77081	69773
39852	03090	03350	24210	56575	04088	01099	06173	93351	65630
61433	18659	22918	75002	66252	31964	46936	35494	36137	31595
96286	39463	84968	28823	88020	43796	97010	66467	63273	16285
34074	97910	60447	47307	17764	88487	93019	57917	34391	33254
78700	25278	87897	21279	96932	36293	87276	11889	70818	50864

25848	35241	58725	06653	92759	31182	05701	89936	11351	42111
70017	53414	04635	15494	52057	23162	30141	34417	20500	75966
88837	88976	56029	64147	17068	17285	43649	93234	82178	22310
44621	85825	37724	72969	09370	85493	45485	67004	62142	82924
39354	95176	22447	95870	40567	76183	53394	52319	60276	22039
02986	87518	91283	88004	93394	37835	03728	27065	62032	59091
08891	80096	29955	56261	46802	34481	74096	34469	73397	21732
16799	78751	41266	56190	00578	52323	97898	85677	52094	66220
98985	17737	71258	19630	66293	80566	17194	53774	14660	47918
16284	39874	03492	54917	79152	35872	00176	80467	03686	94453
25490	45407	31748	60299	61630	71676	70037	73673	12928	87820
12604	03591	76173	06926	32724	41465	76664	59440	03464	08510
62975	56837	00043	87252	98522	63513	47592	74285	49195	62324
02618	29977	98112	05840	43753	68171	70742	04304	93583	94727
97927	47649	56927	12030	08295	55539	46518	43260	86737	09075
83352	32101	77214	14614	47858	09567	94570	10754	57488	86936
12466	63391	04618	42869	71896	62125	88254	18714	63919	35082
51441	07861	80492	09445	18047	88141	84619	76593	64133	10604
92686	18791	23100	54104	15316	48427	34004	61615	74248	05619
30893	63356	68018	67122	42246	75783	52778	13230	35426	55937
20946	80838	17446	84884	84706	82612	28752	88861	11063	28802
91684	70872	39617	84769	44794	27234	62489	41641	45980	25121
08300	00386	67190	88090	39402	54035	73243	96758	46363	40715
84817	17189	48297	23982	31682	25956	08687	52354	19310	90959
82539	50783	75834	71126	85767	39681	17765	54056	64851	27529
86676	36124	28891	41647	56610	21007	37558	67402	70490	57530
61066	22855	19373	88518	51954	50434	77547	54676	32387	03002
02384	62743	99930	59022	49925	67053	31047	21576	72837	76235
07712	82563	03398	64881	03256	17002	75557	33993	30301	44750
12761	27252	29466	95118	95764	01440	36127	88857	25655	76542
55228	88633	04674	94544	39759	00050	65201	89546	87760	07834
79600	20700	02051	85474	92293	18511	40079	12166	59137	91368
70545	69461	84671	77135	48023	34257	34017	30729	10662	74464
44532	29113	71095	53301	70484	67183	30501	27005	54122	36506
85956	72982	16232	58925	52924	06945	11493	62706	47887	82718
75178	18607	16908	18326	86421	32895	71223	87503	50025	58179
54077	86394	10862	95679	48291	86055	17876	55823	77586	46302
80611	69955	26456	31043	54050	89810	63910	54305	67544	11164
75950	31417	53846	42243	03872	23880	22213	26997	28682	66610
75693	71229	15862	55745	25574	33334	01614	22249	93778	36997
94237	56768	93392	56523	17908	12930	88813	67954	75909	82124
04815	05216	62417	00402	24087	49908	40155	37909	73856	31701
12610	63929	33119	85377	52027	43136	71324	13972	81033	55283
75351	27152	25876	20919	58105	75210	84572	49391	08714	82582
38999	59294	30595	81404	93287	02306	81745	09295	67559	02205
13391	22459	97824	31345	28167	07730	42077	16804	40003	30472
26578	92091	65728	38951	99246	41652	53550	83136	09265	09923
19769	27009	81110	78870	13632	18307	11985	14456	97746	64331
18805	72178	66372	25847	83456	87939	20409	94661	03235	27414
29233	12588	14226	36832	69264	19207	59323	81481	60703	46560

64567	00980	40755	18056	44516	55231	14323	02404	12868	50461
68241	66114	98027	15314	00150	83005	85028	57072	66571	41750
00152	65088	18121	34813	44233	63740	13409	96318	11561	04638
68343	44121	52626	73424	22074	28774	60510	41864	97376	30566
30332	87819	53264	62254	78335	32679	97578	86653	61354	77466
71562	72311	44533	64426	90036	95694	06846	48827	31434	75488
08451	27405	81860	99528	74186	20981	25520	27132	22839	23725
98876	84284	65994	34715	02872	25584	88384	21500	76341	71890
26536	54215	41792	38715	56593	23979	71311	48199	48682	15573
14010	76193	99557	51562	58219	82449	09034	88735	36049	95906
34379	62141	69287	20922	89695	07858	66625	75277	75727	04428
39381	91997	58799	91677	85827	46073	05717	24675	87838	88340
47366	15926	25531	63784	76304	82607	45902	79674	54756	13957
46510	61373	35889	98425	79327	11615	44497	92482	89637	78794
88416	67266	23401	78034	71140	97020	98172	37489	90450	30430

Source: Adapted from RAND. (1955). *A million random digits with 100,000 normal deviates.* New York: The Free Press. Copyright © 1955 by RAND. Reprinted by permission.

TABLE E-2   RANDOM ASSIGNMENT TABLE (RANDOM NUMBERS TABLE)

How To Use This Table: Each 5-line block represents a random ordering of the numbers 1–100. For ease of reading the rows are broken into groups of 5 numbers. To randomly assign subjects, drop a pencil on any 5-line block. Asterisks represent subject 100. Starting at the beginning of the block, assign the subject associated with the first number to the first group, the subject associated with the second number to the second group, and so forth until all 100 subjects are assigned.

3	92	64	82	40	95	20	28	62	43	25	8	23	41	85	7	81	54	6	39
59	79	70	18	71	55	66	15	72	75	96	34	24	93	51	63	77	94	45	98
27	31	32	91	21	73	68	50	26	90	42	61	60	14	17	12	99	69	11	97
19	84	44	56	49	80	58	83	88	76	53	52	5	47	16	29	57	2	10	67
78	33	48	86	37	35	89	38	87	65	13	46	36	1	*	74	30	4	22	9
96	95	70	74	84	81	75	64	89	50	86	1	10	34	47	91	53	36	8	32
93	63	5	78	56	2	48	22	68	21	31	59	88	25	90	26	80	39	71	69
24	16	41	28	17	19	99	61	94	38	79	20	7	83	40	14	42	30	23	52
4	3	46	45	98	44	27	97	35	62	54	18	*	51	6	29	55	37	33	9
85	12	58	49	11	82	92	57	76	60	72	87	67	13	65	66	43	73	15	77
88	6	13	94	89	11	91	65	26	64	73	24	27	67	46	*	17	71	39	70
41	78	35	38	3	95	4	63	10	43	59	50	97	8	93	9	82	75	57	52
51	96	77	98	30	40	32	60	20	66	62	12	37	33	1	55	90	2	25	23
84	45	34	86	28	19	72	31	61	22	69	74	99	29	21	16	76	49	85	7
68	18	81	47	87	15	42	79	83	92	53	80	44	54	56	48	14	36	5	58
*	82	66	90	41	68	86	79	48	46	18	61	94	73	12	70	1	34	97	30
17	92	13	32	49	76	25	38	43	96	91	7	40	54	20	60	51	5	88	37
42	53	77	59	15	85	52	24	3	9	28	57	80	2	55	67	64	89	95	69
35	78	10	23	83	99	8	75	26	11	84	36	16	31	62	63	74	45	19	6
98	14	21	93	39	29	33	71	47	27	56	50	87	72	81	44	58	22	65	4
54	38	88	61	69	25	34	7	26	22	90	2	96	35	41	83	72	50	31	98
42	21	77	92	46	17	68	19	14	65	8	85	45	74	60	9	81	1	51	30
64	4	49	71	78	86	28	94	47	16	89	10	52	82	37	24	6	32	91	99
36	87	*	76	93	5	75	84	79	13	63	70	11	57	80	97	95	15	18	23
39	29	58	12	59	67	27	66	20	62	43	73	44	33	40	48	3	53	56	55
2	37	85	27	68	99	17	50	30	44	23	64	46	69	22	26	49	4	29	62
1	66	21	71	86	10	51	89	95	43	60	24	42	88	84	36	25	19	72	20
14	15	94	92	93	52	8	97	5	54	48	81	12	79	56	73	6	80	98	40
33	11	39	3	35	82	53	65	63	9	45	18	78	16	34	41	7	32	28	47
96	75	91	76	87	58	61	90	57	55	59	38	67	31	70	77	*	74	83	13
42	30	28	59	4	76	44	87	58	13	97	27	23	47	98	72	33	94	21	1
45	55	3	35	39	38	66	84	70	69	81	24	34	46	77	99	86	96	7	91
2	50	5	17	10	92	57	95	52	32	49	85	40	14	79	29	19	65	60	83
89	88	37	48	90	12	8	6	62	20	75	25	11	22	56	80	9	26	93	36
78	51	82	15	61	63	54	*	68	31	64	53	67	41	74	16	18	73	43	71
16	88	90	83	96	18	58	89	35	78	15	47	13	80	36	93	39	54	40	95
49	75	8	25	74	11	23	42	37	6	9	27	79	57	87	97	73	46	68	43
48	34	63	*	26	21	82	29	76	85	1	72	14	86	41	53	33	56	70	84
28	2	31	20	98	22	69	52	7	5	61	59	4	44	51	10	24	55	99	19
62	81	32	64	12	65	91	66	94	77	30	38	3	67	71	17	60	45	92	50

```
80 74 69 10  8    51 17 91 59 41    82 65 19 81  7    30 55 13 63 89
71 38 76 48  6     4 60 64  * 45    99 85 78 12 49    46 66 40 88 35
15 73 37 96 54    34 52 56 84 25    27 36 18 97 28     9 29 86  3 14
39 50 43 57 93    47 94 32 79 92    90 53 23 33 75    26 24 61 21 77
 5 83 22 16 31    95 70 42 98 44    68  1 11 58 87    67  2 62 20 72

95 10 76 45 31    21 40 86 48 71    53 49 50 69 13    16  8 96 74  *
36 80 33 24 30    37 73 20 22 89    57 99 75 79 85    55 42 59  6 35
29 91 38 98 41    81 93 72 44 47     9 34 14 32 77    97 23 67 54 94
64 26 51  7 70    25 66 68 43 58    61 88 84  3 27     2 17 19 11 82
78  4 15 83 46    90 92 56 60 52    65 12 18 39  1    62 63  5 28 87

52 85 30 99 75    37 54 10 25 84    79 14  8 87  9    38 21 49 61 64
20 71 92 36 80     * 28 15 83 77    76 55 66 19 74    81 58 51  7 27
67 65 41 23  1    11 73 40 53  2    70 39 43 56 50    62 45 22 42 47
17 35 60 63 94    68 69 90 97 12    16 33  5 59  3    78 44 29  4 82
 6 86 91 95 18    31 93 32 89 96    98 34 26 24 13    57 88 48 72 46

32 65 53 44 38    64 87 17 63 90     3 91 27 23 74    24 94 37 16 28
89 93  2  9 52     1 54  8 66 85    10 76 40 34 11    98 62 47 30 31
 * 69 39 86 73    41 50 14 48  6    83 56 20 45 12    99 70 95 33 21
 4 57 75 43 97    18 84 26 82 22     5 35 29 19 79    81 78 59 71 15
55 36 61 88 80    58  7 77 96 25    67 42 49 13 92    60 51 68 72 46

 2 11 12 44 62    54 88 25 60 16    24 51 97 69 77    14 48 99 89 90
 7  4  1 53 80     * 21 78 96 86    55 93  8 91 26    22 94 79 63 85
45 35 73 71 18    83 33 61 95 50    41 36 13 37 27    17 74 23 28 39
64 92 59 31 68    56 58  3  5 40    76 70 46 32 65    47 57 42 30 66
15 72 34 75  6    10 19 81 52 20    49 43 87 82  9    38 84 29 98 67

61 27 28  5 78    56 38 30 11  4    76 63 75 36 42    51  1 92 25 26
12 64 53 45 14    67 72 22 74 46    62 85 77 34 13    23 35 48 98 58
19 55 16 80 20    71 43  7 41 97    21 57 96 65 91    86  8 44 40 29
59 60 94 88 83    93  3  * 49 99    73 18 37 17 32    81 50 95 82 54
 2 33 89  9 52    79  6 47 10 39    70 66 24 69 31    15 87 90 84 68

29 63 18 57  1    21 54 76  2 86    98 89 35 70  *    23 71 58 82 65
96 48 30 22  6    39 66 42 90 61    83 24 69 43 16    80 59 75 34 64
62 25 19  7 85     5 33 37 74 92    20 51  8 60 12     3 81 26 87 56
72 50 97 95 14    52 10 49 79 28    40 46 73 45 31    13 36 53 77 41
94 78 93  9 17    67 47 27 99 88    32 91 68 44 38    11 15  4 84 55

18 71 78 10 48     * 28 73 22 68    80 35 17 34 61    86 15 33 97 60
 7 66 95 92 77    65 91 40 84  3    75 98  1  4 74    19  6 11 52 94
14 64 93 56 49    99 25 13 36 23    85 37 44 96 20    30 41 88 87 89
55 83 63 24 43    26 76 90 81 82    21 29 70 62 32    67 72 45  5  8
57 12 53 50 27    51 58 38 16 47     9 31 46 42 79    39 59  2 54 69

39 10 34 46 84     5 47 85 70  4    76 11 74 66 19     * 13 48 62 72
57 44 94 90 77    38 80 60 36 54    31  2 21 53 92    17 15 67 25 83
71 41 56 42 26    37 27 86 18 14    65 75 28 61 59     8 43 89 73 55
96 68 82 79 50    51 87 29 64 95    58 69 91 35  7    45  9 22 20 30
32 81 33 52 99    88 24 63 40  6     1 23 98 97  3    93 78 12 49 16

60 12  7 62 97    98 85 69 80 91     9 95 42 21 93    88  5 51 57 20
25 29 68  4 16    22 53 99 89 50    59 72 43 26 49    24 18 55 44  *
41 67 23 84 77    90  2 33  1 34    75 83 10 96 40    82 76 71  3 74
19  8 65 32 66    47 81 94 54  6    17 28 56 37 92    78 58 70 14 63
52 45 38 36 86    35 15 11 30 46    64 73 27 31 13    87 39 48 79 61
```

70	93	11	46	27	71	28	59	29	78	12	56	67	95	80	13	87	86	16	97
50	2	75	51	88	53	47	68	85	98	58	61	72	49	96	73	8	20	65	*
32	42	18	92	52	69	76	3	41	45	48	77	33	30	14	17	23	63	21	1
81	40	66	5	39	79	57	25	74	7	35	24	94	31	89	36	9	60	22	83
54	34	19	44	91	99	84	43	15	10	38	4	64	62	26	37	55	6	82	90
15	20	66	85	28	76	45	12	51	94	96	81	63	53	58	29	95	72	17	86
75	60	35	13	26	25	56	71	73	7	39	55	68	43	41	5	27	37	33	47
67	21	18	44	24	87	32	40	80	50	14	23	61	93	90	22	64	42	10	2
46	57	79	31	6	98	89	16	99	11	49	3	19	97	84	1	65	91	8	69
48	34	30	82	62	74	92	88	83	36	70	*	78	38	4	9	52	77	59	54
4	48	79	82	98	64	59	84	81	19	30	58	44	91	32	2	35	61	23	67
77	57	86	99	43	27	87	55	54	12	62	63	70	40	22	10	74	33	97	11
21	92	3	69	15	85	39	93	18	68	71	13	53	78	56	34	14	49	89	41
36	6	28	65	20	9	83	90	24	75	38	96	47	46	26	51	94	7	76	72
42	95	8	66	37	50	88	*	25	73	52	5	17	29	16	31	1	60	80	45
87	92	33	57	55	34	70	42	81	65	39	46	49	7	16	80	91	32	47	11
6	12	54	98	53	14	72	75	4	73	31	85	43	18	77	13	76	56	20	74
23	97	68	25	8	10	83	38	22	51	27	89	79	93	29	36	62	52	66	2
82	71	96	41	35	63	24	60	94	95	45	86	9	44	21	58	40	28	*	67
19	3	5	26	88	15	1	99	84	90	17	59	37	78	50	61	48	64	69	30
98	29	86	16	90	33	59	54	62	93	99	76	69	56	7	22	46	11	74	72
70	83	97	*	26	55	3	57	21	95	39	67	6	81	38	14	52	10	24	13
96	2	73	61	71	37	84	35	31	12	49	44	85	88	5	48	80	30	17	50
79	40	32	68	91	94	77	4	60	18	45	36	8	34	42	78	75	47	23	15
28	19	20	53	66	9	27	25	65	89	64	51	87	43	82	92	58	1	41	63
39	91	64	86	18	6	37	93	52	28	13	29	67	60	77	94	62	33	14	41
47	5	3	34	24	38	79	58	65	68	42	15	61	36	45	95	78	20	51	84
55	46	32	2	89	63	87	98	83	57	90	80	50	96	26	35	17	43	92	69
97	25	19	12	4	21	8	44	16	81	27	70	59	9	40	23	99	48	7	73
71	53	75	88	10	22	72	54	66	82	76	85	74	49	11	30	*	31	1	56

Source: Adapted from Tables of Random Permutations, by Lincoln E. Moses and Robert V. Oakford, with the permission of the publishers, Stanford University Press. Copyright © 1963 by the Board of Trustees of the Leland Stanford Junior University.

TABLE E-3   z SCORES AND PERCENTAGES IN A NORMAL DISTRIBUTION

How To Use This Table: Find the desired z score in the first column. The second column provides the percentage of z scores falling between the given z value and 0. The third column provides the percentage falling further out on the tail of the distribution than the given z value. These percentages are only appropriate if the distribution is normal.

z	Percent between 0 and z	Percent beyond z	z	Percent between 0 and z	Percent beyond z	z	Percent between 0 and z	Percent beyond z
0.00	0.000	50.000	0.45	17.364	32.636	0.90	31.594	18.406
0.01	0.399	49.601	0.46	17.724	32.276	0.91	31.859	18.141
0.02	0.798	49.202	0.47	18.082	31.918	0.92	32.121	17.879
0.03	1.197	48.803	0.48	18.439	31.561	0.93	32.381	17.619
0.04	1.595	48.405	0.49	18.793	31.207	0.94	32.639	17.361
0.05	1.994	48.006	0.50	19.146	30.854	0.95	32.894	17.106
0.06	2.392	47.608	0.51	19.497	30.503	0.96	33.147	16.853
0.07	2.790	47.210	0.52	19.847	30.153	0.97	33.398	16.602
0.08	3.188	46.812	0.53	20.194	29.806	0.98	33.646	16.354
0.09	3.586	46.414	0.54	20.540	29.460	0.99	33.891	16.109
0.10	3.983	46.017	0.55	20.884	29.116	1.00	34.134	15.866
0.11	4.380	45.620	0.56	21.226	28.774	1.01	34.375	15.625
0.12	4.776	45.224	0.57	21.566	28.434	1.02	34.614	15.386
0.13	5.172	44.828	0.58	21.904	28.096	1.03	34.849	15.151
0.14	5.567	44.433	0.59	22.240	27.760	1.04	35.083	14.917
0.15	5.962	44.038	0.60	22.575	27.425	1.05	35.314	14.686
0.16	6.356	43.644	0.61	22.907	27.093	1.06	35.543	14.457
0.17	6.749	43.251	0.62	23.237	26.763	1.07	35.769	14.231
0.18	7.142	42.858	0.63	23.565	26.435	1.08	35.993	14.007
0.19	7.535	42.465	0.64	23.891	26.109	1.09	36.214	13.786
0.20	7.926	42.074	0.65	24.215	25.785	1.10	36.433	13.567
0.21	8.317	41.683	0.66	24.537	25.463	1.11	36.650	13.350
0.22	8.706	41.294	0.67	24.857	25.143	1.12	36.864	13.136
0.23	9.095	40.905	0.68	25.175	24.825	1.13	37.076	12.924
0.24	9.483	40.517	0.69	25.490	24.510	1.14	37.286	12.714
0.25	9.871	40.129	0.70	25.804	24.196	1.15	37.493	12.507
0.26	10.257	39.743	0.71	26.115	23.885	1.16	37.698	12.302
0.27	10.642	39.358	0.72	26.424	23.576	1.17	37.900	12.100
0.28	11.026	38.974	0.73	26.730	23.270	1.18	38.100	11.900
0.29	11.409	38.591	0.74	27.035	22.965	1.19	38.298	11.702
0.30	11.791	38.209	0.75	27.337	22.663	1.20	38.493	11.507
0.31	12.172	37.828	0.76	27.637	22.363	1.21	38.686	11.314
0.32	12.552	37.448	0.77	27.935	22.065	1.22	38.877	11.123
0.33	12.930	37.070	0.78	28.230	21.770	1.23	39.065	10.935
0.34	13.307	36.693	0.79	28.524	21.476	1.24	39.251	10.749
0.35	13.683	36.317	0.80	28.814	21.186	1.25	39.435	10.565
0.36	14.058	35.942	0.81	29.103	20.897	1.26	39.617	10.383
0.37	14.431	35.569	0.82	29.389	20.611	1.27	39.796	10.204
0.38	14.803	35.197	0.83	29.673	20.327	1.28	39.973	10.027
0.39	15.173	34.827	0.84	29.955	20.045	1.29	40.148	9.852
0.40	15.542	34.458	0.85	30.234	19.766	1.30	40.320	9.680
0.41	15.910	34.090	0.86	30.511	19.489	1.31	40.490	9.510
0.42	16.276	33.724	0.87	30.785	19.215	1.32	40.658	9.342
0.43	16.640	33.360	0.88	31.057	18.943	1.33	40.824	9.176
0.44	17.003	32.997	0.89	31.327	18.673	1.34	40.988	9.012

z	Percent between 0 and z	Percent beyond z	z	Percent between 0 and z	Percent beyond z	z	Percent between 0 and z	Percent beyond z
1.35	41.149	8.851	1.86	46.856	3.144	2.38	49.134	0.866
1.36	41.309	8.692	1.87	46.926	3.074	2.39	49.158	0.842
1.37	41.466	8.534	1.88	46.995	3.005	2.40	49.180	0.820
1.38	41.621	8.379	1.89	47.062	2.938	2.41	49.202	0.798
1.39	41.774	8.226	1.90	47.128	2.872	2.42	49.224	0.776
1.40	41.924	8.076	1.91	47.193	2.807	2.43	49.245	0.755
1.41	42.073	7.927	1.92	47.257	2.743	2.44	49.266	0.734
1.42	42.220	7.780	1.93	47.320	2.680	2.45	49.286	0.714
1.43	42.364	7.636	1.94	47.381	2.619	2.46	49.305	0.695
1.44	42.507	7.493	1.95	47.441	2.559	2.47	49.324	0.676
1.45	42.647	7.353	1.96	47.500	2.500	2.48	49.343	0.657
1.46	42.786	7.215	1.97	47.558	2.442	2.49	49.361	0.639
1.47	42.922	7.078	1.98	47.615	2.385	2.50	49.379	0.621
1.48	43.056	6.944	1.99	47.671	2.330	2.51	49.396	0.604
1.49	43.189	6.811	2.00	47.725	2.275	2.52	49.413	0.587
1.50	43.319	6.681	2.01	47.778	2.222	2.53	49.430	0.570
1.51	43.448	6.552	2.02	47.831	2.169	2.54	49.446	0.554
1.52	43.575	6.426	2.03	47.882	2.118	2.55	49.461	0.539
1.53	43.699	6.301	2.04	47.933	2.068	2.56	49.477	0.523
1.54	43.822	6.178	2.05	47.982	2.018	2.57	49.492	0.508
1.55	43.943	6.057	2.06	48.030	1.970	2.58	49.506	0.494
1.56	44.062	5.938	2.07	48.077	1.923	2.59	49.520	0.480
1.57	44.179	5.821	2.08	48.124	1.876	2.60	49.534	0.466
1.58	44.295	5.705	2.09	48.169	1.831	2.61	49.547	0.453
1.59	44.408	5.592	2.10	48.214	1.786	2.62	49.560	0.440
1.60	44.520	5.480	2.11	48.257	1.743	2.63	49.573	0.427
1.61	44.630	5.370	2.12	48.300	1.700	2.64	49.585	0.415
1.62	44.738	5.262	2.13	48.341	1.659	2.65	49.598	0.402
1.63	44.845	5.155	2.14	48.382	1.618	2.66	49.609	0.391
1.64	44.950	5.050	2.15	48.422	1.578	2.67	49.621	0.379
1.645	45.000	5.000	2.16	48.461	1.539	2.68	49.632	0.368
1.65	45.053	4.947	2.17	48.500	1.500	2.69	49.643	0.357
1.66	45.154	4.846	2.18	48.537	1.463	2.70	49.653	0.347
1.67	45.254	4.746	2.19	48.574	1.426	2.71	49.664	0.336
1.68	45.352	4.648	2.20	48.610	1.390	2.72	49.674	0.326
1.69	45.449	4.551	2.21	48.645	1.355	2.73	49.683	0.317
1.70	45.544	4.457	2.22	48.679	1.321	2.74	49.693	0.307
1.71	45.637	4.363	2.23	48.713	1.287	2.75	49.702	0.298
1.72	45.728	4.272	2.24	48.746	1.255	2.76	49.711	0.289
1.73	45.819	4.182	2.25	48.778	1.222	2.77	49.720	0.280
1.74	45.907	4.093	2.26	48.809	1.191	2.78	49.728	0.272
1.75	45.994	4.006	2.27	48.840	1.160	2.79	49.736	0.264
1.76	46.080	3.920	2.28	48.870	1.130	2.80	49.744	0.256
1.77	46.164	3.836	2.29	48.899	1.101	2.81	49.752	0.248
1.78	46.246	3.754	2.30	48.928	1.072	2.82	49.760	0.240
1.79	46.327	3.673	2.31	48.956	1.044	2.83	49.767	0.233
1.80	46.407	3.593	2.32	48.983	1.017	2.84	49.774	0.226
1.81	46.485	3.515	2.33	49.010	0.990	2.85	49.781	0.219
1.82	46.562	3.438	2.34	49.036	0.964	2.86	49.788	0.212
1.83	46.638	3.363	2.35	49.061	0.939	2.87	49.795	0.205
1.84	46.712	3.288	2.36	49.086	0.914	2.88	49.801	0.199
1.85	46.784	3.216	2.37	49.111	0.889	2.89	49.807	0.193

z	Percent between 0 and z	Percent beyond z	z	Percent between 0 and z	Percent beyond z	z	Percent between 0 and z	Percent beyond z
2.90	49.813	0.187	3.06	49.889	0.111	3.21	49.934	0.066
2.91	49.819	0.181	3.07	49.893	0.107	3.22	49.936	0.064
2.92	49.825	0.175	3.08	49.897	0.104	3.23	49.938	0.062
2.93	49.831	0.169	3.09	49.900	0.100	3.24	49.940	0.060
2.94	49.836	0.164	3.10	49.903	0.097	3.25	49.942	0.058
2.95	49.841	0.159	3.11	49.906	0.094	3.30	49.952	0.048
2.96	49.846	0.154	3.12	49.910	0.090	3.35	49.960	0.040
2.97	49.851	0.149	3.13	49.913	0.087	3.40	49.966	0.034
2.98	49.856	0.144	3.14	49.916	0.084	3.45	49.972	0.028
2.99	49.861	0.139	3.15	49.918	0.082	3.50	49.977	0.023
3.00	49.865	0.135	3.16	49.921	0.079	3.60	49.984	0.016
3.01	49.869	0.131	3.17	49.924	0.076	3.70	49.989	0.011
3.02	49.874	0.126	3.18	49.926	0.074	3.80	49.993	0.007
3.03	49.878	0.122	3.19	49.929	0.071	3.90	49.995	0.005
3.04	49.882	0.118	3.20	49.931	0.069	4.00	49.997	0.003
3.05	49.886	0.114						

Source: Adapted from Tables II, III, IV, and VII of Fisher & Yates; Statistical Tables for Biological, Agricultural and Medical Research. Published by Longman Group UK Ltd., 1974. I am grateful to the Longman Group UK Ltd., on behalf of the Literary Executor of the late Sir Ronald A. Fisher, F. R. S. and Dr. Frank Yates, F. R. S. for permission to adapt Tables II, III, IV, and VII from *Statistical Tables for Biological, Agricultural and Medical Research 6/E* (1974).

Terms in italics are also in the glossary.

alpha level   the acceptable *probability* of a *Type I error*.

alternative hypothesis   a guess concerning the value of a *parameter* which suggests the presence of some pattern or relationship of interest.

analysis of variance   a set of *statistical* procedures for which the common element is the division of the variability in a set of scores into meaningful subcomponents.

bar graph   a representation of the *frequency* or relative frequency associated with each value of a *discrete variable* via the height of bars in a graph.

beta level   the acceptable *probability* of a *Type II error*.

binomial distribution   a *sampling distribution* of a *dichotomous variable*.

block   a set of associated scores across all groups.

Central Limit Theorem   a theorem which states that as the *sample size* increases, the corresponding *sampling distribution of the mean* increasingly resembles a *normal* distribution.

chi-square distribution   a *sampling distribution* of chi-square values for all *random samples* of a given *sample size* from some *population*.

computational formula   a formula used for computational purposes.

conditional probability   the *probability* of some outcome given that some other outcome has occurred.

confidence interval   an *interval* of values associated with an established level of confidence of including some *parameter*.

confound   an unmeasured *variable* that offers an alternative explanation for an observed pattern or relationship to that explanation preferred by the researcher.

constant   a *datum* that has a fixed value in a given context.

construct validity   the extent to which the activities and conditions associated with each *variable* in a *research study* are likely to represent those variables accurately.

continuous variable   a *variable* for which there are no boundaries between adjoining values.

control group   the group of *subjects* that serves as a comparison group for an *experimental group*.

convenience sampling   selecting a *sample* of *subjects* because it is a group to which the researcher has ready access.

criterion variable   in *regression analysis*, the *variable* to be estimated from *predictor variables*.

critical region   the set of values in the *sampling distribution* which would allow rejection of the *null hypothesis* at a desired *alpha level*.

critical value   the value in the *sampling distribution* that represents the dividing line between rejection and non-rejection of the *null hypothesis* at a desired *alpha level*.

cumulative frequency   the *frequency* of values or *intervals* less than or equal to a given value or interval.

cumulative frequency distribution   a variant of the *ungrouped* or *grouped frequency distribution* which uses *cumulative frequencies*.

data set   the entire set of information generated by a *research study*.

datum   a single piece of information.

definitional formula   a formula which corresponds closely to the definition of a *statistic*.

degrees of freedom   a *variable* which determines the shape of a *sampling distribution*.

degrees of freedom between groups   the denominator of the *mean square between groups*.

degrees of freedom residual   the denominator of the *mean square residual*.

degrees of freedom total   the denominator of the *variance* estimate based on the entire *sample*.

degrees of freedom within groups   the denominator of the *mean square within groups*.

dependent groups   groups for which each *subject* in the first group is in some way associated with a subject in the second group.

dependent outcomes   two outcomes for which the *probability* of one possible outcome depends upon the outcome of another event.

dependent variable   a *variable* which is measured by a researcher after manipulation of the *independent variable*.

descriptive statistics   *statistics* used to describe characteristics of a *sample*.

dichotomous variable   a *discrete variable* with only two possible values.

direct effect   a relationship between *variables* in which differences in one variable produce differences in the second variable.

directional hypothesis   a *statistical hypothesis* that suggests a direction for a hypothesized pattern or relationship.

discrete variable   a *variable* for which boundaries between values are clearly defined.

effect size   a measure of the true size, or strength, of a pattern or relationship in the *population*.

equalization of group conditions   a method of enhancing *internal validity* by insuring equivalence across groups on potential *situational confounds*.

error of estimate   in *regression analysis*, the difference between a *criterion variable* score and the estimated criterion variable score.

experimental group   the group of *subjects* that is exposed to the central treatment in *true experiments* or *quasi-experiments*.

external validity   the extent to which the researcher can generalize the results of a *research study* to the *population* of interest.

 distribution   a *sampling distribution* of *F* values for all *random samples* of a given *sample size* from some *population*.

factor   a *discrete variable* in a *factorial ANOVA*.

factorial ANOVA   an *analysis of variance* with more than one *discrete variable*.

family-wise error rate   the *probability* of at least one *Type I error* across a set, or family, of *hypothesis tests*.

frequency   the number of times a particular *variable* value occurred in a *data set*.

frequency distribution   a summary of the *frequency* of occurrence for each value of a single *variable*.

frequency polygon   a representation of the *frequency* or relative frequency associated with each *interval* of a *continuous variable* via the heights of points in a line graph.

group size   the number of *subjects* at each value of a *discrete variable*.

grouped frequency distribution   a table based on the *frequency distribution* in which values are grouped into equal *intervals*.

histogram   a representation of the *frequency* or relative frequency associated with each *interval* of a *continuous variable* via the height of bars in a graph.

homogeneity of variance assumption   a *parametric assumption* that the *variances* of the *populations* are equal.

hypothesis testing statistics   *inferential statistics* that are used to evaluate the accuracy of a *statistical hypothesis*.

independent groups   groups for which the *subjects* in one group are not associated with subjects in the other group.

independent outcomes   two outcomes for which the *probability* of one possible outcome does not depend upon the outcome of the other event.

independent variable   a *variable* that is manipulated by the researcher.

index of association   the *proportion* of the *variance* of one *variable* accounted for by another variable.

inferential statistics   *statistics* used to draw conclusions about a *population* on the basis of a *sample*.

interaction   the *omnibus test* of a *moderator effect* in *factorial ANOVA*.

internal validity   the extent to which alternative explanations of research findings can be ruled out.

interval   a *range* of values grouped together for practical purposes.

interval estimation statistics   *inferential statistics* that use *statistics* from a *sample* to estimate an *interval* of scores in which a *parameter* is likely to fall.

interval variable   a *variable* for which equal *intervals* between variable values indicate equal differences in amount of the characteristic being measured.

leptokurtic distribution   a bell-shaped *symmetrical distribution* in which the relative *frequency* of values in the tails is lower than in the *normal distribution*.

level of significance   another term for the *alpha level*.

linear relationship   a relationship between two *variables* which can be approximated using a straight line.

lower real limit   the lower endpoint of an *interval*.

main effect   the *omnibus test* of a single *factor* ignoring all other factors in *factorial ANOVA*.

matched groups study   a *true experiment* in which *random assignment* occurs within *blocks* of *subjects* who are approximately equivalent on some potential *subject confound*, to equalize groups on the confound.

mathematical model of variables   a model for classifying *variables* based on whether there are clear distinctions between variable values.

mean   the sum of the scores in a *frequency distribution* divided by the *sample size*.

mean square   a *population variance* estimate computed for the *analysis of variance*.

mean square between groups   a *population variance* estimate based on the variability among group *means*.

mean square residual   a *mean square* used in the one-way *dependent groups analysis of variance*.

mean square within groups   a *population variance* estimate based on the variability within the groups.

measurement model of variables   a model for classifying *variables* based on the extent to which variable values demonstrate the mathematical qualities of true numbers.

measures of central tendency   *descriptive statistics* which indicate the most representative value in a *frequency distribution*.

measures of dispersion   another term for *measures of variability*.

measures of linear relationship   *descriptive statistics* which indicate the strength and direction of a *linear relationship* between *variables*.

measures of variability   *descriptive statistics* which describe the amount of variability in a *frequency distribution*.

median   the value which separates the lower half of the scores in a *frequency distribution* from the upper half.

method of least squares   a procedure for computing the *regression coefficient* and *regression constant* that minimizes the sum of the squared *errors of estimate*.

midpoint   the value halfway between the *upper* and *lower real limits* of an *interval*.

mode   the value or *interval* in a *frequency distribution* with the highest *frequency*.

moderator effect   a relationship involving three *variables* in which the relationship between two of the variables differs depending upon the third variable.

modified random assignment   a method of enhancing *internal validity* by modifying the *random assignment* procedure to insure equivalence across groups on potential *subject confounds*.

multiple comparison tests   *hypothesis testing statistics* designed to control the *family-wise error rate* across a set of comparisons.

multiple regression   a *regression analysis* involving more than one *predictor variable*.

mutually exclusive outcomes   *variable* outcomes which cannot occur simultaneously.

mutually exhaustive outcomes   the set of all possible *variable* outcomes.

negative linear relationship   a *linear relationship* between two *variables* and , where higher scores on variable tend to be associated with lower scores on variable , and lower scores on variable tend to be associated with higher scores on variable .

negatively skewed distribution   a *frequency distribution* for which the *frequency polygon* has a tail at the lower end.

nominal variable   a *variable* for which different values indicate only a qualitative difference in the characteristic being measured.

nondirectional hypothesis   a *scientific hypothesis* that does not suggest the direction of a hypothesized pattern or relationship.

nonparametric test   a *hypothesis test* which requires no assumptions about the shape of the *frequency distribution* for the *population*.

normality assumption   a *parametric assumption* required by many *inferential statistics* that the *population* from which a *sample* was drawn is *normally distributed*.

normal distribution   a theoretical bell-shaped *symmetrical distribution* of a *continuous* variable with a specific relationship between the elevation of the tails and the body of the bell.

null hypothesis   a guess concerning the value of a *parameter* which suggests the absence of some pattern or relationship of interest.

observational study   a *research study* in which all *variables* are allowed to vary freely.

omnibus test   an *analysis of variance* test that includes all the s of interest, to determine whether there is evidence of differences in a set of s.

one-tailed test   a test of the *null hypothesis* in which the *critical region* falls in one tail of the *sampling distribution* created by assuming the *null hypothesis* is true.

ordinal variable   a *variable* for which different values indicate a difference in relative amount of the characteristic being measured.

parameter   a mathematical method for organizing and summarizing information in a *population*.

parametric assumption   an assumption about the *distribution* of scores for the *population* from which a *sample* was drawn.

parametric test   a *hypothesis test* which requires *parametric assumptions*.

Pearson product-moment correlation coefficient   a *measure of linear relationship* based on the *standard scores* for two *variables*.

percentage   the *proportion* multiplied by 100.

phi coefficient   a *computational formula* for the *Pearson product-moment correlation coefficient* which may be used when both *variables* are *dichotomous variables*.

pie chart   is a representation of the *proportion* associated with each value of a *discrete variable* via the relative size of pie slices.

pilot study   a trial run of a *research study* with a small *sample* to evaluate the adequacy of the design.

placebo condition   a treatment applied to *subjects* in a *control group* which is considered relatively ineffective, but which creates expectations similar to those of *experimental group* subjects.

planned comparison   a comparison of *means* planned on the basis of the central *scientific hypothesis*.

platykurtic distribution   a bell-shaped *symmetrical distribution* in which the relative *frequency* of values in the tails is greater than in the *normal distribution*.

point-biserial correlation coefficient   a *computational formula* for the *Pearson product-moment correlation coefficient* which may be used when one *variable* is a *dichotomous variable* and the other is an *ordinal*, *interval*, or *ratio* variable.

pooled variance formula   a formula that pools *variance* estimates from multiple groups under the assumption that variances for the *populations* represented by the groups are equal.

population   the complete set of observations of interest to a researcher.

positive linear relationship   a *linear relationship* between two *variables* and , where higher scores on variable tend to be associated with higher scores on variable , and lower scores on variable tend to be associated with lower scores on variable .

positively skewed distribution   a *frequency distribution* for which the *frequency polygon* has a tail at the upper end.

power   the *probability* of correctly rejecting the *null hypothesis* when the *alternative hypothesis* is true.

predictor variable in *regression analysis*, a *variable* used to estimate values of another variable.

probability the expected *proportion* associated with each value of a *variable*.

proportion the *frequency* of some *variable* value relative to the total *sample size*.

quantitative variable any *variable* that is either a *ratio variable*, *interval variable*, or *continuous ordinal variable*.

quasi-experiment a *research study* in which 1) the researcher does not *randomly assign* the *subjects* their values on an *independent variable*, and 2) the impact of manipulating the independent variable on the *dependent variable* is then evaluated.

random assignment a process that occurs when the researcher assigns *subjects* their *independent variable* values at random.

random sampling a procedure for selecting a *sample* which insures that all members of the *population* have an equal chance of being chosen.

range the difference between the highest and lowest value in a *frequency distribution*.

rating scale a method of collecting *data* in which people rate their opinions on topics of interest to the researcher.

ratio variable a *variable* for which ratios of variable values indicate proportional amounts of the characteristic being measured.

regression analysis *statistical* procedures for which the primary purpose is the estimation of scores on one *variable* from scores on other variables.

regression coefficient the slope of the *regression line*.

regression constant the -intercept for the *regression line*.

regression equation the formula for the *regression line*.

regression line a line that is used to estimate *criterion variable* values from *predictor variable* values.

relative frequency distribution a variant of the *ungrouped* or *grouped frequency distribution*, *cumulative* or not, which lists *proportions* or *percentages* rather than *frequencies*.

repeated measures study a *quasi-experimental* study in which the same *subjects* experience all values of the *independent variable*.

research study a set of conditions and activities which produce a *data set*.

robust a condition of a *parametric test* when, under certain conditions, violation of a *parametric assumption* does not affect the *probability* of a *Type I error* associated with the *critical value*.

sample a subset of a *population*.

sample size the number of *subjects* in a *research study*.

sampling distribution the *probability* distribution of a *sample statistic* for all *random samples* of a given *sample size* from some *population*.

sampling distribution of the mean a *sampling distribution* of *means* for all *random samples* of a given *sample size* from some *population*.

scatterplot a graphical representation of the relationship between two *variables*.

scientific hypothesis a guess about some *variable* pattern, or relationship among variables, in a given *population* which can be tested by a *research study*.

scientific theory an integrated model describing the occurrence of certain natural events.

significant result a *hypothesis test* result which allows one to reject the *null hypothesis* at a desired *alpha level*.

simple regression a *regression analysis* involving a single *predictor variable*.

situational confound a *confound* created by differences between groups in the conditions under which a *variable* is measured.

Spearman rank-order correlation coefficient a *computational formula* for the *Pearson product-moment correlation coefficient* which may be used when both *variables* represent rank orders without tied ranks.

standard deviation the square root of the *variance*.

standard error the *standard deviation* of a *sampling distribution*.

standard error of estimate the *standard deviation* of the *errors of estimate*.

standard error of the mean the *standard deviation* of a *sampling distribution of the mean*.

standard score a transformation of *variable* scores into *standard deviation* units.

statistic   is a number derived using mathematical methods that organize and summarize information in a *sample*.

statistical equalization   a method of enhancing *internal validity* by statistically analyzing *data* as if *subjects* were equivalent on potential *subject confounds*.

statistical hypothesis   a guess concerning the value of a *parameter*.

statistics   the plural of *statistic*, or the branch of mathematics that has to do with statistical methods.

stratified random sampling   a variant of *random sampling* in which the researcher insures that the random sample reflects the *population* on important *variables*.

subject   a member of a *sample*.

subject confound   a *confound* having to do with differences between *subjects* prior to any treatment.

sum of squares   the sum of a set of squared differences from the *mean*.

sum of squares between groups   the numerator of the *mean square between groups*.

sum of squares residual   the numerator of the *mean square residual*.

sum of squares total   the numerator of the *variance* estimate based on the entire *sample*.

sum of squares within groups   the numerator of the *mean square within groups*.

summation symbol   a symbol used to indicate the sum of a series of *variable* values.

symmetrical distribution   a *frequency distribution* in which the left half of the *frequency polygon* is a mirror image of the right half.

***t* distribution**   a *sampling distribution* of values for all *random samples* of a given *sample size* from some *population*.

true experiment   a *research study* in which 1) the researcher *randomly assigns* the subjects their values on an *independent variable*, and 2) the impact of manipulating the independent variable on the *dependent variable* is then evaluated.

two-tailed test   a test of the *null hypothesis* in which a *critical region* is defined in each tail of the *sampling distribution* created by assuming the *null hypothesis* is true.

Type I error   incorrect rejection of the *null hypothesis* when the null hypothesis is true.

Type II error   incorrect non-rejection of the *null hypothesis* when the null hypothesis is false.

ungrouped frequency distribution   a table based on the *frequency distribution* which provides the *frequency* for each *variable* value that appears in the *sample*.

unplanned comparison   a comparison of *means* which does not follow from the central *scientific hypothesis*.

unpooled variance formula   a formula for computing a *statistic* that does not assume *population variances* are equal.

upper real limit   the upper endpoint of an *interval*.

variable   a *datum* that can vary in value from one observation to the next.

variance   the average squared difference from the *mean*.

within-subjects study   another term for a *repeated measures study*.